American ENGLISH FILE

3

Teacher's Book

Christina Latham-Koenig
Clive Oxenden

with Anna Lowy
Beatriz Martín García

Paul Seligson and Clive Oxenden are the original co-authors of
English File 1 and *English File 2*

OXFORD
UNIVERSITY PRESS

OXFORD
UNIVERSITY PRESS

198 Madison Avenue
New York, NY 10016 USA

Great Clarendon Street, Oxford, OX2 6DP, United Kingdom

Oxford University Press is a department of the University of Oxford.
It furthers the University's objective of excellence in research, scholarship,
and education by publishing worldwide. Oxford is a registered trade
mark of Oxford University Press in the UK and in certain other countries.

© Oxford University Press 2014

The moral rights of the author have been asserted.

First published in 2014

2018 2017 2016 2015 2014

10 9 8 7 6 5 4 3 2 1

Photocopying

General Manager: Laura Pearson
Executive Publishing Manager: Erik Gundersen
Senior Managing Editor: Louisa van Houten
Associate Editor: Yasuko Morisaki
Design Director: Susan Sanguily
Executive Design Manager: Maj-Britt Hagsted
Associate Design Manager: Michael Steinhofer
Senior Designer: Yin Ling Wong
Electronic Production Manager: Julie Armstrong
Production Artists: Elissa Santos, Julie Sussman-Perez
Image Manager: Trisha Masterson
Image Editors: Liaht Pashayan
Production Coordinator: Brad Tucker

ISBN: 978 0 19 477575 5 TEACHER'S BOOK (PACK COMPONENT)
ISBN: 978 0 19 477635 6 TEACHER'S BOOK (PACK)
ISBN: 978 0 19 477659 2 TESTING PROGRAM CD-ROM (PACK COMPONENT)

Printed in China

This book is printed on paper from certified and well-managed sources.

ACKNOWLEDGEMENTS

Cover Design: Yin Ling Wong

*The authors and publisher are grateful to those who have given permission to reproduce
the following extracts and adaptations of copyright material:*

p.218 "Our House" Words and Music by Christopher Foreman and Cathal
Smyth © 1982, Reproduced by permission of EMI Music Publishing Ltd,
London W8 5SW. p.219 "I'm Gonna be (500 Miles)". Words and Music by
Charles Stobo Reid and Craig Morris Reid. Zoo Music Ltd. (PRS). All rights
administered by Warner/Chappell Music Ltd. p.220 "You Can't Hurry Love"
Words and Music by Brian Holland, Lamont Herbert Dozier and Edward
Holland Jr © 1965, Reproduced by permission of EMI Music Publishing Ltd,
London W8 5SW. p.221 "We Are The Champions" Words and Music by Freddie
Mercury © 1977, Reproduced by permission of EMI Music Publishing Ltd/
Queen Music Ltd, London W8 5SW. p.222 "Ain't got no – I got life" (from
the musical *Hair*) Words and music by Gerome Ragni, Galt MacDermot
and James Rado © 1968 EMI Catalogue Partnership, EMI U Catalog Inc,
EMI United Partnership Ltd, USA. Reproduced by permission of EMI Music
Publishing Ltd, London W8 5SW. p.223 "If I Could Build My Whole World
Around You" Words and Music by Vernon Bullock, Johnny William Bristol
and Harvey Fuqua © 1967, Reproduced by permission of Jobete Music Co Inc/
EMI Music, London W8 5SW. p.224 "Piano Man" Words and Music by Billy Joel
© 1973, Reproduced by permission of EMI Music Publishing Ltd, London W8
5SW.p.225 "Karma" Words and Music by Alicia Auguello-Cook, Kerry Brothers
Jr and Taneisha Smith © 2003, Reproduced by permission of EMI Music
Publishing Ltd, London W8 5SW. p.226 "The Greatest Love Of All" Words and
Music by Michael Masser and Linda Creed © 1977, Reproduced by permission
of EMI Music Publishing Ltd, London W8 5SW.

Illustrations by:

Cover: Chellie Carroll; Echo Chernik/Illustration Ltd; Paul Boston p.218; Camille
Corbetto/Colagene pp.161, 189; Mark Duffin p.151 (exercise 'b'); Joy Gosney
pp.155, 201; Anna Hymas/New Division pp.160, 203; Sophie Joyce pp.183, 187;
Sarah Kelly p.222; Adam Larkum/Illustration pp.142, 148, 159; Tim Marrs
pp.224, 225; Jerome Mireault/Colagene pp.144, 149, 174, 179, 204; Roger Penwill
Cartoons pp.146, 147, 151 (exercise 'a'), 177; Dave Smith pp.152, 163, 176, 180;
Lucy Truman/Meiklejohn Illustration pp.157, 200, 211; Kath Walker p.178.

*We would also like to thank the following for permission to reproduce the following
photographs:*

Cover Gemenacom/shutterstock, Andrey_Popov/shutterstock,
Wavebreakmedia/shutterstock, Image Source/Getty Images, Lane Oatey/
Blue Jean Images/Getty Images, BJI/Blue Jean Images/Getty Images, Image
Source/Corbis, Yuri Arcurs/Tetra Images/Corbis, Wavebreak Media Ltd./Corbis;
pg. 143 PHOVOIR/Alamy; pg. 150 (tennis) Ghislain & Marie David de Lossy/
Getty Images, (computer) naphtalina/Getty Images; pg. 153 (bike) Keenpress/
National Geographic Society/Corbis, (coffee) Image Source/Getty Images;
pg. 154 Columbia Pictures/The Kobal Collection; pg. 156 (Annie) OUP/Image
Source, (Katie) OUP/Fancy; pg. 158 Hemant Mehta/India Picture/Corbis; pg.
162 (perfume) Metta image/Alamy, (ring) Corbis Super RF/Alamy, (dancing)
Rob Lewine /Getty Images, (picnic) George Marks/Retrofile/Getty Images, (dog)
John Churchman/Getty Images, (lotto) Nicemonkey/shutterstock; pg. 182 (car)
Sutton Images/Corbis, (bike) Tim De Waele/Corbis; pg. 185 (1) Matthew Lloyd/
Getty Images, (2) Geoff Pugh/Rex Features, (3) Richard Gardner/Rex Features,
(4) Geraint Lewis/Rex Features, (5) James Higgins/Splash News/Corbis, (6) Mike
Marsland/WireImage/Getty Images; pg. 194 (coffee) JGI/Jamie Grill/Blend Images/
Corbis, (cake) Elena Elisseeva/shutterstock; pg. 207 (wedding) Lambert/Getty
Images, (date) Bill Sykes Images/Getty Images, (children) OJO Images Ltd/Alamy;
pg. 208 (popcorn) Tetra Images/Corbis, (reel) Randall Fung/Corbis; pg. 219 Cath
Ager/Alamy; pg. 220 Gilles Petard/Redferns/Getty Images; pg. 221 (race) Marit
Hommedal/AFP/Getty Images, (trophy) Michael Steele/Getty Images, (boxer)
Gene Blevins/LA Daily News/Corbis; pg. 223 Echoes/Redferns/Getty Images;
pg. 226 Ethan Miller/Reuters/Corbis.

Contents

Syllabus checklist

Introduction

American English File Second Edition is an integrated skills series that gets students talking — in class, and everywhere.

Our goal with this Second Edition has been to make every lesson better and more student- and teacher-friendly. We've created a blend of completely new lessons, updated texts and activities, and refreshed and fine-tuned some favorite lessons from New English File.

In addition to Student Book Lessons A and B, there is a range of material that you can use according to your students' needs and the time and resources you have available:

- Practical English video and exercises (also available on the audio CD, class DVD for home-study)
- Review and Check pages, with video (also available on the audio CD and class DVD for home-study)
- Photocopiable Grammar, Vocabulary, Communicative, and Song activities (in the Teacher's Book).

STUDY LINK Online Practice, Workbook, iChecker, and the Pronunciation app provide multimedia review, support, and practice for students outside of class.

The Teacher's Book also suggests different ways of exploiting many of the Student Book activities depending on the level of your class.

What do Intermediate students need?

The intermediate level is often a milestone for students: at this point, many students really begin to "take off" in terms of their ability to communicate. Some students, however, may see the intermediate level as a "plateau" and feel that they are no longer making the progress they were before. Students at this level need fresh challenges to help them to realize how much they know and to make their passive knowledge active, together with a steady input of new language.

Grammar, Vocabulary, and Pronunciation

At any level, the basic tools students need to speak English with confidence are Grammar, Vocabulary, and Pronunciation (G, V, P). In *American English File* Second Edition, all three elements are given equal importance. Each lesson has clearly stated grammar, vocabulary, and pronunciation goals. This keeps lessons focused and gives students concrete learning objectives and a sense of progress.

Grammar

Intermediate students need

- to review and extend their knowledge of the main grammatical structures.
- to practice using different tenses together.
- student-friendly reference material.

American English File Second Edition puts as much emphasis on consolidating and putting into practice known grammar as learning new structures. It provides contexts for new language that will engage students, using real-life stories and situations, humor, and suspense. The **Grammar Banks**, at the back of the book, give students a single, easy-to-access grammar reference section, with clear rules, example sentences with audio, and common errors. There are at least two practice exercises for each grammar point.

Vocabulary

Intermediate students need

- systematic expansion of topic-based lexical areas.
- to "build" new words by adding prefixes and suffixes.
- practice in pronouncing new lexis correctly.
- to put new vocabulary into practice.

Every lesson in American English File has a clear lexical aim. Many lessons are linked to the **Vocabulary Banks** which help present and practice high-frequency, topic-based vocabulary in class, give an audio model of each word, and provide a clear reference so students can review and test themselves on their own.

Pronunciation

Intermediate students need

- practice in pronouncing sounds and words clearly.
- to be aware of rules and patterns.
- to be able to use phonetic symbols in their dictionary.
- an awareness of word and sentence stress.

Clear, *intelligible* pronunciation (not perfection) should be the goal of students at this level. Students who studied with *American English File* 1 and 2 will already be familiar with American English File's unique system of sound pictures, which give clear example words to help identify and produce sounds. *American English File* 3 integrates this focus on individual sounds with a regular focus on word and sentence stress where students are encouraged to copy the rhythm of English. Pronunciation is also integrated into Grammar and Vocabulary activities, offering more practice for students, and often preparing students for a speaking activity.

Speaking

Intermediate students need

- topics that will motivate them to speak.
- the key words and phrases necessary to discuss a topic.
- to feel their pronunciation is clear and intelligible.
- practice in more extended speaking.
- time to organize their thoughts before speaking.

We believe that a good topic or text is very important in motivating students to speak in class. Every lesson in *American English File* 3 has a speaking activity which enables students to contribute their own knowledge or experience.

Confidence in speaking comes from knowing students are using the language correctly and pronouncing it correctly. So each speaking activity activates grammar, vocabulary, and pronunciation, and the tasks are designed to help students to feel a sense of progress and to show that the number of situations in which they can communicate effectively is growing.

For students who have time to do further practice, there are extra speaking activities available in Online Skills.

Listening

Intermediate students need

- interesting, integrated listening material.
- confidence-building, achievable tasks.
- to practice getting the gist and listening for detail.
- to practice dealing with authentic spoken language.

At Intermediate level, students need confidence-building tasks which are progressively more challenging in terms of speed, length, and language difficulty, but are always achievable. Longer listenings are broken into separate parts with different tasks, to avoid memory overload. Students are exposed to a wide variety of accents, including some non-native speakers of English.

For students who have time to do further practice, there are extra listening activities available in Online Skills.

Reading

Intermediate students need

- engaging topics and stimulating texts.
- exposure to a wide variety of authentic test types.
- challenging tasks which help them read better.

Many students need to read in English for their work or school, and reading is also important in helping to build vocabulary and to consolidate grammar. The key to encouraging students to read is to give them motivating but accessible material and tasks they can do. In *American English File* 3 reading texts have been adapted from a variety of real sources (newspapers, magazines, news websites) and have been chosen for their intrinsic interest.

For students who have time to do further practice, there are extra reading activities available in Online Skills.

Writing

Intermediate students need

- clear models.
- an awareness of register, structure, and fixed phrases.
- a focus on "micro" writing skills.

The growth of the Internet, email, and social networking means that people worldwide are writing in English more than ever before both for business and personal communication. *American English File* 3 provides guided writing tasks in each File, which consolidate grammar and lexis taught in the File.

For students who have time to do further practice, there are extra writing activities available in Online Skills.

Practical English

Intermediate students need

- to consolidate and extend their knowledge of functional language.
- to know what to say in typical social situations.
- to get used to listening to faster, more colloquial speech.

The five Practical English lessons review and extend common situations such as introducing yourself and others, or making polite requests, and introduce and practice the language for new situations, like expressing opinions or apologizing. The story line involving the two main characters, Jenny and Rob, continues from where it left off in *American English File* 2 but it is self-standing, so it can be used equally with students who did not use that level. The lessons also highlight other key "Social English" phrases such as *Could you tell me why… ?* and *I think I'll go home if you don't mind*. The Practical English lessons are on the ***American English File* 3 DVD** and **iTools**. Teachers can also use the Practical English Student Book exercises with the **Class Audio CD**. Using the video will provide a change of focus and give the lessons a clear visual context. The video will make the lessons more enjoyable and will also help students to role-play the situations.

Review

Intermediate students need

- regular review.
- motivating reference and practice material.
- to feel a sense of progress.

Intermediate students need to feel they are increasing their knowledge and improving their skills. After every two Files, there is a two-page Review & Check section. The left-hand page reviews the grammar, vocabulary, and pronunciation of each File. The right-hand page provides a series of skills-based challenges, including video interviews, and helps students to measure their progress in terms of competence. These pages are designed to be used flexibly according to the needs of your students. There are also a separate short movies available on video for students to watch and enjoy. Students can also review and consolidate after each lesson using the iChecker.

Student Book Files 1–10

The Student Book has ten Files, or units. Each File is organized like this:

A and B lessons

Each file contains two four-page lessons that present and practice **Grammar**, **Vocabulary**, and **Pronunciation** with a balance of reading and listening activities, and a lot of opportunity for speaking. These lessons have clear references to the Grammar Bank, Vocabulary Bank, and Sound Bank at the back of the book.

Practical English

After every odd-numbered File, there is a two-page lesson that teaches high-frequency, everyday English (e.g., language for asking for permission and making requests) and also social English (useful phrases like *How come you're so late?* and *I think I'll go home if you don't mind*). Integrated into every Practical English lesson is a motivating drama which can be found on the *American English File* 3 DVD.

Review & Check

After every even-numbered File, there is a two-page section reviewing **Grammar**, **Vocabulary**, and **Pronunciation** of each File and providing **Reading**, **Listening**, and **Speaking** *"Can you…?"* challenges to show students what they can achieve.

The back of the Student Book

The lessons contain references to these sections: Communication, Writing, Listening, Grammar Bank, Vocabulary Bank, and Sound Bank.

STUDY LINK

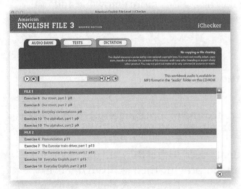

Workbook

For practice after class

- All of the Grammar, Vocabulary, Pronunciation, and Practical English
- Extra reading
- A listening exercise for every lesson
- Pronunciation exercises with audio
- Useful Words and Phrases
- Audio for Pronunciation and Listening exercises (on iChecker)

iChecker CD-ROM

Each workbook is packaged with an iChecker CD-ROM for students to check their progress and receive immediate feedback

- A Progress Check with 30 multiple choice questions for each File
- A Dictation exercise for each File
- All of the audio for the Workbook listening and pronunciation activities

Online Practice

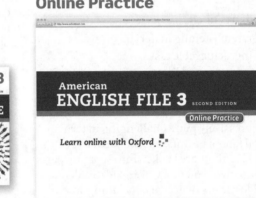

There is an access card on the inside back cover of each Student Book. Students register for engaging LMS-powered practice with immediate feedback on:

- Reading and Listening exercises for every File
- Writing and Speaking models and tasks for every File

Pronunciation app

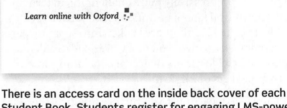

Students can purchase an engaging app through the iTunes or Google Android online stores for tablet- or phone-based practice. Students can learn and practice the sounds of English

- Individual sounds
- Sounds in useful phrases
- Speak and record

For teachers

Teacher's Book

Detailed lesson plans for all the lessons, including:

- an optional "books-closed" lead-in for every lesson
- **Extra idea** suggestions for optional extra activities
- **Extra challenge** suggestions for exploiting the Student Book material in a more challenging way if you have a stronger class
- **Extra support** suggestions for adapting activities or exercises to make them work for students who need extra support

Extra activities appear in green type so you can see at a glance what is core material and what is extra when you are planning and teaching your classes.

All lesson plans include keys and complete audio scripts.

Seventy pages of photocopiable activities are in the Teacher's Book.

Grammar

see pages 140 –163

- An activity for every Grammar Bank, which can be used in class or for self-study extra practice
- An Activation section to help students use the new language in class

Communicative

see pages 164 –195

- Extra speaking practice for every A and B lesson

Vocabulary

see pages 196 –214

- Extra practice of new vocabulary, for every Vocabulary Bank

Songs

see pages 215 –226

- A song for every File
- Provides the lyrics of the song, with task to do before, during, or after listening

iTools – bring your classroom to life

- The Student Book, Workbook, and Teacher's Book (photocopiables only) onscreen
- All class audio (including songs) and video, with interactive scripts
- Answer keys for Student Book, Workbook, and Teacher's Book
- Resources including Grammar PowerPoints, maps, and a CEFR Mapping Guide

Testing Program CD-ROM

- A Quick Test for every File
- A File test for every File covering G, V, P, Reading and Listening
- An Entry Test, two Progress Tests, and an End-of-course Test
- A and B versions of all the main tests
- Audio for all the Listening tests

Class Audio CDs

- All of the listening materials for the Student Book

DVD

Practical English

- A sitcom-style video that goes with the Practical English lessons in the Student Book

On the street

- Short real-world interviews to accompany the Review & Check sections

Short movies

- Short documentary films for students to watch after the Review & Check sections

G simple present and continuous, action and nonaction verbs
V food and cooking
P vowel sounds

1A Mood food

Lesson plan

The topic of this first lesson is food and restaurants. The lesson begins with a quiz to brainstorm food words Sts already know, and leads them to the Vocabulary Bank where they extend their knowledge of words and phrases related to food and cooking. There is then a pronunciation focus on vowel sounds, which is both very relevant to this lexical area, and will be especially useful if your Sts are not familiar with the *American English File* sound picture system. Sts then listen to people answering questions about food, which serves as a model for them to then answer the questions themselves, and they then read an article about new research on how different foods can affect your mood.

In the second half of the lesson, Sts listen to an interview with a chef who has his own restaurant in Spain. Extracts from the interview lead to the grammar focus, which is on the simple present and continuous, and Sts are introduced to the concept of action and nonaction verbs. The lesson ends with a speaking activity where Sts discuss statements related to food and cooking.

If you would like to begin the first lesson without the book, there is a Communicative photocopiable "Getting to know you" activity on *pages 172–173* (instructions *page 164*), two photocopiable review Grammar activities on *pages 142–143* (answers *page 140*), and one Vocabulary photocopiable "Classroom language" activity on *page 200* (instructions *page 196*).

There is an Entry Test on the *Testing Program CD-ROM*, which you can give the Sts before starting the course.

STUDY LINK
- Workbook 1A

Extra photocopiable activities

- **Grammar** Introduction a *page 142*
  Introduction b *page 143*
  simple present and continuous *page 144*
- **Communicative** Getting to know you *pages 172–173*
  (instructions *page 164*)
  Spot the difference *page 174* (instructions *page 164*)
- **Vocabulary** Classroom language *page 200* (instructions *page 196*)
  Food and cooking *page 201* (instructions *page 196*)

Optional lead-in (books closed)

- Write FRUIT on the board. Then put Sts in pairs and give them a minute to write down five words for different kinds of fruit.
- Check answers and write them on the board (eliciting the spelling from Sts if you want to review the alphabet).
- Then ask Sts which fruit they think is the most popular in their country.

1 VOCABULARY food and cooking

a Books open. Focus on the quiz. Quickly go through the questions and then set a time limit of about five minutes for Sts to answer in pairs.

Extra idea
- You could divide the class into teams and make this a contest.

Check answers and write them on the board, getting Sts to spell some of the words.

Possible answers
1 red – apple / strawberry / cherry
  yellow – banana / lemon
  green – apple / pear / grapes
2 eggs, nuts, seafood, etc.
3 cheese, cream, yogurt, ice cream, etc.
4 lettuce, tomatoes, carrots, onions, beans, potatoes, etc.
5 a package, a bag, a can, a box, a jar, etc.
6 toast, bread, cereal, eggs, croissant, fruit, etc.

b Tell Sts to go to **Vocabulary Bank** *Food and cooking* on *page 152*.

Focus on **1 Food** and get Sts to do **a** individually or in pairs.

1 2)) Now do **b**. Play the audio for Sts to check answers. Play the audio again, pausing for Sts to repeat. Practice any words your Sts find difficult to pronounce, modeling and drilling as necessary. You could use the audio to do this.

1 2))
Food and cooking
Food

Fish and seafood		**Fruit and vegetables**	
1	crab	23	beet
5	mussels	12	cabbage
2	salmon	22	cherries
6	shrimp	16	cucumber
3	squid	18	eggplant
4	tuna	21	grapes
Meat		25	green beans
10	beef	24	lemon
11	chicken	17	mango
8	duck	13	melon
9	lamb	19	peach
7	pork	14	pear
		26	raspberries
		15	red pepper
		20	zucchini

Get Sts to do **c** in pairs and then get some feedback.

Do **d** as a whole class.

Now focus on **2 Cooking** and get Sts to do **a** individually or in pairs.

1 3)) Now do **b**. Play the audio for Sts to check answers. Play the audio again, pausing for Sts to repeat. Practice any words your Sts find difficult to pronounce, modeling and drilling as necessary. You could use the audio to do this.

Cooking
4 boiled
3 roasted
1 baked
6 grilled
2 fried
5 steamed

Sts may ask what the difference is between *baked* and *roast*, as both mean cooked in the oven: *baked* is usually for bread, cakes, and most sweet, though chicken and fish can also be baked. *Roast* usually means cooked by exposing to dry heat as in an oven, and is usually a method for cooking meat and vegetables.

Now focus on **c** and get Sts to tell a partner how they like the four items cooked. Get some feedback from the class.

Finally, focus on the **Phrasal verbs** box and go through it with Sts.

You may want to immediately get Sts to test themselves or each other before going back to the main lesson.

Ways of testing

Sts can test themselves by covering the words and looking at either the definitions or pictures (or sometimes fill-in-the-blank texts or sentences) and trying to remember the words.

Alternatively, Sts can take turns testing each other. **B** closes his / her book and **A** defines or explains a word for **B** to try and remember, e.g., **A** *What do you call food that is cooked in hot water?* **B** *Boiled food.* After a few minutes, Sts can change roles.

In a monolingual class, Sts could also test each other by saying the word in their L1 for their partner to say in English.

Expanding Sts' vocabulary

In this lexical group, as in many others, there are large numbers of useful words and a selection has been made in order not to overwhelm Sts. However, words which are important in your Sts' country may have been left out. It is important to teach these very common or popular foods and to get Sts to add them to the Vocabulary Bank page, so that they are equipped with the vocabulary they need to do the speaking activities that follow.

Tell Sts to go back to the main lesson **1A**.

Extra support

• If you think Sts need more practice, you may want to give them the Vocabulary photocopiable activity at this point or leave it for later as consolidation or review.

c **1 4**)) Tell Sts to look at the list of adjectives that are used to describe food, and play the audio. Elicit the meaning of each adjective and drill pronunciation.

1 4))
See adjectives in Student Book on *page 4*.

Give Sts time, in pairs, to think of a food item for each adjective.

Check answers.

Possible answers
canned: tomatoes, tuna, etc.
fresh: fish, vegetables, etc.
frozen: peas, fish, pizza, etc.
low-fat: yogurt, cheese, etc.
raw: fish, vegetables, etc.
spicy: sauce, chicken, etc.
take-out: pizza, Chinese, etc.

2 PRONUNCIATION

vowel sounds

Pronunciation notes
• Sts work on distinguishing eight common vowel sounds in American English.

a Focus on the eight sound pictures. If your Sts are not familiar with them, explain that the sound pictures give a clear example of a word with the target sound and they help them remember the pronunciation of the phonetic symbol (there is one for each of the 46 sounds of American English).

Now put Sts in pairs and get them to work out the eight words and sounds.

Check answers.

| 1 fish /ɪ/ | 3 cat /æ/ | 5 clock /ɑ/ | 7 bull /ʊ/ |
| 2 tree /i/ | 4 car /ɑr/ | 6 horse /ɔr/ | 8 boot /u/ |

b Now focus on the instructions and the example. Give Sts a few moments in pairs to find the word with the sound that's different from the others in each list. Remind Sts that this kind of exercise is easier if they say the words aloud to themselves.

Extra support

• You could play the audio first for Sts to hear the words <u>before</u> they try to find the word that doesn't have the same sound as the picture word.

c **1 5**)) Play the audio once for Sts to listen and check.

Check answers.

2 breakfast	5 roast	8 duck
3 grapes	6 boiled	
4 warm	7 food	

(1 5))

See words in Student Book on *page 4*

Now play the audio again, pausing after each group of words for Sts to listen and repeat.

d   Tell Sts to go to the **Sound Bank** on *page 166*. Explain that here they can find all the sounds and their symbols and also the typical spellings for these sounds plus some more irregular ones.

Tell Sts to go back to the main lesson **1A**.

3   LISTENING & SPEAKING

a   **(1 6))** Focus on the instructions and the *Food & Eating* questions. Give Sts time to read the questions and make sure they understand them. Elicit / explain the meaning of *ready-made food* and *feeling a little down*.

Play the audio once all the way through for Sts just to listen.

Now play the audio again, pausing after each speaker for Sts to match each one to a question. Play again if necessary.

Check answers.

Extra support

• Before playing the audio, go through the listening script and decide if you need to preteach / check any lexis to help Sts when they listen.

Speaker B: 2	Speaker D: 5
Speaker C: 1	Speaker E: 3

(1 6))

(script in Student Book on *page 122*)

A

I usually have meat or seafood. Usually shrimp or something as an appetizer and then maybe lamb for the main course.

B

I often have ready-made vegetable soups that you just have to heat up – in fact, they're the only vegetables I ever eat! And I usually have a couple of frozen pizzas in the freezer for emergencies. I don't really order takeout when I'm on my own, but if I'm with friends in the evening, we sometimes order Chinese food for dinner.

C

Eggs and soda. I have eggs for breakfast at least twice a week, and I drink a couple of cans of soda every day.

D

If I'm feeling down, chicken soup, with nice big pieces of chicken in it. It's warm and comforting. Uh, I usually have a banana before going to the gym. If I know I'm going to have a really long meeting, I usually have a coffee and a cup cake because I think it will keep me awake and give me energy.

E

Fruit – cherries, strawberries, raspberries, and apples. Vegetables – peppers, tomatoes, and cucumbers. The only thing I really don't like is zucchini. I can't even stand the smell of it.

b   Tell Sts that they are going to listen to the five speakers again and that this time they must write down in note form the answer the speakers give.

Play the audio, pausing after each speaker to give Sts time to write.

Get Sts to compare with a partner and then check answers.

See script 1.6

c   Put Sts in pairs and get them to ask and answer the questions in *Food & Eating*, giving as much information as possible. They should see if they have anything in common.

Monitor and help with any food vocabulary.

Get feedback from different pairs to find out if they have anything in common.

Extra challenge

• Before Sts give feedback, you may want to teach them the phrases *Both of us* and *Neither of us*, which they can use to show what they have in common.

Extra support

• Demonstrate the activity by answering one or two of the questions yourself before putting Sts in pairs.

4   READING

a   Focus on the instructions and make sure Sts understand the words *carbohydrate* and *protein*. Write the two words on the board. Model and drill their pronunciation. You may want to tell Sts that native speakers often just say *carbs* for *carbohydrates*.

First, get Sts to match the four food items in the list with the right food category.

Then check answers.

carbohydrates: cake, pasta
proteins: chicken, salmon

Now put Sts in pairs and get them to add four food items to each category.

Check answers and write them on the board.

Possible answers
carbohydrates: bread, potatoes, rice, cereal, etc.
proteins: beef, tuna, eggs, cheese, etc.

b   Focus on the instructions and the four questions. In pairs, Sts answer the questions.

Do <u>not</u> check answers.

c Focus on the title of the article and ask Sts what they think it means. Do <u>not</u> tell Sts if they are right.

Now tell Sts to read the article to find out the meaning of the title and to check their answers to **b**, to see if they are eating the right things.

Check answers.

Extra support

- Before Sts read the article, check it for words and phrases that your Sts might not know and be ready to help with these while they are answering the questions or afterwards. You may even want to preteach / check a few words / phrases to lighten the load.

> The title means that certain foods can affect your mood – how you think and feel.
>
> b
> for lunch before an exam or meeting: proteins
> for breakfast: proteins
> for your evening meal: carbohydrates
> if you are stressed: carbohydrates

d Tell Sts to read the article again and to find why the people 1–5 are mentioned.

Get Sts to discuss the five people or groups of people with a partner. Remind them to use their own words.

Check answers.

> 1 Dr. Paul Clayton is a food expert from Middlesex University. He says that our brains are affected by the things we eat and drink, and that some foods affect how we think and feel.
> 2 People on diets often begin to feel depressed after two weeks because they are eating fewer carbohydrates, and carbohydrates make us feel happy.
> 3 Schoolchildren who have protein for breakfast do better at school because protein makes us feel awake and focused.
> 4 Paul and Terry are former chess champions. In an experiment they did before a match, Paul had a plate of *prosciutto* and salad (full of protein from the red meat), and Terry had pasta with a creamy sauce (full of carbohydrates). In the chess match Terry felt sleepy and took longer than Paul to decide what moves to make.
> 5 Swiss researchers found that eating dark chocolate reduced stress. They also proved that chocolate improves mood and reduced high blood pressure.

e Tell Sts to look at the verbs and nouns in the list and to then look for the equivalent adjectives in the article.

Get Sts to compare with a partner and then check answers. Model and drill pronunciation.

> stress, stressful, stressed
> relax, relaxed
> wake, awake
> sleep, sleepy
> power, powerful
> benefit, beneficial

Elicit the difference between *stressful* and *stressed* (stressful = something that makes you feel stressed, e.g., your job, a problem).

Finally, help with any other new vocabulary and encourage Sts to write down any useful new lexis from the article.

f Put Sts in pairs to answer the questions and then get feedback from the class.

Extra support

- Demonstrate the activity by answering the questions yourself.

5 LISTENING & SPEAKING

a Focus on the *Restaurants* questionnaire and make sure Sts understand all the questions – for example, make sure Sts are clear about the difference between *food* (meat, fish, pasta, etc.) and *dish* (mushroom pizza, chicken curry, spaghetti carbonara, etc.).

Put Sts in pairs and get them to interview each other. Tell them that they can use their L1 for dishes from their country which may not have a translation.

Get some feedback from the class.

Extra support

- Answer the first two questions yourself to demonstrate the activity.

b (1 7))) Focus on the instructions. Give Sts time to read the introduction and then ask them some questions, e.g., *Who taught Steve how to cook?* (his mother and several famous chefs) *What nationality is Steve's mother?* (half Burmese) *Who is Alastair Little?* (the chef who employed Steve as a trainee chef), etc.

Now focus on the photos and elicit what Sts can see. Preteach *snails* and *a casserole* for photos C and E, and elicit that a casserole is made of meat or fish with vegetables all cooked together slowly in one pot in the oven.

Tell Sts that when they listen the first time, they should just try to get a general understanding of what Steve says and number the photos in the order that they are mentioned.

Play the audio once for Sts to number the photos 1–6.

Check answers, getting Sts to tell you what each photo shows.

Extra support

- Before playing the audio, go through the listening script and decide if you need to preteach / check any lexis to help Sts when they listen.

> 1 C snails and shrimp with garlic
> 2 F the market
> 3 A Steve's restaurant
> 4 B mussels
> 5 E a casserole
> 6 D desserts

(1 7)))

(script in Student Book on *page 122*)
I = interviewer, S = Steve

Part 1

I What was your favorite food when you were a child?

S Well, I always liked unusual things, at least things that most English children at the time didn't like. For instance, when I was six or seven my favorite things were snails, oh and prawns with garlic.

I Funny things for a six-year-old English boy to like!

S Well, the thing is my parents liked traveling and eating out a lot, and I first tried snails in France, and the prawns, my first prawns, I had at a Spanish restaurant in the town where we lived.

I So you were interested in Spanish food right from the start. Is that why you decided to come to Spain?

S Partly, but of course, I suppose like a lot of British people I wanted to see the sun! The other thing that attracted me when I got here were all the fantastic ingredients. I remember going into the market for the first time and saying "Wow!"

I When you opened your restaurant, how did you want it to be different from typical Spanish restaurants?

S Well, when I came to Spain, all the good restaurants were very formal, very traditional. In London then, the fashion was for informal places where the waiters wore jeans, but the food was amazing. So I wanted a restaurant a bit like that. I also wanted a restaurant where you could try more international food, but made with some of these fantastic local ingredients. For example, Spain's got wonderful seafood, but usually here it's just grilled or fried. I started doing things in my restaurant like cooking Valencian mussels in Thai green curry paste.

I What do you most enjoy cooking?

S What I most enjoy cooking, I think are those traditional dishes which use quite cheap ingredients, but they need very long and careful cooking, and then you turn it into something really special... like a really good casserole, for example.

I And is there anything you <u>don't</u> like cooking?

S Maybe desserts. You have to be very very precise when you're making desserts. And that's not the way I am.

c Now tell Sts to listen again and write down why Steve mentions each item.

Get Sts to compare with a partner, and then check answers.

1 snails and prawns with garlic: they were his favorite food when he was six or seven – unusual things for a British child to like.

2 the market: he remembers going to the market in Spain for the first time and being impressed by all the wonderful ingredients.

3 the restaurant: he wanted a restaurant that was informal, but served fantastic food.

4 mussels: they are an example of the kind of food he makes. He cooks Valencian mussels with Thai green curry paste.

5 a casserole: something which uses cheap ingredients, but can be wonderful with long careful cooking and what he most enjoys cooking.

6 desserts: he doesn't like making desserts because you have to be very precise.

d **(1 8)))** Tell Sts they are now going to listen to **Part 2** of the interview. Focus on the questions and quickly go through them.

Play the audio once all the way through. You could pause after each question is answered to give Sts time to make notes. Play again if necessary.

Get Sts to compare with a partner and then check answers.

1 the best thing: making people happy
the worst thing: the long hours

2 British customers always say that everything is lovely even if they don't actually eat it all, whereas Spanish customers are honest and say what they think.

3 Customers who want him to cook something in a way that he doesn't think is very good, for example a well-done steak.

4 He thinks they are getting worse. People are eating more unhealthily.

(1 8)))

(script in Student Book on *page 122*)

Part 2

I What's the best thing about running a restaurant?

S I think the best thing is making people happy. That's why even after all this time I still enjoy it so much.

I And the worst thing?

S That's easy, it has to be the long hours. This week for example I'm cooking nearly every day. We usually close on Sundays and Mondays, but this Monday is a public holiday, when lots of people want to eat out, so we're open.

I *Seu Xerea* is in all the British restaurant guides now. Does that mean you get a lot of British customers?

S Yes, we get a lot of British people, especially at the weekends, but then we get people from other countries too.

I And are the British customers and the Spanish customers very different?

S Yes, I think they are. The British always say that everything is lovely, even if they've only eaten half of it. The Spanish, on the other hand, are absolutely honest about everything. They tell you what they like, they tell you what they don't like. I remember when I first opened, I had sushi on the menu, which was very unusual at that time, and I went into the dining room and I said to people, "So what do you think of the sushi?" And the customers, who were all Spanish, said "Oh, it was awful! It was raw fish!" Actually, I think I prefer that honesty, because it helps us to know what people like.

I What kind of customers do you find difficult?

S I think customers who want me to cook something in a way that I don't think is very good. Let's see, a person who asks for a really well-done steak, for instance. For me that's a difficult customer. You know, they'll say, "I want a really really well-done steak," so I give them a really really well-done steak and then they say, "It's tough." And I think well, of course it's tough. It's well done! Well-done steak is always tough.

I People say that the Mediterranean diet is very healthy. Do you think people's eating habits in Spain are changing?

S Well, I think they are changing. Unfortunately, I think they're getting worse. People are eating more unhealthily.

I How do you notice that?

S I see it with, especially with younger friends. They often eat in fast-food restaurants, they don't cook... and actually the younger ones come from a generation where their mothers don't cook either. That's what's happening now, and it's a real pity.

Extra support

• If there's time, you could get Sts to listen again with the scripts on *page 122*, so they can see exactly what they understood / didn't understand. Translate / explain any new words or phrases.

e Put Sts in pairs and have them tell each other their answers to the four questions.

Get feedback from individual pairs or you could simply ask the whole class. You could also tell them about yourself.

6 GRAMMAR simple present and continuous, action and nonaction verbs

a   Focus on the instructions. Give Sts a minute, in pairs, to circle the correct form in each sentence.

Play the audio for Sts to listen and check.

See words in **bold** in script 1.9

---

1 9))

1 This week for example **I'm cooking** nearly every day. We **usually close** on Sundays and Mondays, but this Monday is a public holiday.
2 The British always **say** that everything is lovely.
3 Actually, I think **I prefer** that honesty, because it helps us to know what people like.
4 Unfortunately, I think **they're getting** worse. People **are eating** more unhealthily.

---

b Give Sts time in pairs to discuss why they think Steve chose each form in the sentences in **a**.

Check answers, getting Sts to explain why (in their L1 if necessary) the other form is wrong. For 3, they may simply "feel" that *prefer* is right without being able to explain why. This would be a good moment to explain about action / nonaction verbs (see **Additional grammar notes** below).

---

1 I'm cooking (It's a temporary action which is only happening this week.)
   close (It usually happens.)
2 say (It's a habitual action.)
3 I prefer (It's a nonaction verb, not usually used in the continuous.)
4 they're getting, are eating (They are actions which are happening right now.)

---

c **1 10)) 1 11)) 1 12))** Tell Sts to go to **Grammar Bank 1A** on *page 132*. If your Sts have not used the *American English File* series before, explain that all the grammar rules and exercises are in this part of the book.

Focus on the example sentences and play the audio for Sts to listen to the sentence rhythm. You could also get Sts to repeat the sentences to practice getting the rhythm right. Then go through the rules with the class.

Additional grammar notes

Simple present

• At this level Sts should be clear about the form and use of the simple present.

• Remind Sts of the difference in pronunciation of the third person *-s*, i.e., /s/ (verbs ending in an unvoiced consonant, e.g., *cooks, eats*), /z/ (verbs ending in a vowel sound or voiced consonant, e.g., *plays, has*), and /ɪz/ (verbs where you have added *-es*, e.g., *watches, finishes*).

• Remind them too of the irregular pronunciation of (*he / she / it*) *says* /sez/ and *does* /dʌz/.

! The simple present is also occasionally used to refer to the future, e.g., *The next train leaves at 7:30.* This use is not dealt with here.

Present continuous

• Sts who don't have a continuous form in their language may need reminding that this is the form they must use when they are talking about temporary actions in progress now, this week, this month, etc.

• Remind Sts of the use of the present continuous for future arrangements. This will be reviewed fully together with the other future forms in **1B**.

Action and nonaction verbs

• These are often called dynamic / stative or progressive / non-progressive verbs. We have called them action / nonaction as we think this helps to make the difference clearer for Sts. There are several other verbs which can be both action and nonaction, e.g., *see*, *look*, and *feel*, but at this level we feel it is best to use *have* and *think* as two clear examples.

Focus on the exercises and get Sts to do them individually or in pairs.

Check answers, getting Sts to read the full sentences.

---

a
1 have
2 Are ... taking
3 don't like
4 Does ... know
5 don't get
6 is / 's ... making
7 are ... thinking
8 is getting
9 do ... eat
10 don't ... cook
b
1 is coming
2 doesn't want
3 isn't working
4 seems
5 aren't speaking
6 thinks
7 Do we need
8 I'm having
9 I love
10 are you cooking

Tell Sts to go back to the main lesson **1A**.

Extra support

• If you think Sts need more practice, you may want to give them the Grammar photocopiable activity at this point or leave it for later as consolidation or review.

d Focus on the question prompts. Elicit that those under **On a typical day** are habitual actions, so should be simple present, and Sts must add *do you*. The ones under **Right now / nowadays** are things in progress, and if the verbs are action verbs, they should be present continuous; if they are nonaction, they should be simple present.

Elicit the questions from the class to check that they are forming the questions correctly, and that they are using the correct rhythm, i.e., stressing the "information" words.

On a typical day

<u>What</u> do you <u>usually</u> <u>have</u> for <u>breakfast</u>?

Do you <u>drink</u> <u>soda</u>? <u>How</u> <u>many</u> <u>glasses</u> do you <u>drink</u> a <u>day</u>?

<u>Where</u> do you <u>usually</u> <u>have</u> <u>lunch</u>?

<u>What</u> do you <u>usually</u> <u>have</u> for <u>lunch</u> <u>during</u> the <u>week</u>?

Do you <u>ever</u> <u>cook</u>? <u>What</u> do you <u>make</u>?

Do you <u>prefer</u> <u>eating</u> at <u>home</u> or <u>eating</u> <u>out</u>?

> **Right now / nowadays**
> Do you <u>need</u> to <u>buy</u> any <u>food</u> <u>today</u>?
> Do you <u>want</u> <u>anything</u> to <u>eat</u> right <u>now</u>? <u>What</u>?
> Are you <u>taking</u> any <u>vitamins</u> or <u>food</u> <u>supplements</u> right <u>now</u>?
> Are you <u>trying</u> to cut <u>down</u> on <u>anything</u> right <u>now</u>?
> Is the <u>diet</u> in your <u>country</u> getting <u>better</u> or <u>worse</u>?

Extra support

- You could write the full questions on the board and underline the stressed words to help Sts get the rhythm right.

Monitor as Sts work in pairs, making sure they are using the simple present and continuous correctly. The focus here should be on accurate practice of the grammar.

Get some feedback from various pairs.

7 SPEAKING

a Focus Sts' attention on sentence 1 and tell them they are going to listen to two people discussing the statement.

Play the audio once all the way through.

Get Sts to discuss in pairs who they agree with most.

Get some feedback.

>
>
> **M = man, W = woman**
> **M** I agree. In most top restaurants the chef is a man. For example Mario Batali, or Marcus Samuelsson.
> **W** I don't agree. There are many more women chefs than before in restaurants. And at home women cook much more than men.
> **M** That's true. But I still think men are better cooks. They're more adventurous in the kitchen.
> **W** In my opinion that's only because they don't cook every day. It's easy to be adventurous if you only cook once a week.
> **M** I'm not sure. I know a lot of men who cook almost every day.
> **W** I think it depends.

b Tell Sts that they are going to give their opinion about the various topics related to food in sentences 2–6. Focus on the **Useful language: Giving your opinion (1)** box and play the audio once all the way through for Sts to listen to all the phrases.

>
> See phrases in Student Book on *page 7*

Elicit / explain what the phrases mean.

Play the audio again, pausing after each phrase for Sts to listen and repeat, getting them to copy the stress and intonation.

c Focus on the instructions, and divide Sts into groups of three if possible. Give them enough time to think of reasons and examples for each statement.

Monitor while Sts are debating and encourage them to use the phrases for giving their opinion. Don't overcorrect, but make a note of any errors that you may want to focus on when they finish speaking.

Get some feedback.

G future forms: present continuous, *going to*, *will / won't*, 🔑*each other*
V family, adjectives of personality
P sentence stress, word stress, adjective endings

1B Family life

Lesson plan

The context of the lesson is the family. Sts begin by reviewing family vocabulary and talking about the way family life is changing in the US and in their country. The grammar focus is on the three most common future forms. Sts will have studied them all separately, but have probably not had to previously distinguish between them. There is then a pronunciation focus on the stress patterns in the future forms, and this first half of the lesson ends with the song *Our House*.

In the second half, the focus shifts to relationships between siblings. Sts read an article about the advantages and disadvantages of being a younger brother and an only child. They then extend their knowledge of adjectives to describe personality and also practice the word stress in these adjectives. The lesson ends with a listening and speaking about how your position in the family affects your personality, and a writing focus on describing a person.

STUDY**LINK**
- **Workbook** 1B
- **iChecker**

Extra photocopiable activities

- **Grammar** future forms *page 145*
- **Communicative** Who is it? *page 175* (instructions *page 165*)
- **Vocabulary** Personality *page 202* (instructions *page 196*)
- **Song** *Our House* page 218 (instructions *page 215*)

Optional lead-in (books closed)

- Review family words by drawing a quick family tree of your direct family and tell Sts a little about them.
- Put Sts in pairs and have them do the same.

1 VOCABULARY & SPEAKING family

a Books open. Focus on the photos and the questions. Put Sts in pairs and get them to describe the photos.

Check answers.

> **Possible answers**
> The photo on the left shows an extended family celebration.
> The middle photo shows a couple and their young family about to go on a trip. The couple appear to be arguing. The photo on the top right shows a woman with her (great) grandson.

b In pairs, Sts discuss the difference between the words in 1–7.

Check answers.

1 A father is a male parent of a child and a parent is a person's mother or father.
2 Your stepmother is the woman who is married to your father, but she isn't your real mother.
3 Your brother-in-law is the brother of your husband / wife or your sister's husband.
4 Your grandfather is the father of your father or mother. Your great grandfather is your father's / mother's grandfather.
5 A nephew is the son of your brother / sister. A niece is the daughter of your brother / sister.
6 A child is a young human who is not yet an adult, and an only child is a child who doesn't have brothers or sisters.
7 Your immediate family is your parents, children, brother, and sisters. Your extended family is your immediate family and uncles, aunts, grandparents, etc.

! You may also want to teach *stepbrother* / *stepsister* (= the children of your stepmother / stepfather, but who don't have the same mother or father as you and are not blood relatives).

c Focus on the instructions and make sure Sts understand *survey* and *statistics*. Read the introduction together, making sure Sts understand it.

Now give Sts time to read the results of the survey and guess what the missing percentages are.

d (**1 15**)) Play the audio for Sts to listen and check.

Check answers.

1	43%	3	60%	5	75%
2	11%	4	67%		

> (**1 15**))
> Family life is changing in the US, but not in the way we might think. The results of several different US surveys expected to find that family relationships were suffering because of the decline in traditional family structures.
> However, some of the results were very surprising ...
> 32% of young adults under 25 and 10% of adults 30-34 still live at home with their parents.
> 43% of families eat together every day.
> 33% say they have the TV on during dinner.
> 50% think a new baby in the family brings more happiness.
> 49% of adults are happy and enjoy their lives without a lot of stress.
> 11% of adults are not happy and have a lot of stress or worry in their lives.
> 60% of teens feel close to their family.
> 67% of teens want to spend more time with their parents.
> 75% of parents stay connected with their children on social networks.
> 40% of parents worry about what their kids post on social networks.
> 17% of elderly women live with a relative such as a daughter, daughter-in-law, or grandchild.

Get feedback on what Sts found surprising.

Remind Sts that the surveys used for this piece were done in the US. Put Sts in pairs and get them to discuss which results they think would be very different for their country.

Get some feedback from various pairs.

e Focus on the **Useful language: Giving your opinion (2)** box and go through it with the class.

Put Sts in small groups of four if possible. Tell Sts to discuss the questions in their groups.

Monitor and help, encouraging Sts to use expressions from the box.

Get some feedback from the class.

2 GRAMMAR future forms

a (1 16)) Focus on the instructions. Play the audio once all the way through. You could pause after each dialogue. Play again if necessary.

Check answers.

1 grandmother to grandson; they are talking about what he's going to do next year.
2 father to daughter; they are talking about where she's going and what she's doing.
3 son to mother; they are talking about if he can borrow her car.

(1 16))

1
A So what are you going to do next year, dear? Are you going to go to college? Adam, can you hear me?
B Sorry, Grandma. What did you say?
A I said, "Are you going to go to college next year?"
B No, Grandma. I've already told you a thousand times. I'm not going to go to college yet. I'm going to look for a job. I need to earn some money.
A All right, dear, you don't need to shout. I can hear perfectly well, thank you. What time is it now?
B Ten to four. I'll I make you a cup of tea.
A Yes, please, dear. That'd be very nice.

2
A Bye. See you tomorrow.
B Bye. Hey, what do you mean <u>tomorrow</u>? Aren't you coming back tonight?
A No, I told you about it yesterday. I'm going to a party at Katie's. I'm staying over night there.
B Who else is going?
A Oh, just the usual crowd. You don't know any of them.
B Well, make sure you don't go to bed too late. And don't forget to...
A Bye.
B Where's your coat? You can't go out like that; it's going to be cold tonight.
A Bye!

3
A Can I use your car tonight?
B No, you can't.
A You said you didn't need it. Why can't I borrow it?
B Because you won't be careful. You'll drive too fast.
A I won't, I promise, I'll drive really slowly. I'll be really careful.
B Well, alright.
A Thanks. See you.

Extra idea

• Alternatively, you could pause the audio after each dialogue, play it again if necessary, and check the answer.

b Go through sentences A–F and make it clear that Sts don't have to number the sentences in order, but simply match two with each dialogue.

Extra challenge

• Get Sts in pairs to decide before they listen again which sentences are from which dialogue.

Play the audio again, pausing after each dialogue.

Check answers.

A 1	B 3	C 1	D 2	E 3	F 2

c Focus on the instructions and make sure Sts understand the difference between, for example, a plan or intention, and an arrangement.

Get Sts to compare with a partner and then check answers.

a plan or intention: C
an arrangement: D
a prediction: B, F
a promise: E
an offer: A

From this, elicit from Sts that generally speaking we use *be going to* for plans and predictions, *will* / *shall* for predictions, offers, and promises, and the present continuous for arrangements.

d (1 17)) (1 18)) (1 19)) (1 20)) Tell Sts to go to **Grammar Bank 1B** on *page 133*. Focus on the example sentences and play the audio for Sts to listen to the sentence rhythm. You could also get Sts to repeat the sentences to practice getting the rhythm right. Then go through the rules with the class.

Additional grammar notes
• Sts often have problems using future forms correctly in American English, mainly because the future form you use depends on what the speaker wants to say, e.g., whether he / she wants to express a plan or pre-arranged event, or make an "instant" decision at that moment. This means that Sts often can't use the same form that they would use in their L1.
• The important thing to emphasize is that we use *be going to* (or present continuous) for things we have already decided to do, i.e., our plans, intentions, or arrangements, whereas *will* / *won't* + infinitive is used for decisions made at the time of speaking, and also for promises, offers, and future facts.
• A typical mistake here is to use the simple present for offers: ~~I carry your bag for you.~~
! You may want to point out that in song lyrics *going to* is usually transcribed as *gonna* (because that is how it sounds when sung quickly).

Focus on the exercises and get Sts to do them individually or in pairs.

Check answers, getting Sts to read the full sentences.

a		
1 ✓		6 ✓
2 I'll make		7 ✓
3 ✓		8 I'm not going to go
4 will be		9 ✓
5 I won't tell		

b		
1 will / 'll write		5 Are, going to get
2 is / 's going to earn		6 will / 'll lend
3 am / 'm working		7 is / 's going to rain / will rain
4 will / 'll have		8 Will, need

Extra idea

• Get Sts to read the dialogues in **b** aloud to practice the rhythm.

Tell Sts to go back to the main lesson **1B**.

Extra support

• If you think Sts need more practice, you may want to give them the Grammar photocopiable activity at this point or leave it for later as consolidation or review.

3 PRONUNCIATION sentence stress

Pronunciation notes

• As Sts should already know, in English, words which are stressed more strongly are the ones which carry information, e.g., I WENT to the MOVIES on FRIDAY NIGHT. These are typically verbs, nouns, adjectives, and adverbs. The other "non-information" words (e.g., personal pronouns, articles, and little words like *to, of, on, as,* etc.) are pronounced less strongly, and these words often get shortened when we speak, e.g., *to* becomes /tə/. It is this mixture of stressed and unstressed words which gives American English its rhythm, and Sts need plenty of practice until correct stress and rhythm becomes instinctive.

a (1 21))) Focus on the **Sentence stress** box and go through it with the class.

Now focus on the dialogues. Point out to Sts that the words that are stressed are in a bigger font.

Play the audio once all the way through for Sts just to listen.

> (1 21)))
> See dialogues in Student Book on *page 9*

Then play it again, pausing after each line for Sts to listen and repeat, copying the rhythm.

b Put Sts in pairs and get them to practice saying the dialogues.

Get some feedback from various pairs.

c Focus on the questions and make sure Sts understand them.

Put Sts in pairs and get them to ask and answer the questions, giving as much information as possible.

Monitor and make sure they are using the right future forms and getting the sentence stress correct.

Get some feedback.

4 (1 22))) SONG *Our House* ♫

This song was made famous by the British group Madness in 1982. For copyright reasons this is a cover version. If you want to do the song in class, use the photocopiable activity on *page 218*.

(1 22)))

Our House

Father wears his Sunday best
Mother's tired she needs a rest
The kids are playing up downstairs
Sister's sighing in her sleep
Brother's got a date to keep
He can't hang around

> *Chorus*
> Our house, in the middle of our street
> Our house, in the middle of our...

Our house it has a crowd
There's always something happening
And it's usually quite loud
Our mum she's so house-proud
Nothing ever slows her down and a mess is not allowed

> *Chorus*

Our house, in the middle of our street
(Something tells you that you've got to move away from it)

Father gets up late for work
Mother has to iron his shirt
Then she sends the kids to school
Sees them off with a small kiss
She's the one they're going to miss in lots of ways

> *Chorus*

I remember way back then when everything was true and when
We would have such a very good time
Such a fine time
Such a happy time
And I remember how we'd play, simply waste the day away
Then we'd say nothing would come between us two dreamers

Repeat first verse

> *Chorus (x 2)*

Our house, was our castle and our keep
Our house, in the middle of our street
Our house, that was where we used to sleep
Our house, in the middle of our street

Tell Sts to go back to the main lesson **1B**.

5 READING

a Ask the questions to the whole class and elicit opinions.

! Do <u>not</u> ask Sts if they are an only child as they will talk about this later.

b Focus on the instructions and tell Sts they are going to read an article written by a journalist about siblings. Put Sts in pairs and tell the **A**s to read *The Younger Brother* and the **B**s *The Only Child*.

Extra support

• Before Sts read the texts, check them for words and phrases that your Sts might not know and be ready to help with these while they are answering the questions or afterwards. You may even want to preteach a few words / phrases to lighten the load (but not the highlighted words).

c Focus on the instructions and the task. Give Sts time to read their text again if necessary.

When they have finished reading, tell them to cover the text they just read and to discuss 1 and 2 with their partner. Alternatively, you could write points 1 and 2 on the board and tell Sts to close their books.

Ask the class *Whose childhood sounds happier?* and get Sts to vote by raising their hands.

d Tell Sts now to re-read their text and also read the other one. As they read, they should guess what the highlighted words mean and then match them with the definitions.

Get Sts to compare with a partner and then check answers. Model and drill pronunciation, paying particular attention to *rivalry* /'raɪvlri/.

1	sick	7	aware of
2	No wonder	8	boarding school
3	rivalry	9	value
4	childhood	10	shared
5	a gathering	11	fight
6	adults	12	a gang

Now focus on the ***each other*** box and go through it with Sts.

Finally, help with any other new vocabulary and encourage Sts to write down any useful new lexis from the texts.

e Focus on the questions. Then give Sts a few minutes to discuss them in pairs.

Get feedback from the class, particularly from only children. You could tell Sts about your own situation and how you feel about it.

6 VOCABULARY adjectives of personality

a Focus on the instructions and the first question. Elicit that Jeff / the brother was *neat*, *responsible*, and *sensible*, and Tim / the journalist was *messy*, *rebellious*, and *emotional*. Then elicit from Sts what the adjectives mean.

Now ask Sts if they would use any of these adjectives to describe themselves.

Extra idea
- You could tell Sts whether or not you would use any of the adjectives to describe yourself.

b Tell Sts to go to **Vocabulary Bank** *Personality* on *page 153*.

Focus on **1 What are they like?** and elicit / teach that the question *What are they like?* = What kind of personality does he / she have?

Give Sts, individually or in pairs, time to complete the definitions in **a**.

Extra support
- Let Sts use their dictionaries to help them with this section.

1 23))) Now do **b**. Play the audio for Sts to check answers. Practice any words your Sts find difficult to pronounce, modeling and drilling as necessary.

---

1 23)))
Personality
What are they like?
1 **Selfish** people think about themselves and not about other people.
2 A **competitive** person always wants to win.
3 **Spoiled** children behave badly because they are given everything they want.
4 An **aggressive** person gets angry quickly and likes fighting and arguing.
5 **Charming** people have an attractive personality and make people like them.
6 A **sensible** person has common sense and is practical.
7 A **sociable** person is friendly and enjoys being with other people.
8 **Anxious** people are often worried or stressed.
9 A **moody** person is happy one minute and sad the next, and is often bad-tempered.
10 **Independent** people like doing things on their own, without help.
11 A **bossy** person likes giving orders to other people.
12 An **affectionate** person shows that he or she loves or likes people very much.
13 A **jealous** person thinks that someone loves another person more than him or her or wants what other people have.
14 A **sensitive** person can be easily hurt or offended.
15 An **ambitious** person wants to be successful in life.
16 A **reliable** person is someone who you can trust or depend on.
17 A **rebellious** person doesn't like obeying rules.
18 A **stubborn** person never changes his opinion or attitude about something.

Extra idea
- If your Sts' L1 is a Latin-based language, many of these adjectives may be quite similar. Get them to underline the ones that are similar and highlight or circle the ones that are completely different.

Focus on **c**. Get Sts to cover the definitions and look at the adjectives in the list. In pairs, they try to remember their meaning.

Now focus on **2 Opposites** and give Sts time to do **a** individually or in pairs.

1 24))) Now do **b**. Play the audio for Sts to check answers. Play the audio again, pausing for Sts to repeat. Practice any words your Sts find difficult to pronounce, modeling and drilling as necessary. You could use the audio to do this.

---

1 24)))
Opposites
generous – cheap
insecure – self-confident
lazy – hardworking
quiet – talkative
shy – outgoing
smart – stupid

Get Sts to cover the **Opposite** column and test themselves.

Finally, do **c** and put Sts in pairs. Tell them to go through all the adjectives again in **1** and **2**, and to decide if each one is a positive, negative, or neutral characteristic. (They may not always agree, e.g., some people see *ambitious* as negative and some as positive.) Elicit answers from the class.

Now focus on **3 Negative prefixes** and explain that with some adjectives of personality, the opposite is a completely different word, but for others you simply add a negative prefix. Get Sts to do **a** individually or in pairs.

1 25)) Now do **b**. Play the audio for Sts to check answers. Play the audio again, pausing for Sts to repeat. Practice any words your Sts find difficult to pronounce, modeling and drilling as necessary. You could use the audio to do this.

---

1 25))
Negative prefixes
unambitious, unclean, unfriendly, dishonest, unimaginative, unkind, disorganized, unreliable, unselfish, unsociable, immature, impatient, irresponsible, insensitive

---

Elicit that *un-* is by far the most common negative prefix. Explain also that *im-* is used before adjectives beginning with *p* or *m*, e.g., *impossible, immature*, and *ir-* before adjectives beginning with *r*, e.g., *irregular*.

Now elicit which adjective has a positive meaning.

Unselfish has a positive meaning.

Focus on **c** and get Sts to cover the columns and test themselves.

Finally, focus on the **False friends** box and go through it with Sts.

Tell Sts to go back to the main lesson **1B**.

Extra support
- If you think Sts need more practice, you may want to give them the Vocabulary photocopiable activity at this point or leave it for later as consolidation or review.

c Tell Sts to close their eyes and try to remember adjectives of personality they have just learned. Then tell them to open their eyes and write down the first three that come to mind.

Now tell Sts to go to **Communication** *Personality* on *page 104*.

In pairs, Sts read the explanation and then tell each other what they think.

Get some feedback from the class. You might want to tell the class that this activity is based on a real personality test.

Extra support
- You could write any useful words and phrases from **Communication** on the board for Sts to copy.

Tell Sts to go back to the main lesson **1B**.

7 PRONUNCIATION
word stress, adjective endings

Adjective endings
- Negative prefixes (e.g., *un-, im-, in-* added to adjectives) are never stressed e.g., <u>un</u>friendly NOT <u>un</u>friendly.
- The common adjective endings -*ous* (e.g., *jealous*), -*able* | -*ible* (e.g., *sociable, responsible*), and -*ive* (e.g., *talkative*) are also unstressed. The pronunciation of -*ous*, -*able* | -*ible* is the /ə/ sound, while -*ive* is pronounce /ɪv/.

---

a **1 26**)) Focus on the task and remind Sts that with multisyllable words they must always learn which syllable is stressed.

Now focus on the adjectives, and elicit / explain that 1–4 are grouped according to their endings, and that 5 is adjectives with negative prefixes. Get Sts, individually or in pairs, to practice saying the adjectives aloud, and then to underline the syllable they think is stressed.

Play the audio once for Sts to listen and check.

Check answers by writing the words on the board and underlining the stressed syllable.

---

1 <u>jea</u>lous, <u>anx</u>ious, am<u>bi</u>tious, <u>gen</u>erous, re<u>bel</u>lious
2 <u>so</u>ciable, re<u>li</u>able
3 re<u>spon</u>sible, <u>sen</u>sible
4 com<u>pet</u>itive, <u>talk</u>ative, a<u>ggres</u>sive, <u>sen</u>sitive
5 un<u>friend</u>ly, inse<u>cure</u>, im<u>pa</u>tient, imma<u>ture</u>

---

1 26))
See words in Student Book on *page 11*

---

b Focus on the phonetics in 1–4 and make sure Sts can pronounce them. Then play the audio again, pausing after each line to elicit an answer.

---

1 -*ous* is pronounced /əs/.
2 -*able* is pronounced /əbl/.
3 -*ible* is pronounced /ɪbl/.
4 -*ive* is pronounced /ɪv/.
5 -*ous*, -*able*, -*ible*, and -*ive* are not stressed.
6 *un-*, *in-*, and *im-* are not stressed.

Finally, play the audio again pausing after each group of words for Sts to listen and repeat.

8 LISTENING & SPEAKING

a Focus on the question and have students raise their hands for each position in the family to create class statistics to see how many oldest children, etc. there are.

b **1 27**)) Focus on the book cover and get Sts to read it. Then focus on the instructions and tell Sts they will hear a journalist talking on the radio about Linda Blair's book.

Now focus on the chart. Point out that Sts should listen for four more adjectives for each column and that they will hear the audio at least twice.

Play the audio once all the way through. Then play it again, pausing after each position in the family has been mentioned and making sure Sts are completing the chart.

Extra support

- Before playing the audio, go through the listening script and decide if you need to preteach / check any lexis to help Sts when they listen.

---

①27))

(script in Student Book on *page 122*)
I = interviewerer, D = Danielle

I This morning, we're talking about family and family life, and now Danielle Barnes is going to tell us about a book she has just read called *Birth Order* by Linda Blair. So what's the book about, Danielle?

D Well, it's all about how our position in the family influences the kind of person we are. I mean whether we're firstborn, a middle child, a youngest child, or an only child. Linda Blair argues that our position in the family is possibly the strongest influence on our character and personality.

I So, tell us more about this, Danielle. What about the oldest children in a family, the firstborn?

D Well, firstborn children often have to take care of their younger brothers and sisters, so they're usually sensible and responsible as adults. They also tend to be ambitious and they make good leaders. Many US Presidents and British Prime Ministers, including for example Abraham Lincoln, were oldest children. On the negative side, oldest children can be insecure and anxious. This is because when the second child was born he or she lost some of his or her parents' attention and maybe he or she felt rejected.

I That's very interesting. What about the middle child?

D Middle children are usually more relaxed than oldest children. That's probably because the parents are more relaxed themselves by the time the second child arrives. They're usually very sociable – the kind of people who get along with everybody, and they're also usually sensitive to what other people need. Now this is because they grew up between older and younger brothers and sisters. For the same reason, they're often good at sorting out arguments, and they're always sympathetic to the ones on the losing side, or in general to people who are having problems. On the other hand, middle children can sometimes be unambitious, and they can lack direction in life.

I And youngest children?

D I was very interested in this part of the book because I'm a youngest child myself. It seems that youngest children are often very outgoing and charming. This is the way they try to get the attention of both their parents and their older brothers and sisters. They're often more rebellious, and this is probably because it's easier for the youngest children to break the rules – by this time their parents are more relaxed about discipline.
On the negative side, youngest children can be immature, and disorganized, and they often depend too much on other people. This is because they have always been the baby of the family.

I Fascinating. And finally, what about only children?

D Only children usually do very well at school because they have a lot of contact with adults. They get a lot of love and attention from their parents, so they're typically self-confident. They're also independent because they're used to being by themselves. And because they spend a lot of time with adults they're usually very organized.

I I'm an only child myself and people always think that I must be spoiled. Is that true, according to Linda Blair?

D Well it's true that only children can sometimes be spoiled by their parents because they're given everything they ask for. Also, on the negative side, only children can be selfish, and they can also be impatient, especially when things go wrong. This is because they're not used to sorting out problems with other brothers and sisters.

---

c Get Sts to compare charts with a partner. Then replay the audio, again pausing after each kind of child, so that Sts can add to / check their answers, and for them to listen for more details.

Check answers and ask Sts for the reasons and examples.

Oldest children	Middle children	Youngest children	Only children
responsible	sociable	charming	independent
ambitious	sensitive	rebellious	organized
insecure	sympathetic	immature	spoiled / selfish
anxious	unambitious	disorganized	impatient

Extra support

- If there's time, you could get Sts to listen again with the script on *page 122*, so they can see exactly what they understood / didn't understand. Translate / explain any new words or phrases.

d Focus on the instructions. Demonstrate the activity by telling Sts about yourself and someone you know, and saying whether the information is true for you and for the other person or not.

Then put Sts in pairs and get them to do the same. Monitor and help with vocabulary if necessary. Don't overcorrect, but encourage Sts to communicate.

Get feedback from a few pairs asking if they agree with what the psychologist said in her book.

9 WRITING a description of a person

This is the first time Sts are sent to the **Writing** at the back of the Student Book. In this section Sts will find model texts, with exercises and language notes, and then a writing task. We suggest that you go through the model and do the exercises in class, but assign the actual writing for homework.

Tell Sts to go to **Writing** *A description of a person* on *page 113*.

a Before Sts read the two *Facebook* messages, you might want to check they know what an *au pair* is. Model and drill its pronunciation /ˌoʊ ˈpɛr/.

Give Sts time to read the two messages and to answer the questions.

Check answers.

1 Because she is looking for an au pair and Sofia's friend told Angela she might be interested in working in the US as an au pair.
2 Yes, she does.

b Tell Sts to read Sofia's email again and correct the five spelling mistakes.

Check answers by getting Sts to spell the correct version and write it on the board.

interrested	interested
responsable	responsible
fotography	photography
independant	independent
forgetfull	forgetful

c Tell Sts to read the two emails once more, then cover them, and answer 1–4 from memory.

Get Sts to compare with a partner and then check answers.

> 1 intelligent, hardworking, friendly, responsible, independent
> 2 She likes going to the movies, listening to music, and taking photos.
> 3 She's quite shy, a little forgetful, and her English isn't very good.
> 4 Yes, she does.

d Tell Sts to look at all the highlighted expressions in the second message and explain that they are all expressions that modify adjectives. Point out the example *very* and highlight that the sentences in the chart should go from very positive to negative.

Give Sts time to complete in the chart.

Check answers.

> incredibly
> really
> very
> a bit

! Highlight that we normally only use *a little* (or *a bit*) with negative adjectives.

e Now focus on the **Useful language: describing a person** box and go through it with Sts.

Tell Sts to imagine they received the message from Angela and they need to write back.

Focus on the plan and go through it with Sts. Remind them to use the **Useful language** box as well as the **Vocabulary Bank** *Personality* on *page 153*.

You may choose to get Sts to do the writing in class or you could assign it as homework. If you do it in class, set a time limit for Sts to write their description, e.g., 15–20 minutes.

f Sts should check their work for mistakes before turning it in.

PRACTICAL ENGLISH
Episode 1 Meeting the parents

Lesson plan

This is the first in a series of five Practical English lessons (one every other File) in which Sts learn and practice functional language.

There is a storyline based on two characters, Jenny Zielinski, an American journalist who works in the New York office of a magazine called *NewYork24seven* and Rob Walker, a British journalist who worked in London for the same magazine, but who is now working in New York City. If your Sts did *American English File* 1 or 2, they will already be familiar with the characters. If they aren't, the first episode begins with a brief summary of the story so far, so they will not be at a disadvantage.

In the first scene, Jenny takes Rob to meet her parents. They arrive late (because of Rob, who has also forgotten the chocolates). Jenny tells her parents about her new promotion, and Sts then practice reacting to what other people say (e.g., to good, bad, interesting, and surprising news). In the second scene, Rob struggles at first to impress Jenny's father, but then they find a shared interest – a jazz musician.

These lessons can be used with *Class DVD, iTools*, or *Class Audio* (audio only).

STUDY LINK
- **Workbook** Meeting the parents

Testing Program CD-ROM

- Quick Test 1
- File 1 Test

Optional lead-in (books closed)

- If your Sts did *American English File* 2, elicit anything they can remember about Rob and Jenny, and write it on the board in columns under their names. Leave it on the board, so when Sts do exercise **b**, they can see if any of the points on the board are mentioned.
- If your Sts didn't do *American English File* 2, introduce this lesson by giving the information in the Lesson plan.

1 ◄ INTRODUCTION

a Books open. Focus on the two photos and tell Sts that Jenny and Rob are the main characters in these lessons.

Get Sts to describe them.

b (1 28)) Focus on the **American and British English** box and go through it with Sts.

Give Sts a few minutes to read the text and think about what the missing words might be.

Now play the DVD or audio once all the way through for Sts just to listen.

Then play it again if necessary.

Get Sts to compare with a partner and then check answers.

1	magazine	5	New York
2	British	6	permanent
3	months	7	find
4	London	8	family

(1 28))

(script in Student Book on *pages 122–123*)

J = Jenny, R = Rob

J My name's Jenny Zielinski. And New York is my city. I live here and I work for a magazine, *NewYork24seven*.

R My name's Rob Walker. I'm a writer on *NewYork24seven*. You can probably tell from my accent that I'm not actually *from* New York. I'm British, and I came over to the States a few months ago.

J I met Rob in London when I was visiting the UK on a work trip. He was writing for the London edition of *24seven*. We got along well right away. I really liked him.

R So why am I in New York? Because of Jenny, of course. When they gave me the opportunity to work here for a month, I took it immediately. It gave us the chance to get to know each other better. When they offered me a permanent job I couldn't believe it!

J I helped Rob find an apartment. And now here we are. Together in New York. I'm so happy. I just hope Rob's happy here, too.

R I really loved living in London. A lot of my friends and family are there, so of course I still miss it. But New York's a fantastic city. I've got a great job and Jenny's here too.

J Things are changing pretty fast in the office. We have a new boss, Don Taylor. And things are changing in my personal life, too. This evening's kind of important. I'm taking Rob to meet my parents for the very first time. I just hope it goes well!

Extra idea

- Ask Sts some comprehension questions, e.g., *Where are Rob and Jenny now?* (in New York), *Who is Don Taylor?* (the new boss), etc.

Extra support

- If there's time, you could get Sts to listen again with the script on *pages 122–123*, so they can see exactly what they understood / didn't understand. Translate / explain any new words or phrases.

2 ◄ REACTING TO WHAT PEOPLE SAY

a (1 29)) Focus on the photos and ask Sts some questions, e.g., *Where are Jenny and Rob?* (in a car) *How does Jenny look?* (not very happy) *Who are Jenny and Rob saying hello to?* (her parents), etc.

Now either tell Sts to close their books and write the questions on the board, or get Sts to focus on the two questions and cover the rest of the page.

Play the DVD or audio once all the way through and then check answers.

> He left the chocolates on his desk at work.
> She was promoted to manager.

---

1 29))
(script in Student Book on *page 123*)
J = Jenny, R = Rob, H = Harry, S = Sally

J   I can't believe we got here so late.
R   I'm sorry, Jenny. I had to finish that article for Don.
J   Don't forget the chocolates.
R   OK... Oh, no!
J   I don't believe it. Don't tell me you forgot them?
R   I think they're still on my desk.
J   You're kidding.
R   You know what my desk's like.
J   Yeah, it's a complete mess. Why don't you ever tidy it?
***
R   We could go and buy some more.
J   How can we get some more? We're already late!... Hi, there!
H   You made it!
J   Sorry we're late. So, this is my mom and dad, Harry and Sally. And this, of course, is Rob.
R   Hello.
S   It's so nice to meet you at last.
H   Yes, Jenny's finally decided to introduce you to us.
S   Come in, come in!
***
J   Mom, I'm really sorry – we bought you some chocolates, but we left them at the office.
S   What a pity. Never mind.
H   Yeah, don't worry about it. We know what a busy young woman you are. And your mom has made way too much food for this evening anyway.
S   Oh, Harry!
J   But I also have some good news.
S   Really? What's that?
J   Well, you know we have a new boss? He's still new to the job and needs support, so today he made me the managing editor of the magazine.
S   So you've got a promotion? How fantastic!
H   That's great news! Hey, does that mean Jenny's going to be your boss, Rob?
R   Uh... yes, I guess so.
J   Well, not exactly. I'm a manager, but I'm not Rob's manager.
S   Let's go and have dinner.
J   What a great idea!

Focus on the **American and British English** box and go through it with Sts.

b   Focus on sentences 1–6. Go through them with Sts and make sure they understand them.

Now play the DVD or audio again all the way through and get Sts to mark the sentences T (true) or F (false). Remind them to correct the false ones.

Get Sts to compare with a partner and then check answers.

---

1   T
2   F (Rob's desk is **always a complete mess**.)
3   F (Rob is meeting Jenny's parents for the **first** time.)
4   T
5   F (Jenny's new job is managing **editor**.)
6   F (She is a manager, but **not** Rob's.)

Extra support

• If there's time, you could get Sts to listen again with the script on *page 123*, so they can see exactly what they understood / didn't understand. Translate / explain any new words or phrases.

c   **1 30**)) Give Sts a minute to read through the extracts from the conversation and to think about what the missing words might be.

Now play the DVD or audio again and get Sts to fill in the blanks.

Get Sts to compare with a partner and then check answers.

> See words in **bold** in script 1.30

---

1 30))
1
J   Don't forget the chocolates.
R   OK... Oh, **no**!
J   I don't **believe** it. Don't tell me you forgot them?
R   I think they're still on my desk.
J   **You're** kidding.
2
J   Mom, I'm really sorry – we bought you some chocolates, but we left them at the office.
S   What a **pity**. **Never** mind.
3
J   But I also have some good news.
S   **Really**? What's that?
4
S   So you've got a promotion? **How** fantastic!
H   That's great **news**!
5
S   Let's go and have dinner.
J   What a **great** idea!

---

d   **1 31**)) Focus on the *How* + adjective, *What* + noun box and go through it with Sts.

Now focus on the **Reacting to what people say** chart and go through it with Sts.

Play the DVD or audio once all the way through for Sts just to listen.

---

1 31))
See chart in Student Book on *page 13*

Now play it again, pausing after each phrase for Sts to listen and repeat with the right intonation.

Then repeat the activity eliciting responses from individual Sts.

e   Put Sts in pairs and tell them to practice the dialogues in **c**.

Monitor and help, encouraging Sts to pay attention to rhythm and intonation.

Make sure Sts change roles.

f   Put Sts in pairs, **A** and **B**, and tell them to go to **Communication** *How awful! How fantastic!*, **A** on *page 104*, **B** on *page 109*.

Go through the instructions with them carefully.

Monitor and help, encouraging Sts to use appropriate intonation.

When they have finished, get some Sts to tell the class a piece of news (real or invented) and get Sts to react to it.

Extra support

• You could write any new and useful words and phrases from **Communication** on the board for Sts to copy.

Tell Sts to go back to the main lesson.

3 📹 HARRY FINDS OUT MORE ABOUT ROB

a **1 32)))** Focus on the photos and ask Sts what they think they are talking about.

Now either tell Sts to close their books and write the question on the board, or get Sts to focus on the question and cover the rest of the page.

Play the DVD or audio once all the way through, and then check the answer.

Extra support

- Before playing the audio, go through the listening script and decide if you need to preteach / check any lexis to help Sts when they listen.

> The evening ends well.

---

1 32)))

(script in Student Book on *page 123*)

J = Jenny, R = Rob, H = Harry, S = Sally

H You know, our Jenny has done incredibly well, Rob. She's the first member of our family to study at Harvard. She's a very capable and ambitious young woman.

J Oh, Dad.

R No, it's true, Jenny.

H But what about you, Rob? How do you see your career? Do you see yourself going into management?

R Me? No. Not really. I'm more of a... a writer.

H Really? What kind of things do you write?

R Umm, you know, interviews, reviews... things like that... and I'm doing a lot of work for the online magazine...

J Rob's a very talented writer, Dad. He's very creative.

H That's great, but being creative doesn't always pay the bills.

J You know, my dad's a very keen photographer. He took all of these photos.

H Oh, Rob won't be interested in those.

R But I am interested. I mean, I like photography. And I think I recognize some of these people.

H That's because most of them are of Jenny.

R But there are some great jazz musicians, too... That's Miles Davis... and isn't that John Coltrane? And that's Wynton Marsalis.

H You know about Wynton Marsalis?

R Know about him? I've interviewed him!

H How incredible! I love that guy. He's a hero of mine.

R Well, he's a really nice guy. I spent a whole day with him, chatting and watching him rehearse.

H Really? I want to hear all about it.

S Have a cookie, Rob.

H Go ahead, son! Sally makes the best cookies in New York!

---

b Focus on the instructions and give Sts time to read questions 1–6. Elicit / explain the meaning of *impressed by*.

Play the DVD or audio again, pausing if necessary to give Sts time to answer the questions.

Get Sts to compare with a partner and then check answers.

> 1 Harvard
> 2 No, he isn't because he thinks creative people, like writers, sometimes don't earn enough money to pay the bills.
> 3 He likes taking pictures.
> 4 Jenny
> 5 Famous jazz musicians
> 6 That he knows about Wynton Marsalis (Harry's idol), interviewed him, and spent the day with him.

Extra support

- If there's time, you could get Sts to listen again with the script on *page 123*, so they can see exactly what they understood / didn't understand. Translate / explain any new words or phrases.

c Focus on the **Social English phrases**. In pairs, get Sts to think about what the missing words might be.

Extra challenge

- In pairs, get Sts to complete the phrases before they listen.

d **1 33)))** Play the DVD or audio for Sts to listen and complete the phrases.

Check answers.

> See words in **bold** in script 1.33

---

1 33)))

Harry	How do you **see** your career?
Rob	Not **really**. I'm more of a writer.
Rob	Umm, you know, interviews, reviews, **things** like that...
Rob	I **mean**, I like photography.
Harry	That's **because** most of them are of Jenny.
Harry	How **incredible**!
Rob	Well, he's a really nice **guy**.
Harry	Go **ahead**, son!

If you know your Sts' L1, you could get them to translate the phrases. If not, get Sts to look at the phrases again in context in the script on *page 123*.

e Now play the DVD or audio again, pausing after each phrase for Sts to listen and repeat.

Finally, focus on the **Can you...?** questions and ask Sts if they feel confident they can now do these things.

G present perfect and simple past
V money
P the letter *o*

2A Spend or save?

Lesson plan

In this lesson Sts review some important uses of the present perfect and how the present perfect contrasts with the simple past. They also learn common words and phrases to talk about money.

The lesson begins with a song which has a rather cynical view of how a certain kind of male and female views money. This provides a lead-in to the vocabulary focus which is followed by a pronunciation activity on different pronunciations of the letter *o*. The new lexis is consolidated through reading and listening activities that ask *Are you a spender or a saver?*

In the second half of the lesson, a dialogue where two people are arguing about money provides the context for the grammar review. Finally, Sts read and talk about the true story about a man who became a successful businessman despite having a very difficult childhood.

STUDY LINK
• **Workbook** 2A

Extra photocopiable activities

• **Grammar** present perfect and simple past *page 146*
• **Communicative** Money, money, money... *page 176* (instructions *page 165*)
• **Vocabulary** Money *page 203* (instructions *page 196*)

Optional lead-in (books closed)

• Put Sts in pairs and give them three or four minutes to brainstorm some titles of songs which are about money.
• Elicit the songs (and singers) onto the board.

Some suggested titles: *Money* (Pink Floyd), *Money, Money, Money* (Abba), *Material Girl* (Madonna), *Can't Buy Me Love* (The Beatles), *Money Makes the World Go Round* (from *Cabaret*), *Money For Nothing* (Dire Straits), *Bills, Bills, Bills* (Destiny's Child), *Money Honey* (Lady Gaga), etc.

1 VOCABULARY money

a (1 34)) Books open. Tell Sts they are going to listen to a song about money by an American band called Good Charlotte.

Focus on the task and phrases A–G. Tell Sts not to worry about the meaning of any phrases they don't know as these will be dealt with later.

Play the audio once all the way through for Sts to fill in the blanks. Play again if necessary.

Check answers.

1 G	2 C	3 E	4 F	5 B	6 D	7 A

(1 34))

Girls & Boys

Educated, with money
He's well-dressed
Not funny
And not much to say in
Most conversations
But he'll foot the bill in
All situations
'Cause he pays for everything

Girls don't like boys, girls like cars and money
Boys will laugh at girls when they're not funny

Paper or plastic
Don't matter
She'll have it
Vacations
And shopping sprees
These are a few
Of her favorite things
She'll get what she wants
If she's willing to please
His type of girl
Always comes with a fee
Hey, now, there's nothing for free

Girls don't like boys, girls like cars and money
Boys will laugh at girls when they're not funny
And these girls like these boys like these boys like these girls
The girls with the bodies like boys with Ferraris
Girls don't like boys, girls like cars and money

Let's go!

Chorus

All of these boys, yeah get all of these girls
Losing their souls in a material world (x3)

---

b Now tell Sts they are going to listen to the song again and they should read the lyrics at the same time.

Play the audio all the way through.

Put Sts in pairs and give them time to match phrases A–G with meanings 1–7.

Check answers.

1 G	2 E	3 B	4 C	5 D	6 F	7 A

c Do this as a whole class. First, explain / elicit the meaning of the three bullets. You might want to check Sts understand *cynical* (= believing that people only do things to help themselves and not for good or honest reasons) and *offensive* (= extremely unpleasant).

Then ask Sts what they think the song is saying and elicit answers.

d Tell Sts to go to **Vocabulary Bank Money** on *page 154*.

Focus on **1 Verbs** and get Sts to do **a** individually or in pairs.

(1 35)) Now do **b**. Play the audio for Sts to check answers. Make sure Sts are clear about the meaning of all the verbs. Remind Sts of the difference between *lend* and *borrow* with these examples: *Can I borrow your book?* | *Can you lend me your book?*

Practice any words your Sts find difficult to pronounce, modeling and drilling as necessary.

> **1 35**))
>
> **Money**
> **Verbs**
> 1 My uncle died and left me $2,000. I'm going to inherit $2,000.
> 2 I put some money aside every week for my next vacation. I **save** money every week.
> 3 My brother promised to give me $50. He promised to **lend** me $50.
> 4 I need to ask my mom to give me $20. I need to **borrow** $20 from my mom.
> 5 I often spend money on stupid things. I often **waste** money.
> 6 I don't have enough money to buy that car. I **can't afford** to buy that car.
> 7 I usually have to pay the mechanic $400 to fix my car. The mechanic **charges** me $400.
> 8 These shoes are very expensive. They are $200. They **cost** $200.
> 9 Jim gave me $100. I haven't paid him back yet. I **owe** Jim $100.
> 10 I want to put money in a bank account. They'll give me 5% interest. I want to **invest** some money.
> 11 I work in a supermarket. They pay me $1,600 a month. I **earn** $1,600 a month.
> 12 I could sell my house for about $200,000. My house **is worth** about $200,000.
> 13 We need to get people to give money to build a new hospital. We want to **raise** money for the new hospital.

Now tell Sts to cover the sentences on the right and see if they can remember the missing verbs.

Focus on **2 Prepositions** and emphasize that Sts must write the preposition in the **Preposition** column, <u>not</u> in the shaded blank in the sentence (This is so they can test themselves later).

1 36)) Now do **b**. Play the audio for Sts to check answers. Point out the silent *b* in *debt* /dɛt/.

> **1 36**))
>
> **Prepositions**
> 1 Would you like to pay **in** cash or **by** credit card?
> 2 I paid **for** the dinner last night. It was my birthday.
> 3 I spent $50 **on** books yesterday.
> 4 My uncle invested all his money **in** real estate.
> 5 I don't like lending money **to** friends.
> 6 I borrowed a lot of money **from** the bank.
> 7 They charged me $120 **for** a haircut!
> 8 I never get **into** debt. I hate owing people money.

Do **c** and tell Sts to cover the **Preposition** column and see if they can remember them.

Next focus on **3 Nouns** and get Sts to do **a** individually or in pairs.

1 37)) Now do **b**. Play the audio for Sts to check answers. Model and drill the pronunciation of any words you think are difficult for your Sts, e.g., *mortgage* /ˈmɔrgɪdʒ/ (pointing out the silent *t*). Make sure Sts are clear that *loan* is the general word for money lent by an individual or bank to another person and *mortgage* is specifically money lent by a bank to buy real estate like a house, a townhouse, or for the construction of a new house.

> **1 37**))
>
> **Nouns**
> 1 coin   5 loan
> 2 bill   6 mortgage
> 3 salary   7 ATM
> 4 tax

Now tell Sts to cover the words and see if they can remember what the definitions mean.

Finally, focus on the **Phrasal verbs** box and go through it with Sts. Highlight that *take out* and *pay back* are separable, i.e., you can also put the particles (*out* and *back*) after the noun, e.g., *When can you* **pay** *me the money* **back**?

Tell Sts to go back to the main lesson **2A**.

Extra support

- If you think Sts need more practice, you may want to give them the Vocabulary photocopiable activity at this point or leave it for later as consolidation or review.

2 PRONUNCIATION the letter *o*

> **Pronunciation notes**
>
> - The letter *o* is quite tricky for Sts as it has several different possible pronunciations. There are some spelling–pronunciation rules you might want to point out / elicit after you have done the exercises and you can also help Sts by highlighting the exceptions.
>
>   – *o* + one consonant + *e* is usually /oʊ/, e.g., *hope, alone*, but there are several common words which have the /ʌ/ sound, e.g., *some, money*.
>
>   – *o* between two or several consonants is often /ɑ/, e.g., *holly, follow*. There are some exceptions, e.g., *worry*.
>
>   – the letters *ol* and *oa* between consonants are usually /oʊ/, e.g., *old, road*.
>
>   – the letters *or* between consonants are usually /ɔr/, e.g., *airport*, but common exceptions are *work* and *world*, which are /ər/.
>
> - Encourage Sts to use a dictionary to check pronunciation when they are not sure.

a Focus on the question and do it as a class, making sure Sts understand the word *rhyme*.

> *funny* rhymes with *money*

b Focus on the activity and elicit the three sounds and words, i.e., *up* /ʌ/, *clock* /ɑ/, and *phone* /oʊ/.

Give Sts two minutes to put the words in the right column. Remind Sts that it is easier to do this kind of exercise if they say the words aloud to themselves.

Get Sts to compare with a partner.

c **1 38**)) Play the audio for Sts to listen and check.

Check answers.

> **1 38**))
>
> up /ʌ/   done, money, nothing, some, won
> clock /ɑ/   dollar, honest, shopping
> phone /oʊ/   clothes, loan, go, owe, sold

Play the audio again, pausing after each group of words for Sts to listen and repeat. Offer more practice if these sounds are a problem for your Sts.

Then repeat the activity eliciting responses from individual Sts.

d Now tell Sts to focus on the words with the letters *or*. In pairs, get Sts to answer the two questions.

Extra challenge

- Elicit the answers to **d** before playing the audio.

e (1 39)) Play the audio for Sts to listen and check.

Check answers.

> The letters *or* are normally pronounced /ər/ when they're stressed.
> The two words that are different are *worth* and *work*.

> (1 39))
> See words in Student Book on *page 15*

Play the audio again for Sts to listen and repeat.

Then repeat the activity eliciting responses from individual Sts.

f Put Sts in pairs and get them to practice saying the sentences.

Extra support

- Model and drill each sentence before putting Sts in pairs.

3 READING & SPEAKING

a Focus on the title of the questionnaire and make sure Sts understand it. Also make sure Sts understand the questions and options, e.g., *I don't have a clue, I have a rough idea, an installment*, etc.

Give Sts time to read the questions and choose the best answers.

b Put Sts in pairs and get them to compare their answers and explain why they have chosen each option.

Get some feedback from various pairs.

c Now tell Sts to go to **Communication** *Spender or saver?* on *page 104*.

Tell Sts to find out which description applies to them depending on whether they have answered mainly with "a," "b," or "c" answers. While they read, go around monitoring and helping with any vocabulary problems, e.g., *trust, manage, budget*, etc.

When they have finished, Sts should tell their partner if they agree with what they read.

Get some feedback from the class.

Finally, with a show of hands find out how many Sts are savers and how many are spenders. You could also tell Sts whether you are a saver or a spender and why.

Extra support

- You could write any useful words and phrases from the questionnaire and **Communication** on the board for Sts to copy.

Tell Sts to go back to the main lesson **2A**.

4 LISTENING

a (1 40)) Tell Sts they are going to listen to six people answering the question *Are you a spender or a saver?* They need to listen to find out how many are savers.

Play the audio once all the way through for Sts to listen.

Extra support

- Before playing the audio, go through the listening script and decide if you need to preteach / check any lexis to help Sts when they listen, e.g., *kids* = children.

Check the answer.

> Two of them are savers.

> (1 40))
> (script in Student Book on *page 123*)
> **Speaker 1**
> I'm a spender, I think. I try to save, but something always seems to come along that I need to buy and I end up broke. I can get by with very little money for myself when I need to, but I don't seem to be good at holding on to it. Also if my kids ask to borrow some money, I always say yes.
> **Speaker 2**
> I would say that I'm a spender. I spend money on things like concerts or on trips because I like having the experience and the memories. I know that I should spend my money on things that last, or save for the future, but I don't want to miss all those good things that are happening right now.
> **Speaker 3**
> I consider myself a spender. I don't have much money, but when I do have some there is always something I need or want to spend it on. I love computers and computer games, so I buy things to make sure my computer's always up to date. I know it's not very sensible, but it's important to me.
> **Speaker 4**
> That's hard to say. I can save money if there's something I really, really want, but usually my money disappears as soon as I get it. I get some money from my parents every week, so I have just enough money to go to the movies with my friends and to buy something for myself, maybe a book or a DVD or some makeup... I usually end up buying something. But, for example, if I want to go on a trip with my friends, then I can make an effort and save some money for a few weeks.
> **Speaker 5**
> Since I was little, I've always saved about a third of the money I get. I would never think of spending all the money I have. You could say that I'm careful about money. When I want to buy something that's expensive I don't use a credit card, I take the money out of the bank, so I never have to worry about getting into debt.
> **Speaker 6**
> I'd say a saver, definitely. I like having some money saved in case I have an emergency. I also think very carefully before I buy something, and I always make sure it's the best I can buy for that price. But I wouldn't describe myself as cheap. I love buying presents for people, and when I do spend my money, I like to buy nice things, even if they're more expensive.

b Tell Sts that they are going to listen to the six speakers again and that this time they must match speakers 1–6 with A–F.

Play the audio, pausing after each speaker to give Sts time to answer. Play the audio again as necessary.

Get Sts to compare with a partner and then check answers.

| A 5 | B 1 | C 6 | D 3 | E 4 | F 2 |

Extra support

- If there's time, you could get Sts to listen again with the script on *page 123*, so they can see exactly what they understood / didn't understand. Translate / explain any new words or phrases.

5 GRAMMAR present perfect and simple past

a Focus on the illustration and elicit what the relationship is between the two people (husband / wife or boyfriend / girlfriend).

Focus on the task and tell Sts to read the conversation quickly and answer the question.

> They are arguing about money.

b (1 41)) Tell Sts to complete the conversation with the verbs in the present perfect or the simple past.

Play the audio for Sts to listen and check.

Check answers.

2	just bought	8	bought
3	did ... cost	9	didn't need
4	were	10	worked
5	Have ... seen	11	needed
6	came	12	needed
7	haven't paid		

(1 41))

D = David, K = Kate

D I haven't seen those shoes before. Are they new?
K Yes. I just bought them. Do you like them?
D They're OK. How much did they cost?
K Oh, not much. They were a bargain. Under $100.
D You mean $99.99. That isn't cheap for a pair of shoes. Anyway, we can't afford to buy new clothes right now.
K Why not?
D Have you seen this?
K No. What is it?
D The phone bill. It came this morning. And we haven't paid the electricity bill yet.
K Well, what about the iPad you bought last week?
D What about it?
K You didn't need a new one. The old one worked just fine.
D But I needed the new model.
K Well, I needed some new shoes.

Extra idea

- Put Sts in pairs and get them to practice reading the dialogue. You could even get a pair to perform in front of the class.

c Now tell Sts to answer questions 1–3 in pairs. Tell them to look at the conversation to help them.

Check answers using the examples in the conservation in **a** to exemplify the rules.

> 1 PS (e.g., *How much did they cost?*)
> 2 PP (e.g., *Have you seen this?*)

d (1 42)) (1 43)) (1 44)) Tell Sts to go to **Grammar Bank 2A** on *page 134*. Focus on the example sentences and play the audio for Sts to listen to the sentence rhythm. You could also get Sts to repeat the sentences to practice getting the rhythm right. Then go through the rules with the class.

Additional grammar notes

- In **Grammar Bank 2A** the main uses of the present perfect are pulled together and contrasted with the simple past. This is all review from *American English File* 2, but it is the first time Sts have compared the two forms in such detail. If you know your Sts' L1, some careful use of L1 / L2 contrast could help here.

Simple past

- The most important point to emphasize is that when we use the simple past, a specific time in the past is mentioned, e.g., *Did you see the game last night?*, or understood between the speakers, e.g., *Did you see the game?* (We both know it was last night). So, for example, a question beginning *What time or When...?* will normally be in the simple past.

- Typical mistakes: ~~Have you see the game last night? When have they arrived? What time have you got up today?~~

- The simple past is frequently used with "just, yet, and already" instead of the present perfect. In this context it is often used to give a piece of news or information. *Did you hear? Lina broke her leg. Guess what! I found a new job! I'm sleepy. I just got up.* (No past time expression is used).

- Typical mistakes: ~~I've been to Paris last year. I already saw that film. Lina has broken her leg this morning.~~

Present perfect

- The most important point to emphasize is that we use the present perfect for a past action or actions where no specific time is mentioned or understood, e.g., *I've been to Paris twice. I've already seen that movie. Have you ever met Jack's wife?*

- Refer Sts to the **Irregular verbs** list on *page 165* and explain that this is their reference list. Get Sts to go through the list quickly in pairs, checking that they know what the verbs mean. Encourage them to highlight verbs they didn't know or whose past forms they had forgotten. Test them periodically on the simple past and past participle forms. You could use audio 5.45 to drill the pronunciation of the irregular verbs.

Focus on the exercises and get Sts to do them individually or in pairs.

Check answers, getting Sts to read the full sentences.

a	
1	Have ... ever booked
2	(have / 've) already saved
3	Have ... paid ... yet, Did ... pay ... yet
4	Have ... ever lent
5	have / 've never used
6	have / ever been
7	(have / 've) already spent
8	have / 've already seen

> **b**
> 1 ✓
> 2 ✓
> 3 ✓
> 4 ✗ When **did** you **buy** that leather jacket?
> 5 ✗ **They finished** paying back the loan last month.
> 6 ✓
> 7 ✓
> 8 ✗ I'm sure I **didn't borrow** any money from you last week.
> 9 ✓
> 10 ✗ **Did** you **see** the Batman movie on TV yesterday?

Tell Sts to go back to the main lesson **2A**.

Extra support

- If you think Sts need more practice, you may want to give them the Grammar photocopiable activity at this point or leave it for later as consolidation or review.

e This questionnaire practices the contrast between the simple past and present perfect and also provides an opportunity for free-speaking.

Put Sts in pairs and focus on the questionnaire and the example speech bubbles under the questionnaire.

Point out that the *Have you ever...?* questions in the questionnaire are in the present perfect because they are asking about your whole life until now.

However, if the answer is *Yes*, then the follow-up questions, asking for more information, should be in the simple past, because you are now referring to a specific time in the past, e.g., *When did you sell it? What happened?*

Set a time limit. You could either get one student to ask all the questions and then Sts change roles or Sts can take turns asking each other a question. The same question can be returned using *What about you?*

Stop the activity when the time limit is up or earlier if you think the activity is losing momentum. If there's time, get some whole-class feedback by finding out, e.g., how many people in the class have sold something on the Internet and asking individual Sts to talk about their experience. However, don't let this stage go on too long.

Extra support

- You could model the activity first by getting Sts to choose a couple of questions to ask you and eliciting follow-up questions.

6 READING & SPEAKING

a Focus on the instructions and give Sts a minute to think of two people they know, or have heard of, who are very rich.

Now put Sts in pairs and get them to discuss the two questions, giving as much information as possible.

Get some feedback from the class.

b Focus on the photo of John DeJoria and the title of the article, making sure Sts know the meaning of the phrase *from the streets*.

Now focus on the questions that Sts have to answer when they read the article.

Give Sts a time limit to read the article once all the way through.

Extra support

- Before Sts read the article, check it for words and phrases that your Sts might not know and be ready to help with these while they are answering the questions or afterwards. You may even want to preteach / check a few words / phrases to lighten the load, e.g., *dyslexia*, *leather*, etc. (but not the highlighted words).

Check answers.

> He became rich selling hair products.
> His success is surprising because he was very poor as a child and homeless as a young adult.
> He participates in charitable organizations that take homeless people off the streets.

c Focus on the instructions and make sure Sts understand the meaning of *event* (= a thing that happens, especially something important). Tell Sts to read the article again and to number A–K in the order in which they happened.

Get Sts to compare with a partner and then check answers.

1 G	3 D	5 H	7 C	9 I
2 B	4 F	6 E	8 A	

d Do this as a whole-class activity.

e Focus on the highlighted words and phrases. Get Sts, in pairs, to guess their meaning. Tell them to read the whole sentence as the context will help them guess.

Check answers, either explaining in English, translating into Sts' L1, or getting Sts to check in their dictionaries.

Explain any other new vocabulary and encourage Sts to write down any useful new lexis from the article.

Finally, ask Sts what new vocabulary they want to remember from the article and write these words and phrases on the board.

f Tell Sts to complete 1–5 with a highlighted word or phrase from the article.

Check answers.

2 door-to-door	4	rejection
3 backer	5	made it

In pairs, Sts answer the questions.

Then get some feedback from the class.

G present perfect + *for / since*, present perfect continuous
V strong adjectives: *exhausted, amazed*, etc.
P sentence stress, stress on strong adjectives

2B Changing lives

Lesson plan

In this lesson Sts review the present perfect (with *for* and *since*) and they are introduced to the present perfect continuous. The context is provided by the story of a family whose vacation to Uganda changed their lives and led them to set up a charity to help build a new school for orphan children.

The lesson begins with an interview with Jane Cadwallader, one of the founding members of the charity *Adelante África*. Then sentences from the listening are used to contextualize the grammar presentation. This is followed by a pronunciation focus on sentence stress in present perfect continuous sentences and a speaking activity where Sts put the grammar into practice.

In the second half of the lesson, Sts read and listen to the story of a TV host who kayaked down the Amazon to raise money for charity. Both the lexical and pronunciation focus in this part of the lesson is on using strong adjectives, like *furious* and *exhausted*. The lesson finishes with a writing activity where Sts write an informal email.

STUDY LINK
• **Workbook** 2B
• **iChecker**

Extra photocopiable activities

• **Grammar** present perfect + *for / since*, present perfect continuous *page 147*
• **Communicative** How long have you...? *page 177* (instructions *pages 165–166*)

Optional lead-in (books closed)

• Review the present perfect with *for* and *since* by writing these prompts on the board.
  1 How long / be a teacher?
  2 How long / work at this school?
  3 How long / live in this town?
  4 How long / know your best friend?

• Give the class two minutes in pairs to decide how to make the questions and then get them to ask you. Make sure Sts use the present perfect tense and not the simple present (How long are you a teacher?).

  1 How long have you been a teacher?
  2 How long have you worked at this school?
  3 How long have you lived in this town?
  4 How long have you known your best friend?

• Answer the Sts' questions using *for* and *since* and elicit from the class when you use these words (*for* = period of time, *since* = a point in time).

• Finally, you could get Sts to ask each other questions 3 and 4.

! If a student (who already knows the tense) uses the present perfect continuous to ask question 3, point out to the class that this is another form of the present perfect which they are going to study in this lesson.

1 LISTENING

a Books open. Focus on the photos and do the questions as an open-class activity.

b (1 45)) Tell Sts to look at the photos while they listen to Jane describing her trip. They should answer the two questions. Emphasize that this is a true story and that the person being interviewed is the real person.

Play the audio once all the way though. Play again if necessary.

Get Sts to compare with a partner, and then check answers.

Extra support

• Before playing the audio, go through the listening script and decide if you need to preteach / check any lexis to help Sts when they listen.

> She went to Africa – to Uganda and Rwanda.
> After the trip she decided to set up an organization to get money to build a new school.

(1 45))
(script in Student Book on *page 123*)
I = interviewer, J = Jane
Part 1
I   Jane, you're an elementary school teacher and a writer. What kind of books do you write?
J   Well, I write books for children who are learning English as a foreign language.
I   How long have you been a writer?
J   Uh, let me see, since 1990. So for about 22 years.
I   Tell us about the trip that changed your life. Where were you going?
J   Well, it was in the summer of 2008, and my family – my husband and I and our three children – decided to have a holiday of a lifetime, and to go to Africa. We went to Uganda and Rwanda, to see the mountain gorillas. It was something we'd always wanted to do. Anyway, about halfway through the trip we were in Uganda, and we were travelling in a lorry when the lorry broke down. So the driver had to find a mechanic to come and help fix it.
I   And then what happened?
J   Well, as soon as we stopped, lots of children appeared and surrounded us. I could see some long buildings quite near, so I asked the children what they were, and they said in English "That's our school." And I was very curious to see what a Ugandan school was like, so I asked them to show it to me.
I   What was it like?
J   I was shocked when I first saw it. The walls were falling down, the blackboards were broken, and there weren't many desks. But the children were so friendly, and I asked them if they would like to learn a song in English. They said yes, and I started teaching them some songs like *Heads, shoulders, knees, and toes* – a song I've used all over the world to teach children parts of the body. Almost immediately the classroom filled up with children of all ages and they all wanted to learn. I was just amazed by how quickly they learned the song!

I Did you meet the teachers?
J Yes, we did, and the headmaster too. He explained that the school was called St. Joseph's, and it was a community school for orphans, very poor children, and refugees. I asked him what the school needed. I thought that he might say, "We need books, or paper", and then later we could send them to him. But he actually said, "What we need is a new school." And I thought yes, of course he's right. These children deserve to have better conditions than this to learn in. So when I got back home, my husband and I, and other people who were with us on the trip, decided to set up an organization to get money to build a new school.

c Give Sts a few minutes to go through the items in 1–6 and to compare with a partner to see what they remember.

Point out the glossed terms holiday, lorry, and headmaster and help Sts understand the American English equivalents.

Then play the audio again for Sts to make notes about why Jane mentions those items.

Check answers.

1 She is an elementary school teacher and a writer.
2 She went to Uganda in 2008 with her family to see the gorillas.
3 Lots of children appeared. They wanted to show Jane their school.
4 It was in a very bad condition – falling down / blackboards broken / not many desks.
5 The children were very friendly. They were all different ages and they all wanted to learn the song (*Heads, shoulders, knees, and toes*). They learned it very quickly.
6 The headmaster told them about the school (St Joseph's – a school for poor children, orphans, and refugees). When Jane asked him what he needed, he said they needed a new school.

d (1 46》) Tell Sts they are now going to listen to **Part 2** of the interview and they need to correct the mistakes in sentences 1–9.

Give Sts time to read the sentences and then play the audio once all the way through.

(1 46》)
(script in Student Book on *pages 123–124*)
Part 2
I So *Adelante África* was born. Why did you decide to call it that?
J Well, we wanted a name that gave the idea of Africa moving forward, and my husband is Spanish, and he suggested *Adelante África*, because in Spanish *Adelante* means "go forward", and *Adelante África* sort of sounded better than "Go forward, Africa."
I How long did it take to raise the money for the new school?
J Amazingly enough, not long really, only about two years. The school opened on the 14th of March 2010 with 75 children. Today it has nearly 500 children.
I That's great! I understand that since the new school opened you've been working on other projects for these children.
J Yes. When we opened the school we realized that although the children now had a beautiful new school, they couldn't really make much progress because they were suffering from malnutrition, malaria, things like that. So we've been working to improve their diet and health, and at the moment we're building a house where children who don't have families can live.
I And are your children involved in *Adelante África*, too?
J Yes, absolutely! They all go out to Uganda at least once a year. My daughter Tessie runs the *Facebook* page, and my other daughter Ana runs a project to help children to go to secondary school, and Georgie, my son, organizes a football tournament there every year.

I And how do you think you have most changed the children's lives?
J I think the school has changed the children's lives because it has given them hope. People from outside came and listened to them and cared about them. But it's not only the children whose lives have changed. *Adelante África* has also changed me and my family. We have been very lucky in life... I feel that life has given me a lot. Now I want to give something back. But it's not all giving. I feel that I get more from them than I give! I love being there. I love their smiles and how they have such a strong sense of community, and I love feeling that my family and the other members of *Adelante África* are accepted as part of that community.
I And, do you have a website?
J Yes, we do. It's www.adelanteafrica.com. We've had the website for about four years. It was one of the first things we set up. If you'd like to find out more about *Adelante África*, please go there and have a look. There are lots of photos there and even a video my son took of me teaching the children to sing on that very first day. Maybe it will change your life too, who knows?

e Get Sts to compare with a partner and then play the audio again.

Check answers.

1 Jane's **husband** chose the name.
2 The new school opened in **2010**.
3 The school has almost **500** children.
4 *Adelante África* has also been trying to improve the children's **diet and health**.
5 They are building a house for the **children who don't have families**.
6 All **three** of Jane's children have been helping.
7 The school has changed children's lives because it has given them **hope**.
8 Jane thinks that she **gets more than she gives**.
9 Jane's **son** took the video of her teaching the children.

Extra support

• If there's time, you could get Sts to listen again with the scripts on *pages 123–124*, so they can see exactly what they understood / didn't understand. Translate / explain any new words or phrases.

f Do this as an open-class activity.

2 GRAMMAR present perfect + *for / since*, present perfect continuous

a Focus on the task and get Sts to match questions 1–3 with answers A–C.

Check answers.

1 B   2 C   3 A

b In pairs, get Sts to answer questions 1 and 2 by referring to the questions and answers in **a**. You could do this in pairs or as a whole-class activity.

Check answers.

1 b: a period of time from the past until now
2 present perfect: *has been, has had* – i.e., auxiliary *have* + past participle
   present perfect continuous: *has been working* – i.e., auxiliary *have* + *been* + (verb + *-ing*)

c (1 47》) (1 48》) Tell Sts to go to **Grammar Bank 2B** on *page 135*. Focus on the example sentences and play the audio for Sts to listen to the sentence rhythm. You could also get Sts to repeat the sentences to practice getting the rhythm right. Then go through the rules with the class.

Additional grammar notes

Present perfect (*How long...?* and *for / since*)

- This use of the present perfect was presented in *American English File* 2 and should be review for most Sts. Sts will need reminding that the simple present tense cannot be used here. (NOT ~~How long do you live in this town?~~)

- Remind them how *for* and *since* are used and the different words or phrases that can be used after them, e.g., *for* two months, three years, a long time, ages; *since* October, I was born, last summer, I was a child, etc.

Present perfect continuous (with *How long...?* and *for / since*)

- For many Sts, including those who used *American English File* 2, this will be the first time they have seen the present perfect continuous.

- Point out to Sts that in the same way that there is a simple and continuous form of the present and the past, there are also two forms of the present perfect (simple and continuous).

- The most important difference between the two forms for Sts at this point is that with *How long...?* and *for / since* we normally use the continuous form with action verbs (e.g., *learn, go, play, do, wait*, etc.) and the simple form is used with nonaction verbs (e.g., *be, have, know*).

- Some typical mistakes include:
  - getting the form wrong, e.g., (forgetting to include *been*) ~~How long have you learning English?~~
  - depending on their L1, using the present tense instead of the present perfect continuous, e.g., ~~I am learning English for a long time~~.
  - using the continuous form of the present perfect with non-action verbs, e.g., ~~I've been knowing my best friend for 15 years~~.
  - confusing *for* and *since*.

Present perfect continuous (for continuous or repeated recent actions)

- We also use the present perfect continuous to talk about recent continuous actions which have either just stopped or are still continuing, e.g., **A** *You look tired.* **B** *Yes, I've been cleaning the house all afternoon* (= I've just finished).
  A *You look tired.* **B** *Yes, I haven't been sleeping well recently* (= I still have problems sleeping at night).

Focus on the exercises and get Sts to do them individually or in pairs. You might want to tell Sts that **a** only focuses on the present perfect.

Check answers, getting Sts to read the full sentences.

a
1. We've had our new apartment **for** six months.
2. Hi, Jackie! How are you? I **haven't seen** you for ages!
3. How long **have you known** your husband?
4. Emily has been a volunteer **for ten years** ~~ago~~.
5. Paul **hasn't eaten** anything since yesterday because he's sick.
6. It hasn't rained **for** two months.
7. How long **have** your parents been married?
8. **They've had** their dog since they got married.
9. I haven't gotten any emails from my brother **since** last winter.
10. My grandmother **has lived** in the same house all her life.

b
1. We've known each other since we were children.
2. The children have been playing computer games for two hours.
3. Has your sister had that hairstyle for a long time?
4. I've loved her since the first day we met.
5. My Internet connection hasn't been working since yesterday.
6. How long have you been waiting?
7. I've been a teacher for three years.
8. It's been snowing since five o'clock this morning.
9. Sam hasn't been studying enough recently.
10. Have you been living in Chicago for a long time?

Tell Sts to go back to the main lesson **2B**.

Extra support

- If you think Sts need more practice, you may want to give them the Grammar photocopiable activity at this point or leave it for later as consolidation or review.

3 PRONUNCIATION sentence stress

Pronunciation notes

- Sts already know, but you may need to remind them, that in English the words which are stressed more strongly in a sentence are the ones that carry the important information, e.g., I've LIVED in the DOWNTOWN for TEN YEARS. These are the words which you hear more clearly when somebody speaks to you and are typically verbs, nouns, adjectives, and adverbs.

  The other "non-information" words (e.g., personal pronouns, articles, and little words like *to, of, in, on, as*, etc.) are pronounced less strongly, and these words often get shortened when we speak, e.g., *for* becomes /fər/. These words are harder for a nonnative speaker to hear. It is this mixture of stressed and unstressed words which gives English its rhythm and Sts need plenty of practice until correct stress and rhythm becomes instinctive.

a **(1 49))** Tell Sts that they are going to hear a dictation of three present perfect continuous questions and three answers. The first time they listen they should try to write down the stressed words they hear.

Play the audio, pausing after each sentence to give Sts time to write.

See script 1.49

1 49))
1 **How long** have you been **learning French**?
2 I've been **learning French** for **three years**.
3 **How long** has it been **raining**?
4 It's been **raining** since **lunchtime**.
5 **How long** have you been **waiting**?
6 I've been **waiting** for **half** an **hour**.

b Now tell Sts to look at the stressed words they have written and try to remember or guess what the complete question or sentence is.

Tell Sts they will listen to the audio again and they should try to complete any parts they are missing. Play the audio again.

Check answers and write the sentences on the board.

See script 1.49

c Play the audio again, pausing after each question and sentence for Sts to listen and repeat, copying the rhythm. Encourage them to pronounce the stressed words (in the large pink rectangles) more strongly and not to stress the other words. Remind Sts that unstressed words are often contracted and are often weak forms, e.g., *for* becomes /fər/.

Then repeat the activity, eliciting responses from individual Sts.

In pairs, Sts practice saying the sentences.

Finally, get some Sts to say the sentences to the class.

d **1 50))** Focus on the instructions and example.

Play the audio, pausing after each sentence for Sts to listen and form the question.

1 50))
1 It's snowing. (*pause*) How long has it been snowing?
2 I'm learning Korean. (*pause*) How long have you been learning Korean?
3 Natalia has been working in Brazil. (*pause*) How long has Natalia been working in Brazil?
4 John is looking for a job. (*pause*) How long has John been looking for a job?
5 They're living with Mary's parents. (*pause*) How long have they been living with Mary's parents?
6 I'm going to salsa classes. (*pause*) How long have you been going to salsa classes?
7 It's raining. (*pause*) How long has it been raining?
8 Justin is going out with Britney. (*pause*) How long has Justin been going out with Britney?

Then repeat the activity, eliciting the questions from individual Sts.

4 SPEAKING

In this speaking activity, Sts practice using both the present perfect and the present perfect continuous.

a Focus on the instructions, and give Sts time to write true information in as many of the circles as they can (e.g., *Twitter* in the first circle). Go around the class, making sure they have completed at least six of the circles.

b Focus on the instructions. Highlight that with an action verb, e.g., *use*, *play*, etc., they should ask the questions in the present perfect continuous. With nonaction verbs, e.g., *be*, *know*, etc., you can't use the continuous form and the present perfect must be used,

e.g., *How long have you known your best friend?* NOT *How long have you been knowing...?*

Remind Sts that with the verb *live* you can use either of the present perfect forms.

Extra support

• Go through the circles before you start and elicit whether the verbs are action or nonaction and the question that Sts should ask in each case. You could demonstrate the activity yourself by copying a couple of circles on the board (one with an action verb, the other with a nonaction verb) and writing something true in them. Then the class could ask you three questions about each one.

Put Sts in pairs. Focus on the speech bubbles. Sts now compare their information and take turns choosing one of their partner's circles and asking him / her about the information in it. Remind them that the first question must be *How long...?*

Monitor and help or take part yourself if there are an odd number of Sts.

Bring the activity to a close before it starts to lose momentum. If there's time, get feedback from one person in each pair about an interesting piece of information about their partner.

5 READING & LISTENING

a Focus on the questions and make sure Sts understand the phrases *to take part in a charity event* and *to raise money for charity*.

Sts could discuss the questions in pairs or you could do it as an open-class activity.

b Focus on the instructions. Give Sts time to read the introduction and to answer questions 1–4.

Get Sts to compare with a partner and then check answers.

Extra support

• Before Sts read the text, check it for words and phrases that your Sts might not know and be ready to help with these while they are answering the questions or afterwards. You may even want to preteach a few words / phrases to lighten the load.

1 She ran the 78-mile ultra marathon in Namibia. / She ran three consecutive marathons.
2 To kayak 1,998 miles down the Amazon (from Nauta in Peru to Almeirim in Brazil).
3 The river is full of crocodiles. She will be a long way from civilization, so if something happens to her, it will take a long time to get to a hospital.
4 She has only been kayaking once before.

c Focus on the instructions and elicit some ideas, e.g., *the weather was too hot*, *she was afraid of the crocodiles*, etc. Write all the ideas on the board.

Now give Sts time to read the three phone calls and see if they were right. Tell Sts not to worry about the missing words at this stage.

Check answers.

she only kayaked half a day; she started late; she's been suffering from the heat and humidity; she went the wrong way; she has problems with her hands; she's been suffering from heat exhaustion because she hasn't been drinking enough water.

d (1 51)) Now tell Sts to read all three phone calls again and to fill in the blanks.

Now play the audio for Sts to listen and check.

Explain any other vocabulary problems and encourage Sts to write down any useful new lexis.

Check answers. Where relevant, elicit from Sts why a particular word is right and what the other words mean.

Extra support
• Before playing the audio, go through the listening script and decide if you need to preteach / check any lexis to help Sts when they listen.

1 b: behind	6 c: chocolate
2 c: boiling	7 b: paddle
3 a: exhausted	8 a: boring
4 b: up	9 c: feeling
5 b: wide	10 a: sick

(1 51))
Phone call 1
Everything went wrong. I only managed half a day on Wednesday, the first day, and on Thursday we started late, so I'm already **behind**. I've been suffering from the heat. It's absolutely **boiling** and the humidity is 100% at lunchtime. I went the wrong way and I had to paddle against the current; I was **exhausted**. They asked me, "Do you want to give **up**?", but I said, no! because I've also been having a wonderful time! There are pink dolphins – pink, not gray – that come close to the boat. I think that if I can do 62 miles a day, then I can make it.

Phone call 2
I've been on the Amazon for a week now, and I've been paddling for six out of the seven days. The river is incredibly **wide**, and it's very hard to paddle in a straight line. The water is so brown that I can't see my paddle once it goes under the surface. It looks like melted **chocolate**. I start at 5:30 in the morning, and I **paddle** for at least ten hours, from 5:30 a.m. until dark, with only a short break for lunch. My hands have been giving me problems – I have big blisters. I now have them bandaged in white tape. I'm usually on the water for at least ten hours; it's **boring** at times and exciting at others. I listen to music on my iPod. I've been listening to *Don't Stop Me Now* by Queen to inspire me!

Phone call 3
I haven't been **feeling** very well this week. The problem is heat exhaustion. They say it's because I haven't been drinking enough water. I've been traveling 62 miles a day, which is my target. But yesterday after 52 miles I was feeling **sick**, and my head was aching, and I had to stop and rest.

e (1 52)) Focus on the instructions and elicit some predictions.

Now play the audio once all the way through.

Check the answer.

Yes, she did.

Extra idea
• Pause the audio after Phone call 5 and ask Sts if they have changed their minds.

(1 52))
(script in Student Book on *page 124*)
Phone call 4
I haven't had any music for the last three days, because my iPod broke, so paddling has been getting more boring. To pass the time I count or I name countries in my head, and sometimes I just look up at the sky. Sometimes the sky is pink with clouds that look like cotton, and other times it's dark like the smoke from a fire, and sometimes it's bright blue. The day that I reached the halfway point in my trip, the sky was bright blue. I'm superstitious, so I didn't celebrate – there's still a very long way to go.

Phone call 5
This week the mosquitoes have been driving me crazy. They obviously think I'm easy food! They especially like my feet. I wake up in the night when they bite me, and I can't stop scratching my feet. But I'm feeling happier now than I've been feeling for weeks. I've seen a lot of amazing wildlife this week. One day I found myself in the middle of a group of dolphins. There were about six pairs jumping out of the water. I've also seen enormous butterflies, iguanas, and vultures that fly above me in big groups. Yesterday a fish jumped into my kayak. Maybe it means I'm going to be lucky. I am starting to feel a little sad that this adventure is coming to an end.
***
The six o'clock news
And finally on the news, TV host Helen Skelton has successfully completed her 1,998-mile trip down the Amazon River in a kayak. She left from Nauta in Peru six weeks ago on a trip that many people said would be impossible. But yesterday she crossed the finish line at Almeirim in Brazil to become the first woman to paddle down the Amazon. Here's Helen: "It's been hard, but I've had an amazing time. The only thing I've really missed is my dog, Barney. So the first thing I'm going to do will be to pick him up and take him for a nice long walk."

f Now tell Sts to look at questions 1–10 for **Phone calls 4** and **5**, and **The 6:00 news**. Give them time to see if they can remember any of the answers.

Play the audio again for Sts to listen and answer the questions. Pause the audio after each section to give Sts time to write. Play again as necessary.

Get Sts to compare with a partner and then check answers.

1	Because her iPod broke.
2	She counts or names countries in her head, and sometimes she just looks up at the sky.
3	Because she is superstitious.
4	mosquitoes
5	dolphins, enormous butterflies, iguanas, and vultures
6	Because her adventure is coming to an end.
7	1,998
8	six weeks
9	her dog
10	Take her dog for a long walk.

Extra support
• If there's time, you could get Sts to listen again with the script on *page 124*, so they can see exactly what they understood / didn't understand. Translate / explain any new words or phrases.

g Focus on the instructions.

Get Sts to answer the questions in pairs. Help them with any new vocabulary they need.

Get some feedback.

Extra support
• Elicit some common adventure sports e.g., *rock climbing, hang-gliding, mountain biking, bungee jumping, canyoning*, etc. and write them on the board. Then put Sts in pairs or small groups to discuss the questions.

6 VOCABULARY & PRONUNCIATION

strong adjectives

a Focus on the **Strong adjectives** box and go through it with the class.

Give Sts time to read dialogues 1–12, which all contain a strong adjective. From the context or their previous knowledge Sts should be able to write synonyms for each one by writing the normal adjective. Sts could work in pairs or individually and then compare answers when they finish.

b (1 53))) Play the audio for Sts to listen and check. Make sure Sts are clear what all the adjectives mean. Point out that *amazed = very surprising*, but *amazing* can mean either *very surprising* or *very good*, e.g., *It was an amazing film.*

See **bold** adjectives in script 1.53

(1 53)))

1 A Was Lisa's father **angry** about the car?
  B Yes, he was furious!
2 A Is Oliver's apartment **small**?
  B Yes, it's really tiny – just a bedroom and a living room.
3 A Are you **afraid** of flying?
  B Yes, I'm terrified! I never fly anywhere.
4 A Was the food **good**?
  B Yes, it was delicious.
5 A Are you very **hungry**?
  B I'm starving! I haven't eaten all day.
6 A Is your parents' house **big**?
  B It's enormous. It has seven bedrooms.
7 A Was it **cold** in Moscow?
  B It was freezing! Minus 20 degrees.
8 A Was Jack's kitchen **dirty**?
  B It was filthy. It took us three hours to clean it.
9 A Are your parents **happy** about the wedding?
  B They're excited. In fact, they want to pay for everything!
10 A Was the movie **funny**?
  B It was hilarious. We laughed all the way through.
11 A Are you **sure** you locked the door?
  B I'm positive. I remember turning the key.
12 A Were you **surprised** to hear that Ted is getting married?
  B I was absolutely amazed! I never thought it would happen.

Now play the audio again pausing after each dialogue for Sts to repeat the questions and responses. Model and drill pronunciation of the adjectives where necessary. Encourage Sts to copy the strong stress on the strong adjectives.

Put Sts in pairs and get them to practice the dialogues.

Get some pairs to perform in front of the class.

Extra support

• If you want to provide more practice, you could ask the class more questions using a normal adjective and get them to respond with a strong one, e.g., *Is the water cold? Is an elephant big? Was the book good? Was the weather bad? Are you frightened of snakes?*, etc.

c Put Sts in pairs, **A** and **B**, and tell them to go to **Communication** *Are you hungry?*, **A** on *page 104*, **B** on *page 109*.

Go through the instructions with them carefully and then demonstrate the activity with a **B** student (you take the part of student **A**).

Point out that when a pair has finished the activity they should repeat it, this time trying to respond as quickly as possible and trying to stress the strong adjective strongly.

Extra support

• You could write any useful words and phrases from **Communication** on the board for Sts to copy.

Tell Sts to go back to the main lesson **2B**.

d Put Sts in pairs and get them to interview each other. Tell them to give as much information as possible.

Monitor and help with vocabulary.

Get some feedback from various pairs.

Extra support

• Choose one of the questions and tell Sts what you think, giving as much information as possible.

7 WRITING an informal email

Tell Sts to go to **Writing** *An informal email* on *page 114*.

a Focus on the photo and see if Sts can guess who they are (they are the people from Writing 1 – Marisol and Angela's children, Austin and Melissa).

Now focus on the instructions and give Sts time to number the sentences in the order in which they think they are mentioned in the email.

b Tell Sts to read Marisol's email to check their answers to **a**. Tell them not to worry about the mistakes in the email.

Check answers.

1 She apologizes for not writing before.
2 She thanks them for her stay.
3 She talks about the nice things that happened.
4 She talks about what she's been doing recently.
5 She promises to send some photos.
6 She thanks them again and invites them to stay.

c Now tell Sts to look at the mistakes underlined in Marisol's email and to correct them.

Check answers.

Grammar: I am I've been, Be Being, for to buy to buy, I send I'll send
Vocabulary: travel trip
Punctuation: english English, dont don't
Spelling: mesages messages

d Now focus on the **Useful language: informal emails** box and go through it with Sts.

Tell Sts to imagine they have some friends in the US, and they stayed with them for a week last month. Now they need to write a thank-you email. Tell Sts to use 1–6 in **a** in the right order as their plan and to use expressions from the **Useful language** box.

You may choose to have Sts do the writing in class or you could assign it as homework. Get them to write the email according to the model. If you do it in class, set a time limit for Sts to write their description, e.g., 15–20 minutes.

e Sts should check their emails for mistakes and then exchange them with another student to read.

There are two pages of review and consolidation after every two Files. The first page reviews the grammar, vocabulary, and pronunciation of the two Files. These exercises can be done individually or in pairs, in class or at home, depending on the needs of your Sts and the class time available. The second page presents Sts with a series of skills-based challenges. First, there is a reading text that is of a slightly higher level than those in the File, but that reviews grammar and vocabulary Sts have already learned. Then Sts can watch or listen to five unscripted street interviews, where people are asked questions related to the topics in the File. You can find these on the *Class DVD*, *iTools*, and *Class Audio* (audio only). Finally, there is a speaking challenge, which measures Sts' ability to use the language of the File orally. We suggest that you use some or all of these activities according to the needs of your class.

In addition, there is a short documentary film available on the *Class DVD* and *iTools* on a subject related to one of the topics of the Files. This is aimed at giving Sts enjoyable extra listening practice and showing them how much they are now able to understand.

Testing program CD-ROM

- Quick Test 2
- File Test 2

GRAMMAR

1 a	5 c	9 a	13 a
2 c	6 c	10 b	14 c
3 a	7 a	11 a	15 b
4 b	8 c	12 b	

VOCABULARY

a 1 duck (The others are seafood.)
   2 crab (The others are meat.)
   3 beet (The others are fruits.)
   4 raspberry (The others are vegetables.)
   5 chicken (The others are ways of cooking.)

b 1 dishonest
   2 generous
   3 unselfish
   4 lazy
   5 talkative / loud

c 1 waste
   2 inherit
   3 earn
   4 borrow
   5 save

d 1 exhausted
   2 starving
   3 freezing
   4 filthy
   5 furious

e 1 out   2 out   3 on   4 back   5 out

PRONUNCIATION

a 1 steak   4 tiny
   2 money   5 worth
   3 account

b 1 <u>s</u>almon   4 de<u>l</u>icious
   2 in<u>v</u>est   5 <u>s</u>ensible
   3 imma<u>ture</u>

CAN YOU UNDERSTAND THIS TEXT?

a It changed after he had a very bad accident

b 1 DS   2 T   3 F   4 DS   5 F   6 T

CAN YOU UNDERSTAND THESE PEOPLE?

 1 54))

1 b   2 c   3 c   4 a   5 b

---

1 54))

Max
I = interviewer, M = Max
I What do you like eating when you're feeling a little down?
M Brownies. I love brownies—chocolate brownies. My sister would always make these brownies, and she would let me eat them—and they sent some to me a little while ago, and they were just fantastic.
I Does it make you feel better?
M Oh, absolutely. They're great. Sometimes I give them to other people who aren't feeling so good, and they feel better, too.

Andrew
I = interviewer, A = Andrew
I How often do you eat out?
A Lately I've been eating out a lot, but I try not to eat out to save money.
I What kind of places do you go to?
A I like any kind of Asian food, and steak is good, but it's kind of expensive.
I Why do you like these kinds of restaurants?
A I like them because they're different. I like to cook, and the food is different from the things that I know how to make.

Samantha
I = interviewer, S = Samantha
I Do you have brothers and sisters?
S I do. I have one younger brother. And he's 16 years old.
I How well do you get along with him?
S Ooh, sometimes I get along better with him depending on how much time we spend together.

Zenobia
I = interviewer, Z = Zenobia
I Are you a spender or a saver?
Z I'm a very big spender.
I Can you give examples?
Z Bags. I have a weakness for bags. I love designer bags, and when I see something in the shops which is on sale, and it's half price or reduced, all my savings for the last three months will go on that item. So bags is a weakness – bags, bags, bags.

Skylar
I = interviewer, S = Skylar
I Have you ever taken part in a charity event?
S I have. I have been a captain at the Relay for Life event in my home state in Kentucky in America, and we raised money for cancer patients.
I How much money did you raise?
S I have raised $15,000 in total.

G comparatives and superlatives
V transportation
P /ʃ/, /dʒ/, and /tʃ/, linking

3A Race across Florida

Lesson plan

The context for this lesson is an episode of the well-known series about cars and driving, *Top Gear*, in which hosts Rutledge Wood, Adam Ferrera, and Tanner Foust organize a race across South Florida using three different methods of transportation.

The lesson begins with vocabulary and Sts learn words and phrases connected to transportation, focusing particularly on road travel. This is followed by a pronunciation focus where the consonant sounds /ʃ/, /dʒ/, and /tʃ/ are contrasted. Sts then read about three of the participants in the race, who traveled by motorboat, airplane, and car. The first half ends with Sts discussing what the result of the race would have been if it had been held in their nearest big city, and finally do a role play where a local person gives a tourist advice about transportation.

In the second half of the lesson, Sts begin by reviewing what they know about comparatives and superlatives, before going to the Grammar Bank where this knowledge is extended. There is another pronunciation focus on linking in fast speech, followed by oral grammar practice. Sts then listen to an expert talking about dangerous things that people do when driving, and discuss other statements to do with road transportation. The lesson ends with a writing focus, where Sts write an article about transportation in their town, and with the song *500 Miles*.

STUDY **LINK**
• **Workbook** 3A

Extra photocopiable activities

• **Grammar** comparatives and superlatives *page 148*
• **Communicative** Questionnaire *page 178* (instructions *page 166*)
• **Vocabulary** Transportation *page 204* (instructions *page 197*)
• **Song** *500 Miles* page 219 (instructions page 215)

Optional lead-in (books closed)

• Play *Hangman* (see Teacher's Book 1 *page 23*) with the phrase PUBLIC TRANSPORTATION.

• Drill the pronunciation. Then have Sts raise their hands to find out how many regularly use public transportation to get to work / school.

1 VOCABULARY & SPEAKING transportation

a Books open. Puts Sts in pairs and get them to think of four different forms of public transportation in towns and cities in their country.

Get some feedback and write the answers on the board.

Possible answers
taxi, bus, subway, bike

b Tell Sts to go to **Vocabulary Bank *Transportation*** on *page 155*.

Focus on **1 Public transportation and vehicles** and make sure Sts know the meaning of *vehicle*. Model and drill its pronunciation /ˈviːkl/. Then get Sts to do **a** individually or in pairs.

2 2)) Now do **b**. Play the audio for Sts to check answers. Play the audio again, pausing for Sts to repeat. Practice any words your Sts find difficult to pronounce, modeling and drilling as necessary. You could use the audio to do this.

2 2))
Transportation
Public transportation and vehicles

2	bus	3	freeway
9	light rail	1	platform
8	scooter	4	subway
6	train	7	truck
5	van		

Point out that light rail is usually a train that is powered by electrical wires that are hung over the train cars. A train is usually much larger and longer is powered by either electricity that runs under the trains along the track or by large engine cars.

Do **c** and tell Sts to cover the words and look at the pictures to see if they can remember them.

Now look at **2 On the road**, focus on the **Compound nouns** box and go through it with Sts. You might also want to tell Sts that occasionally compound nouns are hyphenated, e.g., *part-time*, or one word, e.g., *sunglasses*.

Get Sts to do **a** individually or in pairs.

2 3)) Now do **b**. Play the audio for Sts to check answers. Play the audio again, pausing for Sts to repeat. Practice any words your Sts find difficult to pronounce, modeling and drilling as necessary. You could use the audio to do this. Point out that the strong stress falls on the first word in compound nouns, e.g., *seat belt*.

2 3))
On the road

1	bicycle lane	8	rush hour
2	car crash	9	seat belt
3	cross walk	10	speed camera
4	gas station	11	speed limit
5	parking ticket	12	taxi stand
6	pedestrian zone	13	traffic light
7	road work	14	traffic jam

41

Tell Sts to cover the compound nouns and look at the photos. Can they remember the compound nouns?

Now focus on **3 How long does it take?** and go through the information box with Sts.

Put Sts in pairs and get them to ask and answer the two questions. Then get some feedback.

Extra idea
* With a show of hands you could see who has the shortest / longest trip to work / school.

Finally, focus on the **Phrasal verbs** box and go through it with Sts.

Tell Sts to go back to the main lesson **3A**.

Extra support
* If you think Sts need more practice, you may want to give them the Vocabulary photocopiable activity at this point or leave it for later as consolidation or review.

2 PRONUNCIATION /ʃ/, /dʒ/, and /tʃ/

> **Pronunciation notes**
> * These three consonant sounds are often confused by Sts.
> – *sh* is always pronounced /ʃ/, (e.g., *shower, ship*), as is *-tion* (e.g., *station, edition*).
> – *j* is always pronounced /dʒ/.
> – *ch* is usually pronounced /tʃ/, but can also be pronounced /ʃ/ in some words mainly of French origin, e.g., *chef, machine*. It is also sometimes pronounced /k/ in words like, e.g., *chemistry, chorus*, etc.

a (2 4))) Focus on the sound pictures and elicit the words and sounds: *shower* /ʃ/, *jazz* /dʒ/, and *chess* /tʃ/.

Then play the audio once for Sts just to listen.

> (2 4)))
> See words in Student Book on *page 24*

Play the audio again, pausing after each word and sound for Sts to repeat.

b Get Sts to look at the list of words and put them in the correct column. Remind Sts that this kind of exercise is easier if they say the words aloud to themselves.

c (2 5))) Get Sts to compare with a partner, and then play the audio to check answers.

> (2 5)))
> shower /ʃ/   crash, rush, station
> jazz /dʒ/   bridge, dangerous, traffic jam
> chess /tʃ/   adventure, catch, each

Now play the audio again, pausing after each group of words for Sts to listen and repeat.

Get Sts to practice saying the words.

d Elicit the sound–spelling rules in **Pronunciation notes** above. Then tell Sts to go to the **Sound Bank** on *page 167*.

Go through the spelling rules for the three sounds.

Tell Sts to go back to the main lesson **3A**.

e (2 6))) Focus on the pairs of words and play the audio once all the way through for Sts just to listen.

> (2 6)))
> See words in Student Book on *page 24*

Play it again, pausing after each pair for Sts to repeat.

f (2 7))) Now tell Sts that this time they will only hear one of the words in each pair. They must circle the one they hear.

Play the audio once the whole way through.

Check answers.

> See words in script 2.7

> (2 7)))
> 1 jeep   3 joke   5 shoes
> 2 chain   4 chip   6 watch

g (2 8))) Tell Sts they are going to hear five sentences and they need to write them down.

Play the audio once all the way through for Sts just to listen.

> (2 8)))
> 1 Do you like potato chips?
> 2 I'm going to wash it.
> 3 You choose.
> 4 Don't joke about it.
> 5 Is it cheap?

Now play the audio again, pausing after each sentence to give Sts time to write. Repeat if necessary.

Check answers and write the sentences on the board.

> See script 2.8

3 READING & LISTENING

a Focus on the photos and ask Sts if they know the TV show *Top Gear*. If they do, ask them what they think of it. If they don't, tell them that it is a TV show about cars and that the presenters do funny and daring things.

Now focus on the instructions and make sure Sts understand *race*. Point out the **Glossary** to Sts and go through it.

Get Sts to read the introduction and answer questions 1–4.

Check answers.

! When you check the answer to 1, focus on the map so that Sts can see the places mentioned. Point out that the distances and positions of Miami and the Florida Keys (the islands the contestants race through) are approximate.

> 1 They go from Jones Boat Yard on the Miami River to the southern-most point in the US, Key West.
> 2 A motorboat, a car, and a combination of transportation including a taxi, an airplane, and a scooter

Elicit Sts' opinions for 3 and 4. You could write their suggestions on the board.

b Now set a time limit for Sts to read the two paragraphs and to see if they want to change their predictions to questions 3 and 4 in **a**.

When they have finished reading, they should tell another student what they think.

Find out if anyone has changed their predictions.

c Focus on the instructions and get Sts to read about the two trips again and to answer questions 1–6.

Set a time limit and when Sts finish, get them to compare their answers with a partner.

Check answers.

1 R	2 A	3 A	4 R	5 A	6 R

d Focus on the highlighted verbs and verb phrases. Get Sts, in pairs, to guess their meaning. Tell them to read the whole sentence as the context will help them guess.

Check answers, either explaining in English, translating into Sts' L1, or getting Sts to check in their dictionaries.

Explain any other new vocabulary and encourage Sts to write down any useful new lexis from the text.

e (2 9)) Focus on the instructions and the map, and ask Sts how Tanner is going to travel. Give them time to look at the map carefully.

Play the audio once all the way through for Sts to listen and mark his route on the map. Play again if necessary.

Check the answer, eliciting what forms of transportation he took.

Extra support

• Before playing the audio, go through the listening script and decide if you need to preteach / check any lexis to help Sts when they listen.

Tanner took a taxi from the boat yard to the airport where the seaplane was leaving from. After landing at the airport in Key West, he rented a scooter for the last three miles of the race to arrive at the southern-most point of the US.

(2 9))
(script in Student Book on *page 124*)
Tanner took a taxi from the boat yard to the airport where the seaplane was leaving from. It took 45 minutes to get from the boat yard to the airport. Once he got on the seaplane, Tanner quickly made up the time he spent riding in the taxi. With the plane flying close to 100 miles an hour, Tanner caught up to Rutledge and Adam near Seven Mile Bridge. After landing at the airport in Key West, Tanner rented a scooter for the last three miles of the race. Just a few more minutes until he arrived at the southern-most point of the US.

f (2 10)) Elicit the three hosts' names and modes of transportation used. Write them on the board: Rutledge – motorboat, Adam – car, Tanner – taxi, airplane, scooter

Tell Sts to number them in the order in which they now think they arrive at the final destination.

Get Sts to compare with a partner.

Now focus Sts' attention on the two questions and tell them to listen to what happened.

! Play the audio once all the way through. Audio 2.10 has not been included in the Listening section of the Student Book so that it works successfully as a guessing activity in class.

(2 10))
Rutledge Wood, who had traveled in the boat, ran from the Key West boat yard to the streets of Key West. After running for a few minutes in the heat, he hailed a taxi which brought him to the southern-most marker in Key West and the US. Unfortunately, Adam and Tanner were already standing next to the marker. Rutledge couldn't believe it! He looked at the other men who were standing nearby laughing. It turns out that Adam, traveling in the Lotus Evora had reached the Key West marker just seconds before Tanner arrived on his rented scooter.
Adam's car had won—which is a good thing because Top Gear, is after all, a program about cars! Tanner's combination of taxi, seaplane, and scooter arrived second several minutes before Rutledge, who ended his boat trip with a ride in a taxi.

First, elicit the order in which everyone arrived.

1 Adam (car)
2 Tanner (taxi, airplane, scooter)
3 Rutledge (motorboat)

With a show of hands find out how many Sts had guessed correctly.

g Put Sts in pairs, **A** and **B**, and tell them to go to **Communication** *I'm a tourist – can you help me?*, **A** on *page 104*, **B** on *page 109*.

Focus on the instructions and set the scene. The **A**s, who are foreign tourists looking to use public transportation in the town, should ask the **B**s, who live in the town, their five questions.

Monitor and help.

Make sure Sts switch roles. Now the **B**s, who are foreign tourists interested in renting a car in the town, should ask the **A**s, who live in the town, their five questions.

Monitor and help.

Get some feedback from the class on some of the information given by the **B**s and then by the **A**s.

Extra support

• You could write any new and useful words and phrases from **Communication** on the board for Sts to copy.

Tell Sts to go back to the main lesson **3A**.

4 GRAMMAR comparatives and superlatives

a Focus on the task and get Sts to do this in pairs or individually.

Get Sts to compare with a partner if they worked individually, and then check answers. Make sure Sts explain why the ✗ sentences are wrong, as well as give the right answer.

1 ✗ the quickest way
2 ✓
3 ✗ as fast as
4 ✓
5 ✗ as many trains as
6 ✗ the most exciting trip
7 ✓
8 ✗ more carefully than

b (2 11))) (2 12))) (2 13))) Tell Sts to go to **Grammar Bank 3A** on *page 136*. Focus on the example sentences and play the audio for Sts to listen to the sentence rhythm. You could also get Sts to repeat the sentences to practice getting the rhythm right. Then go through the rules with the class.

Additional grammar notes

• Sts will almost certainly have been taught the basic rules regarding comparative and superlative forms of adjectives and adverbs, so this grammar focus should be mainly review and consolidation. Sts may still mix up comparative and superlative forms and make mistakes with the rules for forming comparatives and superlatives.

• Some typical mistakes include:

– mixing up comparative and superlative forms (*This is the older building in the town.*)

– confusing *as* and *than* (*The train isn't as cheap than the bus.*)

– omitting the definite article (*He's best player in the team.*)

– confusing adjectives and adverbs (*You drive more quick than me.*)

Focus on the exercises and get Sts to do them individually or in pairs.

Check answers, getting Sts to read the full sentences.

a			
1	easier than	6	The farthest/furthest
2	more powerful than	7	older than
3	the most relaxing	8	the hottest
4	more slowly than	9	the best
5	The worst		

b			
1	as	6	most
2	the	7	as
3	than	8	more
4	ever	9	as
5	him	10	in

Tell Sts to go back to the main lesson **3A**.

Extra support

• If you think Sts need more practice, you may want to give them the Grammar photocopiable activity at this point or leave it for later as consolidation or review.

5 PRONUNCIATION linking

a (2 14))) Focus on the **Linking** box and go through it with Sts.

Now tell Sts to listen to and read the five sentences at the same time. Play the audio once all the way through.

(2 14)))
See sentences in Student Book on *page 26*

Now play the audio again for Sts to listen and repeat.

You could then get individual Sts to say the sentences.

b Put Sts in pairs. Focus on the task and demonstrate what Sts have to do.

First, Sts have to choose one of the things, make a superlative sentence using the given adjective, and give a reason. Then they must compare the other two remaining things, as in the example.

Extra challenge

• Get pairs to compare with another pair to see if they agree and get them to defend their choices.

Get some feedback from the class.

6 LISTENING

a Focus on the instructions and check that Sts understand all the vocabulary, e.g., *a simulator*, *setting*, or *adjusting a GPS*, and *doing your hair*.

Give Sts a few minutes to read the text and answer the questions with a partner.

Get some class feedback.

Extra idea

• Get a show of hands for each one and write the top three on the board.

b (2 15))) Focus on the task and play the audio for Sts to number the activities 1–7. To add suspense, you could pause the audio just before the expert says which thing is the most dangerous, second most dangerous, etc. and elicit from the class what they think is going to be next.

Check answers.

Extra support

• Before playing the audio, go through the listening script and decide if you need to preteach / check any lexis to help Sts when they listen.

1	Sending or receiving text messages
2	Setting or adjusting a GPS
3	Doing your hair or putting on makeup
4	Talking on a cell phone (not hands free) **and** Eating or drinking
6	Listening to your favorite music
7	Listening to music you don't know

(2 15)))
(script in Student Book on *page 124*)
T = TV host, E = expert

T And on tonight's program we talk to Tom Dixon, who is an expert on road safety. Tom, new technology like GPS devices has meant new distractions for drivers, hasn't it?

E That's right, Nicky, but it isn't just technology that's the problem. Car drivers do a lot of other things while they're driving that are dangerous and that can cause accidents. Remember, driver distraction is the number one cause of road accidents.

T Now I know you've been doing a lot of tests with simulators. According to your tests, what's the most dangerous thing to do when you're driving?

E The tests we did in a simulator showed that the most dangerous thing to do while you're driving is to send or receive a text message. This is incredibly dangerous, and it is, of course, illegal. In fact, research done by the police shows that this is more dangerous than drinking and driving.

T Why is that?

E Well, the reason is obvious – many people use two hands to text, one to hold the phone and the other to type. Which means that they don't have their hands on the wheel, and they are looking at the phone, not at the road. Even for people who can text with one hand, it's still extremely dangerous. In the tests we did in the simulator, two of the drivers crashed while texting.

T And which is the next most dangerous?

E The next most dangerous thing is to set or adjust your GPS. This is extremely hazardous too because although you can do it with one hand, you still have to take your eyes off the road for a few seconds.

T And number three?

E Number three was putting on makeup or doing your hair. In fact, this is something that people often do, especially women, of course, when they stop at traffic lights, but if they haven't finished when the lights change, they often continue when they start driving again. It's that fatal combination of just having one hand on the steering wheel, and looking in the mirror, not at the road.

T And number four?

E In fourth place, there are two activities that are equally dangerous. One of them is making a phone call on a cell phone. Our research showed that when people talk on the phone they drive more slowly (which can be just as dangerous as driving fast), but their control of the car gets worse, because they're concentrating on the phone call and not on what's happening on the road. But the other thing, which is just as dangerous as talking on your cell phone, is eating and drinking. In fact, if you do this, you double your chance of having an accident, because eating and drinking always involves taking at least one hand off the steering wheel. And the thing that's most worrying here is that people don't think of this as a dangerous activity at all and it isn't even illegal.

T And in fifth, well actually sixth place. It must be listening to music, but what kind?

E Well, it's listening to music you know.

T Oh, that's interesting.

E We found in our tests that when drivers were listening to music they knew and liked, they drove either faster or slower depending on whether the music was fast or slow.

T So fast music made drivers drive faster.

E Exactly. And a study in Canada also found that if the music was very loud, then drivers' reaction time was 20% slower. If you are listening to very loud music, you're twice as likely to go through a red light.

T So the safest of all the things on the list is to listen to music we <u>don't</u> know.

E Exactly. If we don't know the music, then it doesn't distract us. In this part of the tests all drivers drove safely.

Find out if anyone guessed the top three correctly. Then find out if the class agrees with the expert's top three.

c Now Sts listen for more detail. Tell Sts they need to find out why each activity is dangerous and get more information.

Play the audio again, pausing where necessary to give Sts time to write the answers.

Get Sts to discuss what they heard with their partner and play the audio again if necessary.

Check answers.

1 Sending or receiving text messages: many people use two hands and look at the phone, not the road.
2 Setting or adjusting a GPS device: you use one hand and you take your eyes off the road.
3 Doing your hair or putting on makeup: you use one hand and you look in the mirror, not at the road.
4 Talking on a cell phone (not hands free): your control of the car gets worse because you concentrate on the phone call and not on the road.
  Eating or drinking: you double your chances of having an accident because you only have one hand on the wheel.
6 Listening to your favorite music: if the music is fast, people drive fast. If the music is slow, they drive slowly. If the music is loud, your reaction time is reduced.
7 Listening to music you don't know: it is much less distracting and safer than listening to music you know.

Extra support

• If there's time, you could play the audio again while Sts read the script on *page 124*, so they can see what they understood / didn't understand. Translate / explain any new words or phrases.

7 SPEAKING

a Focus on the statements and go through them with Sts.

Give Sts time to decide if they agree or disagree with them and to think of their reasons.

b Focus on the **Agreeing and disagreeing** box and go through it with Sts.

Put Sts in small groups of three or four. Appoint a group secretary, whose job it is to read the sentence aloud and then invite opinions from the other Sts as well as giving his / her own opinion. The secretary should also write down how many people agreed or disagreed with each statement.

Monitor and help, encouraging Sts to use the expressions in the box.

Get feedback to find out if there was a general consensus of agreement or disagreement on each statement.

8 WRITING an article for a magazine

Tell Sts to go to **Writing** *An article for a magazine* on *page 115*.

a Focus on the instructions and questions.

Put Sts in pairs or small groups and get them to discuss the questions.

Get some feedback from the class.

b Tell Sts to read the article to check their answers to **a** and then tell them to answer 1–3.

the least expensive: subway
the healthiest: bike
the best if you want to see New York City: (double-decker) bus
the safest to use late at night: taxi

1 For the subway and buses
2 Cash (but no pennies and no paper money)
3 Car service is a normal car which works for a company, and which you have to call. It is much cheaper than a taxi.

c Now tell Sts to read the article again and to fill in the blanks with prepositions from the list.

Check answers.

2	on	6	with
3	next to	7	in
4	on	8	at
5	on the top of		

d Focus on the **Useful language: transportation in your town** box and go through it with Sts.

Now tell Sts they are going to write a similar article about public transportation in their (nearest) town / city for foreign Sts.

Tell Sts to plan the headings they are going to use and what they are going to say about each form of transportation. Remind them to use the **Useful language** box and the **Vocabulary Bank Transportation** on *page 155*.

You may choose to have Sts do the writing in class or you could assign it as homework. If you do it in class, set a time limit for Sts to write their description, e.g., 15–20 minutes.

e Sts should check their work for mistakes before turning it in.

Tell Sts to go back to the main lesson **3A**.

9 (2 16)) **SONG** *500 Miles* ♫

This song was originally made famous by the Scottish band The Proclaimers in 2000. For copyright reasons this is a cover version. If you want to do this song in class, use the photocopiable activity on *page 219*.

(2 16))

500 Miles

When I wake up, well I know I'm gonna be,
I'm gonna be the man who wakes up next to you.
When I go out, yeah I know I'm gonna be,
I'm gonna be the man who goes along with you.

If I get drunk, well I know I'm gonna be,
I'm gonna be the man who gets drunk next to you.
And if I haver, yeah I know I'm gonna be,
I'm gonna be the man who's havering to you.

> **Chorus**
> But I would walk five hundred miles
> And I would walk five hundred more
> Just to be the man who walked a thousand miles
> To fall down at your door

When I'm working, yes I know I'm gonna be,
I'm gonna be the man who's working hard for you.
And when the money comes in for the work I do,
I'll pass almost every penny on to you.

When I come home (when I come home),
Oh I know I'm gonna be,
I'm gonna be the man who comes back home to you.
And if I grow old, well I know I'm gonna be,
I'm gonna be the man who's growing old with you.

> **Chorus**

Da da da da, *etc.*

When I'm lonely, well I know I'm gonna be,
I'm gonna be the man who's lonely without you.
And when I'm dreaming, well I know I'm gonna dream,
I'm gonna dream about the time when I'm with you.

When I go out (when I go out), well I know I'm gonna be,
I'm gonna be the man who goes along with you.
And when I come home (when I come home),
Yes, I know I'm gonna be,
I'm gonna be the man who comes back home with you,
I'm gonna be the man who's coming home with you.

> **Chorus**

Da da da da, *etc.*

> **Repeat chorus**

G articles: *a / an, the*, no article
V collocation: verbs / adjectives + prepositions
P /ə/, sentence stress, /ðə/ or /ði/?

3B Stereotypes – or are they?

Lesson plan

This lesson challenges common stereotypes about men and women. It begins with a split reading: one article about whether women really talk more than men, and another about what men and women talk about, which Sts read and then tell each other about. This leads to a grammar focus on articles: when (and when not) to use an article, and which article to use. This is followed by a pronunciation focus on the schwa in unstressed syllables and words, and on the two pronunciations of *the*. The first half of the lesson ends with a speaking activity to see if Sts can prove the stereotypes wrong.

In the second half of the lesson, Sts read and listen about a new book called *Commando Dad*, which challenges the idea that women are better than men at caring for young children. This is followed by a speaking activity on stereotypes, with a special focus on generalizing. The lesson ends with a vocabulary focus on verbs and adjectives with dependent prepositions.

STUDY **LINK**
- **Workbook** 3B
- **iChecker**

Extra photocopiable activities

- **Grammar** articles *page 149*
- **Communicative** Generally speaking *page 179* (instructions *page 166*)
- **Vocabulary** Dependent prepositions *page 205* (instructions *page 197*)

Optional lead-in (books closed)

- Write the following sentences on the board:

  WHERE ARE MY SOCKS? I CAN'T SEE THEM ANYWHERE.

  YOU JUST RELAX. I'LL PLAN THE SUMMER VACTION THIS YEAR.

  WE NEED TO TALK.

  THAT WASN'T A TOUCHDOWN! HE WAS DEFINITELY OUT OF BOUNDS.

- Then ask Sts who they think would probably say each sentence – a man to a woman or a woman to a man? Have Sts try to explain their reasons.

1 READING & SPEAKING

a Books open. Put Sts in pairs and get them to discuss the questions, giving as much information as possible.

Get some feedback from various pairs. You could write some of their conclusions on the board and also say if you agree or not with Sts.

b Focus on the definition of *stereotype* and go through it with the class. Model and drill the pronunciation.

Put Sts in pairs, **A** and **B**. Make sure Sts understand the four questions.

Now tell the **A**s to read *Men talk just as much as women* and the **B**s *Gossip with the girls?*

Extra support

- Before Sts read the articles, check them for words and phrases that your Sts might not know and be ready to help with these while they are answering the questions or afterwards. You may even want to preteach / check a few words / phrases to lighten the load, e.g., *a recorder*, *trivial*, etc. (but not the highlighted words).

c Now tell Sts to tell their partner what they found out in the article, using questions 1–4 as a guide for how to give the information.

Then check answers to 1–4 for both articles.

Men talk just as much as women
1   That women talk more than men.
2   At the University of Arizona.
3   They fitted hundreds of students with recorders.
4   That men speak only slightly fewer words a day than women.

Gossip with the girls?
1   That women often talk about trivial things.
2   At University College London.
3   A professor interviewed over 1,000 women.
4   That women's conversations are not trivial at all, that they have a wide variety of conversation topics, and that they move quickly from one subject to another.

d Tell Sts to now read both articles and then to complete 2–10 (1 has been done for them) with a highlighted word or phrase from either article.

Check answers.

2	reduce	7	according to
3	tend to	8	range from
4	slightly	9	almost
5	whereas	10	been skeptical of
6	claim		

Explain any other new vocabulary and encourage Sts to write down any useful new lexis from the articles.

e Focus on the question and the three options. Make sure Sts understand *credible*. Model and drill its pronunciation.

Give Sts time to choose one piece of research for each option.

Put Sts in pairs or small groups and get them to share their ideas, giving their reasons.

Get some feedback.

Extra idea

• Write the idiom at the end of the first article on the board: SILENCE IS GOLDEN. Ask Sts what they think it means (It is often best not to say anything). Then ask Sts if they have a similar idiom in their L1 and whether they agree with it or not.

2 GRAMMAR articles: *a / an*, *the*, no article

a Focus on sentences 1–4 and tell Sts to fill in the blanks with *a*, *an*, or – (no article at all).

Get them to compare with a partner and then check answers. Don't give any grammar explanations now as these will be given later.

> 1 ***A*** hamburger and ***a*** French fry walk into ***a*** coffee shop. ***The*** waitress says, "I'm sorry. We don't serve food here."
> 2 "I just read ***an*** article on ***the*** Internet about how eating **–** strawberries makes you look younger…"
> 3 "I'm sure there's something wrong between us because we never go out to **–** dinner or to ***the*** movies anymore."
> 4 "Did you watch ***the*** game **–** last night? I can't believe that ***the*** referee didn't see that it was ***a*** penalty…"

b Now focus on the question and give Sts a few minutes to discuss it with a partner, or do this as a whole-class activity.

Check answers.

> 1 Man   2 Woman   3 Woman   4 Man

c (2 17)) (2 18)) (2 19)) Tell Sts to go to **Grammar Bank 3B** on *page 137*. Focus on the example sentences and play the audio for Sts to listen to the sentence rhythm. You could also get Sts to repeat the sentences to practice getting the rhythm right. Highlight that the articles are not stressed. Then go through the rules with the class.

> **Additional grammar notes**
>
> • Sts have learned rules for using articles before, but here the main ones are brought together. Most nationalities will have some problems using articles correctly, but especially those who don't have articles in their language.
>
> • In this lesson the basic rules are covered. Other more specific uses, e.g., with geographical names, are introduced in *American English File* 4.
>
> • Some typical mistakes include:
>
> – omitting the article, e.g., ~~I saw old man with dog~~.
>
> – the incorrect use of the definite article when generalizing, e.g., ~~The~~ men usually love ~~the~~ football.

Focus on the exercises and get Sts to do them individually or in pairs.

Check answers, getting Sts to read the full sentences.

> a
> 1 a nurse, The hospital
> 2 a horrible day, the car
> 3 love stories, war movies
> 4 the theater, once a month
> 5 dinner, next Friday
> 6 a chef, the best cook
> 7 the windows, home
> 8 dogs, the dogs
> 9 school, last week
> 10 happiness, success
> b
> 1 the, a, –   4 the, the, the   7 a, a, –
> 2 the, a, the   5 –, –, the   8 a, the, –
> 3 a, –, –   6 –, –, the   9 the, the, –

Tell Sts to go back to the main lesson **3B**.

Extra support

• If you think Sts need more practice, you may want to give them the Grammar photocopiable activity at this point or leave it for later as consolidation or review.

3 PRONUNCIATION /ə/, sentence stress, /ðə/ or /ði/?

> **Pronunciation notes**
>
> • /ə/ is the most common sound in English.
>
> • /ə/ can be spelled by any vowel. It always occurs in unstressed syllables, or unstressed words, e.g., articles and prepositions.
>
> • You may want to give Sts some simple rules, e.g., that:
> -*tion* is always pronounced /ʃən/.

a (2 20)) Elicit the sound and picture word: /ə/ *computer*.

Play the audio once for Sts just to listen.

> (2 20))
> See words in Student Book on *page 29*

Now play the audio for Sts to listen and repeat.

b (2 21)) Now focus on the instructions and the sentences.

Play the audio once for Sts just to listen.

> (2 21))
> See sentences in Student Book on *page 29*

Play the audio again for Sts to listen and repeat.

Then repeat the activity, eliciting the sentences from individual Sts.

c (2 22)) Focus on the instructions and the phrases in the list. Demonstrate clearly the two different pronunciations of *the*, /ðə/ and /ði/.

Play the audio once for Sts to listen and underline the five phrases where *the* is pronounced /ði/.

Check answers.

> 1 the end   3 the Internet   5 the Earth
> 2 the other day   4 the answer

2 22 》
See phrases in Student Book on *page 29*

Next ask Sts why *the* is pronounced differently in those five phrases and elicit that it is because the words start with a vowel sound.

Play the audio again for Sts to listen and repeat the phrases.

4 SPEAKING

This speaking task is meant to be a light-hearted response to the article, but will also provide practice of not using the definite article *the* when you generalize.

Focus on the task. Either put Sts in groups of three or pairs. If you have a more or less equal number of men and women in your class, put them in mixed groups. They could each try all three topics, or simply choose one each.

If your class is mainly one gender, simply get them to try to talk about one of their three topics for two minutes.

Monitor and correct, especially if Sts use the article incorrectly when speaking in general.

Get feedback to find out which topic men or women found most difficult to talk about.

5 READING & LISTENING

a Ask these questions to the whole class and elicit answers, or if you prefer, put Sts in pairs to discuss the questions.

b Focus on the instructions and give Sts a few minutes, in pairs, to write down as many things as they can.

Check answers.

> a bottle of aspirin, wet wipes, a first-aid kit, bibs, a pacifier, a baby food jar, a baby bottle, a baby spoon, a changing mat, an adult's car / house keys, a container of powdered milk, a blanket, a jar of baby lotion, a thermometer

c Tell Sts they are going to read the beginning of an article about a book written by Neil Sinclair. Point out the **Glossary** to Sts and go through it.

Give Sts time to read the beginning of the article and answer the two questions.

Get Sts to compare with a partner and then check answers.

> 1 Because when his first child was born, he had absolutely no idea how to take care of him, and he wanted to help other men in this situation.
> 2 It is written like a military training manual, with very precise instructions and it includes diagrams.

Extra idea

• You could begin by focusing on the title of the book and eliciting from Sts what they think it might be about.

Extra support

• Ask Sts more questions about the article, e.g., *At what precise moment did Neil realize he didn't know what to do? What did Neil and his wife decide when Neil left the army? What kind of book does he compare* Commando Dad *to? For what age children is it written?*

Finally, help with any other new vocabulary in the article. You may want to focus on the expressions *a basic training manual, with military precision,* etc.

d **2 23** 》 Tell Sts they are now going to listen to two men talking about the book. Give them time to read sentences 1–8.

Play the audio once all the way through for Sts to listen and mark the sentences T (true) or F (false).

Get Sts to compare with a partner and then play the audio again if necessary.

Check answers.

Extra support

• Before playing the audio, go through the listening script and decide if you need to preteach / check any lexis to help Sts when they listen.

| 1 | F | 3 | F | 5 | T | 7 | F |
| 2 | T | 4 | F | 6 | T | 8 | F |

2 23 》
(script in Student Book on *page 124*)
A = Miranda's father, B = Stephen's father

A Excuse me, is this seat free?
B Yes, sure, sit down. Ah, he's cute. Is he yours?
A Yes, yes. Actually, he's a *she*. Miranda.
B Oh. Three months?
A Three and a half. How about yours?
B Stephen. He's four months. Did you have a bad night?
A Yes, Miranda was crying <u>all</u> night. You know, that noise gets to you. It drives me crazy.
B Do you know what you need? These.
A What are they? Earplugs?
B Yes. Earplugs! When the baby starts crying, you just put these in. You can still hear the crying, but the noise isn't so bad and it's not so stressful.
A That's a great idea! Who told you to do that?
B It's all in this book I read. You should get it.
A Yeah? What's it called?
B It's called *Commando Dad*. It was written by an ex-soldier. He was a commando in the army, and it's especially for men with babies or small children. It's pretty good.
A Really? So what's so good about it?
B Well, it's like a military manual. It tells you exactly what to do with a baby in *any* situation. It makes everything easier. There's a website, too, that you can go to – commandodad.com. It has a lot of advice about taking care of babies and small kids, and I really like the forums where men can write in with their problems, or their experiences.
A What kind of things does it help you with?
B All kinds of things. How to change diapers – he has a really good system – how to dress the baby, how to get the baby to sleep, the best way to feed the baby, how to know if the baby is sick. It's really useful and it's pretty funny, too, I mean he uses a kind of military language, so, for example, he calls the baby a BT which means a baby trooper, and the baby's bedroom is base camp, and taking the baby for a walk is maneuvers, and taking the diapers to the trash is called bomb disposal.
A What else does it say?
B Well, it has all kinds of stuff about...
***

A And what does he think about men taking care of children? Does he think we do it well?
B He thinks that men are just as good as women at taking care of children in almost everything.
A Almost everything?
B Yeah, he says the one time when women are better than men is when the kids are sick. Women kind of understand better what to do. They have an instinct... Oh. Now it's my turn. OK, I know exactly what that cry means. It means he's hungry.
A Wow! What was that book called?

e Now have Sts listen again and correct the wrong information in the false sentences.

Play the audio again all the way through.

Get Sts to compare with a partner and then check answers.

1 Miranda is **younger** than Stephen. She is three and a half months old, and he is four months old.
3 Stephen's father recommends **earplugs**.
4 Stephen's father **has** read *Commando Dad*.
7 "Base Camp" means the **baby's bedroom**.
8 The author of *Commando Dad* thinks that women are only better than men when the baby is **sick**.

Extra support
• If there's time, you could play the audio again while Sts read the script on *page 124*, so they can see what they understood / didn't understand. Translate / explain any new words or phrases.

f Do this as an open-class activity.

6 SPEAKING

a **(2 24))** Focus on the instructions and the paragraph. Tell Sts that a woman is discussing the first statement in *Men & Women: stereotypes or true?* in **b**. Give Sts time to read the paragraph and encourage them to guess what the missing words might be.

Now play the audio once all the way through. Play it again and give Sts time to fill in the blanks.

Get Sts compare with a partner and then either check answers or play the audio again.

Check answers. Point out that the highlighted expressions are useful for when you are talking in general.

See words in **bold** in script 2.24

(2 24))
Generally **speaking**, I think women worry more about their appearance than men. They **tend** to spend hours choosing what to wear, doing their hair, and putting on makeup. Women are also **usually** better at making themselves look more attractive. But I think that in **general**, men are more worried than women about their body image. They feel more insecure about their hair, for instance, especially when they're going bald.

Now ask Sts if they agree or disagree with what the woman said, and elicit opinions.

b Focus on the instructions and on the nine other statements and make sure Sts understand them.

Then put Sts in groups of three or four and get them to discuss each statement (starting with the second one, as Sts will have already discussed the first one in **a**).

Monitor and check, correcting any misuse of articles and encouraging Sts to use the highlighted expressions for generalizing from **a**.

Get quick feedback from a different group for each topic. Tell Sts if you agree or not and why.

7 VOCABULARY
collocation: verbs / adjectives + prepositions

a Focus on the instructions and remind Sts that they have to remember which prepositions to use after certain verbs and adjectives, e.g., you talk *to* a person *about* a subject.

Get Sts to cover the ten sentences in *Men & Women: stereotypes or true?* and complete 1–3, and then check answers.

1 about   2 at   3 in

b Tell Sts go to **Vocabulary Bank** *Dependent prepositions* on *page 156*.

Focus on **1 After verbs** and get Sts to do **a** individually or in pairs. Remind them to write the prepositions in the column on the right, <u>not</u> in the sentence.

(2 25)) Now do **b**. Play the audio for Sts to check answers.

(2 25))
Dependent prepositions
After verbs
1 He apologized **to** the police officer **for** driving fast.
2 We're arriving **in** Miami on Sunday.
3 We're arriving **at** O'Hare Airport at 3:45.
4 Who does this book belong **to**?
5 I never argue **with** my husband **about** money.
6 Could you ask the waiter **for** the check?
7 Do you believe **in** ghosts?
8 I can't choose **between** these two bags.
9 We might go out. It depends **on** the weather.
10 I dreamed **about** my childhood last night.
11 Don't laugh **at** me! I'm doing my best!
12 I'm really looking forward **to** the party.
13 If I pay **for** the gas, can you pay for the parking?
14 This music reminds me **of** our honeymoon in Italy.
15 I don't spend a lot of money **on** clothes.

Extra support
• You could play the audio again, pausing after each sentence for Sts to listen and repeat, to give them extra practice with sentence rhythm.

Do **c** and tell Sts to cover the **Preposition** column on the right and say the sentences with the correct preposition.

Now focus on **2 After adjectives** and get Sts to do **a** individually or in pairs.

(2 26)) Now do **b**. Play the audio for Sts to check answers.

> **2 26)))**
> **After adjectives**
> 1 My brother is afraid **of** bats.
> 2 She's really angry **with** her boyfriend **about** last night.
> 3 I've never been good **at** sports.
> 4 Eat your vegetables. They're good **for** you.
> 5 I'm very close **to** my older sister.
> 6 This exercise isn't very different **from** the last one.
> 7 We're really excited **about** going to Brazil.
> 8 I'm fed up **with** listening to you complaining.
> 9 Krakow is famous **for** its main square.
> 10 My sister is very interested **in** astrology.
> 11 I'm very fond **of** my little nephew. He's adorable.
> 12 She's very passionate **about** riding her bike. She does about 30 miles every weekend.
> 13 I don't like people who aren't kind **to** animals.
> 14 She used to be married **to** a pop star.
> 15 I'm really happy **with** my new motorcycle.
> 16 My dad was very proud **of** learning to ski.
> 17 Why are you always rude **to** waiters and salespeople?
> 18 Rachel is worried **about** losing her job.
> 19 I'm tired **of** walking. Let's stop and rest.

Extra support

- You could play the audio again, pausing after each sentence for Sts to listen and repeat, to give them extra practice with sentence rhythm.

Do **c** and tell Sts to cover the **Preposition** column on the right and say the sentences with the correct preposition.

Finally, focus on the **Gerunds after prepositions** box and go through it with Sts.

Tell Sts to go back to the main lesson **3B**.

Extra support

- If you think Sts need more practice, you may want to give them the Vocabulary photocopiable activity at this point or leave it for later as consolidation or review.

c Focus on the **When are prepositions stressed?** box and go through it with Sts.

Tell Sts to complete questions 1–8 with a preposition.

d **2 27)))** Play the audio for Sts to listen and check.

Check answers, making sure Sts understand the questions.

> See words in **bold** in script 2.27

> **2 27)))**
> 1 When you're with friends of the same sex, what do you usually talk **about**?
> 2 Are there any sports or games that you're good **at**?
> 3 Is there anything you're really looking forward **to**?
> 4 Who in your family are you closest **to**?
> 5 What kind of movies are you interested **in**?
> 6 Are there any animals or insects that you're afraid **of**?
> 7 What's your town famous **for**?
> 8 Are there any superstitions that you believe **in**?

Then play the audio again for Sts to repeat the questions, making sure they say the strong form of the prepositions.

Now put Sts in pairs and get them to ask and answer the questions, giving as much information as possible.

Get some feedback from various pairs.

Extra support

- Get Sts to choose a few questions to ask you first.

Function giving opinions, agreeing / disagreeing / responses
Language *To be honest..., I don't think that's right.*, etc.

PRACTICAL ENGLISH
Episode 2 A difficult celebrity

Lesson plan

In this lesson the functional focus is on learning more ways of expressing opinions and agreeing and disagreeing with other people's opinions.

In the first scene, Rob interviews Kerri, a British singer who is visiting New York City. Then in the second scene Don, the new boss, Jenny, and Rob take Kerri out to lunch. During the lunch Kerri is critical of what she considers the "fake friendliness" of people in New York City, and compares New York City unfavorably to London. Don strongly disagrees; however, Rob sides with Kerri. In the final scene Kerri has to eat her words, as a genuinely friendly taxi driver comes to the restaurant to bring her her phone, which she had left in the cab.

STUDY LINK
• **Workbook** A difficult celebrity

Testing program CD-ROM

• **Quick Test 3**
• **File 3 Test**

Optional lead-in (books closed)

• Before starting Episode 2 elicit what Sts can remember about Episode 1. Ask *Who's Harry?, What does he think of Rob?, Where did Rob and Jenny go in the last episode?*, etc.

• Alternatively, you could play the last scene of Episode 1.

1 ◄ ROB'S INTERVIEW

a (2 28)) Books open. Focus on the photo and ask Sts to guess who the woman is.

Now either tell Sts to close their books and write the question on the board, or get Sts to focus on the question and cover the rest of the page.

Play the DVD or audio once all the way through and then check answers.

She is happy to talk about her new album, but not about what happened with the band or her private life.

(2 28))
(script in Student Book on *pages 124–125*)
R = Rob, K = Kerri, J = Jenny, D = Don

K (*singing*) You work hard, but your money's all spent
Haven't got enough to pay the rent
You know it's not right and it makes no sense
To go chasing, chasing those dollars and cents
Chasing, chasing those dollars and cents
R That was great, Kerri.
K Thanks.
R Kerri, you used to be in a band, now you play solo. Why did you change?

K What happened with the band is private. I've already said I don't want to talk about it in interviews. All I'll say is that I have a lot more freedom this way. I can play – and say – what I want.
R Did your relationship with the band's lead guitarist affect the break up?
K No comment. I never talk about my private life.
R Your dad was in a famous punk band and your mom's a classical pianist. Have they influenced your music?
K Of course they have – what do you think? Isn't everyone influenced by their parents?
R When did you start playing?
K I started playing the guitar when I was about four.
R Four? That's pretty young.
K Yeah, the guitar was nearly as big as me!
R I think that your new album is your best yet. It's a lot quieter and more experimental than your earlier albums.
K Thank you! I think it's my best work.
R So, what have you been doing recently?
K Well, I've been writing and recording some new songs. And I've played at some of the summer festivals in the UK.
K And what are you doing while you're in the States?
K I'm going to play at some clubs here in New York, then I'm doing some small gigs in other places. I just want to get to know the country and the people. It's all very new to me.
***
J Good job, Rob. She isn't the easiest person to interview.
R She's OK. And this video clip will work great online.
***
D Well, thank you for coming in today, Kerri. Now I suggest we have some lunch. Rob, could you call a taxi?
R Uh, sure.

b Now focus on sentences 1–8. Go through them with Sts and make sure they understand them.

Play the DVD or audio again all the way through, and get Sts to mark the sentences T (true) or F (false). Remind them to correct the ones that are false.

Get Sts to compare with a partner and then check answers.

Extra support

• Before playing the audio, go through the listening script and decide if you need to preteach / check any lexis to help Sts when they listen.

1 F (The song is about **money**.)
2 F (She **used to play** in a band, she now plays **solo**.)
3 T
4 F (Her father was in a band and her mother is a pianist.)
5 F (She started playing the guitar when she was about **four**.)
6 T
7 T
8 F (She is going to play **at some clubs** in New York City.)

Extra support

• If there's time, you could get Sts to listen again with the script on *pages 124–125*, so they can see exactly what they understood / didn't understand. Translate / explain any new words or phrases.

52

2 📹 GIVING OPINIONS

a (2 29)》 Focus on the photos and ask Sts *Who are the people?* (Don and Kerri), *Where are they?* (At a restaurant).

Now either tell Sts to close their books and write the question on the board, or get Sts to focus on the question and cover the rest of the page.

Play the DVD or audio once all the way through and then check the answer.

> They disagree about which city is better, New York City or London.

(2 29)》

(script in Student Book on *pages 125*)
D = Don, K = Kerri, J = Jenny, R = Rob, W = waitress

D So when will you be coming back to New York, Kerri?
K Oh, I don't know...
W Hi guys, is everything OK?
D Yes, it's delicious, thank you.
W That's great!
K New York waiters never leave you alone! I really don't like all this "Hi guys! Is everything OK?" stuff.
D What? You mean waiters aren't friendly in London?
R Oh, they're very friendly!
K Yes, they're friendly, but not <u>too</u> friendly. They don't bother you all the time.
W Can I get you anything else? More drinks, maybe?
D No, thanks. We're fine.
W Fantastic.
K See what I mean? Personally, I think people in London are a lot more easygoing. London's just not as hectic as New York.
D Sure, we all like peace and quiet. But in my opinion, New York is possibly... well, no, is definitely the greatest city in the world. Don't you agree?
K To be honest, I definitely prefer London.
D Come on, Rob. You've lived in both. What do you think?
R Um, well, I have to say, London's very special. It's more relaxed, it's got great parks and you can cycle everywhere. It's dangerous to cycle in New York!
D Why would you cycle when you can drive a car?
K You can't be serious.
D OK, I agree, London has its own peculiar charm. But if you ask me, nothing compares with a city like New York. The whole world is here!
K But that's the problem. It's too big. There are too many people. Everybody's so stressed out. And nobody has any time for you.
J I don't think that's right, Kerri. New Yorkers are very friendly...
K Oh sure, they can sound friendly with all that "Have a nice day" stuff. But I always think it's a little bit... fake.
D You've got to be kidding me!
R I'm sorry. I'll just have to take this... Hello?... Yes... You're who?... The taxi driver?... What did she leave?... Her cell phone... right. OK. Yes, we're still at the restaurant. See you in about five minutes.

---

b Focus on the instructions and give Sts time to read questions 1–3.

Play the DVD or audio again, pausing if necessary to give Sts time to answer the questions.

Get Sts to compare with a partner and then check answers.

Extra support

• Before playing the audio, go through the listening script and decide if you need to preteach / check any lexis to help Sts when they listen.

> 1 a: The waiters in New York City never leave the customers alone. London waiters are friendly, but not too friendly. They don't bother you.
> b: The people in New York City are less easygoing.
> 2 Rob agrees. Don and Jenny disagree. Don thinks New York is the greatest city in the world, and Jenny thinks New Yorkers are very friendly.
> 3 The taxi driver calls Rob about Jenny or Kerri's phone.

Extra support

• If there's time, you could get Sts to listen again with the script on *page 125*, so they can see exactly what they understood / didn't understand. Translate / explain any new words or phrases.

c (2 30)》 Give Sts a minute to read through the extracts from the conversation and to think about what the missing words might be.

Now play the DVD or audio again and get Sts to fill in the blanks.

Get Sts to compare with a partner and then check answers.

> See words in **bold** in script 2.30

(2 30)》

1
K **Personally**, I think people in London are a lot more easygoing. London's just not as hectic as New York.
D Sure, we all like peace and quiet. But in my **opinion**, New York is possibly... well, no, is definitely the greatest city in the world. Don't you **agree**?
K To be **honest**, I definitely prefer London.
D Come on, Rob. You've lived in both. What do you **think**?

2
D OK, I **agree**, London has its own peculiar charm. But if you **ask** me, nothing compares with a city like New York. The whole world is here!
K But that's the problem. It's too big. There are too many people. Everybody's so stressed out. And nobody has any time for you.
J I don't think that's **right**, Kerri. New Yorkers are very friendly.
K Oh **sure**, they can sound friendly with all that "Have a nice day" stuff.

---

d (2 31)》 Tell Sts to focus on the highlighted phrases in the extracts. They should listen and repeat the phrases, copying the rhythm and intonation.

Play the DVD or audio, pausing for Sts to listen and repeat.

(2 31)》

See highlighted phrases in Student Book on *page 33*

Then repeat the activity, eliciting responses from individual Sts.

e Put Sts in pairs and tell them to practice the dialogues in **c**.

Monitor and help, encouraging Sts to pay attention to rhythm and intonation.

Make sure Sts exchange roles.

f Focus on the instructions and the four statements. Give Sts a few minutes to think about ideas for each statement.

Now put Sts in small groups of four and ask them to discuss each statement in turn.

Get some feedback from various groups.

3 📹 A SURPRISE FOR KERRI

a (2 32))) Focus on the photos and the question.

Before playing the DVD or audio, focus on the **American and British English** box and go through it with the class.

Play the DVD or audio once all the way through and then check the answer.

> Kerri is surprised because the taxi driver returned to the restaurant to give her back her phone, which she had left in the taxi.

> **(2 32)))**
> (script in Student Book on *page 125*)
> **D = Don, K = Kerri, J = Jenny, R = Rob, W = waitress,**
> **T = taxi driver**
>
> **K** Thank you for a nice lunch, Don.
> **D** You're welcome.
> **W** Thanks for coming, guys! Have a nice day.
> **D** See? Nice, friendly service.
> **K** Maybe. But I think she saw the big tip you left on the table!
> ***
> **J** Did you mean what you said in the restaurant, Rob?
> **R** Did I mean what?
> **J** About missing London.
> **R** Sure, I miss it, Jenny.
> **J** Really?
> **R** But hey, not _that_ much! It's just that moving to a new place is always difficult.
> **J** But you don't regret coming here, do you?
> **R** No... no... not at all.
> **J** It's just that... you seemed homesick in there. For the parks, the cycling...
> **R** Well, there are some things I miss but... Oh, hang on a minute. Look over there. Our taxi's come back.
> ***
> **T** Excuse me, Ma'am.
> **K** Who me? What is it?
> **T** I believe this is your cell phone. You left it in my cab.
> **K** What?... Oh, wow... thank you!
> **T** Have a nice day!
> **K** That was so kind of him!
> **D** See? New Yorkers are really friendly people.

b Focus on sentences 1–3 and give Sts time to read them.

Now play the DVD or audio again, so Sts can listen a second time and complete the sentences.

Get Sts to compare with a partner and then check answers.

Extra support

- Before playing the audio, go through the listening script and decide if you need to preteach / check any lexis to help Sts when they listen.

> 1 left a big tip.
> 2 misses London.
> 3 kind.

Extra support

- If there's time, you could get Sts to listen again with the script on *page 125*, so they can see exactly what they understood / didn't understand. Translate / explain any new words or phrases.

c Focus on the **Social English phrases**. In pairs, get Sts to think about what the missing words could be.

Extra challenge

- In pairs, get Sts to complete the phrases before they listen.

d (2 33))) Play the DVD or audio for Sts to listen and complete the phrases.

Check answers.

> See words in **bold** in script 2.33

> **(2 33)))**
> **Jenny** Did you **mean** what you said in the restaurant, Rob?
> **Jenny** It's **just** that... you seemed homesick in there.
> **Rob** Oh, **hang** on a minute.
> **Rob** Our taxi's come **back**.
> **Kerri** That was so **kind** of him!

If you know your Sts' L1, you could get them to translate the phrases. If not, get Sts to look at the phrases again in context in the script on *page 125*.

e Now play the DVD or audio again, pausing after each phrase for Sts to listen and repeat.

Finally, focus on the **Can you...?** questions and ask Sts if they feel confident they can now do these things.

G *can, could, be able to,* 🔑reflexive pronouns
V *-ed / -ing* adjectives
P sentence stress

4A Failure and success

Lesson plan

The grammatical focus of this lesson is for Sts to learn how to use *be able to* in the tenses / forms where *can / can't* cannot be used. The main context is failure and success, and the new grammar is presented through a magazine article about three people who have tried unsuccessfully to learn something. This is followed by a pronunciation focus on sentence stress in sentences with *can / could / be able to*, and then the new language is put into practice in Speaking where Sts talk about things they have tried to learn to do or would like to be able to do.

In the second half of the lesson, there is a vocabulary focus on adjectives which have both *-ed* and *-ing* forms, e.g., *disappointed / disappointing*. Sts then read about a young student who was in the news because of his talent for learning foreign languages (he can speak 11). This is followed by a short grammar spot on the use of reflexive pronouns. Finally, Sts listen to some advanced students who each give a tip for improving one's English. Sts then discuss how useful they think the tips are.

STUDY LINK
• **Workbook** 4A

Extra photocopiable activities

• **Grammar** *can, could, be able to page* 150
• **Communicative** Language learning *page* 180 (instructions *page* **166**)

Optional lead-in (books closed)

• Write on the board:

NOUN: **SUCCESS**   OPPOSITE NOUN: _____

ADJ: _____

VERB: _____   OPPOSITE VERB: _____

• Put Sts in pairs. First, elicit the meaning of *success* (= something you wanted or planned to do and that you have done well), that it's a noun, and that the stress is on the second syllable. Then get Sts to try to complete the chart. Check answers and drill pronunciation.

> Adj: suc<u>cess</u>ful
> Verb: suc<u>ceed</u>
> Opposite noun: <u>fail</u>ure
> Opposite verb: fail

• Make sure Sts understand the meaning of all the words and model and drill pronunciation.

1 GRAMMAR *can, could, be able to*

a Books open. Focus on the instructions and get Sts, in pairs or as a whole class, to say what they think this well-known saying means.

Elicit answers. (It means that you shouldn't give up too easily, but should keep trying.) You could tell Sts that the origin of this saying is from the 1800s and it was originally used to encourage American schoolchildren to do their homework.

b Focus on the instructions and make sure Sts understand all the different ways of continuing the saying.

Now give Sts time to look at all the new versions of the saying and to choose the one they like best.

Get Sts to compare their choice with a partner's.

Get some feedback. You could see with a show of hands if one ending is more popular than the others.

c Focus on the definition of *be able to* and elicit that it is similar in meaning to *can*. Tell Sts that now they are going to see how *be able to* is used and to compare it with *can*.

d Focus on the task and on A–G. Set a time limit for Sts to read about the three people and to fill in the blanks with the missing phrases. Tell them to read each text first before they try to complete it.

Get Sts to compare with a partner, and then check answers.

> 1 C   2 B   3 D   4 F   5 A   6 E   7 G

Extra support

• You could do the first text with the whole class.

e Tell Sts to read the article again and answer the questions.

Get Sts to compare with a partner and then check answers.

> 1 Bea suffered from claustrophobia. Sean dances like a robot. Joaquin found Japanese too difficult.
> 2 Bea and Joaquin have given up. Sean still tries to dance salsa if nobody is watching.

Now find out if any Sts have ever tried to learn something and given up. Make sure they explain why.

f Focus on the instructions. Then take each phrase and elicit the answer.

> **A** and **C** are in the simple past.
> **B** is a gerund.
> **D** is a future tense.
> **E** and **G** are conditional sentences.
> **F** is in the present perfect.
> ***Can*** can be used in the present or the past (= *could*).

g (2 34)) (2 35)) Tell Sts to go to **Grammar Bank 4A** on *page 138*. Focus on the example sentences and play the audio for Sts to listen to the sentence rhythm. You could also get Sts to repeat the sentences to practice getting the rhythm right. Then go through the rules with the class.

Extra idea

• In a monolingual class you could get Sts to translate the example sentences and compare the forms / verbs they would use in their L1.

> **Additional grammar notes**
>
> • Sts should all be perfectly familiar with the verb *can* for ability and possibility (or permission). *Can / can't* is a modal verb, which has a past and conditional structure (*could / couldn't*), but has no present perfect or past perfect forms nor does it have an infinitive or *-ing* form. In these situations *be able to* must be used.
>
> ! For the future you can often use *can* or *will be able to*, e.g., *I can't go to the meeting tomorrow / I won't be able to go to the meeting tomorrow.*
>
> • Some typical mistakes include:
>
> – trying to use *can* where *be able to* should be used, e.g., ~~I want to can speak English well.~~ / ~~I won't can come to your party on Saturday.~~
>
> – leaving out *to*, e.g., ~~I won't be able help you.~~
>
> ! There is a very small difference between *could* and *was able to*. In a ⊞ simple past sentence, if we want to refer to something that someone succeeded in doing, something difficult on a specific occasion, we use *be able to* (or *managed to*), e.g., *Although the space was very small, he was able to* (or *managed to*) *park there.* In this context it is not possible to use *could*. With a strong class you may want to point this out.

Focus on the exercises and get Sts to do them individually or in pairs.

Check answers, getting Sts to read the full sentences.

a			
1	haven't been able to	6	not being able to
2	being able to / to be able to	7	were able to
3	will / 'll be able to	8	won't be able to
4	Will ... be able to	9	Have ... been able to
5	to be able to	10	isn't able to
b			
1	✓	6	✓
2	be able to	7	✓
3	been able to	8	be able to
4	being able to	9	✓
5	be able to	10	✓

Tell Sts to go back to the main lesson **4A**.

Extra support

• If you think Sts need more practice, you may want to give them the Grammar photocopiable activity at this point or leave it for later as consolidation or review.

h Put Sts in pairs, **A** and **B**, and tell them to go to **Communication** *Guess the sentence*, **A** on *page 105*, **B** on *page 109*.

Demonstrate the activity by writing in large letters on a piece of paper the following sentence:

SORRY. I WON'T BE ABLE TO SEE YOU TONIGHT.

Don't show the piece of paper to the Sts yet. Then write on the board:

SORRY. I WON'T _____ YOU TONIGHT.

Tell Sts that what's missing is a form of *be able to* + a verb. Tell them that they must guess the exact sentence that you have written on a piece of paper. Elicit ideas. If they are wrong, say "Try again," until someone guesses the right answer. Then show them your piece of paper with the sentence on it and complete the sentence on the board with *be able to see*.

Tell Sts to look at instruction **a**. Give them a few minutes to think of the correct form of *be able to* + a verb to complete their sentences in a logical way. Emphasize that their partner has the same sentences already completed and the aim is to try and complete the sentences in the same way. Monitor and help while they are doing this. Emphasize that Sts should write their ideas next to the sentence and tell them <u>not</u> to show their sentences to their partner.

Now tell Sts to look at instruction **b**. Tell **A** to read out his / her first sentence for **B** to tell him / her if he / she has guessed the sentence correctly. If not, he / she has to guess again. If the sentence is correct, he / she writes the missing words in the blank.

When they finish, Sts **B** read his / her sentences to Sts **A**, etc.

Extra support

• You could write any useful words and phrases from **Communication** on the board for Sts to copy.

Tell Sts to go back to the main lesson **4A**.

2 PRONUNCIATION sentence stress

> **Pronunciation notes**
>
> • If necessary, remind Sts about sentence stress in English (See **Pronunciation notes** in **Lesson 2B** on *page 36*).

a (2 36)) Here Sts practice stress and rhythm in sentences with *be able to*. Play the audio once all the way through for Sts just to listen.

> (2 36))
> See sentences in Student Book on *page 35*

Now play it again, pausing after each sentence for Sts to listen and repeat.

Then repeat the activity, getting individual Sts to say the sentences.

b (2 37)) Go through the instructions. Explain (or show on the board) that they will first hear an example sentence, e.g., *I'd love to be able to ski*. Then they will hear a verb or verb phrase (e.g., *Ride a horse*). Sts then have to make a new sentence using that verb / verb phrase, i.e., *I'd love to be able to ride a horse*. At the same time, they should try to copy the rhythm of the original sentence.

When Sts are clear what they have to do, play the audio and get the whole class to respond.

(2 37))

1 I'd love to be able to ski. Ride a horse (*pause*) I'd love to be able to ride a horse.
2 We won't be able to come. Park (*pause*) We won't be able to park.
3 I've never been able to dance. Speak French (*pause*) I've never been able to speak French.
4 She hates not being able to drive. Cook (*pause*) She hates not being able to cook.
5 Will you be able to find it? Afford it (*pause*) Will you be able to afford it?
6 He'd love to be able to snowboard. Windsurf (*pause*) He'd love to be able to windsurf.
7 I love being able to understand everyone. Speak to everyone (*pause*) I love being able to speak to everyone.
8 They haven't been able to finish. Come (*pause*) They haven't been able to come.

Repeat the activity for extra practice, this time getting individual Sts to respond.

3 SPEAKING

a Focus on the instructions and on the things which Sts have to talk about, making sure they understand them all.

Give Sts time to make some notes or think about what they are going to say for two or three of the topics they have chosen.

b Put Sts in pairs and give them time to tell each other about each of the things they chose in **a**. Encourage them to ask each other for more information and to give as much detail as possible. If there is an odd number of Sts in the class, you can take part yourself or have one group of three. Monitor and correct any misuse of *can / could / be able to*.

Get some feedback afterwards to find how many people, for example, have learned to do something after a lot of effort, etc.

Extra support

• Demonstrate the activity by choosing one of the topics and telling the Sts about your experience.

4 VOCABULARY *-ed / -ing* adjectives

a Focus on the photo and on the two sentences and elicit answers. Elicit / explain / translate the meaning of the two adjectives in each case.

1 The movie was **boring**. 2 The audience was **bored**.

Point out that:

– the *-ing* adjective is used for a person or thing who causes the feeling.

– the *-ed* adjective is used for the person who has the feeling. In other words, a *boring* person makes us feel *bored*.

b Focus on the instructions and go through the *-ed* and *-ing* **adjectives** box with Sts.

Give Sts a couple of minutes to choose the right adjective endings for 1–10.

c (2 38)) Play the audio for Sts to listen and check answers. Make sure Sts know what the correct adjective means. Give Sts practice in pronouncing the adjectives, making sure they stress them on the right syllable. You could play the audio again pausing after each question and getting Sts to repeat just the adjective.

(2 38))

1 What do you think is the most **exciting** sport to watch?
2 What's the most **amazing** scenery you've ever seen?
3 What music do you listen to if you feel **depressed**?
4 Have you ever been **disappointed** by a birthday present?
5 Which do you find more **tiring**, speaking English or listening to English?
6 What's the most **embarrassing** thing that's ever happened to you?
7 Are you **scared** of spiders?
8 Do you feel very **tired** in the morning?
9 Who's the most **boring** person you know?
10 Do you ever get **frustrated** by technology?

Remind Sts that *amazing / amazed* are strong adjectives (See the Student Book **Lesson 2B Vocabulary** *page 21*). This means that you cannot use *very* with these words. *Amazing* can mean either *very surprised* or *very good*.

Now play the audio again and get Sts to underline the stressed syllable in the adjectives.

Check answers.

See underlining in script 2.38

d Focus on the questions in **b** and get Sts to ask you a couple of questions first. Make sure they ask for more information.

Put Sts in pairs and get them to ask and answer the questions. Monitor and correct any mistakes with word stress.

Get some feedback from the class for each question.

Extra idea

• Get feedback with a show of hands for number 5. You could also ask Sts why they find one more tiring than the other.

5 READING & SPEAKING

a Do this as an open-class activity or put Sts in pairs. If you know someone yourself, tell Sts about him / her.

b (2 39)) Focus on the photo and the instructions.

Put Sts in pairs and give them time to look at the word *hello* written in 11 languages and to decide which language each one is.

Play the audio for Sts to listen and check.

See script 2.39

2 39)))

1	Afrikaans, *Hallo*	7	Greek, *Yassou*
2	German, *Guten Tag*	8	Catalan, *Bon dia*
3	French, *Bonjour*	9	Spanish, *Hola*
4	Hebrew, *Shalom*	10	Dutch, *Goedendag*
5	Russian, *Privet*	11	Italian, *Ciao*
6	English, *Hello*		

c Now tell Sts to read the article and answer questions 1–7. Point out the **Glossary**.

Get Sts to compare with a partner and then check answers.

Extra support

- Before Sts read the article, check it for words and phrases that your Sts might not know and be ready to help with these while they are answering the questions or afterwards. You may even want to preteach / check a few words / phrases to lighten the load (but not the highlighted ones).

1	English, Greek, and French
2	German and Russian
3	Greek
4	Arabic
5	Japanese
6	Dutch
7	Russian

d Focus on the highlighted words and phrases. Get Sts, in pairs, to guess their meaning. Tell them to read the whole sentence as the context will help them guess.

Check answers, either explaining in English, translating into Sts' L1, or getting Sts to check in their dictionaries.

Explain any other new vocabulary and encourage Sts to write down any useful new lexis from the text.

Now put Sts in pairs and get them to answer the questions.

Get some feedback from the class. You could tell the Sts if you would like to be able to speak other languages and why.

e Focus on the **Reflexive pronouns** box and go through it with Sts. Highlight that reflexive pronouns are made by adding *self* (or *selves* in the plural) to the possessive adjective (*my, your,* etc.). The exceptions are *himself* and *themselves* where *self / selves* are added to the object pronouns *him* and *them*.

! You may want to teach Sts the expression *by* + reflexive pronoun = alone, e.g., *I cooked it by myself.*

Now focus on the exercise and give Sts time to do it individually or in pairs.

Check answers.

1	myself	3	itself	5	herself
2	himself	4	yourself		

6 LISTENING & SPEAKING

a **2 40**))) Focus on the instructions and make sure Sts understand the word *tip* (= a useful piece of advice).

Play the audio once all the way through for Sts to listen and fill in the blanks. Play the audio again as necessary.

Get Sts to compare with a partner and then check answers.

Extra support

- Before playing the audio, go through the listening script and decide if you need to preteach / check any lexis to help Sts when they listen.

Tip 1	Change the language to English on all the **gadgets** you have, for example on your **phone**, or **laptop**, or **tablet**.
Tip 2	Do things that you **like doing**, but in English.
Tip 3	Try to find an English-speaking **boyfriend** or **girlfriend**.
Tip 4	Get a **vocabulary learning** app for your phone.
Tip 5	Book yourself a **vacation** in an **English-speaking country**.
Tip 6	Listen to as many **songs** as possible in English, and then **learn to sing** them.

2 40)))

(script in Student Book on *page 125*)

1
One very easy thing you can do is just change the language to English on all the gadgets you have, for example on your phone, or laptop, or tablet. That way you're reading English every day and without really noticing you just learn a whole lot of vocabulary, for example the things you see on your screen like "Are you sure you want to shut down now?," things like that.

2
My tip is to do things that you like doing, but in English. So for example if you like reading, then read in English, if you like movies, watch them in English with subtitles, if you like computer games, play them in English. But don't do things you don't enjoy in your language, I mean if you don't like reading in your language, you'll enjoy it even less in English, and so you probably won't learn anything.

3
What really helped me to improve my English was having an American boyfriend. He didn't speak any Japanese – well, not many foreigners do – so we spoke English all the time, and my English improved really quickly. We broke up when he went back to the US, but by then I could speak pretty fluently. We didn't exactly end up as friends, but I'll always be grateful to him for the English I learned. So my tip is try to find an English-speaking boyfriend or girlfriend.

4
I've always thought that learning vocabulary is very important, so I bought a vocabulary flashcard app for my phone. I write down all the new words and phrases I want to remember in French and in English, and then when I get a quiet moment I test myself. It really helps me remember new vocabulary. So that's my tip. Get a vocabulary learning app for your phone.

5
I think one of the biggest problems when you're learning something new is motivation, something to make you continue and not give up. So my tip is to book yourself a vacation in an English-speaking country or a country where people speak very good English, like the Caribbean, as a little reward for yourself and so you can actually practice your English. It's really motivating when you go somewhere and find that people understand you and you can communicate! Last year I went to the Bahamas for a weekend and I had a great time and I spoke a lot of English.

6
If you love music, which I do, my tip is to listen to as many songs as possible in English and then learn to sing them. It's so easy nowadays with *YouTube*. First, I download the lyrics and try to understand them. Then I sing along with the singer and try to copy the way he or she sings – this is fantastic for your pronunciation. Then once I can do it well, I go back to *YouTube* and get a karaoke version of the song, and then I sing it. It's fun and your English will really improve as a result.

b Tell Sts to listen again and this time to write down as many details as possible about each tip.

Play the audio, pausing after each speaker to give Sts time to write.

Get Sts to compare with a partner and then check answers.

> **Tip 1** **Change the language to English on all the gadgets you have.** That way you're reading English every day and you just learn a lot of vocabulary, especially technology vocabulary.
>
> **Tip 2** **Do things that you like doing, but in English.** If you don't like reading in your language, you'll enjoy it even less in English, and so you probably won't learn anything.
>
> **Tip 3** **Try to find an English-speaking boyfriend or girlfriend.** If you speak English all the time with him / her, your English will improve really quickly.
>
> **Tip 4** **Get a vocabulary learning app for your phone.** Write down all the new words and phrases you want to remember in your language and in English, and then when you get a quiet moment test yourself.
>
> **Tip 5** **Book yourself a vacation in an English-speaking country** or a country where people speak very good English. You can practice your English. It's really motivating when you go somewhere and find that people understand you and you can communicate!
>
> **Tip 6** **Listen to as many songs as possible in English and then learn to sing them.** It's easy nowadays with *YouTube*. Download the lyrics and try to understand them. Then sing along with the singer and try to copy the way he or she sings – this is fantastic for your pronunciation. Then, go back to *YouTube* and get a karaoke version of the song, and then sing it. It's fun and your English will really improve.

Extra support

- If there's time, you could play the audio again while Sts read the script on *page 125*, so they can see what they understood / didn't understand. Translate / explain any new words or phrases.

c Put Sts in pairs or small groups and get them to discuss the questions.

Extra idea

- For the question *Which do you think is the best tip?* get a show of hands for each one and see which is the most popular.

Get some feedback from the class. If Sts use apps, websites, etc., that they recommend, write them on the board for all Sts to make a note of. Get Sts who use them to say why they are useful.

G modals of obligation: *must, have to, should,* 🔑*should have*
V phone language
P silent consonants, linking

4B Modern manners?

Lesson plan

The main topic of this lesson is on manners in today's world – how people should behave in a variety of common situations.

In the first half of the lesson the focus is on cell phone etiquette. The lesson begins with a vocabulary focus on words and phrases related to cell phones and then Sts speak about their own phones and phone experiences. A short reading text extracted from *Debrett's Guide to cell Phone Etiquette* provides the context for Sts to practice common ways of expressing obligation using *must, have to,* and *should*. Sts will have met these verbs separately, but will probably not have contrasted them before. In Pronunciation and Speaking, Sts first work on silent letters in, for example, *should* and *listen*, and later practice linking in phrases with modals of obligation. Then they put the new grammar into practice in a speaking activity about phone manners.

In the second half of the lesson, Sts read a newspaper article about an email written by a boy's mother to his fiancée criticizing her lack of manners. The email went viral on the Internet causing the family great embarrassment. In Listening the focus is on how different nationalities can have a different idea of what are good and bad manners. This leads into an extended speaking activity where Sts discuss "modern manners" and their relative importance in different situations. The lesson finishes with a song, *You Can't Hurry Love.*

STUDY LINK
- **Workbook** 4B
- **iChecker**

Extra photocopiable activities
- **Grammar** modals of obligation: *must, have to, should page* 151
- **Communicative** Tell us about... *page* 181 (instructions pages 166–167)
- **Song** *You Can't Hurry Love page* 220 (instructions *page* 215)

Optional lead-in (books closed)
- Do a quick survey to find how many Sts in the class are carrying a cell phone. Then find out which make is the most popular. Take the opportunity to make sure everybody's cell phone is switched off!

1 VOCABULARY & SPEAKING
phone language

a **2 41**)) Books open. Focus on the instructions and sentences A–G. Give Sts time to go through them in pairs and say what they think the bold words and phrases mean. Clarify the meaning of any words or phrases they don't know.

Now play the audio, pausing after the first sound effect, and elicit that the sounds they are hearing are different ringtones, so the answer is D.

Now continue playing the audio to the end and give Sts time to compare answers. Play again if necessary.

Check answers. You might like to tell Sts that *She's texting a friend* is the same as *She's sending a text to a friend.*

Extra support
- Alternatively, you could pause the audio after each sound effect and let Sts, in pairs, choose the right sentence.

| 1 D | 2 C | 3 G | 4 F | 5 A | 6 E | 7 B |

2 41))
1 *several different ringtones*
2 **Woman** Goodbye. (*hangs up.*)
3 *busy signal*
4 **Jack** Please leave a message after the tone.
Sandra Hi Jack, it's Sandra. I was just calling to confirm that meeting.
5 *dial tone and dialing a number*
6 **Man** Hello?
James Oh, hi. It's James. I called half an hour ago, but Ann wasn't there. Is she there now?
7 *texting*

Get Sts to close their books and play the audio again. Pause after each sound effect and get the class (or individual Sts) to say the sentence.

b In pairs, Sts look at the words in the list and tell each other what they mean.

Elicit answers.

Skype: a telephone system that works by direct communication between users' computers on the Internet
a screensaver: a computer program that replaces a screen display on a computer with another, moving, display after a particular length of time, to stop the screen from being damaged
silent / vibrate mode: the mode on a cell phone that makes it move from side to side very quickly and with small movements
quiet zones: are places where you aren't allowed to use a cell phone, e.g., in certain sections of a train
instant messaging: a system on the Internet that allows people to exchange written messages with each other very quickly

c Focus on the questionnaire and go through the questions with Sts.

In pairs, Sts interview each other and ask for more information.

Extra idea
- If you have a cell phone, get Sts to ask you the questions first.

60

2 GRAMMAR

modals of obligation: *must, have to, should*

a Focus on the title of the article. Elicit / explain the meaning of *etiquette*, and model and drill pronunciation.

Now read the introduction together to make sure Sts understand what Debrett's is and what it produces.

Tell Sts to read the extract and then, in pairs, they should discuss questions 1–4.

Get some feedback.

b Get Sts to read the text again and then match the highlighted phrases with A–D.

Get Sts to compare with a partner, and then check answers.

> You should change it = D
> You must not use your phone = B
> You don't have to shout = A
> You have to keep your phone on = C
> You must take a call = C

Explain any other new vocabulary.

c (2 42))) (2 43))) (2 44))) (2 45))) Tell Sts to go to **Grammar Bank 4B** on *page 139*. Focus on the example sentences and play the audio for Sts to listen to the sentence rhythm. You could also get Sts to repeat the sentences to practice getting the rhythm right. Then go through the rules with the class.

Extra idea

- In a monolingual class if you know your Sts' L1, you could get Sts to translate the example sentences and compare the forms / verbs they would use in their L1.

Additional grammar notes

Obligation and necessity: *have to* and *must*

- *have to* / *must* and *should* / *shouldn't* were taught separately in *American English File* 2.
  In this lesson they are reviewed and contrasted in more detail.

- Some typical mistakes include:

  – saying *must to*, e.g., ~~I must to be on time tomorrow~~.

  – confusing *must not* (prohibition) and *don't have to* (not necessary / not obligatory).

  – using *must* (not *had to*) in the past tense, e.g., ~~I must study last night~~.

Advice or opinions: *should* / *shouldn't*

- The important point to emphasize here is that *should* isn't as strong as *have to* / *must* and it is normally used to express a personal opinion or give advice.

  Compare:

  – *You should talk to your teacher about the problem.*
    (= I think it's a good idea)

  – *You must talk to your teacher about the problem.*
    (= I think it's <u>very</u> important you do this)

Focus on the exercises and get Sts to do them individually or in pairs.

Check answers, getting Sts to read the full sentences.

> a
> 1 have to   6 had to
> 2 Did ... have to   7 won't have to
> 3 has to   8 have to
> 4 Have ... had to   9 Does ... have to
> 5 not having to   10 didn't have to
>
> b
> 1 ✓   4 must not
> 2 must not   5 ✓
> 3 ✓   6 don't have to

Tell Sts to go back to the main lesson **4B**.

Extra support

- If you think Sts need more practice, you may want to give them the Grammar photocopiable activity at this point or leave it for later as consolidation or review.

3 PRONUNCIATION & SPEAKING

silent consonants, linking

Pronunciation notes

- Silent consonants are a feature of English. Sts will be aware of some or most of these, but probably not all of them. Sometimes Sts may have been pronouncing, for example, the *l* in *calm*, since they learned the word without realizing that it is a silent consonant (even though they probably don't pronounce the *l* in *half* or *walk*).

- Here Sts also practice linking and sentence rhythm again. If you want to remind them when linking occurs, refer them back to the information box on linking in the Student Book **Lesson 3A**, **5 Pronunciation** on *page 26*.

a In pairs, Sts look at the words in the list and decide which consonant (or consonants) is silent in each one.

b (2 46))) Play the audio for Sts to listen and check.

Check answers (the silent consonants are marked in green in the key), and write them on the board.

> should, talk, wrong, listen, half, dishonest, knowledge, design, whole, rhythm, doubt, foreign, calm, island

> (2 46)))
> See words in Student Book on *page 39*

Extra challenge

- You could elicit other words from the class which have silent consonants (in **bold** here), e.g., *thumb, castle, sword, science, knee, answer, sign, climb, scissors, exhausted*, etc.

c (2 47)) Focus on the sentences and point out how the words are linked.

Play the audio once all the way through for Sts to just listen.

> (2 47))
> See sentences in Student Book on *page 39*

Point out that:

– *must* can have either a strong or weak pronunciation. It normally has a weak pronunciation unless we want to give special emphasis. Compare:

  1 I must <u>go</u> to the <u>bank</u> this <u>morning</u>. (= It is something I need to do this morning.) – weak stress on *must*.

  2 I <u>must</u> <u>go</u> to the <u>bank</u> this <u>morning</u>. (= It is very important I do this.) – strong stress on *must* to emphasize the importance.

– in ⊞ sentences *should* is not usually stressed and is pronounced /ʃəd/.

– the weak form of *to* in *have to* /tə/.

– the negative forms *must not*, *don't have*, and *shouldn't* are always stressed.

Remind Sts of the silent *l* in *should* /ʃʊd/.

Play the audio, pausing after each sentence for Sts to listen and repeat, copying the rhythm and linking the words where necessary.

Then repeat the activity getting individual Sts to repeat the phrases.

d Focus on the instructions and the definition of *manners* and go through it with Sts.

Now focus on the phrases and make sure Sts understand them.

For phrase 1 elicit from the class *You have to turn off your phone in a theater.* (rule)

Sts continue in pairs making sentences with *should* / *shouldn't*, *must* / *must not*, or *have to*.

> **Possible answers for the US (answers may vary in different countries)**
> You shouldn't talk loudly on a cell phone in public. (good manners)
>
> You must not send text messages when you are driving. (law)
>
> You shouldn't reply to a message on your phone. (manners)
>
> You shouldn't play noisy games on a phone in public. (manners or rule depending on the public place)
>
> You must not use your phone at a gas station. (law)
>
> You shouldn't video people without their permission. (manners)
>
> You should set your phone to silent mode on a train. (manners or rule depending on the train)
>
> You shouldn't send or receive texts in the movies. (rule or manners)
>
> You have to / must turn off your phone on a plane. (law)

4 READING

a Focus on the instructions. Then put Sts in pairs and get them to discuss the situation.

Elicit some answers and write them on the board. Try to get at least four or five.

> **Possible answers**
> not bring a present, use your cell phone at the dinner table, not say *please* or *thank you*, use bad language, say that you don't like the food, etc.

b Focus on the instructions and give Sts time to read the article to see if their ideas from **a** are there.

Check answers, by eliciting what Heidi did wrong.

> She told Mrs. Bourne food that she liked and disliked; she said she didn't have enough food; she started eating before everyone else; she helped herself to more food before Mrs. Bourne had offered her more; she stayed in bed late; and she didn't send a handwritten card after the visit.

Now tell Sts to focus on the title and elicit / explain the meaning of *two sides to every story* (i.e., there is more than one opinion to everything).

Ask Sts if they think this is a true story and then tell them it is.

c Focus on the ***should have*** box and go through it with Sts. This is normally considered more advanced grammar, but it is pointed out here as it occurs several times in the article and comments. Sts should not have too many problems deducing the meaning.

Tell Sts to match 1–7 with words and phrases in the article.

Get Sts to compare with a partner, and then check answers. Model and drill pronunciation where necessary.

> | | | | |
> |---|---|---|---|
> | 1 a fiancé | 3 criticize | 5 a guest | 7 forwarded |
> | 2 nasty | 4 lack | 6 a host | |

Remind Sts that *fiancé* is a word that has been imported into English from the French and point out that a *fiancée* is a woman to whom you are going to be married. Highlight the silent *u* in *guest*. Help with any other vocabulary problems and encourage Sts to write down any useful new lexis from the article.

d Ask Sts what Heidi did when she received the email from Mrs. Bourne and elicit that she forwarded it to some of her friends. Then ask Sts what happened and elicit that the friends also forwarded it to other people.

Finally, tell Sts that they are going to read some comments that were posted on the Internet by various people. Focus on the instructions and make sure Sts understand the expression *to support somebody* (i.e., took her side in the argument). Model and drill the pronunciation of *support* /sə'pɔrt/.

Give Sts time to read the comments.

Get Sts to compare with a partner and then check answers.

> | | | | | | | |
> |---|---|---|---|---|---|---|
> | 1 H | 2 H | 3 C | 4 H | 5 H/C | 6 H | 7 C |

e Tell Sts to get a piece of paper and to write a comment of their own, either supporting Heidi or Mrs. Bourne. They should write at least 25 words.

When they have finished, get them to exchange pieces of paper with their partner. Did they both support the same person?

With a show of hands find out how many people support Heidi. Ask Sts what they think Heidi should do now.

f Tell Sts to go to **Communication** *The big day* on *page 105*.

In pairs, Sts read about what happened at Heidi and Freddie's wedding and then tell each other what they think.

Get some feedback from the class.

Finally, ask Sts which words and phrases they want to try and remember from both the article and posted comments.

Extra support
- You could write any new and useful words and phrases from **Communication** on the board for Sts to copy.

Tell Sts to go back to the main lesson **4B**.

5 LISTENING

a (2 48)) Ask Sts if they think good manners are the same everywhere in the world and elicit some ideas.

Tell Sts they are going to listen to Caroline, an American woman dating a Burmese man, talking about manners. Focus on the questions and make sure Sts understand them.

Now play the audio once all the way through. Play again if necessary.

Check answers.

Extra support
- Before playing the audio, go through the listening script and decide if you need to preteach / check any lexis to help Sts when they listen.

> They have a different idea of what manners are. Caroline thought it was rude that Jason wouldn't spend time with her alone, and she doesn't understand why Jason won't write romantic messages on her Facebook page. He thinks you shouldn't have one best friend because it makes your other friends feel bad.
>
> They have agreed to disagree about manners.

(2 48))

(script in Student Book on *page 125*)
I always thought that good manners were good manners wherever you were in the world. But that was until I met my boyfriend Jason, who is from Burma – also known as Myanmar. We met in upstate New York, when we were both students in college. When we first got to know each other, we were always surrounded by a group of friends. I liked Jason because he was funny and kind, and I could tell he liked me, but we never spent any time alone.
The first time I suggested that we hang out without our friends, he said no without an explanation, which I thought was kind of rude. My feelings were hurt, so I didn't talk to him as much. The next time I saw Jason in our big group, he was just as friendly and happy as usual. I was confused.
Finally, I asked him why he wouldn't hang out with me. He apologized and then he told me that in Burma, it's custom to

"date" in a group situation. Since he had only been in the US for a few years, he was still having trouble navigating the two cultures he lived in – the more reserved Burmese culture and the more open American culture.
A few months later, after we started dating, I asked him why he never responded to my cute, romantic Facebook posts with more than "cool" or "thanks." It seemed weird to me that his responses weren't romantic. And honestly, I was a little jealous of the sweet posts my American friends' boyfriends left on their Facebook pages.
But Jason told me in Burma, it's considered bragging to express your feelings in public, especially on a social networking site. He didn't want his family and friends to think he was bragging about his American girlfriend. From an American point of view, I thought he was being a bit cold; however from a Burmese point of view, he was actually being respectful.
As confused as I was about what's considered good and bad manners in Jason's culture, he felt the same way about American culture. He thought it was bad manners to refer to have a "best friend," and he would argue with me whenever I called my friend Rachel, my best friend. Jason said there is no such thing as a "best friend" in Burmese culture. There are only "close friends." It would be inconsiderate to name one person as a "best friend" because your other friends would feel offended.
Anyway, we've been together for two years, and we still have disagreements. But, we've learned that as long as we're a couple, we'll never completely agree about whether our manners are good or bad, and that most importantly it's OK to agree to disagree!

b Focus on sentences 1–7. Go through them with Sts and make sure they understand them.

Now play the audio again all the way through, and get Sts to mark the sentences T (true) or F (false). Remind them to correct the false ones.

Get Sts to compare with a partner and then check answers.

> 1 F (Caroline thought Jason was rude.)
> 2 F (In Burma, it's the custom to date in large groups.)
> 3 T
> 4 F (He wrote very short responses.)
> 5 F (Jason didn't talk about Caroline at all to his friends and family.)
> 6 T
> 7 F (They still have disagreements,)

! If you have any students from Myamar/Burma in your class, ask them if they agree with Jason.

Extra support
- If there's time, you could play the audio again while Sts read the script on *page 125*, so they can see what they understood / didn't understand. Translate / explain any new words or phrases.

c Put Sts in pairs, small groups, or do this as an open-class activity to find out if people in your Sts' country behave more like the Burmese or more like Americans.

6 SPEAKING

Divide Sts into groups of three or four and focus on the instructions and the example speech bubbles.

Then focus attention on the section **When you are invited to somebody's house**. Elicit opinions from the whole class, encouraging Sts to use *I think people should…*, *I don't think people should…*, *I don't think it's necessary to…*, *You have to…*

Get Sts to talk about each thing in the other two sections of the questionnaire in their groups.

If there's time, get some feedback from various groups to see if Sts agree with each other.

7 (2 49»)) **SONG** *You Can't Hurry Love* ♫

This song was originally made famous by the American singing group The Supremes in 1966. For copyright reasons this is a cover version. If you want to do this song in class, use the photocopiable activity on *page 220*.

(2 49»))

You Can't Hurry Love

I need love, love
To ease my mind
I need to find, find someone to call mine
But mama said,

> *Chorus*
> "You can't hurry love
> No, you just have to wait"
> She said, "Love don't come easy
> It's a game of give and take."

You can't hurry love
No, you just have to wait
You've got to trust, give it time
No matter how long it takes

But how many heartaches
Must I stand
Before I find a love
To let me live again?
Right now the only thing
That keeps me hanging on
When I feel my strength, yeah
Is almost gone

I remember mama said,

> *Chorus*

How long must I wait
How much more can I take
Before loneliness will cause my heart
Heart to break?

No, I can't bear to live my life alone
I grow impatient for a love to call my own
But when I feel that I, I can't go on
These precious words keep me hanging on
I remember mama said,

> *Chorus*

You can't hurry love
No, you just have to wait
She said, "Trust, give it time
No matter how long it takes"

No love, love don't come easy
But I keep on waiting
Anticipating for that soft voice
To talk to me at night
For some tender arms
To hold me tight
I keep waiting
I keep on waiting
But it ain't easy
It ain't easy
But mama said,

You can't hurry love
No, you just have to wait
She said, "Trust, give it time
No matter how long it takes"

> *Chorus*

3&4 Revise and Check

For instructions on how to use these pages see *page 40*.

Testing Program CD-ROM

- Quick Test 4
- File 4 Test

GRAMMAR

1 c	6 a	11 a
2 a	7 b	12 a
3 c	8 b	13 c
4 a or b	9 c	14 b
5 a	10 b	15 b

VOCABULARY

a 1 in
2 for
3 in
4 at
5 of

b 1 limit
2 belt
3 lanes
4 rush
5 stand

c 1 stuck
2 van
3 platform
4 set
5 take

d 1 boring
2 amazing
3 excited
4 disappointed
5 depressing

e 1 leave
2 busy
3 hung
4 screensaver
5 ringtones

PRONUNCIATION

a 1 want
2 the end
3 machine
4 gossip
5 argue

b 1 <u>free</u>way
2 disa<u>ppoint</u>ed
3 pe<u>des</u>trian
4 <u>vi</u>brate
5 em<u>barra</u>ssing

CAN YOU UNDERSTAND THIS TEXT?

a It was a classical concert. Someone's mobile phone rang.

b 1 It rang during the fourth movement. It was a marimba riff.
2 No.
3 a) The audience members were horrified. A lot of people stood up. They wanted the man with the phone to leave.
b) They applauded him.
4 No.
5 No, he started a little before the place where he had stopped the performance.
6 Yes.

CAN YOU UNDERSTAND THESE PEOPLE?

2 50))
1 c   2 b   3 c   4 a   5 c

2 50))

Christopher
I = interviewer, C = Christopher
I   How do you get to work?
C   I take the subway every day. I take two trains. I live in Brooklyn. I take a train from Brooklyn to Washington Square. And then I switch to a train that takes me to midtown Manhattan.
I   How long does it take?
C   It takes about 30 to 40 minutes.
I   What do you think is the best way to get around New York City?
C   I think subways are an excellent way to get around New York. They serve all five boroughs and they're open 24 hours a day, so they're very convenient and they don't get stuck in traffic.

Maria
I = interviewer, M = Maria
I   Do you think women are better than men with young children, or do you think that's just a stereotype?
M   I think women are, they have a, they're more natural with young children, they have a natural ability with them, they're better at sort of knowing what they need, and perhaps knowing if they need hugs or food or things like that, and perhaps their manner is better with young children. I think men can do it, but perhaps it takes a bit more practice.

Harry
I = interviewer, H = Harry
I   Some new research says that men talk just as much as women. Do you think that's true?
H   I definitely think that's true. I would say that I know men who talk more than women talk, especially in my family it's the men who do most of the talking, especially repeating the same story time and time again.
I   Do you think men and women talk about different things?
H   Yes, I think they do talk about different things. I think they have different interests, and so they will try and control the conversation to topics that interest them rather than everyone else.

Skylar
I = interviewer, S = Skylar
I   Is there anything you've tried to learn, but failed?
S   I've always wanted to learn to paint very well. But I have never been very good at it. So, it's not my thing.
I   Have you stopped trying?
S   I still paint for fun, but I still...I'm not very good. So I just do it for leisure activity.

Cristina
I = interviewer, C = Cristina
I   Is there anything that people do with their phones that really annoys you?
C   Yeah, lots of things, but what really, really gets to me is when people are interacting with you, but they're looking at the phone at the same time, or you know, when you're having dinner if they keep checking their phone. That bothers me.

65

G past tenses: simple, continuous, perfect
V sports
P /ɔr/ and /ər/

5A Sports superstitions

Lesson plan

The topic of this lesson is sports. The lesson begins with a vocabulary focus on words and phrases connected with sports and then a pronunciation focus on two vowel sounds, which Sts often have problems with, /ɔr/ and /ər/. Sts then have a speaking activity about sports, which caters to both Sts who like and do sports, and those that do not. This is followed by a reading about the superstitions that many sportspeople have.

The angle in the second half of the lesson is cheating in sports. Sts listen to an interview with a soccer referee, and then the grammar, narrative tenses (simple past, past continuous, and past perfect), is presented through stories about famous cheaters. Sts then practice telling anecdotes, and the lesson ends with a writing focus on stories, and the song *We Are the Champions*.

STUDY LINK
• **Workbook** 5A

Extra photocopiable activities

• **Grammar** past tenses *page 152*
• **Communicative** What a cheat! *page 182* (instructions *page 167*)
• **Vocabulary** Sport *page 206* (instructions *page 197*)
• **Song** *We Are the Champions page 221* (instructions *pages 215–216*)

Optional lead-in (books closed)

• Write on the board the names of the three most popular sports in your Sts' country, and drill the pronunciation. Then get a show of hands to find out a) how many people in the class like watching these sports and b) how many do these sports.

• Then ask Sts if they think the class statistics are typical of their country as a whole.

1 VOCABULARY sports

a Books open. Focus on the quiz.

Put Sts in small groups of three or four and set a time limit for them to answer the questions.

Check answers, getting Sts to spell the names of the sports and checking pronunciation.

Extra challenge

• You could also elicit / teach the names of the equipment shown in the photos (see answers in parentheses in the key).

1	badminton (a birdie)
2	basketball (basketball hoop)
3	ice hockey (a hockey stick and puck)
4	ice skating (ice skates)
5	riding a bike (a bike helmet)
6	skateboarding (a skateboard)
7	gymnastics (a ribbon and ball)
8	baseball (a glove and ball)
9	table tennis or ping-pong (a paddle and ball)
10	judo / karate / tae kwon do (a black belt)

b Tell Sts to go to **Vocabulary Bank** *Sports* on *page 157*.

Focus on **1 People and places** and get Sts to do **a** individually or in pairs.

 Now do **b**. Play the audio for Sts to check answers. Play the audio again, pausing for Sts to repeat. Practice any words your Sts find difficult to pronounce, modeling and drilling as necessary. You could use the audio to do this.

Sports
People and places

3	captain	9	spectators / the crowd
7	coach	4	team
1	fans	8	stadium
5	players	6	sports arena
2	referee / umpire		

Point out that the *coach* is the non-playing person in charge of a sports team. He / she is in charge of training, tactics, and team selection.

Now tell Sts to cover the words and look at the pictures to see if they can remember the lexis.

Sts do **c** individually or in pairs.

 Now do **d**. Play the audio for Sts to check answers. Play the audio again, pausing for Sts to repeat. Practice any words your Sts find difficult to pronounce, modeling and drilling as necessary. You could use the audio to do this.

1	tennis court / basketball court
2	soccer field / baseball field
3	swimming pool / diving pool
4	running track / horse racing track
5	golf course
6	ski slope

Point out that you usually use both words to describe the place where you play a sport, e.g., *tennis court, soccer field*.

Now put Sts in pairs and get them to test each other. Make sure Sts change roles.

Focus on **2 Verbs** and go through the **win and beat** box with Sts.

Make sure Sts know the meaning of the verbs and then get them to do **a** and **b** individually or in pairs. Highlight that in **b** Sts should write the verbs in the **Verb** column, <u>not</u> in the shaded blanks in the sentence. By doing this they can later use the sentences to test their memory.

 Now do **c**. Play the audio for Sts to check answers to **a** and **b**. Play the audio again, pausing for Sts to repeat. Practice any words your Sts find difficult to pronounce, modeling and drilling as necessary. You could use the audio to do this.

>
> **Verbs**
> a
> beat, beat, beaten
> win, won, won
> lose, lost, lost
> tie, tied, tied
>
> b
> 1 Costa Rica **beat** the US 3 to nothing.
> 2 Costa Rica **won** the game 3 to nothing.
> 3 The Chicago Bulls **lost** 78–91 to the Boston Celtics.
> 4 Spain **tied** with Brazil 2 to 2.

Sts do **d** individually or in pairs. Remind them to write in the **Verb** column.

 Now do **e**. Play the audio for Sts to check answers. Play the audio again, pausing for Sts to repeat. Practice any words your Sts find difficult to pronounce, modeling and drilling as necessary. You could use the audio to do this.

>
> 1 Professional sportspeople have to **train** every day.
> 2 Don't play tennis on a wet court. You might **get injured**.
> 3 A soccer player has to try to **kick** the ball into the goal.
> 4 I've started going to the gym because I want to **get in shape**.
> 5 Our new striker is going to **score** a lot of goals.
> 6 Would you like to **go** swimming this afternoon?
> 7 My brothers **do** yoga and tai-chi.
> 8 In basketball, players **throw** the ball to each other.

Get Sts to cover the **Verb** columns in **b** and **d** to test themselves.

Finally, go through the **Phrasal verbs** box with Sts.

Tell Sts to go back to the main lesson **5A**.

Extra support

• If you think Sts need more practice, you may want to give them the Vocabulary photocopiable activity at this point or leave it for later as consolidation or review.

2 PRONUNCIATION /ɔr/ and /ər/

Pronunciation notes
• Here the focus is on two sounds which are often mispronounced especially because of the sometimes irregular relationship between sound and spelling. The biggest problem is -or which is sometimes /ɔr/ and sometimes /ər/.

a Focus on the sound pictures and elicit the words and sounds: *horse* /ɔr/ and *bird* /ər/.

Give Sts a few minutes to put the words in the right column. Warn them to be careful with the -or words which may go in one or other of the columns.

b Play the audio for Sts to listen and check.

Check answers.

See words in script 3.6

>
> horse /ɔr/ court, four, score, shorts, sport, warm up
> bird /ər/ girl, hurt, serve, shirt, world, worse, work out

Play the audio again, pausing after each group of words for Sts to listen and repeat.

c Tell Sts to go to the **Sound Bank** on *page 166*. Go through the different spellings. Emphasize that -or is usually pronounced /ɔr/, but that after the letter *w* it is often pronounced /ər/, e.g., *world*, *work*, *word*, and *worse | worst*.

Tell Sts to go back to the main lesson **5A**.

d Tell Sts they are going to hear six sentences and they must write them down.

Play the audio all the way through for Sts to listen.

>
> 1 I got hurt working out at the gym.
> 2 Her serve's worse than the other girl's.
> 3 It was a tie – the score was four to four.
> 4 It's the worst sport in the world.
> 5 We warmed up on the court.
> 6 They wore red shirts and white shorts.

Then play it again, pausing after each sentence to give Sts time to write it down. Repeat if necessary.

Check answers by writing the sentences on the board.

See sentences in script 3.7

If necessary, play the audio for Sts to listen and repeat.

3 SPEAKING

This topic-based speaking activity takes into account the fact that not all Sts are interested in sports!

Focus on the instructions and the flow chart. Point out the two alternative "routes," and the last three questions for all Sts to discuss whichever route they took.

Extra support

• Get Sts to interview you with the first few questions. Elicit possible follow-up questions.

Monitor while Sts interview each other. Correct any pronunciation errors with the vocabulary they have just learned and help them with any new vocabulary they need. Make a note of any common mistakes and have a correction spot at the end of the activity.

Get some feedback from a few individual Sts.

Extra support

• You could do the last three questions as an open-class activity.

4 READING

a Elicit / explain the meaning of *superstitious*. Model and drill its pronunciation. Do the questions as an open-class activity.

Extra idea

- Now focus on the title of the article. Elicit the meaning of *bounce* and then ask Sts how they think the sentence might continue (*I'll win the point / game*, etc.)

b Now focus on the instructions and phrases A–F. Make sure Sts understand the word *ritual* and *confined to*. Before Sts start, point out the **Glossary**.

Now explain that A–F are the first sentences from paragraphs 1–6. They tell you what each paragraph is about and are known as topic sentences. Tell Sts that in order to match the topic sentences with their paragraphs, they must read each paragraph carefully to understand what it is about.

Give Sts time to read the article and fill in the blanks.

Get Sts to compare with a partner and then check answers.

Extra support

- Before Sts read the article, check it for words and phrases that your Sts might not know and be ready to help with these while they are answering the questions or afterwards. You may even want to preteach / check a few words / phrases to lighten the load, e.g., *fate*, *a lucky charm*, etc.

2 B	3 E	4 A	5 C	6 D

Explain any new vocabulary.

c Tell Sts to read the article again and to answer the question.

Check the answer.

All of them.

d Tell Sts to look at the article and choose five words or phrases that they would like to remember. They should underline these words and phrases and write them in a notebook.

e Focus on the photos and elicit anything Sts know about the sportspeople. If they don't know anything, tell them not to worry as they will find out later.

In pairs, get Sts to discuss what the sportspeople's superstitions might be.

Elicit a few ideas, but do <u>not</u> tell Sts if they are right.

f Put Sts in pairs, **A** and **B**, and tell Sts to go to **Communication** *Other sports superstitions*, **A** on *page 106*, **B** on *page 110*.

Tell the **A**s to read about Sydney Crosby and Kolo Touré, and the **B**s read about Jason Terry and Alexander Wurz.

When they have finished reading, Sts should cover the text or close their books and tell their partner about the sportspeople's superstitions.

Get four Sts to tell the class about each sports player.

In their pairs, Sts decide which superstition is the strangest and which is the most impractical.

Get some feedback.

Extra support

- You could write any new and useful words and phrases from the article and **Communication** on the board for Sts to copy.

Tell Sts to go back to the main lesson **5A**.

g Do this as an open-class activity, and elicit Sts' own superstitions. If you have or used to have any, tell Sts about them.

5 LISTENING

a Do these as open-class questions and elicit some opinions on referees in general.

b (3 8))) Focus on the photo and the instructions. Give Sts a few minutes to read the questions and the three options and make sure they understand them.

Then play the audio once all the way through.

Play the audio again, pausing after the referee's answers to the first two questions, and then after each of his other answers (see ✱✱✱ in the audioscript).

Get Sts to compare with a partner and then check answers.

Extra support

- Before playing the audio, go through the listening script and decide if you need to preteach / check any lexis to help Sts when they listen.

1 c	2 b	3 b	4 a	5 a

(3 8)))

(script in Student Book on *pages 125–126*)
I = interviewer, JA = Juan Antonio

Part 1

I What made you want to become a soccer referee, or football referee as you would call it?

JA My father was a referee, but that didn't influence me – in fact, the opposite because I saw all the problems that he had as a referee. But as a child I was always attracted by the idea of being a referee and at school I used to referee all kinds of sports, basketball, handball, volleyball, and of course football. I was invited to join the Referees' Federation when I was only 14 years old.

I Were you good at sports yourself?

JA Yes. I was a very good handball player. People often think that referees become referees because they are frustrated sportsmen, but this is just not true in most cases in my experience.

I What was the most exciting match you ever refereed?

JA It's difficult to choose <u>one</u> match as the most exciting. I remember some of the Real Madrid–Barcelona matches, for example the first one I ever refereed. The atmosphere was incredible in the stadium. But really it's impossible to pick just one – there have been so many.

✱✱✱

I What was the worst experience you ever had as a referee?

JA The worst? Well, that was something that happened very early in my career. I was only 16 and I was refereeing a match in a town in Spain and the home team lost. After the match, I was attacked and injured by the players of the home team and by the spectators. After all these years I can still remember a mother, who had a little baby in her arms, who was trying to hit me. She was so angry with me that she nearly dropped her baby. That was my worst moment, and it nearly made me stop being a referee.

✱✱✱

I Do you think that there's more cheating in soccer than in the past?

JA Yes, I think so.

I Why?

JA I think it's because there's so much money in football today that it has become much more important to win. Also football is much faster than it used to be so it's much more difficult for referees to detect cheating.

***

I How do soccer players cheat?

JA Oh, there are many ways, but for me the worst thing in football today is what we call "simulation." Simulation is when a player pretends to have been fouled when in fact he hasn't. For example, sometimes a player falls over in the penalty area when, in fact, nobody has touched him and this can result in the referee giving a penalty when it wasn't a penalty. In my opinion, when a player does this he's cheating not only the referee, not only the players of the other team, but also the spectators, because spectators pay money to see a fair contest.

c **(3 9)))** Now tell Sts they are going to hear **Part 2** of the interview. Give them time to quickly read sentences 1–6. Make sure Sts know that they must fill in the blanks with one to three words.

Play the audio once all the way through. Then play it again, pausing after each answer is given.

Get Sts to compare their answers with a partner and then play the audio again if necessary.

Check answers.

1	the right decisions	4	the exceptions
2	fast	5	with the ball
3	the rules	6	typical superstar

(3 9)))

(script in Student Book on *page 126*)

Part 2

I What's the most difficult thing about being a referee?

JA The most difficult thing is to make the right decisions during a match. It's difficult because you have to make decisions when everything's happening so quickly – football today is <u>very</u> fast. You must remember that everything is happening at 100 kilometres an hour. Also important decisions often depend on the referee's *interpretation* of the rules. Things aren't black and white. And of course making decisions would be much easier if players didn't cheat.

I Do you think that the idea of fair play doesn't exist anymore?

JA Not at all. I think fair play <u>does</u> exist – the players who cheat are the exceptions.

I Finally, who do you think is the best player right now?

JA I think most people agree that the best footballer today is Leo Messi.

I Why do you think he's so good?

JA It's hard to say what makes him so special, but a study was done on him which showed that Messi can run faster <u>with</u> the ball than many footballers can do <u>without</u> the ball. Apart from his great ability, what I also like about him is that he isn't the typical superstar footballer. You can see that he enjoys playing football and he behaves in public and in his personal life in a very normal way. That's unusual when you think how famous he is. And what's more he doesn't cheat – he doesn't need to!

Extra support

• If there's time, you could play the audio again while Sts read the scripts on *pages 125–126*, so they can see what they understood / didn't understand. Translate / explain any new words or phrases.

d Either get Sts to answer in pairs, or do the questions as an open-class activity. Encourage Sts to give reasons to justify what they say.

6 GRAMMAR past tenses: simple, continuous, perfect

a Do these as an open-class activity and elicit sports where cheating is common and different ways of cheating.

b Focus on the instructions and the question. Elicit the meaning of *take a short cut*.

Give Sts time to read the article and answer the question.

Get Sts to compare with a partner and then check the answer.

> In the Boston Marathon, she jumped out of the crowd during the last half mile. In the New York City Marathon, she took the subway.

Extra support

• You could read each text aloud, eliciting or translating / explaining any new words, and ask a few more comprehension questions to check understanding, e.g., *Which marathon was Rosie Ruiz running in? Did she win?*, etc.

c Focus on the highlighted verbs. Get Sts to answer the questions individually or in pairs.

Check answers.

> 1 was, finished
> 2 had happened, had also cheated, had taken
> 3 wasn't sweating

d **(3 10)))** **(3 11)))** **(3 12)))** **(3 13)))** Tell Sts to go to **Grammar Bank 5A** on *page 140*. Focus on the example sentences and play the audio for Sts to listen to the sentence rhythm. You could also get Sts to repeat the sentences to practice getting the rhythm right. Then go through the rules with the class.

Additional grammar notes

• In *American English File* 2 Sts learned the simple past, the past continuous, and the past perfect in separate lessons, so this will be the first time Sts see the three tenses together.

• Highlight that these three tenses are the ones that we normally use to tell a story / anecdote in the past. Most verbs tend to be in the simple past, when we are describing consecutive actions (First… then…, etc.), but we often use the simple past in conjunction with either the past continuous and past perfect or both, e.g., *I got home late and my wife had already finished her lunch and was watching the news on TV.*

You may want to draw a timeline on the board to show Sts how the three tenses work together:

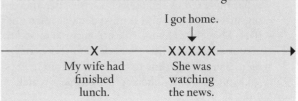

Focus on the exercises and get Sts to do them individually or in pairs.

Check answers, getting Sts to read the full sentences.

a
1	had trained	6	was playing
2	was driving	7	had stopped
3	cleaned	8	hadn't lost
4	started	9	was raining
5	hadn't scored		

b
1 happened, were driving
2 cheered, blew
3 didn't recognize, had changed
4 stopped, wasn't wearing
5 weren't listening, was talking
6 couldn't, hadn't snowed
7 weren't able to, hadn't booked
8 got, had taken off / took off

Tell Sts to go back to the main lesson **5A**.

Extra support
• If you think Sts need more practice, you may want to give them the Grammar photocopiable activity at this point or leave it for later as consolidation or review.

e Focus on the photo, the task, and text, and ask Sts if they know what happened.

Then tell them to read the text once all the way through, and then to go back and fill in each blank with the verb in parentheses in the right tense.

Give Sts time to fill in the blanks.

Get Sts to compare with a partner and then check answers.

2	were playing	7	had scored
3	was	8	said
4	scored	9	scored
5	protested	10	won
6	gave		

7 SPEAKING

a Focus on the instructions and make sure Sts understand what an anecdote is (an informal true story about something that happened to you).

Give Sts time to choose which two topics they are going to talk about and to plan the stories. Encourage them to think about the vocabulary they are going to need, especially verbs.

Monitor and help Sts with their planning and with any specific vocabulary.

Extra idea
• Tell Sts that one anecdote should be true and the other invented. **A** then tells both his / her anecdotes one after the other and **B** must decide which one is true. They then change roles. You could model the activity first by telling them two anecdotes of your own. Pause from time to time and encourage Sts to ask you questions. Then get Sts to guess which one is true.

b Focus on the **Starting an anecdote** box and go through it with Sts.

Put Sts in pairs (or threes). **A** should start by telling his / her first anecdote and **B** should ask questions. **B** then tells his / her first anecdote.

Monitor while Sts are telling their anecdotes, but don't correct too much as the aim here is to encourage fluency, and Sts are unlikely to use all the tenses perfectly.

Extra idea
• Tell Sts to look back at the language for reacting to what people say in **Practical English** Episode 1 on Student Book *page 13*. Encourage them to use this language when they listen to the anecdotes.

If Sts are enjoying the activity (and you have time), you could get them to change partners and tell their stories again.

8 WRITING telling a story

Tell Sts to go to **Writing *Telling a story*** on *page 116*.

a Focus on the instructions and give Sts time to read the story and answer the questions.

Check answers.

> They got lost because her husband followed the instructions given by the GPS, which sent them in the wrong direction.
> They left their dog under the table in the cafe on the road.

b Focus on the instructions and the connecting words or phrases in the list.

Give Sts time to read the story again and fill in the blanks.

Get Sts to compare with a partner and then check answers.

2	when	6	because
3	instead of	7	as soon as
4	but	8	although
5	So		

c Focus on the **Useful language: getting lost** box and go through it with Sts.

Now tell Sts they are going to write about a trip when they got lost. If Sts can't think of a trip, they can invent one.

Focus on the plan and go through it with Sts.

Sts should write three paragraphs as in the model, and use the **Useful language** box to help them.

You may like to get Sts to do the writing in class or you could assign it as homework. If you do it in class, set a time limit for Sts to write their description, e.g., 15–20 minutes.

d Sts should check their work for mistakes before turning it in.

Tell Sts to go back to the main lesson **5A**.

9 (3 14)) **SONG** *We Are the Champions* ♫

This song was originally made famous by the British rock group Queen in 1977. For copyright reasons this is a cover version. If you want to do this song in class, use the photocopiable activity on *page 221*.

(3 14))

We Are the Champions

I've paid my dues
Time after time
I've done my sentence
Committed no crime
And bad mistakes
I've made a few
I've had my share of sand kicked in my face
But I've come through
(And we can go on and on and on and on)

> *Chorus*
> We are the champions, my friend
> And we'll keep on fighting till the end
> We are the champions
> We are the champions
> No time for losers
> 'Cause we are the champions of the world

I've taken my bows
And my curtain calls
You brought me fame and fortune and everything that goes with it
I thank you all

But it's been no bed of roses
No pleasure cruise
I consider it a challenge before the whole human race
That I'd never lose
(And we can go on and on and on and on)

> *Chorus* (x2)

G *usually* and *used to*
V relationships
P linking, the letter s

5B Love at Exit 19

Lesson plan

Different kinds of relationships provide the main theme for this lesson. It begins with a newspaper article about a couple who met in an unusual place. Sts then listen to four more people talking about where they met their partners, and extracts from the listening provide a lead-in to the grammar, which reviews and consolidates the use of *used to* for past habits and states, and contrasts it with the way we express present habits. The pronunciation focus is on linking in fast speech, with a special focus on the pronunciation of *used to*, and this is followed by a controlled oral grammar practice stage.

The angle of the second half of the lesson is social networks. It begins with a vocabulary focus on words and phrases related to relationships and is followed by a pronunciation focus on the different ways the letter *s* can be pronounced. Sts then listen to a radio program where people talk about friendships on *Facebook*, and the lesson ends with a speaking activity where Sts discuss various aspects of friendship.

STUDY **LINK**
• **Workbook** 5B
• **iChecker**

Extra photocopiable activities

• **Grammar** *usually* and *used to* *page 153*
• **Communicative** How did they change our world? *page 183* (instructions *pages 167–168*)
• **Vocabulary** Relationships *page 207* (instructions *page 197*)

Optional lead-in (books closed)

• Write the following sentences on the board:

I _____ MY BEST FRIEND AT ELEMENTARY SCHOOL.

WE'VE _____ EACH OTHER FOR ABOUT 15 YEARS NOW.

• Now ask Sts what words they think are missing (*met* and *known*). Then ask Sts to explain what the difference is between the verbs *meet* and *know*.

1 READING

a Books open. Focus on the task and make sure Sts know what a partner is (a husband / boyfriend or wife / girlfriend).

Get Sts to number phrases A–E in order according to how likely people are to meet friends and partners that way.

Get Sts to compare with a partner, and then elicit answers from the class.

b (3 15))) Tell Sts they are going to read and listen to an article about how Sonya Baker and Michael Fazio met. Focus on the **Glossary** and go through it with Sts.

Sts must read and listen at the same time to find the answer to the question. Play the audio once all the way through.

Get Sts to compare with a partner and then check the answer.

Extra support

• Before Sts read the article, check it for words and phrases that your Sts might not know and be ready to help with these while they are answering the questions or afterwards. You may even want to preteach a few words / phrases to lighten the load (but not the highlighted ones).

> Because Michael changed his working hours from daytime to nighttime.

> (3 15)))
> See the article in the Student Book on *page 48*

c Now tell Sts to read the article again and to number events A–J in the order in which they happened. Point out that the first one (G) has been done for them.

Get Sts to compare with a partner and then check answers.

| 2 A | 4 F | 6 E | 8 D | 10 J |
| 3 H | 5 B | 7 I | 9 C | |

d Focus on the instructions, and set a time limit for Sts to re-read the article, guess the meaning of the highlighted words and phrases, and then match them with definitions 1–10.

Get Sts to compare with a partner and then check answers. Model and drill the pronunciation of any tricky words, e.g., *courage* /ˈkərɪdʒ/.

1 shifts	6 likely
2 a commuter	7 a candle
3 cute	8 exchange a few words
4 it turned out	9 their eyes met
5 runs	10 found the courage

Explain any other new vocabulary and encourage Sts to write down any useful new lexis from the article.

2 GRAMMAR *usually* and *used to*

a Focus on the instructions and give Sts time to think about how a couple they know met.

Put Sts in pairs and get them to share their stories.

Get some feedback and if you know a couple who met in unusual circumstances, tell the class.

b (3 16))) Focus on the instructions and on places A–E in **1a**.

Extra support

• Write A–E on the board for easier reference.

Play the audio once, pausing after each speaker for Sts to write the correct letter.

Get them to compare with a partner and then play the audio again if necessary.

Check answers.

Extra support

• Before playing the audio, go through the listening script and decide if you need to preteach / check any lexis to help Sts when they listen.

1 B	2 C	3 E	4 D

③ 16))

1

Sara and I met in college when we were cast in the University of New Hampshire theater department's production of Susanna Centiliver's *The Basset Table*. We met on stage at the Hennessy Theater during the first play rehearsal. We became good friends, and I started walking her home after rehearsal ended on most nights. We fell in love and continued to date each other throughout college. After we graduated, we moved to Chicago together to start a small theater company. Once we decided to get married, we moved back to New Hampshire and had our ceremony on the stage in the Hennessy Theater where we first met.

2

Back in 2005, I was doing the online dating thing. But this is no online dating story. One morning, I received an email from a guy named Dan in Chicago. Apparently, he thought I was the perfect match for his friend Greg in Boston. I can't remember whether I was feeling really optimistic or really desperate that morning, but I agreed to email Greg. We exchanged a few emails, met, and got along really well. I thought it was amazing that Greg's friend was able to pick me out of thousands of women. Well, it turns out that Dan wasn't so amazing. He had actually emailed over 20 women for Greg on the dating site. So, to all of the women out there who didn't respond to Dan and take a chance on Greg, thank you! He is the love of my life...my husband...and soon-to-be father of my first child.

3

Pete and I were both single and we used to go to clubs together on Saturday night, but then he started going out with a girl, who he had met at work. After a few weeks he said to me, "Why don't you come out with us on Saturday? My girlfriend is going to bring one of her friends." To be honest, I wasn't all that enthusiastic about the idea – I'd never been on a blind date before, and I just couldn't imagine it would be a success. On the evening of the date I was feeling very pessimistic and I almost canceled. Pete and I had arranged to meet the girls in a club. We got to the club early and I remember my friend saying, "Here they are now." I looked towards the door and I thought "Well, I really hope the girl on the right is my date." Fortunately, she was. The evening went really well, and two years later we got married. Pete and his girlfriend got married too and we're still good friends – we usually meet for dinner about once a month.

4

I was born in Egypt to an Italian father and French mother, but we came to live in London in the early 60s when I was 20. I got a job in a bank, but I didn't have many friends. In those days it used to be difficult to meet people if you were a foreigner. One evening I went to a dance at a restaurant, and I saw this gorgeous 18-year-old girl get up from her table and start dancing. I thought I had nothing to lose, and I wrote her a note saying that I was standing by the window and if she would agree to come out with me, could she please smile at me. I then left the note on her chair. When the music stopped she went back to her chair, read the note, and smiled at me. That was how it all started. When we decided to get married, at first her mother was totally against the idea – mainly because I was a foreigner and also I was 11 years older than Lesley. But little by little she got to like me, and in the end she treated me like a son.

c Now tell Sts they will listen again and they must write down more details about how the people met.

Play the audio and pause it after the first speaker. Get Sts to compare their notes with a partner and then elicit as many details as possible.

Repeat for the other three speakers.

See script 3.16

Find out with a show of hands which meeting Sts found the most romantic.

d Focus on the task and the two questions. Do this as an open-class activity and elicit answers.

> 1 We use *used to* to talk about past habits or states, i.e., things that were true over a period of time in the past (e.g., when you were a child), but are often not true anymore.
> ⊟ *didn't use to*, e.g., *I didn't use to have short hair. I didn't use to exercise.*
> ? *Did (you) use to*, e.g., *Did you use to have short hair? Did you use to exercise?*
> 2 We usually go to bars and clubs together on Saturday night.
> It is usually quite difficult to meet people.

e **③ 17))** Tell Sts to go to **Grammar Bank 5B** on *page 141*. Focus on the example sentences and play the audio for Sts to listen to the sentence rhythm. You could also get Sts to repeat the sentences to practice getting the rhythm right. Then go through the rules with the class.

> **Additional grammar notes**
>
> • *Used to* is a grammar point that was presented in *American English File* 2 and is reviewed and consolidated here. This is a "late assimilation" structure as Sts can express more or less the same idea by using the past tense + a time expression. Compare: *I used to go to that elementary school* and *I went to that elementary school (when I was a child)*. In that sense *used to* is a sophisticated structure and its correct use helps to give the impression of having a good level of English. In this lesson *used to* is contrasted with the use of the simple present with *usually* to talk about present habits.
>
> • Sts may have problems with this structure as their language may either use a tense which doesn't exist in English for past habits, or may have a verb that can be used both for present and past habits, unlike *used to* which can only be used in the past.
>
> • Emphasize the way we often don't repeat the main verb, but just use the auxiliary verb with *anymore / any longer* when we contrast the past and present habits, e.g., *I used to like cartoons, but I don't anymore.*
>
> Some typical mistakes include:
>
> – using *use to* instead of *usually* for present habits and states, e.g., ~~I use to go to bed about 11:00~~.
>
> – making mistakes of spelling such as ~~We didn't used to~~ wear a uniform at my school.
>
> – confusing *used to* + base form with *be/get used to (doing something)*.

Focus on the exercises and get Sts to do them individually or in pairs.

Check answers, getting Sts to read the full sentences.

a

1	used to have	6	didn't use to be
2	didn't use to spend	7	Did ... use to argue
3	Did ... use to wear	8	didn't use to like
4	used to go out	9	used to get along
5	did ... use to work	10	didn't use to speak

b

1	✗ split up	6	✗ don't usually go
2	✓	7	✗ did your parents meet
3	✓	8	✗ used to work
4	✗ didn't use to like	9	✓
5	✓		

Tell Sts to go back to the main lesson **5B**.

Extra support

- If you think Sts need more practice, you may want to give them the Grammar photocopiable activity at this point or leave it for later as consolidation or review.

3 PRONUNCIATION & SPEAKING linking

> **Pronunciation notes**
> - You might want to remind Sts when words are linked in English. To do this, ask Sts to refer back to **Lesson 3A**, **5 Pronunciation** on Student Book *page 26*.

a ③ 18))) Focus on the *used to* box and go through it with Sts. Then focus on the instructions.

Play the audio once all the way through for Sts just to listen.

> ③ 18)))
> See sentences in Student Book on *page 49*

Now play the audio again, pausing after each sentence for Sts to listen and repeat.

Then repeat the activity eliciting the sentences from individual Sts.

Extra support

- You could get Sts to listen and repeat after the audio and then practice in pairs.

b Focus on the task and give Sts a few minutes to choose their three topics and plan what they are going to say.

Put Sts in pairs, **A** and **B**. Tell the **A**s to start talking about their first topic, giving as much information as they can. The **B**s can ask for more information too.

Then the **B**s tell the **A**s about their first topic, etc.

Extra support

- Choose one of the topics yourself and tell Sts a little about it. This way you both demonstrate what you want them to do and give Sts extra listening practice.

As Sts are talking, move around monitoring and helping, and correcting any mistakes with *used to*.

Get some feedback.

4 VOCABULARY relationships

a Either put Sts in pairs and get them to discuss 1–3 or do it as an open-class activity. You could leave out 1 if you did the **Optional lead-in**.

Check answers.

> 1 to meet somebody = to see somebody for the first time
>   to know somebody = you have met before
> 2 a colleague = a person that you work with
>   a friend = a person you know well and like, and who is not usually a member of your family
> 3 to argue with somebody = to speak angrily to somebody because you disagree with them
>   to discuss something with somebody = to talk about something with somebody, especially in order to decide something

b Tell Sts to go to **Vocabulary Bank** *Relationships* on *page 158*.

Focus on **1 People** and get Sts to do **a** individually or in pairs.

③ 19))) Now do **b**. Play the audio for Sts to check answers. Play the audio again, pausing for Sts to repeat. Practice any words your Sts find difficult to pronounce, modeling and drilling as necessary. You could use the audio to do this. Remind Sts that *fiancé(e)* is a word "borrowed" from French, which explains the pronunciation, and why it has an accent.

> ③ 19)))
> **Relationships**
> **People**
> | | | | | | |
> |---|---|---|---|---|---|
> | 1 | couple | 4 | roommate | 7 | close friend |
> | 2 | partner | 5 | colleague | 8 | classmate |
> | 3 | fiancé(e) | 6 | ex | | |

Now tell Sts to cover the definitions, look at the words, and see if they can remember what they mean.

Extra idea

- You might also want to teach *coworker* as an alternative to *colleague*.

Now focus on **2 Verbs and verb phrases** and get Sts to do **a** individually or in pairs. Remind Sts to change the verb to the simple past.

Extra support

- Elicit the past tense of all the verbs first.

③ 20))) Now do **b**. Play the audio for Sts to check answers. Practice any words your Sts find difficult to pronounce, modeling and drilling as necessary.

> ③ 20)))
> **Verbs and verb phrases**
> 1 I **met** Mark when I was studying at Boston University.
> 2 We **got to know** each other quickly because we went to the same classes.
> 3 We soon **became friends**, and we discovered that we **had** a lot **in common**. For example, we both liked art and music.
> 4 We **went out together** in our second sezmester and we fell in love.
> 5 We **were together** for two years, but we argued a lot, and in our last semester of school we **broke up**.
> 6 After we graduated from college, we **lost touch** because I moved to Chicago and he stayed in Boston.
> 7 Five years later, we **got in touch** again on *Facebook*. We were both still single, and Mark had moved to Chicago, too.
> 8 This time we **got along** better than before, maybe because we were older.
> 9 After two months, Mark **proposed** and I accepted.
> 10 We **got married** last summer. A lot of our old college friends came to the wedding!

For **c** tell Sts to look at the pictures and see if they can remember the story.

Finally, focus on the **Colloquial language** and the **Phrasal verbs** box and go through it with Sts.

Tell Sts to go back to the main lesson **5B**.

Extra support
- If you think Sts need more practice, you may want to give them the Vocabulary photocopiable activity at this point or leave it for later as consolidation or review.

c Focus on the task and give Sts a couple of minutes to think about a close friend and how they will answer the questions.

Put Sts in pairs and they take turns interviewing each other about their close friend. While they are doing this, go round monitoring and helping if necessary.

Get some feedback from individual Sts.

5 PRONUNCIATION the letter s

> **Pronunciation notes**
> - Many learners of English tend to always pronounce the letter s as the unvoiced sound /s/ as in *bus*. In fact, s in the middle or at the end of a word is often pronounced /z/, e.g., *music, jobs*, and -*se* is very often pronounced /z/, e.g., *lose, wise*, etc. At the beginning of a word, s is almost always /s/ with the exceptions of *sugar* and *sure*, where the s is pronounced /ʃ/. Double s is also always pronounced /s/.

a (3 21)) Focus on the task and elicit the four picture words (*snake, zebra, shower*, and *television*).

Now play the audio, pausing after each word for Sts to write them in the correct column.

Get them to compare with a partner.

> **(3 21))**
> See words in Student Book on *page 50*

b (3 22)) Play the audio for Sts to listen and check.

Check answers.

> See script 3.22 – *close* (adj) is pronounced with /s/ and *close* (verb) with /z/

> **(3 22))**
> | | |
> |---|---|
> | snake /s/ | close, conversation, discuss, promise, school, somebody, sport, summer, used to, various |
> | zebra /z/ | busy, close, eyes, friends, lose, music, raise |
> | shower /ʃ/ | sugar, sure |
> | television /ʒ/ | decision, pleasure, unusual, usually |

c Put Sts in pairs and get them to answer 1–3.

Check answers.

> 1 At the beginning of a word, the letter s is usually pronounced /s/. The exceptions are *sugar* and *sure*.
> 2 At the end of a word, s or es can be pronounced /s/ or /z/.
> 3 In -*sion*, the letter s is pronounced /ʒ/.

6 LISTENING

a Put Sts in pairs and get them to discuss the three statements.

Elicit some answers, but do <u>not</u> tell Sts if they right.

Extra idea
- You could get Sts to vote for each one saying whether it is true or false with a show of hands.

b (3 23)) Focus on the task and tell Sts that the program is about *Facebook*. They must listen for the answers to 1–3 in **a**.

Play the audio once all the way through for Sts to listen.

Get Sts to compare with a partner, and then check answers.

Extra support
- Before playing the audio, go through the listening script and decide if you need to preteach / check any lexis to help Sts when they listen.

> | 1 T | 2 F | 3 T |
> |---|---|---|

Extra challenge
- Ask Sts to discuss why women may have more online friends than men.

> **(3 23))**
> (script in Student Book on *page 126*)
> **H = host, M = Martha**
> **H** Hello and welcome to *Forum*, the program that asks you what <u>you</u> think about current topics. Today Martha Park will be talking about the social networking site *Facebook*, how we use it, how much we like it – or dislike it. So get ready to call us or text us and tell us what you think. The number as always is 555–4318. Martha.
> **M** Hello. Since *Facebook* was first launched in 2004, a lot of research has been done to find out what kind of people use it, what they use it for, and what effect it has on their lives. According to a recent study by consumer research specialist Intersperience, the average 22-year-old in Britain has over 1,000 online friends. In fact, 22 seems to be the age at which the number of friends peaks. It also appears that women have slightly more online friends than men. And another study from an American university shows that people who spend a lot of time on *Facebook* reading other people's posts tend to feel more dissatisfied with their own lives, because they feel that everyone else is having a better time than they are.
> So, over to you. Do you use *Facebook*? How do you feel about it? Can you <u>really</u> have 1,000 friends? Are social networking sites making us unhappy? Call in and share your experiences...

c (3 24)) Focus on the task.

Play the audio once all the way through for Sts to listen.

Get Sts to compare with a partner and then check answers.

> The most positive person is Young.
> The most negative person is Beth.

3 24)))

(script in Student Book on *page 126*)

H = host, M = Martha, Y = Young, B = Beth, E = Emma,
N = Ned

H And our first caller is Young. Go ahead, Young.

Y Hi. Uh, yeah, I use *Facebook* a lot, every day really. I think it's a great way to, uh, organize your social life and keep in touch with your friends. I have a lot of friends...

M How many friends do you have, Young?

Y Right now, I have 1,042.

M And how many of them do you know personally?

Y About half, maybe?

M And what do you use *Facebook* for?

Y For me it's a good way to get in touch with my friends without having to use the phone all the time. When I'm having a busy week at school, I can change my status so I can let my friends know I can't go out. That's a lot easier than wasting time telling people "Sorry, I'm too busy to get together." It's just easier and quicker than using the phone.

H Thanks, Young. We have another caller. It's Beth. Hello, Beth.

B Hi. Um, I don't use *Facebook* or any other social networking site.

M Why's that, Beth?

B Well, two reasons. First, I don't spend much time online. I play a lot of sports – I'm on a hockey team, so I meet my teammates almost every day, and we don't need to communicate on *Facebook*.

M And the other reason?

B I just don't really like the whole idea of social networking sites. I mean, why would I want to tell the whole world everything that I am doing? I don't want to share my personal information with the world and become friends with people I don't even know. And I don't want to read what other people had for breakfast or lunch or dinner or what they're planning to do this weekend.

H Thanks for that, Beth. Our next caller is Emma. It's your turn, Emma.

M Hi, Emma.

E Hi, Martha.

M And do you use *Facebook*, Emma?

E I use it once in a while, but not very much. I only really use it to keep up with friends who have moved abroad or live too far away for us to meet regularly. For example, one of my best friends recently moved to Canada and we chat on *Facebook*. But I never add "friends" who are people I hardly know. I just can't understand those people who collect hundreds or even thousands of *Facebook* friends! I think it's just competition, people who want to make it seem that they are more popular than everybody else.

M So you think the *Facebook* world is kind of unreal?

E Absolutely. I think people write things and post photos of themselves just to show everyone they know what a fantastic time they're having and what exciting lives they lead. But they're probably just sitting at home in front of the computer all the time.

H Thanks for that, Emma. We have time for one more caller before the news, and it's Ned. Hi, Ned. You'll have to be quick.

M Hi, Ned.

N Hi. When I started off with *Facebook* I thought it was great, and I used it to communicate with close friends and with family, and I got back in touch with old friends from school. It was good because all the people I was friends with on *Facebook* were people I knew, and I was interested in what they were doing. But then I started adding friends, people I hardly knew who were friends of friends, people like that – in the end, I had more than a 1,000 – and it just became too much. It was just too many people leaving updates, writing messages on my wall. So last month I decided to delete most of them. It took me about half an hour to delete, and in the end, the only people I left were actual, real-life friends and family, and old school friends. I got it down to 99. It was really liberating.

H Thanks, Ned, and we'll be back after the news, so keep those calls coming...

d Tell Sts they are going to listen to the audio again and they must answer questions 1–8 with the speakers' initials.

Give Sts time to read the questions.

Play the audio again, pausing after each speaker. Play again if necessary.

Get Sts to compare with a partner and then check answers.

1 B	2 N	3 Y	4 E	5 E	6 N	7 Y	8 B

Extra support

- If there's time, you could play the audio again while Sts read the scripts on *page 126*, so they can see what they understood / didn't understand. Translate / explain any new words or phrases.

e Put Sts in pairs and get them to discuss the two questions.

Get some feedback from the class.

7 SPEAKING

a Focus on the task and go through sentences A–F.

Give Sts time to put a check mark or an X next to each sentence according to their own opinions. Tell them to think about their reasons. They can write notes if they want.

b Focus on the **Giving examples** box and go through it with Sts.

Put Sts in groups and tell them to discuss each sentence in turn giving their opinion.

Get some feedback from the whole class.

PRACTICAL ENGLISH
Episode 3 Old friends

Lesson plan

In this third Practical English lesson, Sts learn some key phrases for asking for permission to do something and asking other people to do something for you.

In the first scene, Jenny meets Monica, an old friend, in the street and they have a coffee together. Monica tells Jenny she is going to get married and Jenny tells Monica about Rob. In the next scene, Rob arrives and joins them, but Monica has to leave. Rob then tells Jenny that an old friend of his, Paul, is coming to stay and asks Jenny if she could meet him at the airport, as he has to work late. Jenny agrees. In the third scene, Jenny brings Paul to Rob's apartment. She is tired because she had to wait at the airport for a long time, and the traffic was terrible, and she leaves Rob and Paul to have a night out together.

STUDY LINK
• **Workbook** Old friends

Testing Program CD-ROM

• **Quick Test 5**
• **File 5 Test**
• **Progress Test Files 1–5**

Optional lead-in (books closed)

• Before starting Episode 3, elicit what Sts can remember about Episode 2. Ask them *Who are Kerri and Don? What did they disagree about? What did Jenny and Rob think? What happened in the end?*, etc.

• Alternatively, you could play the last scene of Episode 2.

1 ■ JENNY HAS COFFEE WITH A FRIEND

a (3 25)) Books open. Focus on the photos and elicit what is happening.

Now either tell Sts to close their books and write the question on the board, or get Sts to focus on the question and cover the rest of the page.

Play the DVD or audio once all the way through and then check answers.

> She got engaged. / She and her boyfriend are getting married.

(3 25))
(script in Student Book on *page 126*)
J = Jenny, M = Monica

J Monica!
M Jenny!
J Wow! How are you? You look great!
M Thanks, Jenny! You look really good, too.
J Hey, why don't we get some coffee?
M I'd love to, but I'm on the way to meet... oh, come on. Five minutes!
***
J So, how is everything?
M Oh, great. Things couldn't be better actually. Scott and I... we're getting married!
J You're what? Congratulations!
M Thank you!
J When did you get engaged?
M Only a few days ago. I'm glad I saw you actually. I was going to call you. We've only told family so far.
J I can't believe it. Monica the wife! And to think you used to go clubbing every night!
M Well, that was a few years ago! All I want to do now is stay in and read wedding magazines.
J And how are the plans coming along?
M I haven't done anything yet. My mom and Scott's mom want to organize the whole thing themselves!
J That's what mothers are for!
M True. But what about you? You look fantastic.
J Well, I guess I'm kind of happy, too.
M Uh huh. What's his name?
J Rob.
M You've been keeping him very quiet! Is it serious?
J Umm, it's kind of, you know...
M So it is!
J It's still early. We haven't been together for long. He only moved here from London a few months ago...
M What? He's British? And you think you can persuade him to stay in New York? That won't be easy!
J I think he likes it here. You know how guys are, you never know what they're thinking.
M When can I meet him?
J Umm... that's him now.

b Focus on the instructions and give Sts time to read questions 1–7.

Play the DVD or audio again, pausing if necessary to give Sts time to answer the questions.

Get Sts to compare with a partner and then check answers.

> 1 Monica's fiancé / Monica's future husband
> 2 a few days ago
> 3 family
> 4 She used to go clubbing; now she stays in and reads wedding magazines.
> 5 The two mothers want to organize the wedding.
> 6 That they haven't been together for long.
> 7 She thinks it will be hard for Jenny to persuade him to stay in New York.

Extra support

• If there's time, you could get Sts to listen again with the script on *page 126*, so they can see exactly what they understood / didn't understand. Translate / explain any new words or phrases.

2 📹 PERMISSION AND REQUESTS

a (3 26))) Focus on the photos and ask Sts some questions, e.g., *Where is Rob? Who is he talking to?*, etc.

Now either tell Sts to close their books and write the question on the board, or get Sts to focus on the question and cover the rest of the page.

Play the DVD or audio once all the way through and then check the answer.

> He asks Jenny to meet his friend, Paul, at the airport and to take him back to his apartment.

> **(3 26)))**
>
> (script in Student Book on *pages 126–127*)
> **J = Jenny, M = Monica, R = Rob, W = waiter**
>
> **R** Do you mind if I join you?
> **M** Of course not. Come on, sit down.
> **R** Thank you.
> **M** I have to leave in a minute anyway.
> **R** Could I have a large latte, please?
> **W** Of course.
> **J** Rob, this is Monica.
> **M** Nice to meet you, Rob.
> **R** You too, Monica. You know, Jenny talks about you a lot. And I've seen college photos of you two together. At Jenny's parents' house.
> **J** Of course you have. My dad's photos.
> **R** You've hardly changed at all.
> **M** What a nice man! I can see why you like him, Jenny. The perfect English gentleman.
> **W** Your latte.
> **R** Oh, thanks. Can you pass the sugar?
> **J** Sure.
> **M** Sorry guys, but I have to go.
> **R** You're sure I haven't interrupted anything?
> **M** Not at all. It's just that I have to meet someone. But let's get together very soon.
> **J** We will!
> **M** Bye, Rob. Nice meeting you.
> **R** Bye.
> **J** Bye. Talk soon!
> **R** She seems like a happy person.
> **J** She is, especially right now – she's getting married.
> **R** That's fantastic news!
> **J** Yeah, it is. I guess we're at that age now, when most of our friends are settling down and getting married.
> **R** Yeah... Oh, speaking of friends, I want to ask you a favor. Is it OK if we change our plans a bit this week?
> **J** Uh... sure. What's up?
> **R** I've just had a call from an old friend of mine, Paul. I haven't seen him since we were at university and he's traveling around the States at the moment. Anyway, he's arriving in New York this evening and uh... I've invited him to stay for the week.
> **J** Cool! It'll be fun to meet one of your old friends! What's he like?
> **R** Oh, Paul's a laugh. He used to be a bit wild, but that was a long time ago. He's probably changed completely.
> **J** Well, I'm looking forward to meeting him.
> **R** Just one other thing. Could you do me a big favor? I have to work late this evening, so... would you mind meeting him at the airport?
> **J** Not at all. I'd like to meet him.
> **R** And do you think you could take him to my flat? I'll give you the keys.
> **J** No problem, Rob.
> **R** Thanks so much, Jenny. You're a real star.

b Focus on sentences 1–8. Go through them with Sts and make sure they understand them.

Now play the DVD or audio again all the way through and get Sts to mark the sentences T (true) or F (false). Remind them to correct the false ones.

Get Sts to compare with a partner and then check answers.

> 1 F (He orders a **large latte**.)
> 2 F (He says she **hasn't changed**.)
> 3 T
> 4 F (She needs **to meet someone**.)
> 5 F (She says that most of their friends are **getting married**.)
> 6 F (He is going to stay for a **week**.)
> 7 F (He used to be **a little wild**.)
> 8 T

Extra support

- If there's time, you could get Sts to listen again with the script on *pages 126–127*, so they can see exactly what they understood / didn't understand. Translate / explain any new words or phrases.

c (3 27))) Give Sts a minute to read through the extracts from the conversation and to think about what the missing words might be.

Now play the DVD or audio again and get Sts to fill in the blanks.

Get Sts to compare with a partner and then check answers.

> See words in **bold** in script 3.27

> **(3 27)))**
>
> **Asking permission**
> 1
> **R** Do you **mind** if I join you?
> **M** Of **course** not. Come on, sit down.
> 2
> **R** Is it **OK** if we change our plans a bit this week?
> **J** Uh... sure.
> **Requests: asking someone to do something**
> 1
> **R** **Can** you pass the sugar?
> **J** **Sure**.
> 2
> **R** Could you do me a big **favor**? I have to work late this evening, so... would you mind **meeting** him at the airport?
> **J** **Not** at all. I'd like to meet him.
> 3
> **R** And do you think you **could** take him to my flat? I'll give you the keys.
> **J** No **problem**, Rob.

d Tell Sts to focus on the highlighted phrases and answer the questions.

Get Sts to compare with a partner and then check answers.

> 1 Of course not. Not at all.
> 2 *Could you...?* and *Would you mind...?*

e (3 28))) Tell Sts to focus on the highlighted phrases in the extracts. They should listen and repeat the phrases, copying the rhythm and intonation.

Play the DVD or audio, pausing for Sts to listen and repeat.

> **(3 28)))**
>
> See highlighted phrases in Student Book on *page 53*

Then repeat the activity, eliciting responses from individual Sts.

f Put Sts in pairs and tell them to practice the dialogues in **c**.

Monitor and help, encouraging Sts to pay attention to rhythm and intonation.

Make sure Sts exchange roles.

g Tell Sts to go to **Communication** *Could you do me a favor?* on *page 105*.

Go through the instructions with them carefully.

Monitor and help.

When they have finished, get feedback. Who got the most people to help them?

Extra support

* You could write any new and useful words and phrases from **Communication** on the board for Sts to copy.

Tell Sts to go back to the main lesson.

3 ▶ PAUL ARRIVES

a (3 29)) Focus on the photos and elicit what is happening.

Now either tell Sts to close their books and write the question on the board, or get Sts to focus on the question and cover the rest of the page.

Play the DVD or audio once all the way through and then check answers.

> Rob is delighted to see him. Jenny seems tired and not very enthusiastic.

> **(3 29))**
> (script in Student Book on *page 127*)
> **P = Paul, R = Rob, J = Jenny**
>
> **P** Hey man!
> **R** Paul!
> **P** It's great to see you, mate.
> **R** You too, Paul. It's been years. You haven't changed at all.
> **P** Just got better looking!
> **R** How come you're so late?
> **J** Paul's flight from LA was delayed. And then the traffic coming back was just awful.
> **P** But that gave us time to get to know each other.
> **J** Yeah. Paul told me <u>all</u> about his travels. Every detail.
> **P** And look at this. Your own New York flat. How cool is that?
> **R** It's good. Really good. But – do you want something to eat? I got some things on my way home.
> **P** Stay in? It's my first night in the Big Apple! Let's go out and have a pizza or something.
> **R** I thought you'd be tired after the flight.
> **P** No way, man! I'm ready for action.
> **R** Great! I'll get my jacket...
> **J** Rob, I think I'll go home if you don't mind. I, uh, I'm exhausted.
> **R** Oh, OK, then.
> **P** So it's a boys' night out!
> **R** Just like the old days!
> **P** And after the pizza we can go on somewhere else. Rob, we've got a lot to talk about!

b Focus on the instructions and on sentences 1–6. Give Sts time to read them.

Now play the DVD or audio again all the way through and get Sts to circle the right answer.

Get Sts to compare with a partner and then check answers.

> 1 hasn't changed much
> 2 late
> 3 talked a lot about himself
> 4 eating in
> 5 full of energy
> 6 doesn't feel like

Extra support

* If there's time, you could get Sts to listen again with the script on *page 127*, so they can see exactly what they understood / didn't understand. Translate / explain any new words or phrases.

c Focus on the **Social English phrases**. In pairs, get Sts to think about what the missing words could be.

Extra challenge

* In pairs, get Sts to complete the phrases before they listen.

d (3 30)) Play the DVD or audio for Sts to listen and complete the phrases.

Check answers.

> See words in **bold** in script 3.30

> **(3 30))**
> **Paul** Hey **man**!
> **Paul** It's great to see you, **mate**.
> **Rob** How **come** you're so late?
> **Paul** No **way**, man!
> **Jenny** Rob, I think I'll go home if you don't **mind**.
> **Rob** Just like the old **days**!
> **Paul** Rob, we've got a lot to talk **about**!

If you know your Sts' L1, you could get them to translate the phrases. If not, get Sts to look at the phrases again in context in the script on *page 127*.

e Now play the DVD or audio again, pausing after each phrase for Sts to listen and repeat.

Finally, focus on the **Can you...?** questions and ask Sts if they feel confident they can now do these things.

G passive (all tenses)
V movies
P sentence stress

6A Shot on location

Lesson plan

The topic of this lesson is movies. The lesson begins with a reading text about locations in the UK, the US, and Canada, where famous films and TV series have been shot. This provides the context for review and extension of the passive forms which are then focused on in Pronunciation.

In the second half of the lesson, movie vocabulary is presented and then put into practice in a questionnaire where Sts talk about their own movie preferences and experiences. Then Sts listen to the true story of a young student who, by chance (and because of her excellent English), got to work for a world-famous film director. Finally, in Writing, Sts write a review of a movie.

STUDY LINK
• **Workbook** 6A

Extra photocopiable activities

• **Grammar** passive *be* + past participle *page 154*
• **Communicative** Give me an answer *page 184* (instructions *page 168*)
• **Vocabulary** Movies *page 208* (instructions *page 198*)

Optional lead-in (books closed)

• Put Sts in pairs or threes.

• Write on the board the names of some movies you think your Sts will know that are set in a different country from where your Sts are studying.

• Then teach Sts the question *Where is the movie set?* (= *In which country does the action take place?*).

• Set a time limit, e.g., three minutes. Tell each pair or group to write down the country in which each movie is set.

> Some possible films to give them an idea (but try to include some recent films known to your Sts): *Lost in Translation* (Japan), *The Mask of Zorro* (Mexico), the Harry Potter films (England), *Braveheart* (Scotland), the *Spider-Man* films (USA), *The Girl with the Dragon Tattoo* (Sweden), *The Descendants* (Hawaii).

1 READING

a Books open. Tell Sts to look at the title of the lesson *Shot on location* and elicit its meaning (= filmed in a real place, not in a studio).

Now focus on the photos and the question. Elicit answers from the class, but do **not** tell them if they are right yet.

b Tell Sts to read the article and find out which movies or TV series have been filmed at the places shown in the photos, and to fill in each blank with the correct past participle of the verbs from the list.

Check answers and elicit the infinitives of each verb (e.g., *own*, *base*, etc.). Model and drill pronunciation, making sure Sts know the meaning of all the verbs.

Extra support

• Before Sts read the article, check it for words and phrases that your Sts might not know and be ready to help with these while they are answering the questions or afterwards. You may even want to preteach a few words / phrases to lighten the load, e.g., (text A) *aristocratic*, *servant*, etc.

> Highclere Castle: *Downton Abbey*, a TV drama
> Cortlandt Alley: Films: *Crocodile Dundee*, *Men in Black 3*; TV series: *Blue Bloods*, *Boardwalk Empire*, *NYPD Blue*, *Law & Order*
> Casa Loma: The X-men movies, Chicago, Scott Pilgrim vs. the World
>
> 2 transformed (transform)
> 3 based (base)
> 4 used (use)
> 5 photographed (photograph)
> 6 inhabited (inhabit)
> 7 designed (design)
> 8 inspired (inspire)
> 9 welcomed (welcome)

c Focus on the questions and make sure Sts understand all the lexis.

Set a time limit for Sts to read the article again and answer the questions.

Get Sts to compare with a partner and then check answers. Tell Sts that the photo next to **c** shows the interior of the Highclere Castle.

> | 1 B | 3 A | 5 B | 7 C |
> | 2 A | 4 C | 6 A | 8 C |

Extra support

• You could now go through the whole article, dealing with any vocabulary problems.

d Do this as an open-class activity. Ask which of the movies and TV series mentioned they have seen and what they thought of them.

Then, with a show of hands, find out which of the three places they would most like to visit and elicit reasons.

2 GRAMMAR passive (all tenses)

a Focus on the instructions. Ask Sts which is the first example of a passive in the *Highclere Castle* text (*has been owned*). Ask Sts what kind of passive it is and elicit that it is the present perfect passive. Then give Sts a few minutes to underline more examples of the passive.

Check answers by eliciting and writing the sentences (or parts of sentences) on the board.

Present passive: ...the castle is used as a hospital... / These scenes are based on a real-life event.
Past passive: ...the castle was transformed into *Downton Abbey*... / Both the interior and exterior scenes were shot in and around the castle itself.
Present perfect passive: ...it has been sold all over the world.
Past perfect passive: ...soldiers who had been wounded...
Passive infinitive: ...to be taken care of in the castle.

Then focus on the two questions which look at how the passive is formed.

the passive = *be* + past participle
be changes

Extra challenge

• You could get Sts to underline more examples of the passive in the other two texts.

b (3 31») Tell Sts to go to **Grammar Bank 6A** on *page 142*. Focus on the example sentences and play the audio for Sts to listen to the sentence rhythm. You could also get Sts to repeat the sentences to practice getting the rhythm right. Then go through the rules with the class.

Additional grammar notes

• If your Sts previously used *American English File* 2, they will already have had an introduction to the passive although only in the present and past tenses.

• The form of the passive (*be* + participle) is quite straightforward and the easiest way to approach this grammar point is to emphasize that there are two ways of saying the same thing (active and passive), but with a different emphasis or focus.

• Depending on your Sts' L1, it may be worth pointing out that we often use the passive in sentences like *These cars are made in Korea. Rice is grown in this area,* where some languages use an impersonal subject. Some contrasting with their L1 may help Sts to see when to use the passive.

• Some typical mistakes include:

– using the active instead of the passive, e.g., ~~The tickets sell at a newsagent's~~.

– problems of form, e.g., leaving out the verb *be* or not using the participle correctly.

– Sts thinking they always have to use *by* (*somebody*) when they make a passive sentence.

Focus on the exercises and get Sts to do them individually or in pairs.

Check answers, getting Sts to read the full sentences.

a
1 are being made
2 inspired
3 hasn't been inhabited
4 is set
5 will be shot
6 aren't recording
7 wasn't being used
8 has transformed
9 hadn't owned
10 was taken

b
1 are subtitled
2 was written by García Márquez
3 is being repaired
4 hasn't been released yet
5 won't be finished until the spring
6 have to be picked up from the box office
7 hadn't been told about the changes in the script
8 was directed by James Cameron
9 has already been recorded
10 was being interviewed about the film

Tell Sts to go back to the main lesson **6A**.

Extra support

• If you think Sts need more practice, you may want to give them the Grammar photocopiable activity at this point or leave it for later as consolidation or review.

3 PRONUNCIATION sentence stress

Pronunciation notes

• Remind Sts that information words are the ones that are usually stressed. These are the words that you hear more clearly when somebody speaks to you. The unstressed words are heard much less clearly or sometimes hardly at all. (See **Pronunciation Notes, Lesson 2B, 3 Pronunciation** on *page 36*)

a (3 32») Focus on the task and tell Sts that they are going to hear six passive sentences which they have to try to write down. The first time they listen they only need to write the stressed words.

Play the audio for Sts just to hear the first sentence and focus on the example.

(3 32»)
1 The <u>movie</u> is <u>based</u> on a <u>famous</u> <u>book</u>.
2 The <u>house</u> was <u>built</u> in the <u>16th</u> <u>century</u>.
3 The <u>castle</u> has been <u>visited</u> by <u>thousands</u> of <u>tourists</u>.
4 The <u>tower</u> was <u>designed</u> by a <u>famous</u> <u>architect.</u>
5 <u>Where</u> is it being <u>filmed</u>?
6 <u>Who</u> was it <u>written</u> by?

Then play the audio all the way through for Sts just to listen.

Now play it again, pausing after each sentence for Sts to listen and write the stressed words.

Check answers.

See words underlined in script 3.32

b Give Sts some time to see if they can remember any of the unstressed words.

Play the audio, pausing after each sentence to give Sts time to write.

Play the audio again for Sts to check their answers.

Check answers by writing the correct sentences on the board.

> See sentences in script 3.32

Finally, play the audio again, pausing for Sts to repeat and copy the rhythm.

4 VOCABULARY movies

a Focus on the task and answer the question as an open-class activity.

> 1 took place / the action happened in
> 2 To make these scenes they used details and facts from a real-life situation.
> 3 were filmed

b Tell Sts to go to **Vocabulary Bank** *Movies* on *page 159*.

Focus on **1 Kinds of movies** and get Sts to do **a** individually, in pairs, or in small groups.

3 33)) Now do **b**. Play the audio for Sts to check answers. Play the audio again, pausing for Sts to repeat. Practice any words your Sts find difficult to pronounce, modeling and drilling as necessary. You could use the audio to do this.

> **3 33**))
> **Movies**
> **Kinds of movies**
> 5 an action movie   2 a musical
> 3 an animated movie   10 a romantic comedy
> 12 a comedy   9 a science-fiction movie
> 1 a drama   7 a thriller
> 11 a historical movie   4 a war movie
> 6 a horror movie   8 a western

Do **c** and elicit answers from the class, making sure Sts pronounce the movie types correctly.

> **Possible answers**
> an action movie: *The Bourne Legacy, Taken*
> an animated movie: *Ice Age, Brave, ParaNorman, Up*
> a comedy: *Ted, Untouchable*
> a drama: *End of Watch, People Like Us, Lawless*
> a historical movie: *Lincoln, J. Edgar, The King's Speech*
> a horror movie: *Resident Evil, The Woman in Black, Sinister*
> a musical: *Les Misérables, Grease, Chicago*
> a romantic comedy: *Ruby Sparks, Bridesmaids*
> a science-fiction movie: *Prometheus, The Hunger Games*
> a thriller: *Red Lights, The Cabin in the Woods*
> a war movie: *War Horse, 300, Battleship*
> a western: *Cowboys & Aliens, True Grit*

Now do **d** as an open-class activity. First, check Sts know the meaning of the adjectives. Then model and drill their pronunciation. You might want to tell Sts that nowadays a lot of people simply say *a sci-fi (movie)* instead of *science fiction movie*.

> | | |
> |---|---|
> | **funny:** | an animated movie, a comedy, a musical |
> | **violent:** | an action movie, a historical movie, a horror movie, a thriller, a war movie, a western |
> | **exciting:** | an action movie, a horror movie, a science-fiction movie, a thriller, a war movie, a western |
> | **scary:** | an action movie, a horror movie, a thriller |
> | **moving:** | a drama, a historical movie, a war movie |

Do **e** as an open-class activity or put Sts in pairs.

Finally, focus on the *movie and film* box and go through it with the Sts.

Now focus on **2 People and things** and get Sts to do **a** individually or in pairs.

3 34)) Now do **b**. Play the audio for Sts to check answers. Play the audio again, pausing for Sts to repeat. Practice any words your Sts find difficult to pronounce, modeling and drilling as necessary. You could use the audio to do this.

> **3 34**))
> **People and things**
> 1 cast   7 sequel
> 2 star   8 special effects
> 3 soundtrack   9 script
> 4 plot   10 extra
> 5 scene   11 subtitles
> 6 audience   12 review

Then tell Sts to cover the definitions and look at the words to see if they can remember the meanings.

Finally, focus on **3 Verbs and phrases** and get Sts to do **a** individually or in pairs.

3 35)) Now do **b**. Play the audio for Sts to check answers. Practice any words your Sts find difficult to pronounce, modeling and drilling as necessary.

> **3 35**))
> **Verbs and phrases**
> 1 **B** It was directed by Tate Taylor. He was the director.
> 2 **D** It was dubbed into other languages. The voices of foreign actors were used.
> 3 **C** Viola Davis played the part of Aibileen Clark. This was her role in the movie.
> 4 **A** The movie is set in Mississippi in the US during the 1960s. It was situated in that place at that time.
> 5 **E** It is based on the novel of the same name by Kathryn Stockett. It was an adaptation of the book.
> 6 **F** It was shot on location in Greenwood, Mississippi. It was filmed in the real place, not in a studio.

Focus on the *be on* box and go through it with the Sts.

Now tell Sts to cover sentences 1–6 and look at A–F to see if they can remember the verbs and phrases.

Tell Sts to go back to the main lesson **6A**.

Extra support

- If you think Sts need more practice, you may want to give them the Vocabulary photocopiable activity at this point or leave it for later as consolidation or review.

c Put Sts in pairs and get them to discuss the difference between the pair of words in 1–4.

Check answers.

1   a plot = the series of events that form the story of a movie
    a script = a written text of a movie
2   a horror movie = a type of movie that is designed to frighten people
    a thriller = a movie with an exciting story, especially one about crime
3   a musical = a movie in which part or all of the story is told using songs and often dancing
    a soundtrack = some of the music, and sometimes some speech, from a movie or musical, that is on CD, the Internet, etc. for people to buy
4   the main cast = the most important people who act in a movie
    the extras = people who are employed to play a very small part in a movie, usually as part of a crowd

5 SPEAKING

a Focus on the movie interview and quickly go through the questions.

Give Sts time to think about what they are going to say.

b Put Sts in pairs and tell them to take turns interviewing each other to find out if they have similar tastes. Emphasize that they should give and ask for as much information as they can.

Get some feedback.

Extra idea

• If there's time, you could get the class to interview you.

6 SPEAKING & LISTENING

a Focus on the instructions. You could do this as an open-class activity or put Sts in pairs. Don't worry if Sts don't know all of these movies.

Elicit what kind of movie each one is and what all the movies have in common (They were made by Steven Spielberg).

War Horse: drama, war
Indiana Jones and the Temple of Doom: action
E.T. the Extra-Terrestrial: drama, science fiction
Minority Report: action, thriller, science fiction
Catch Me If You Can: drama, comedy

b Focus Sts' attention on the photos and the task. Get Sts to quickly discuss the questions in pairs.

Elicit some ideas, but do <u>not</u> tell Sts if they are right yet.

c (3 36)) This interview is with a Polish woman, Dagmara, who became Steven Spielberg's interpreter when he was making the movie *Schindler's List*. The movie is based on the true story of Emil Schindler, a Pole who saved the lives of many Jews during the Second World War by employing them in his factory. The movie stars Liam Neeson and Ben Kingsley and won nine Oscars in 1993.

Play the first part of the interview for Sts to listen and check answers to 1 and 2 in **b**.

Check answers. You could tell Sts that the music they heard at the beginning of the audio is from the soundtrack of the movie *Schindler's List*.

Extra support

• Before playing the audio, go through the listening script and decide if you need to preteach / check any lexis to help Sts when they listen.

1   They are on a movie set in Poland.
2   The movie is *Schindler's List*.

(3 36))
(script in Student Book on *page 127*)
I = interviewer, D = Dagmara

I So, tell me, how did you get involved in the movie, Dagmara?
D Well, as you probably know, *Schindler's List* was shot in Krakow, in Poland, and which is where I live. I was a university student at the time studying English. And the film company set up their production office here three months before they started shooting the film, and I got a job there as a production assistant, preparing and translating documents and the script.
I But how did you get the job as Steven Spielberg's interpreter?
D Well, it was a complete coincidence. Just before the shooting started, there was a big party in one of the hotels in Krakow for all the actors and the film crew, and I was invited too. When I arrived at the party the Polish producer of the film came up to me and said, "The woman who was going to interpret for Steven Spielberg can't come, so we need you to interpret his opening speech."
I How did you feel about that?
D I couldn't believe it! I was just a student – I had no experience of interpreting – and now I was going to speak in front of hundreds of people. I was so nervous that I drank a couple of glasses of champagne to give myself courage. I must have done a pretty good job though, because soon afterwards Spielberg came up to me to say thank you and then he said, "I'd like you to be my interpreter for the whole film." I was so stunned I had to pinch myself to believe that this was happening to me.

---

d Tell Sts they are now going to listen to the first part of the interview again and they must mark the sentences T (true) or F (false). Give them time to read 1–5.

Play the audio once all the way through for Sts to listen.

Get Sts to compare with a partner, and then play the audio again if necessary.

Check answers.

Extra support

• Before playing the audio, go through the listening script and decide if you need to preteach / check any lexis to help Sts when they listen.

1   F (She was a **student**.)
2   T
3   F (The party was for **all the actors and the movie crew**.)
4   F (The interpreter **couldn't come**.)
5   T

e (3 37)) Now tell Sts they are now going to listen to the second part of the interview. They need to listen to check their answers to questions 3 and 4 in **b**.

Play the audio once all the way through.

Get Sts to compare with a partner and then check answers.

3   She is playing an extra in a party scene.
4   Yes, he was demanding, but very nice.

3 37))

(script in Student Book on *page 127*)

I   So what exactly did you have to do?

D   I had to go to the film set every day and translate Spielberg's instructions to the Polish actors, and also to the extras. I had to make them understand what he wanted them to do. It was really exciting, and I often felt as if I was a director myself.

I   So, was it a difficult job?

D   Sometimes it was really hard. The worst thing was when we had to shoot a scene again and again because Spielberg thought it wasn't exactly right. Some scenes were repeated as many as 16 times – and then sometimes I would think that maybe it was my fault – that I hadn't translated properly what he wanted, so I'd get really nervous. I remember one scene with lots of actors in it which we just couldn't get right and Spielberg started shouting at me because he was stressed. Eventually we got it right and then he apologized, and I cried a little, because I was also very stressed – and after that it was all right again.

I   So, was Spielberg difficult to work with?

D   Not at all. I mean he was very demanding, I had to do my best every day, but he was really nice to me. I felt he treated me like a daughter. For instance, he was always making sure that I wasn't cold – it was freezing on the set most of the time – and he would make sure that I had a warm coat and gloves and things.

I   Did you ever get to be an extra?

D   Yes, twice! I was going to be in two party scenes, and I got to wear beautiful long dresses and high heels. Unfortunately, one scene didn't make it to the final cut of the film, and before we started shooting the other one I tripped walking down some stairs and twisted my ankle really badly. I was in so much pain that I couldn't take part in the filming. And that was the end of my "acting career." I still have the photos of me looking like a girl from the 40s, though!

I   Have you ever worked with Spielberg again?

D   Yes. A year later he invited me to interpret for him again, this time during the premiere of *Schindler's List* in Poland, which was broadcast live on national television! Before that, he had also asked me come to work as a production assistant on his next movie in Hollywood. I was very tempted and thought really hard about it, but I hadn't finished my studies yet, and all my family and friends were in Poland – so in the end I decided not to go.

I   Do you regret it?

D   Not at all. I had my moment, and it was unforgettable, but that was it!

f   Focus on the task and go through the headings under which Sts have to take notes. Tell them just to listen and to make notes <u>after</u> they have heard the audio.

Play the audio once all the way through.

Elicit answers and write them on the board.

The worst thing about the job
When they had to shoot a scene many times, she would think it was her fault – maybe she hadn't translated correctly.

One especially difficult scene
In one scene with lots of actors they had to repeat it so many times that Spielberg got stressed and shouted at her. Later he apologized.

What it was like to work with Spielberg
He was demanding, but he treated her well – like a daughter, e.g., he made sure she was warm enough. It was hard work, but she enjoyed it.

Being an extra
She was going to be an extra in two party scenes, but one didn't make it to the final cut of the film, and then before the other scene she hurt her ankle just before filming, so she couldn't be in it.

What happened after the film was finished
She interpreted for Spielberg again at the premiere in Poland. He also invited her to work for him in Hollywood, but she didn't go.

Extra support

• If there's time, you could play the audio again while Sts read the scripts on *page 127*, so they can see what they understood / didn't understand. Translate / explain any new words or phrases.

g   Finally, do the questions as an open-class activity. You could also ask Sts which director they would like to interpret for.

7   WRITING a movie review

Tell Sts to go to **Writing** *A movie review* on *page 117*.

a   Focus on the movie title and with a show of hands find out how many Sts have seen it. Do <u>not</u> ask Sts any questions about it or their opinions as they will be doing this later.

Then elicit / explain the meaning of *classic* in the title (= sth that is accepted as being of very high quality and one of the best of its kind).

Now tell Sts to read the movie review and fill in the blanks with the words in the list.

Check answers.

2	directed	6	recommend
3	stars	7	action
4	set	8	soundtrack
5	location	9	sequels

b   Tell Sts to read the review again, paying particular attention to layout. They must number the paragraphs 1–4 in the order in which they appear.

Check answers.

Paragraph 1	The name of the movie, the director, the stars, and any prizes it won
Paragraph 2	Where and when it is set Where it was filmed
Paragraph 3	The plot
Paragraph 4	Why you recommend the movie

c   Do this as a whole-class activity.

Check the answer.

the simple present

d   In pairs, get Sts to answer the questions.

Get some feedback. If possible, ask at least one student who has seen the movie and another who hasn't.

e   Focus on the **Useful language: describing a movie** box and go through it with Sts.

Now tell Sts they are going to write a similar movie review for a movie they would recommend people to buy on DVD or see at the movies. They should write four paragraphs as in the model, and use the **Useful language** box and **Vocabulary Bank** *Movies* on *page 159* to help them.

You may like to get Sts to do the writing in class or you could assign it as homework. If you do it in class, set a time limit for Sts to write their description, e.g., 15–20 minutes.

f   Sts should check their work for mistakes before turning it in.

G modals of deduction: *might, can't, must*
V the body
P diphthongs

6B Judging by appearances

Lesson plan

The overall topic of this lesson is the image that people choose to give of themselves to the world and how we tend to judge people at first sight according to their appearance.

The lesson begins with a reading text about how people choose their profile photos on social networking sites according to the image they wish to project to their friends and family. This is followed by vocabulary that focuses on the body, and verbs related to parts of the body like *touch* and *point*. Pronunciation looks at diphthongs (combinations of two vowel sounds) and the first half of the lesson finishes with a song *I Got Life*.

In the second half of the lesson, the grammar of modals of deduction is presented through the context of making deductions about people based only on their physical appearance. This topic is further developed in Listening and Reading where Sts listen and read about two situations where an erroneous deduction was made through judging someone purely by their appearance. The lesson finishes with a short related speaking activity.

STUDY LINK

- **Workbook** 6B
- **iChecker**

Extra photocopiable activities

- **Grammar** modals of deduction: *might / may, can't, must* *page 155*
- **Communicative** Who do you think they are? *page 185* (instructions *page 168*)
- **Vocabulary** The body *page 209* (instructions *page 198*)
- **Song** *I Got Life* *page 222* (instructions *page 216*)

Optional lead-in (books closed)

- Review the difference between *look* and *look like* by asking Sts to complete these sentences with the correct form of either verb:

1 DO YOU _____ YOUR MOTHER OR YOUR FATHER?
2 YOU _____ VERY TIRED. ARE YOU OK?
3 YOUR GRANDMOTHER _____ VERY YOUNG FOR HER AGE. SHE DOESN'T _____ 70!
4 JACK _____ A FOOTBALL PLAYER – HE'S ENORMOUS.
5 WHAT _____ MARK'S WIFE _____?
   SHE'S QUITE TALL WITH VERY LONG, DARK HAIR.

1 look like
2 look
3 looks, look
4 looks like
5 does... look like

- Ask Sts if they can remember the grammatical difference between *look* and *look like* (*look* is followed by an adjective and *look like* by a noun).

1 READING & SPEAKING

a Books open. Focus on the questions and make sure Sts understand them, especially *profile photo*. Put Sts in pairs and get them to answer the three questions.

Get some feedback.

b Focus on the instructions and the four photos, and elicit Sts' opinions as to why the people have chosen these photos.

c Focus on the title of the article and read the beginning of the article on *page 58* to the class as they follow it.

Focus on the task and headings A–F, and give Sts time to read the rest of the article and fill in the blanks with the headings.

Get Sts to compare with a partner and then check answers.

Extra support

- Before Sts read the article, check it for words and phrases that your Sts might not know and be ready to help with these while they are answering the questions or afterwards. You may even want to preteach / check a few words / phrases to lighten the load, e.g., *visual, logo, a celebrity*, etc. (but not the highlighted ones).

2 F	3 E	5 B	6 A	10 D	12 C

Now ask Sts which of the 12 categories they think the four profile photos they looked at in **b** belong to and elicit ideas.

Annabel 6	Martin 5	Sean 4	Sarah 3

d Focus on the highlighted phrases. Get Sts, in pairs, to read the article again and guess their meaning.

Check answers, either explaining in English, translating into Sts' L1, or getting Sts to check in their dictionaries.

Explain any other new vocabulary and ask Sts what words or phrases they want to try and remember from this article.

e Focus on the questions and make sure Sts understand them. Put Sts in pairs and get them to answer the four questions.

Get some feedback and find out if any Sts want to change their profile picture now and why.

2 VOCABULARY the body

a ③ 38))) This exercise reviews the basic language of physical appearance, which Sts learnt in *American English File* 2.

Focus on the four pictures. Explain that two women witnessed a robbery and Sts are going to hear them describing the man they saw to the police.

Before listening, get Sts in pairs to describe the four men.

Play the audio once all the way through, and let Sts discuss who they think the thief is and why. Play the audio again as necessary.

Check answers and get Sts to tell you why they are sure that the person they say is the thief.

> The thief is 3.

> **3 38**)))
>
> **P = police officer, W1 = woman 1, W2 = woman 2**
>
> P   OK, ladies, now can you describe the man you saw in the bank?
> W1 Well, he was, uh kind of tall, you know, he had very long legs. And very skinny, you know thin.
> W2 Yes. Very narrow shoulders. And he had a beard and a little mustache.
> W1 No, he didn't. He had a mustache, but not a beard. It's just that I think he hadn't shaved.
> W2 No, it was a beard, I'm sure.
> W1 And anyway, Doris, you weren't wearing your glasses, so you can't have seen him very well.
> W2 I could see perfectly well.
> P   Ladies, ladies, please. So, no mustache, then.
> W1 No, he had a mustache, but he didn't have a beard.
> P   And what about his hair?
> W2 Dark.
> W1 Yes, short, dark hair.
> P   Straight?
> W1 No, curly, I'd say. Wouldn't you say, Doris?
> W2 Yes, very curly.
> P   So, dark, curly hair?
> W1 Yes. That's what we said. Are you deaf or something?
> P   What about his eyes? Did you notice what color they were?
> W2 Brown eyes. Nothing special. And very small. But he had a big nose.
> W1 Yes, a very big nose.
> P   And what time was it when you saw this man...?

b   Tell Sts to go to **Vocabulary Bank** *The body* on *page 160*.

Focus on **1 Parts of the body** and get Sts to do **a** individually or in pairs.

3 39))) Now do **b**. Play the audio for Sts to check answers. Play the audio again, pausing for Sts to repeat. Practice any words your Sts find difficult to pronounce, modeling and drilling as necessary. You could use the audio to do this. Highlight the irregular pronunciations of *stomach* /ˈstʌmək/ and *tongue* /tʌŋ/, and the silent *k* in *knees*.

> **3 39**)))
> **The body**
> **Parts of the body**
>
> | 6 | arms | 17 | legs |
> | 8 | back | 20 | lips |
> | 16 | ears | 1 | mouth |
> | 13 | eyes | 4 | neck |
> | 9 | face | 18 | nose |
> | 7 | feet | 12 | shoulders |
> | 14 | fingers | 10 | stomach |
> | 5 | hands | 11 | teeth |
> | 2 | head | 3 | toes |
> | 19 | knees | 15 | tongue |

Focus on the **Possessive pronouns with parts of the body** box and go through it with Sts.

Focus on **c** and get Sts to cover the words and test themselves or a partner.

Now focus on **2 Verbs related to the body** and get Sts to do **a** individually or in pairs. Remind them to put the verb in the right form.

Elicit which two verbs are irregular in the past.

> bite – bit, throw – threw

3 40))) Now do **b**. Play the audio for Sts to check answers. Practice any words your Sts find difficult to pronounce, modeling and drilling as necessary. Point out the silent *t* in *whistle*.

> **3 40**)))
> **Verbs related to the body**
> 1 Don't be scared of the dog. He won't **bite**.
> 2 Jason **kicked** the ball too hard, and it went over the wall into the next yard.
> 3 Don't **throw** stones – you might hit somebody.
> 4 Mmm! Something **smells** delicious! Are you making a cake?
> 5 The stranger **stared** at me for a long time, but he didn't say anything.
> 6 Can you **taste** the rice? I'm not sure if it's cooked yet.
> 7 My dad **whistled** a tune as he raked the leaves.
> 8 Don't **touch** the oven door! It's really hot.
> 9 The audience **clapped** when I finished singing.
> 10 The teacher suddenly **pointed** at me and said, "What's the answer?"
> 11 In Russia if you **smile** at strangers, people think you're crazy!
> 12 Everybody **nodded** in agreement when I explained my idea.

Now elicit which parts of the body you use for each verb.

> | bite: teeth | smile: mouth / lips |
> | clap: hands | stare: eyes |
> | kick: feet | taste: mouth / tongue |
> | nod: head | throw: arms |
> | point: finger | touch: hands |
> | smell: nose | whistle: lips |

Tell Sts to go back to the main lesson **6B**.

Extra support

• If you think Sts need more practice, you may want to give them the Vocabulary photocopiable activity at this point or leave it for later as consolidation or review.

3 PRONUNCIATION diphthongs

> **Pronunciation notes**
>
> • With diphthongs the tongue glides from one short vowel sound to another, making one longer sound. The most common problem for Sts is that they may not make the sound long enough or may pronounce it as just one sound.

a   **3 41**))) Focus on the **Diphthongs** box and go through it with Sts.

Now play the audio for Sts just to listen to the five words and sounds.

3 41 🔊
1 bike /aɪ/
2 train /eɪ/
3 phone /oʊ/
4 owl /aʊ/
5 boy /ɔɪ/

Then play the audio again, pausing for Sts to repeat.

Then repeat the activity, eliciting responses from individual Sts.

b In pairs or individually, Sts put the words in the list in the correct columns in **a**. This exercise recycles words from **Vocabulary Bank** *The body* which have diphthongs.

c **3 42** 🔊 Play the audio for Sts to listen and check.

Check answers.

3 42 🔊
1	bike /aɪ/	bite, eyes, smile
2	train /eɪ/	face, taste
3	phone /oʊ/	nose, shoulders, throw, toes
4	owl /aʊ/	mouth, outgoing
5	boy /ɔɪ/	pointy, voice

Then play the audio again, pausing after each group of words for Sts to listen and repeat.

Extra challenge

- Write these extra body words on the board: ELBOW, NAIL, THIGH, THROAT, WAIST. Check Sts know what they are.

- Now get Sts to put them in the right columns:

1 bike /aɪ/   thigh
2 train /eɪ/   waist, nail
3 phone /oʊ/   elbow, throat

Focus on the six phrases and elicit / explain what a *Roman nose* is (= a nose that curves out at the top).

In pairs, Sts now practice saying the phrases.

Get individual Sts to say them.

Extra support

- Read each phrase first and get Sts to repeat after you. Then put Sts in pairs and get them to practice saying them.

d Put Sts in pairs and get them to take the quiz.

Put two pairs together and get them to compare answers.

Check answers.

1 You wear a ring on your fingers / thumb; you wear gloves on your hands; you wear socks on your feet; you wear a cap on your head.
2 Ballet dancers stand on their toes.
3 Soccer players often injure their legs / feet / toes.
4 Women put makeup on their face, lips, and eyes.
5 People brush their hair and teeth.
6 People carry a backpack on their back or shoulders.

Extra idea

- Do **d** as a contest. The first pair to finish with all correct answers wins. Or set a time limit and when it is up, get pairs to exchange answer sheets. The pair with the most correct answers wins.

4 **3 43** 🔊 **SONG** *I Got Life* ♫

This song was made famous by the American singer Nina Simone in 1968. For copyright reasons this is a cover version. If you want to do the song in class, use the photocopiable activity on *page 222*.

3 43 🔊
I Got Life

I ain't got no home, ain't got no shoes
I ain't got no money, ain't got no class
Ain't got no skirts, ain't got no sweater
Ain't got no perfume, ain't got no beer
Ain't got no man

Ain't got no mother, ain't got no culture
Ain't got no friends, ain't got no schooling
Ain't got no love, ain't got no name
Ain't got no ticket, ain't got no token
Ain't got no god

What have I got?
Why am I alive anyway?
Yeah, what have I got
Nobody can take away?

I've got my hair, got my head
I've got my brains, got my ears
I've got my eyes, got my nose
I've got my mouth, I got my smile

I've got my tongue, got my chin
I've got my neck, got my lips
I've got my heart, got my soul
I've got my back, I got myself

I've got my arms, got my hands
I've got my fingers, got my legs
I've got my feet, got my toes
I've got my liver, got my blood

I've got life, I've got my freedom
I've got life
I've got life
And I'm gonna keep it
I've got life
And nobody's gonna take it away
I've got life

5 **GRAMMAR** modals of deduction

a Ask Sts if they think it is true that we often judge other people, particularly when we first meet them, by their appearance, i.e., by the way they look.

Focus on the nine sentences. Elicit / explain that *He | she may | might | could* = it's possible that he / she … and that *He | she must be* = it's very probable or certain. Also make sure Sts understand the lexis, e.g., *Scandinavian*, *dyed*, and *retired*.

Now focus on the photos and tell Sts they have two minutes to match three sentences with each person.

b When time is up, get Sts to compare with a partner and tell them to give reasons.

Now elicit some opinions from the class.

c Tell Sts to go to **Communication** *Judging by appearances* on *page 106* to check their guesses.

Sts read the information and then, in pairs, tell each other what they think, e.g., whether they are surprised.

Get some feedback from the class.

Extra support

- You could write any new and useful words and phrases from **Communication** on the board for Sts to copy.

Tell Sts to go back to the main lesson **6B**.

d Focus on the task and get Sts to do this either individually or in pairs.

Check answers.

1	may, could	2	must	3	can't

e (3 44))) (3 45))) (3 46))) Tell Sts to go to **Grammar Bank 6B** on *page 143*. Focus on the example sentences and play the audio for Sts to listen to the sentence rhythm. You could also get Sts to repeat the sentences to practice getting the rhythm right. Then go through the rules with the class.

> **Additional grammar notes**
>
> - Sts are already familiar with these modal verbs in other contexts, e.g., *may / might* to express a possibility (e.g., *I might go*), *must* for obligation (e.g., *You must wear a seat belt*), and *can't* for permission (e.g., *You can't take photos in the museum*). Here the same modal verbs are used in a different way to speculate and make deductions.
>
> - Although these verbs are often used with *be* in the presentation, they can be used with any verb, e.g., *She must have a lot of money.*
>
> - The most common mistakes include:
>   – using *must not* instead of *can't* for something that's impossible, e.g., *It must not be true.*
>   – using *can* instead of *might / may* for a possibility, e.g., *I think he's speaking Spanish, so he can be Spanish or South American.*

Focus on the exercises and get Sts to do them individually or in pairs.

Check answers to **a** and **c**, getting Sts to read the full sentences.

a					
1	I	4	C	7	F
2	J	5	H	8	E
3	A	6	B	9	G

c			
1	must	6	must
2	might not	7	might not
3	must	8	can't
4	can't	9	might
5	might	10	can't

Tell Sts to go back to the main lesson **6B**.

Extra support

- If you think Sts need more practice, you may want to give them the Grammar photocopiable activity at this point or leave it for later as consolidation or review.

6 **LISTENING & READING**

a Focus on the instructions and the adjectives in the list. Tell Sts, in pairs, they must talk about the man in the photo using the adjectives and *might / may / could (not) be, must be,* or *can't be.*

After a few minutes, elicit sentences from each pair. If they use *can't be* or *must be*, encourage them to say why, e.g., *He can't be British. He isn't dressed very well.* Do <u>not</u> say if Sts are right or wrong in their deductions at this point.

b (3 47))) Focus on the instructions and then give Sts time to read the five questions.

Now play the audio once all the way through.

Get Sts to compare answers with a partner.

Play the audio again if necessary and then check answers.

Extra support

- Before playing the audio, go through the listening script and decide if you need to preteach / check any lexis to help Sts when they listen, e.g., *a bench, a mess, a tramp*, etc.

1	They were in West Hollywood, which is a famous part of Los Angeles, California.
2	They were sitting in a cafe.
3	He looked like a mess – He had a beard, long messy brown hair, and he was wearing a winter hat in the middle of summer.
4	She wanted to give the man some money.
5	She told her friend not to give the man any money.

> **(3 47)))**
> (script in Student Book on *page 127*)
> A few months ago I was with a Vietnamese friend of mine named Ny in California, and we were driving around the West Hollywood area, which is a pretty famous part of Los Angeles – you know – the Sunset Strip, Melrose Avenue, lots of cool shops and restaurants...and lots of movie stars!! Anyway, it was a hot, sunny day, and we were thirsty, so we stopped at a cafe for a cold drink and a snack. So, we sat down at an outside table waiting for the server when we saw a man walking toward us. He was wearing a crazy combination of clothing, and he kind of looked like a mess. He had a beard, long messy brown hair, and he was wearing a winter hat in the middle of summer! Ny said, "Oh, look at that poor man. He must be homeless. He looks like he hasn't taken a shower for some time. He's also really thin. He must be hungry – should I give him some money? She started to look in her bag for some money, but I looked at him again and just said, "Don't!" She couldn't understand why I didn't want her to give the man some money, and she thought I was being very mean and unfriendly.

c (3 48))) Focus on the question and elicit some ideas. Do <u>not</u> tell Sts if they are right.

Play the audio all the way through for Sts to listen.

Check the answer. You might want to tell Sts that Russell Brand is known in the British media for his eccentricity and for a trail of controversies. He has been both criticized and praised for his behavior as presenter of various award ceremonies. His drug use and publicly acknowledge alcoholism have influenced his comedic material and public image. He is also widely known for his short marriage to Katy Perry which ended in 2012.

The speaker stopped Ny because the man wasn't homeless. He was a famous actor and comedian, Russel Brand.

> **(3 48)))**
> (script in Student Book on *page 127*)
> When the man had gone past, I said, "Ny, that man isn't homeless. He's Russell Brand, the British comedian and actor." He's one of the funniest people in show business. And he definitely isn't homeless – he has a house in the Hollywood Hills and an apartment in New York City! And he definitely doesn't need any money! He just enjoys wearing comfortable, old, mismatched clothing. In fact, Russell Brand often talks to the homeless people he sees on the streets and gives <u>them</u> money or buys <u>them</u> food. Even though he looks a little messy and scary, he's actually a very kind person. Ny was really surprised. She said that she thought all US celebrities dressed

in designer clothes and had perfect hair and makeup all the time. I told her that in the US, you can't always judge people by their appearance. A lot of people, even famous celebrities, like to dress in old, mismatched clothing because it's comfortable, and it helps them blend in with the crowd better so they can go quietly about their business.

Extra support

- If there's time, you could play the audio again while Sts read the scripts on *page 127*, so they can see what they understood / didn't understand. Translate / explain any new words or phrases.

d Tell Sts that Susan Boyle is a Scottish singer who came to international public attention when she appeared on the TV program *Britain's Got Talent* in 2009 and who has become a successful singer. When she first appeared, she was laughed at for looking old-fashioned, and since then she has considerably changed her appearance.

Do this as an open-class activity.

Do <u>not</u> tell Sts if they are right.

e Focus on the title of the article and elicit what it means.

Now tell Sts to read the article and decide which statement 1–3 is the best summary.

Check the answer.

Extra support

- Before Sts read the article, check it for words and phrases which your Sts might not know and be ready to help with these while they are answering the questions or afterwards. You may even want to preteach / check a few words / phrases to lighten the load, e.g., *to stereotype somebody*, *dominant*, etc.

The best summary is 2.

f Tell Sts to read the article again and to mark sentences 1–6 T (true) or F (false). You could ask them to underline the part of the article that gave them the answer.

Check answers.

1 F (Nobody thought for a minute that she had a chance of doing well on the show, or could ever become a star.)
2 T (Journalists started talking about how wrong it is to stereotype people.)
3 T This was vitally important.
4 F (In the past people needed to judge whether a person was dangerous or not.)
5 F (It often gives us generally accurate information.)
6 T (She has started to change her appearance.)

g Focus on the instructions and tell Sts to read the article again and find words or phrases for the five definitions.

Get Sts to compare with a partner, and then check answers.

1 went viral
2 judge a book by its cover
3 vitally important
4 socio-economic level
5 underdogs

Extra idea

- If you are teaching a monolingual class, you could elicit from Sts the equivalent idiom to *Don't judge a book by its cover* in their L1.

Explain any other new vocabulary and encourage Sts to write down any useful new lexis from the text.

h In pairs, Sts discuss the questions.

Get some feedback.

For instructions on how to use these pages see *page 40*.

Testing Program CD-ROM

- Quick Test 6
- File 6 Test

GRAMMAR

1 a	6 c	11 a
2 b	7 a	12 b
3 c	8 b	13 a
4 b	9 c	14 c
5 b	10 a	15 b

VOCABULARY

a 1 lips / mouth
  2 eyes
  3 nose
  4 hands
  5 teeth

b 1 beat
  2 court
  3 get injured
  4 scored
  5 go

c 1 close
  2 common
  3 touch
  4 got
  5 fiancé

d 1 soundtrack
  2 subtitles
  3 special effects
  4 star
  5 scene

e 1 out
  2 at
  3 up
  4 about
  5 on

PRONUNCIATION

a 1 couple   3 eyes   5 shoe
  2 taste   4 doctor

b 1 ref<u>ere</u>e   3 spect<u>a</u>tors   5 <u>colleague</u>
  2 rev<u>iew</u>   4 dir<u>ec</u>tor

CAN YOU UNDERSTAND THIS TEXT?

1 b 2 a 3 c

CAN YOU UNDERSTAND THESE PEOPLE?

3 49)))

1 b 2 a 3 c 4 b 5 b

---

3 49)))

Andrew

I = interviewer, A = Andrew

I Do you prefer playing sports or watching them?

A I prefer playing sports rather than watching them.

I What sports do you play?

A I play soccer, basketball, lacrosse, volleyball, frisbee, golf. Anything, really.

I What sports do you like watching the most?

A I prefer playing sports to watching it. But if I am watching sports, I like soccer or women's volleyball.

I Why?

A They're very interesting team sports.

Adrian

I = interviewer, A = Adrian

I Do you know anyone who has gone out with someone they met on the Internet?

A Yes, I do. I know of a couple of people.

I How did it work out?

A One person, an old friend of mine, it didn't work out that well because the person I think looked better on the Internet than they did in real life. And the second person, they went on and got married, so I think it can work well.

Ryder

I = interviewer, R = Ryder

I Have you ever cheated on an exam?

R Yes, many.

I How did you cheat?

R Oh, I've used all different types of techniques. Sometimes I've written things on my palm, other times I've just put a book on my lap, sometimes I've put answers on my cell phone, but it was only for subjects that I really didn't like and I knew that would never have anything to do with my career, so I didn't feel bad about cheating on a math test.

I Were you caught?

R I don't think I've ever been caught, no. I'm really good at it.

Helen

I = interviewer, H = Helen

I What's your favorite movie of all time?

H My favorite film is *Dirty Dancing*.

I How many times have you seen it?

H Probably about 25.

I Why do you like it so much?

H Because it has romance, it has dancing, which I like, and it has nice, good-looking men.

Rebekah

I = interviewer, R = Rebekah

I Do you have a profile photo?

R I do, yes.

I What is it?

R It's a photo of me and my four siblings at my sister's wedding a few weeks ago making silly faces.

I Why did you choose it?

R I chose it because I think it really captures the sense of fun my siblings and I have together and the way we like to be silly and goof off.

G first conditional and future time clauses + *when*, *until*, etc., 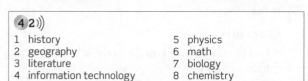*make* and *let*
V education
P the letter *u*

7A Extraordinary school for boys

Lesson plan

This lesson is about education and provides two different angles on the topic. The lesson begins with a vocabulary focus which reviews and extends Sts' knowledge of vocabulary related to education. This is followed by a pronunciation focus on the letter *u*, and a speaking activity where Sts talk about their own education. Sts then read and listen to the account of a televised educational experiment where a well-known TV personality, who is a choirmaster and educator, went into an elementary school for a quarter and attempted to improve the literacy level of the boys. Sts then have a debate on various topics related to education.

In the second half of the lesson, the grammar, first conditional sentences, and future time clauses, *when*, *until*, etc., is presented through the context of exams. Sts then read and discuss an article about a book called *Battle Hymn of the Tiger Mother*, which describes a controversial way of educating girls.

STUDY LINK
• **Workbook** 7A

Extra photocopiable activities

• **Grammar** first conditional and future time clauses *page 156*
• **Communicative** Finish the sentences *page 186* (instructions *page 168*)
• **Vocabulary** Education *page 210* (instructions *pages 198–199*)

Optional lead-in (books closed)

• Put Sts in pairs. Write SCHOOL SUBJECTS on the board and give pairs three or four minutes to think of as many subjects as they can, e.g., *history*, *geography*, etc.

• When time is up, write Sts' ideas on the board and drill the pronunciation.

1 VOCABULARY education

a Books open. Focus on the eight questions and give Sts one minute to answer them individually or in pairs.

Check answers.

1	six	5	Albert Einstein
2	Brasília	6	22½ (or 22.5)
3	F. Scott Fitzgerald	7	six
4	1,024	8	hydrogen and oxygen

Find out which pair got the most correct answers.

b **4 2))** Now give Sts a little more time to match questions 1–8 with the school subjects by writing the correct number in each box.

Then play the audio for Sts to listen and check.

Model and drill pronunciation, especially *geography* /dʒiˈɑgrəfi/ and *literature* /ˈlɪtərətʃər/.

See script 4.2

4 2))
1	history	5	physics
2	geography	6	math
3	literature	7	biology
4	information technology	8	chemistry

c Tell Sts to go to **Vocabulary Bank** *Education* on *page 161*.

Focus on **1 The school system in the US and the UK** and get Sts to do **a** individually or in pairs.

4 3)) Now do **b**. Play the audio for Sts to check answers. Practice any words your Sts find difficult to pronounce, modeling and drilling as necessary.

2	elementary	8	public
3	high	9	private
4	grades	10	religious
5	kindergarten	11	college
6	twelfth	12	graduate
7	semesters		

4 3))
Education

The school system in the US and the UK
In the US
Many children start their education between the ages of two and four in preschool. Once a child turns five, he or she enters the US school system, which is divided into three levels, elementary school, middle school (sometimes called junior high school), and high school. In almost all schools at these levels, children are divided by age groups into grades. The youngest children begin in kindergarten (followed by first grade) and continue until twelfth grade, the final year of high school. The school year is divided into two semesters.
Most US schools (about 75%) are public schools, which means they are supported by US tax dollars and education is free. The other 25% are private schools, where parents have to pay. Many of these schools are religious schools, where the teachers may be priests or nuns.
If you want to go to college, you have to apply. Admission depends on high school grades, college aptitude test scores, and extracurricular activities. A person who has completed college and has earned a degree is called a college graduate.

Sts now do **c** individually or in pairs.

4 4)) Now do **d**. Play the audio for Sts to check answers. Practice any words your Sts find difficult to pronounce, modeling and drilling as necessary.

1	primary	5	pupils
2	nursery	6	head
3	secondary	7	terms
4	boarding	8	university

4 4))

In the UK

Children start primary school when they are five. Before that, many children go to nursery school. From 11–18, children go to secondary school. Some children go to boarding schools, where they study, eat, and sleep. School children are usually called pupils (not "students" which only refers to people who are at university), and the person who is in charge of a school is called the head teacher. The school year is divided into three terms. Higher education is often called university.

For **e**, put Sts in pairs and tell them to cover the two texts. Sts then tell each other about the school system in both countries.

Extra idea

• Get the class to tell you about the school system in their country.

Now focus on **2 Verbs** and get Sts to do **a** individually or in pairs.

4 5)) Now do **b**. Play the audio for Sts to check answers. Practice any words your Sts find difficult to pronounce, modeling and drilling as necessary.

4 5))

Verbs

1 Discipline is very strict in our school. If students **behave** badly, for example if they **cheat** on an exam, they will probably **be punished,** and might even **be suspended.**

2 Marc has to **take** an important English exam next week. He hopes he'll **pass**, but he hasn't had much time to **study**, so he's worried that he might **fail**.

Now get Sts to cover the texts and look at the pictures, and try to remember as much information from the texts as possible.

Finally, focus on the *educate* or *bring up?* and *learn or study?* box and go through it with Sts.

Tell Sts to go back to the main lesson **7A**.

Extra support

• If you think Sts need more practice, you may want to give them the Vocabulary photocopiable activity at this point or leave it for later as consolidation or review.

2 PRONUNCIATION & SPEAKING

the letter *u*

Pronunciation notes

• The letter *u* has several different pronunciations, but between consonants it is usually (but not <u>always</u>) /ʌ/, e.g., *sun, luck, summer* or /yu/, e.g., *music, uniform, usual.*

• Sts often don't realize that there is a kind of "hidden sound" – /y/ – in words like *music* and tend to pronounce them /ˈmuzɪk/ or /ˈuʒuəl/.

• Students are also reminded here about the rule governing the use of the indefinite article *a* or *an* before words beginning with *u*. If the *u* is pronounced /ʌ/ (i.e., a vowel sound), then *an* is used, e.g., *an umbrella, an uncle*, but if *u* is pronounced /yu/ (i.e., a consonant sound) then *a* is used, e.g., *a uniform, a university, a useful book.*

a Focus on the **letter *u*** box and go through it with Sts.

Focus on the task and make sure Sts are clear how the four sounds are pronounced. Give Sts a few minutes to put the words in the right column.

b **4 6))** Play the audio once all the way through for Sts to listen and check.

Check answers.

4 6))

boot /u/	rude, rules, student, true
up /ʌ/	lunch, nun, study, subject
bull /ʊ/	full, put
/yu/	future, music, uniform, university

You may want to point out here that the /ʊ/ pronunciation is the least common.

Then play the audio again, pausing after each group of words for Sts to listen and repeat.

Give Sts time to practice saying the words.

Finally, focus on the question about the article *a* / *an* before words beginning with *u* and elicit answers (see **Pronunciation notes**).

We use *a* when *u* at the beginning of a word is pronounced /yu/ and *an* when it is pronounced /ʌ/.

c **4 7))** Focus on the task and tell Sts that they are going to hear four sentences which they have to try to write down.

Play the audio once all the way through for Sts just to listen. Repeat if necessary.

4 7))

1 What subjects did you study in high school?
2 Do students at your school wear uniforms?
3 Most students have lunch in the cafeteria.
4 I usually get good grades on my music exams.

Then play it again, pausing after each sentence to give Sts time to write.

Check answers and write the correct sentences on the board.

See script 4.7

Extra support

• Play the audio again, pausing for Sts to repeat and copy the rhythm. Put Sts in pairs and get them to practice saying the sentences.

d Education vocabulary is now put into practice in a free-speaking activity. Sts interview their partner, asking the questions in the questionnaire.

Focus on the question prompts. Remind Sts that if they are currently in high school, they should use the present tense (i.e., add *do* or *is* / *are* to the prompts). If they are no longer in school, they should use the past tense (i.e., add *did* or *was* / *were* to the prompts).

Extra support

• Elicit the questions in the questionnaire before you start the activity, by getting Sts to ask you the questions.

Sts take turns interviewing each other. Remind the student who is interviewing to react to the interviewee's answers and ask for more information where possible (*Really? | That's interesting, etc. | Why didn't you like it?*, etc.).

Get some whole class feedback at the end by finding out, e.g., how many people like / liked / don't / didn't like their high school and what their best / worst subjects are / were.

3 LISTENING

a Focus on the photos and elicit from Sts what they can see. Now focus on the title of the text and make sure Sts understand the adjective *extraordinary*.

Tell Sts to read the text to find out what the Extraordinary School for Boys is.

Explain any new vocabulary, e.g., *choirmaster, accomplished, challenge, mixed, behind*. Then ask a few questions to check comprehension, e.g., *Who is Gareth Malone? What TV show made him famous? What was it about? What's his new show called? What did he try to do in the show?*

Then find out from the class if they think boys are usually behind girls in reading and writing in schools in their country. You could teach the opposite of *be behind (be ahead)*.

b (4 8)) Tell Sts they are going to listen to **Part 1** of a radio program about Gareth's experiment. They must listen and then answer questions 1–3.

Play the audio once all the way through.

Get Sts to compare answers with a partner, and then play the audio again.

Check answers.

Extra support

- Before playing the audio, go through the listening script and decide if you need to preteach / check any lexis to help Sts when they listen.

> 1 eight weeks
> 2 His aim was to improve the boys' reading age by six months.
> 3 i to make the work feel like play
>   ii competition
>   iii to allow the boys to take risks

Extra challenge

- For question 3 get Sts to also explain why he believed those three things were important.
  i   Because if he can do that, the boys will learn.
  ii Because learning to lose and to fail and to come back from that will help the boys later in life.
  iii Because doing things which are a little scary is very motivating if you manage to do them.

(script in Student Book on *page 127*)

Part 1
Gareth had only eight weeks for the experiment, during which time he would be teaching three days a week. His aim was to try to improve the boys' reading age by six months. On the other two days the boys would have normal classes with the girls.

His plan was based on his own experience of being a learner and from talking to educational experts. He had three main principles:
First, that it was essential to make the work feel like play. "If I can do that, the boys will learn," said Gareth.
The second principle was competition. Gareth says, "Boys absolutely love competition! It has gone out of fashion in many schools, but I think it's really important. Boys have to learn to lose and to fail and to come back from that. If you've never done that until you go for your first job interview and don't get the job, then you've got a problem."
The third thing Gareth thought was important was to allow boys to take risks. All kinds of risks. Not just physical risks like climbing trees, but doing things like acting in front of other people. Doing things that are a little scary, but that are very motivating if you manage to do them.

Extra support

- Play the audio in sections, pausing after each principle is explained and playing again if necessary. Elicit the answers from the whole class.

c (4 9)) Sts now listen to **Part 2** of the radio program and complete the chart.

Play the audio once all the way through.

Get Sts to compare with a partner and then play the audio again if necessary.

Check answers.

> 1 The boys spent a lot of time outside and did physical education every day before regular classes began.
> 2 Gareth tried to involve the boys' parents as much as possible in their education.
>
> 1 A **school debating** competition
> 2 A **reading** "World Cup"
> 3 A **play**

(4 9))
(script in Student Book on *page 127*)

Part 2
When Gareth started, he made some changes to the way the children were learning. The boys spent a lot of time outside, and they had PE (physical education) every day before regular classes began. They even made their own outdoor classroom. Gareth also tried to involve the boys' parents as much as possible in their education, and he visited them at their homes on several occasions.
Gareth set up three major activities for the boys to help improve their language skills. The first activity was a school debating competition against the girls. The topic that the children had to debate was "Computer games should be banned."
When they started to prepare for the debate, the boys weren't very enthusiastic, but soon they started to get more involved. In the end the girls won the debate, but the boys had learned to argue and make points to express themselves better. They were disappointed not to have won, but they wanted to do it again.
Next Gareth organized a Reading "World Cup", where the boys had to read in teams. Some of the boys couldn't read very well, but they all got very excited about the World Cup, and became much more enthusiastic readers! There was a prize for the winners, and this really motivated the boys.
Finally, the boys, working with the girls had to write their own play and perform it at the local theater. The play they wrote was about Romans and aliens. All the children, boys and girls, worked really hard and although some of them felt very nervous before they performed the play, it was a great success and the boys especially were thrilled. Gareth said afterwards, "It was a risk, and it was scary – but it was good scary."

d Tell Sts to listen again and find out how successful each activity was.

Play the audio once all the way through.

Get Sts to compare with a partner and then check answers.

> The school debating competition: the boys lost, but they wanted to do it again.
> The reading "World Cup": this really motivated the boys.
> The play: it was a great success.

e (4 10))) Tell Sts they are now going to hear how well Gareth did in the experiment. Ask, with a show of hands, if Sts think the boys' reading improved.

Play the audio once all the way through.

Get Sts to compare with a partner, and then check the answer.

> All of the boys' reading had improved by six months and some of them had advanced the equivalent of two years.

(4 10)))

(script in Student Book on *page 128*)

Part 3

The boys had a great time with Gareth as their teacher. But at the end of the eight weeks, had their reading really improved? In the last week of the quarter, they had to take their national reading exams. The exams were independently marked, and when the results were announced the boys had made great progress – all of them had improved by six months and some of them had advanced the equivalent of two years in just eight weeks!

Extra support

• If there's time, you could play the audio again while Sts read the scripts on *pages 127–128*, so they can see what they understood / didn't understand. Translate / explain any new words or phrases.

f Do these as open-class questions.

4 SPEAKING

a Put Sts in small groups (three or four). Go through the instructions and the discussion topics in the list, making sure Sts understand them.

Give Sts time in their groups to each choose a different topic from the list.

Focus on the **Debating a topic: organizing your ideas** box and go through it with Sts.

Then give them time (e.g., five minutes) to think of at least three reasons why they agree or disagree with the sentence they have chosen and to prepare what they are going to say. Help Sts with any vocabulary they may need.

b Sts in each group now take turns saying whether they agree or disagree with the sentence they have chosen in **a** and why. The other Sts should listen and at the end say if they agree or disagree with the student who introduced the topic, and why. Finally, each group votes on whether they agree or disagree.

Get feedback to find out who argued which topic in each group and if they managed to convince the others in their group. If there's time, you could have a brief open-class discussion on each topic.

5 GRAMMAR first conditional and future time clauses + *when, until,* etc.

a Focus on the questions and make sure Sts understand them. Then get Sts, in pairs, to answer the questions.

Get some feedback from the class and tell them how you feel or felt about exams.

b (4 11))) (4 12))) Tell Sts they are going to listen to two interviews with people who have just taken important exams. Highlight that in the interviews the speakers use several examples of time clauses with *if, when, as soon as,* etc.

First, focus on the **Exams** box and go through it with Sts.

Now tell Sts that they are going to listen to Olivia first. Focus on the questions and play audio 4.11 once all the way through for Sts to listen.

Play the audio again for Sts to answer questions 1–5 about Olivia, pausing if necessary after each answer is given.

Get them to compare with a partner and then play the audio again if necessary.

Check answers.

Extra support

• Before playing the audio, go through the listening script and decide if you need to preteach / check any lexis to help Sts when they listen.

Olivia

1 She is sure she has passed, but she is worried about her scores.
2 She gets her scores next week online.
3 She doesn't want to plan any celebrations until she gets the results.
4 She wants to study medicine at the University of California.
5 She will apply to some schools that don't require such high scores.

(4 11)))

J = journalist, O = Olivia

J What test did you take?
O I just took the main parts of the SAT–the Scholastic Aptitude Test–um, the critical reading, math, and writing parts.
J Do you think you did well?
O I'm pretty sure I did OK, but I'm worried about what scores I'll get.
J Why?
O Because I want to be a doctor, and I want to get into a pre-med program at one of the big universities, like maybe the University of California. They probably won't admit me unless I get a 2100 or higher.
J Do you think you'll get them?
O I don't know. I think I did OK, but I'm a little worried about math.
J When will you get your results?
O They'll go online next week. Believe me, as soon as they're online, I'll look up my scores.
J And how will you celebrate if you get high scores?
O I don't want to plan any celebrations until I get the results.
J What will you do if you don't get the scores you need?
O I don't want to think about it. If I don't get into a good college, my parents will kill me. No, I'm joking. I suppose I could apply to some schools that don't require such high scores.
J Well, good luck!
O Thanks.

Extra challenge

* You could ask Sts a few more questions, e.g., *Which test did Olivia take?* (the SAT–the Scholastic Aptitude Test–the critical reading, math, and writing parts.), *What scores does Olivia need to get?*, etc.

(4 12))) Now repeat the process for Woo-sung with audio 4.12.

> **Woo-sung**
> 1 He thinks he has passed and is optimistic.
> 2 In the mail in about six to seven weeks.
> 3 He will go out for dinner with his girlfriend.
> 4 He wants to work as an air traffic controller.
> 5 He will take the test again in June.

> **(4 12)))**
>
> **J = journalist, WS = Woo-sung**
>
> J   What exam did you take?
> WS The TOEFL. That's the Test of English as a Foreign Language.
> J   Was it difficult?
> WS Well, not really, but I need at least 550 to get into a college. One of the schools I've applied to requires 640!
> J   Do you think you'll get it?
> WS I think so. I'm optimistic. I think I did pretty well.
> J   When will you get the results?
> WS When they score the tests, they'll mail the results. It takes about six or seven weeks!
> J   How will you celebrate if you get a high score?
> WS I'll go out for dinner with my girlfriend.
> J   And what will you do if you don't get a high enough score? Will you continue studying English?
> WS Yes, of course, I need it. I'll continue studying, and I'll take the test again in June.
> J   Good luck.

Extra challenge

* You could ask Sts a few more questions, e.g., *What test did Woo-sung take?* (The TOEFL - the Test of English as a Foreign Language), *What score does Woo-sung need?* (at least a 550), etc.

c **(4 13)))** Focus on the five sentences from the interviews and elicit who said them (Olivia said sentences 1–4 and Woo-sung said sentence 5).

Then play the audio, pausing after each sentence for Sts to complete them.

Check answers.

Extra challenge

* Get Sts to try and complete the sentences before they listen.

> 1 I get a 2100
> 2 they are online
> 3 I get the results
> 4 my parents will kill me
> 5 they score the tests

> **(4 13)))**
> 1 They probably won't admit me unless I get a 2100.
> 2 As soon as they're online, I'll look up my scores.
> 3 I don't want to plan any celebrations until I get the results.
> 4 If I don't get into a good college, my parents will kill me.
> 5 When they score the tests, they'll mail the results.

Elicit / explain the meaning of *unless* (= if not) and *as soon as* (= the minute when).

Then ask Sts what forms the verbs are after the bold words (simple present) and if the verbs refer to the present or to the future (the future).

d **(4 14)))** Tell Sts they will now find out what scores Olivia and Woo-sung got. They must listen for the results and also find out what they are going to do.

Play the audio once all the way through.

Get Sts to compare with a partner and then check answers.

> Olivia got a 700 on critical reading and 620 on math. She is going to wait and see if one of the universities will accept her. If not, she'll try to find other schools that will take her. Woo-sung got a 650. He's going to celebrate by going to his favorite restaurant with his girlfriend.

> **(4 14)))**
>
> **J = journalist, O = Olivia, WS = Woo-sung**
>
> J   Olivia, I can see from your face that the results, uh, weren't exactly what you wanted – am I right?
> O   Yeah. I got a 700 on critical reading, but only 620 on math.
> J   So what are you going to do now?
> O   Well, my reading score was pretty good, so I'm going to wait and see if one of the universities I want will still accept me. If not, I'll try to find other schools that will take me.
> J   Were your parents angry?
> O   No, they've been really nice about it. They know how disappointed I am. Besides, it's not like my scores were really bad.
> ***
> J   Well Woo-sung, how did you do?
> WS I got a 650. I'm really really happy. It's even better than I expected.
> J   So have you booked the restaurant?
> WS Yes – well, my girlfriend has! We're going to my favorite place, and I'm really looking forward to it.

e **(4 15)))** **(4 16)))** Tell Sts to go to **Grammar Bank 7A** on *page 144*. Focus on the example sentences and play the audio for Sts to listen to the sentence rhythm. You could also get Sts to repeat the sentences to practice getting the rhythm right. Then go through the rules with the class.

> **Additional grammar notes**
>
> * Sts should be familiar with basic first conditional type sentences (*if* + present, future (*will*)) from their *American English File* 2 course. Here they also learn to use *unless* (instead of *if…not*) in conditional sentences and that other future time clauses (i.e., beginning with *when, as soon as, unless*, etc.) work in the same way as *if*-clauses, i.e., they are followed by a present tense although they actually refer to the future. This may be new for your Sts.
>
> * Emphasize that in the other (main) clause the verb form is usually *will* + infinitive, but it can also be an imperative or *going to*.
>
> * A typical mistake is: using a future form after *when, unless*, etc., e.g., *I'll call you when I'll arrive*.

Focus on the exercises and get Sts to do them individually or in pairs.

Check answers, getting Sts to read the full sentences.

a			
1	will get	6	don't know
2	won't grade	7	shouts
3	are / 're	8	will graduate
4	doesn't improve	9	won't go out
5	hurry	10	need

b			
1	until	6	as soon as
2	before	7	until
3	when	8	when
4	after	9	unless
5	unless	10	before

Tell Sts to go back to the main lesson **7A**.

Extra support

- If you think Sts need more practice, you may want to give them the Grammar photocopiable activity at this point or leave it for later as consolidation or review.

f Put Sts in pairs and focus on the questions. Tell Sts that they should make true sentences beginning with the phrases in the question, e.g., *As soon as I get home I'll…, If I don't pass my English exam, I'll…,* etc.

Give Sts a few minutes to think about their sentences. Then they should ask each other the questions and answer with full sentences.

Get some feedback.

g Put Sts in groups of three or four, calling each team **A** or **B**. An **A** team will work with a **B** team in this activity. Tell Sts to go to **Communication** *Three in a row* on *page 106*.

Go through the instructions. Tell teams **A** that they will mark the square with an **X** and teams **B** will mark the square with an **O**.

As they are playing, walk around monitoring and helping with any questions.

Find out which teams won and elicit some example sentences.

Tell Sts to go back to the main lesson **7A**.

6 READING & SPEAKING

a Focus on the article and photo, and on the title and subheading. Ask Sts how they would feel if their mother or father asked them if they wanted to practice for five hours or six.

Then ask them what kind of mother they think Amy Chua is and elicit ideas.

Now get Sts to read the article once to find out what a "tiger mother" is.

Get Sts to compare with a partner and then check the answer.

Extra support

- Before Sts read the article, check it for words and phrases which your Sts might not know and be ready to help with these while they are answering the questions or afterwards. You may even want to preteach / check a few words / phrases to lighten the load, e.g., *a hug, prestigious,* etc. (but not the highlighted ones).

A "tiger mother" is a very strict mother who makes her children study very hard and doesn't really allow them any free time. She wants her children to be the best in everything.

b Focus on the task. Set Sts a time limit to read the article again, e.g., five minutes, and to put phrases A–H in the correct places.

Get Sts to compare with a partner and then check answers.

2 E	3 G	4 H	5 B	6 D	7 F	8 A

c Focus on the highlighted words and phrases. Get Sts, in pairs, to work out their meaning. Tell them to read the whole sentence as the context will help them guess.

Check answers, either explaining in English, translating into Sts' L1, or getting Sts to check in their dictionaries.

Explain any other new vocabulary and encourage Sts to write down any useful new lexis from the text.

d Focus on the responses. You may want to explain that with online newspapers readers are encouraged to respond to articles and leave their opinions.

Put Sts in pairs and get them to read the responses and then say which, if any, they agree with. Alternatively, ask the whole class.

If Sts did this in pairs, get some feedback.

e Focus on the *make* **and** *let* box and go through it with Sts.

Then focus on the questions and put Sts in pairs or small groups to discuss them.

Get some feedback.

Extra idea

- If some of your Sts have children, ask them if they are as strict as Amy Chua.

G second conditional
V houses
P sentence stress

7B Ideal home

Lesson plan

The topic of this lesson is people's homes. In the first half of the lesson the grammar, the second conditional, is presented through a blog post where young people who are living with their parents say whether they would like to leave and live independently or not. This is followed by a pronunciation focus on sentence stress and rhythm, and oral practice of the second conditional. There is then a vocabulary focus on lexis related to houses and where people live.

In the second half of the lesson Sts read and listen to an audio guide about Tchaikovsky's house, and focus on some more house-related vocabulary. They then listen to some architecture students describing their ideal house and describe their own dream houses. The lesson ends with writing, where Sts write a description of their house or apartment for a house rental website, and with the song *If I Could Build My Whole World Around You*.

STUDY LINK
- **Workbook** 7B
- **iChecker**

Extra photocopiable activities

- **Grammar** first and second conditionals *page 157*
- **Communicative** If you had to choose… *page 187* (instructions *page 169*)
- **Vocabulary** Houses *page 211* (instructions *page 199*)
- **Song** *If I Could Build My Whole World Around You page 223* (instructions *page 216*)

Optional lead-in (books closed)

- Write the following on the board:

  PEOPLE BETWEEN 25 AND 34 WHO LIVE WITH THEIR PARENTS IN THE US:

  MEN   WOMEN
  _____ %   _____ %

- Ask Sts to guess what the statistics were for 2011. Elicit ideas, and then tell them that they were 19% of men and 10% of women (source http://www.census.gov/newsroom/releases/archives/families_households/).

- Then ask Sts if they think the statistics would be the same in their country. Elicit other places where young people live, e.g., in a shared apartment with friends, in a college dormitory, etc.

1 GRAMMAR second conditional

a Books open. Focus on the photos and the instructions, and put Sts in pairs. Encourage them to describe how they think the people are feeling as well as what they can see in the photos.

Get some feedback from the class.

b Focus on the title of the article and the task.

Now give Sts some time to read the article to find out how many of the people would like to leave home.

Check the answer.

> Three of them would like to leave home.

c Focus on the four questions and make sure Sts understand *a conflict* and *to decorate*.

Give Sts time to read the article again.

Check answers.

1	Carlos	3	Mauro
2	Andrea	4	Vivienne

Extra idea

- Depending on the age of your class, you could ask Sts how many of them live with their parents and whether they agree with any of the writers.

d Tell Sts to look at the highlighted phrases in the article. In pairs or individually, Sts answer questions 1–3.

Check answers.

> 1 the simple past
> 2 the conditional form (*would* + base form)
> 3 a: a situation they are imagining

e (4 17)) Tell Sts to go to **Grammar Bank 7B** on *page 145*. Focus on the example sentences and play the audio for Sts to listen to the sentence rhythm. You could also get Sts to repeat the sentences to practice getting the rhythm right. Then go through the rules with the class.

Additional grammar notes

- Sts who previously used *American English File* 2 or a course of a similar level will have already been introduced to second conditional sentences (*if* + past, conditional (*would* / *wouldn't* + base form)). Here they both review it and contrast it with the first conditional.

- What is also introduced here is the use of the conditional tense without *if* in sentences like *I would never buy a car as big as my brother's*. This use should not be too problematic as Sts may well have a conditional form of the verb in their L1, and they have also already met this use of the conditional in the phrase *I would like…*

Focus on the exercises and get Sts to do them individually or in pairs.

Check answers, getting Sts to read the full sentences. In exercise **b** ask Sts after each sentence if it is a first or second conditional.

---

a
1 Nick wouldn't have to commute every day if he worked from home.
2 If they didn't have such a noisy dog, they'd get along better with their neighbors.
3 I wouldn't buy that bike if I were you – it's too expensive.
4 We'd sell our house if somebody offered us enough money.
5 If my mother-in-law lived with us, we'd get divorced.
6 Would you share an apartment with me if I paid half the rent?
7 If my sister cleaned her room more often, it wouldn't be such a mess.
8 You wouldn't treat me like this if you really loved me.
9 If we painted the kitchen white, it would look bigger.
10 Would you think about camping if you couldn't afford to stay in a hotel?

b
1 would get up (2nd)
2 will ... live (1st)
3 will / 'll do (1st)
4 lose (1st)
5 didn't have (2nd)
6 sell (1st)
7 won't get (1st)
8 would ... be (2nd)
9 doesn't find (1st)
10 wouldn't stay up (2nd)

Tell Sts to go back to the main lesson **7B**.

Extra support

- If you think Sts need more practice, you may want to give them the Grammar photocopiable activity at this point or leave it for later as consolidation or review .

2 PRONUNCIATION & SPEAKING

sentence stress

Pronunciation notes

- Sts continue work on sentence stress and are given more practice in pronouncing the words in a sentence more strongly that convey important information (e.g., nouns, verbs, adjectives, and adverbs).

- Other, shorter words (e.g., articles and pronouns) should be pronounced less strongly. Getting this balance right will help Sts pronounce English with the correct rhythm.

See **Pronunciation Notes** in **Lesson 2B** on *page 36*.

a (4 18)) Tell Sts they are going to work on sentence stress. Play the audio once all the way through for Sts just to listen.

(4 18))
See sentences in Student Book on *page 69*

Now play the audio again, pausing after each sentence for Sts to listen and repeat.

Then repeat the activity eliciting responses from individual Sts.

Extra support

- In pairs, Sts practice saying the sentences.

b Put Sts in pairs, **A** and **B**, and tell Sts to go to **Communication** *Guess the sentence*, **A** on *page 107*, **B** on *page 111*.

Demonstrate the activity by writing in large letters on a piece of paper the following sentence:

IF I HAD A JOB, I'D RENT MY OWN APARTMENT.

Don't show the piece of paper to the Sts yet. Then write on the board:

IF I HAD A JOB, I _____ MY OWN APARTMENT. (+)

Tell Sts that they must guess the exact sentence that you have written on a piece of paper. Elicit ideas. If they are wrong, say *Try again*, until someone guesses the right answer. Then show them your piece of paper with the sentence on it and complete the sentence on the board with *'d rent*.

Tell Sts to look at instruction **a**. Give them a few minutes to complete their sentences in a logical way. Emphasize that their partner has the same sentences already completed and the aim is to try and complete the sentences in the same way. Monitor and help while they are doing this. Emphasize that Sts should write their ideas next to the sentence and tell Sts not to show their sentences to their partner.

Now tell Sts to look at instruction **b**. Tell **A** to read out his / her first sentence for **B** to tell him / her if he / she has guessed the sentence correctly. If not, he / she has to guess again. If the sentence is correct, he / she writes the missing words in the blank.

When they finish, Sts **B** read their sentences to Sts **A**, etc.

Extra support

- You could write any useful words and phrases from **Communication** on the board for Sts to copy.

Tell Sts to go back to the main lesson **7B**.

c Focus on the task and give Sts time to choose their three sentences and complete them. Go around making sure that Sts are writing correct sentences.

d Focus on the speech bubbles. Put Sts in pairs, **A** and **B**. **A** tells **B** his / her first sentence. **B** should ask for more information. Then **B** says his / her first sentence, etc.

Monitor and encourage them to get the right sentence rhythm.

Get some feedback from the class. Find out if any Sts had the same endings as their partner.

3 VOCABULARY houses

a Put Sts in pairs and get them to write down five things / pieces of furniture, etc. for each room.

Elicit answers and write them on the board in columns.

b Tell Sts to go to **Vocabulary Bank** *Houses* on *page 162*.

Focus on **1 Where people live** and get Sts to do **a** individually or in pairs. Make sure they write in the **Preposition** column and not in the sentences.

4 19)) Now do **b**. Play the audio for Sts to check answers. Practice any words your Sts find difficult to pronounce, modeling and drilling as necessary.

---

4 19))

Houses

Where people live

1 I live **in** the country, surrounded by fields.
2 I live **on** the outskirts of Boston, about 5 miles from the center of the city.
3 I live **in** a village.
4 I live in Del Mar, a small town **on** the West Coast.
5 I live **on** the second floor of a large apartment building.
6 I live **in** Littleton, a suburb of Denver about 11 miles from the center of the city.

Focus on the *suburbs* or *outskirts?* box and go through it with Sts.

Do **c** and tell Sts to cover the **Preposition** column. Can they remember sentences 1–6 with the prepositions?

Sts do **d** in pairs.

Now focus on **2 Parts of a house or an apartment building** and get Sts to do **a** individually or in pairs.

4 20)) Now do **b**. Play the audio for Sts to check answers. Play the audio again, pausing for Sts to repeat. Practice any words your Sts find difficult to pronounce, modeling and drilling as necessary. You could use the audio to do this.

---

4 20))

Parts of a house or an apartment building

An apartment building		A house	
2	balcony	1	chimney
5	basement	3	deck/patio
3	entrance	7	gate
4	first floor	2	roof
1	top floor	4	steps
		5	walkway
		6	wall

Finally, tell Sts to cover the words, look at the pictures, and see if they can remember the words.

Now focus on **3 Describing a house or an apartment** and get Sts to do **a** individually or in pairs.

4 21)) Now do **b**. Play the audio for Sts to check answers. Focus on the highlighted words and practice any words your Sts find difficult to pronounce, modeling and drilling as necessary.

---

4 21))

Describing a house or an apartment

2 I live in a cabin in the woods. It's old, and made of logs. The rooms have very low ceilings. There's a fireplace in the living room, and it's very cozy in the winter.

1 I live in a modern apartment in the city. It's spacious and very light, with wood floors and big windows.

Focus on the *chimney* or *fireplace?* and *roof* or *ceiling?* box and go through it with Sts.

Do **c** and tell Sts to cover the descriptions and look at the photos. They can test themselves or a partner by describing the rooms.

Tell Sts to go back to the main lesson **7B**.

Extra support

• If you think Sts need more practice, you may want to give them the Vocabulary photocopiable activity at this point or leave it for later as consolidation or review.

c Put Sts in pairs and get them to discuss the difference between the words.

Check answers.

---

1 the outskirts = the area around a town or city that is the farthest from the downtown
the suburbs = a residential area outside the center of a large city
2 a village = a very small town located in a country area
a town = a place where people live and work, which is larger than a village, but smaller than a city
3 a roof = the structure that covers the whole house
a ceiling = the top inside surface of a room
4 a balcony = a platform that is built on the upstairs outside wall of a building, with a wall or rail around it.
a deck = a wooden floor that is built outside the back of a house where you can sit and relax
5 a chimney = a structure through which smoke is carried up away from a fire, etc. and through the roof of a building
a fireplace = an open space for a fire in the wall of a room
6 the first floor = the floor of a building that is at the same level as the ground outside
the ground floor = in British English the ground floor = the first floor, and the first floor is one level above the ground level.
7 wood = noun; the hard material that the trunk and branches of a tree are made of; this material when it is used to build or make things with, or as a fuel
wooden = adjective; made of wood

---

4 READING

a Ask the question to the whole class and elicit answers. Be ready to answer the question yourself if Sts are slow to volunteer anything.

Tchaikovsky was from Russia and was a composer of classical music.

You might want to tell Sts that Pyotr Illyich Tchaikovsky was born in 1840 and died in 1893.

b Focus on the task and the photos. Elicit answers to the question, but do <u>not</u> tell Sts if they are right or not yet.

c **4 22))** Now tell Sts to listen and read at the same time to find out which photos show a–c.

Play the audio once all the way through.

Check answers. You could tell Sts that the music they heard at the beginning and end of the audio is Tchaikovsky's *Symphony No. 6* (the *Pathétique*).

Extra support

• Before playing the audio, go through the text and decide if you need to preteach / check any lexis to help Sts when they listen (but not the highlighted words.)

---

a = his writing desk / bedroom (photo 3)
b = the living room and study (photo 2)
c = the yard (photo 1)

---

4 22))

See text in Student Book on *page 71*.

---

d Now tell Sts to just read the guide again.

Then put Sts in pairs, **A** and **B**, and tell them to cover the text. **A** tells **B** why 1–3 are mentioned and **B** tells **A** why 4–6 are mentioned in connection with Tchaikovsky's house.

Check answers.

> 1 Maidanovo: the village where Tchaikovsky rented a small house after leaving Moscow; it was too full of tourists and visitors and this is why he later moved to the house in Klin.
> 2 The *Pathétique* symphony: he wrote it in the house in Klin.
> 3 Alexei: he was Tchaikovsky's servant and lived on the first floor of the house.
> 4 Lilies of the valley: Tchaikovsky's brother planted thousands of lilies in the yard after Tchaikovsky's death as Tchaikovsky adored flowers, particularly lilies of the valley.
> 5 Doroshenko: he was an anarchist who lived in Tchaikovsky's house after the Bolshevik Revolution. People say he shot at a painting in one of the bedrooms.
> 6 The International Tchaikovsky Competition: the winner goes to Klin, plays on Tchaikovsky's piano, and plants a tree in his yard.

e Focus on the highlighted words. Tell Sts to first try to figure out what they mean from the context and then to match them with definitions 1–8.

Check answers, and model and drill the pronunciation.

> | | | | |
> |---|---|---|---|
> | 1 | neat | 5 | turn into |
> | 2 | remain | 6 | plain |
> | 3 | overlooking | 7 | property |
> | 4 | hanging | 8 | bookcase |

Explain any other new vocabulary and encourage Sts to write down any useful new lexis from the text.

f In pairs, small groups, or as an open-class activity, Sts answer the questions.

Get some feedback.

5 LISTENING & SPEAKING

a (4 23)) Focus on the task and make sure Sts understand the four options.

Play the audio for Sts to match the four speakers with their "dream house" by writing numbers 1–4 in the appropriate box.

Check answers.

Extra support

- Before playing the audio, go through the listening script and decide if you need to preteach / check any lexis to help Sts when they listen.

> | | |
> |---|---|
> | 3 | the most hi-tech |
> | 4 | the most luxurious |
> | 1 | the most eco-friendly |
> | 2 | the most romantic |

> **(4 23))**
> (script in Student Book on *page 128*)
> **1**
> My dream house would be in one of our national parks like Yellowstone or Redwood. It would be totally green – I'd have solar panels and wind turbines, and I'd collect rainwater. The house would be made of wood and would be heated by wood fires. I would try to live off the land as much as possible and I'd plant vegetables and fruit, and maybe have chickens. It would all be organic, with no pesticides or anything like that.
> **2**
> My dream house would be in Paris. It'd be on the top floor of an old apartment building and I'd have a view of the Eiffel Tower or Notre Dame. It would be full of furniture that I'd found in antique shops-places like that, and amazing paintings, one of which would turn out to be an undiscovered Picasso or Matisse. There would be a beautiful old dining table and chairs for candlelit dinners... then all I'd need would be the right person to share it with.
> **3**
> My dream house would be an apartment in SoHo in New York City. It wouldn't be too big, it'd just have a couple of bedrooms, and a huge living room with a home theater. It would be very modern and incredibly practical, with things like automatic temperature control, a kitchen with all the latest gadgets – and if possible, a stove that would produce amazing meals on its own – I'm a lazy kind of guy.
> **4**
> If I had to choose where to live, I'd choose Hawaii. So, my dream house would be made of glass with the most amazing view of the beach from every room in the house, and it'd have indoor and outdoor pools, and maybe a tennis court – I'm really into sports. It would also have a big indoor aquarium. There's something so peaceful about looking at fish. And fabulous bathrooms of course.

b Now Sts listen for more detail. Make sure the two categories are clear.

Play the audio again, pausing after each speaker to give Sts time to write down the information.

Check answers.

> **Speaker 1**
> **Location:** in a national park like Yellowstone or Redwood
> **Special features:** solar panels, wind turbines, rainwater collected. House made of wood and heated by wood fires. Land with vegetables and fruits, chickens – all organic.
>
> **Speaker 2**
> **Location:** Paris
> **Special features:** the top floor of an old apartment building with a view of the Eiffel Tower or Notre Dame in Paris. Full of furniture from antique shops and amazing paintings. A beautiful old dining table and chairs.
>
> **Speaker 3**
> **Location:** SoHo in New York City
> **Special features:** not too big an apartment – a couple of bedrooms, and a very big living room with a home theater. Very modern and incredibly practical, with e.g., automatic temperature control, a kitchen with all the latest gadgets.
>
> **Speaker 4**
> **Location:** Hawaii
> **Special features:** made of glass with amazing view of the beach from every room, indoor and outdoor pools, a tennis court, a big indoor aquarium, fabulous bathrooms

Extra support

- If there's time, you could play the audio again while Sts read the script on *page 128*, so they can see what they understood / didn't understand. Translate / explain any new words or phrases.

c (4 24)) Tell Sts they are going to hear four sentences and they must decide why the speakers use *would* in each one.

Play the audio once all the way through.

Get Sts to compare with a partner and then play the audio again.

Check answers.

> The speakers use *would* + infinitive because they are talking about something hypothetical / imaginary, i.e., their dream houses.

> (4 24))
> 1 It would be totally green.
> 2 There would be a beautiful old dining table.
> 3 It wouldn't be too big.
> 4 It'd have indoor and outdoor pools.

d Focus on the speaking task and give Sts a few minutes to think about what they are going to say. Go around the class, helping Sts with any vocabulary they might need which isn't in **Vocabulary Bank** *Houses* on *page 162*.

e Put Sts into small groups of three to five. They take turns describing their dream house in as much detail as possible. They must also say which of the other houses they like best.

When the activity has finished, you could get feedback from each group to find out which house was the most popular.

6 WRITING describing a house or apartment

Tell Sts to go to **Writing** *Describing a house or apartment* on *page 118*.

a Focus on the instructions. Tell Sts to read the two posts and decide which one they would choose for a two-week vacation. You might want to elicit / teach what a *villa* is (a house in the country, usually with a large garden/yard).

In pairs, Sts tell each other which one they have chosen and why.

Get some feedback from various pairs. You could have a vote for each place to see if there is a favorite.

b Focus on the instructions and make sure the task is clear.

Give Sts time to read about the apartment in Mexico City.

Check answers, making sure Sts can remember what the adjectives mean.

> quiet, cozy, spacious, modern, well-equipped, beautiful, flower-filled, big, large, lively, non-smoking

c Sts now read about the Thai beach villa and improve the ad with the adjectives in the list.

Get Sts to compare with a partner and then check answers.

Possible answers
Our house is **spacious**.
It has … a **beautiful** / **luxurious** / **superb** kitchen
There is a **beautiful** / **spacious** patio
There are **amazing** / **breathtaking** / **magnificent** / **superb** views
There is a **superb** / **pretty** / **beautiful** yard / garden
The house is near a / an **amazing** / **magnificent** / **superb** beach

d Focus on the **Useful language: describing location** box and go through it with Sts.

Now tell Sts they are going to write a description of their house or apartment for the website. If Sts don't want to write about their own house or apartment, they can invent a description.

Focus on the plan and go through it with Sts.

Sts should write four paragraphs as in the model, and use the **Useful language** box and **Vocabulary Bank** *Houses* to help them.

You may choose to get Sts to do the writing in class or you could assign it as homework. If you do it in class, set a time limit for Sts to write their description, e.g., 15–20 minutes.

e Sts should check their work for mistakes before turning it in.

Tell Sts to go back to the main lesson **7 B**.

7 (4 25)) **SONG** *If I Could Build My Whole World Around You*

This song was originally made famous by American singers Marvin Gaye and Tammi Terrell in 1967. For copyright reasons this is a cover version. If you want to do this song in class, use the photocopiable activity on *page 223*.

> (4 25))
>
> ***If I Could Build My Whole World Around You***
>
> Oh, if I could build my whole world around you, darling
> First I'd put heaven by your side
> Pretty flowers would grow wherever you walked, honey
> And over your head would be the bluest sky
> And I'd take every drop of rain
> And wash all your troubles away
> I'd have the whole world wrapped up in you, darling
> And that would be all right, oh yes, it would
>
> If I could build my whole world around you
> I'd make your eyes the morning sun
> I'd put so much love where there is sorrow
> I'd put joy where there's never been love
> And I'd give my love to you
> For you to keep for the rest of your life
> Oh, and happiness would surely be ours
> And that would be all right, oh yes, it would
>
> Doo doo doo doo doo, doo doo doo doo
> Doo doo doo doo doo, doo doo doo doo
>
> Oh, if I could build my whole world around you
> I'd give you the greatest gift any woman could possess
> And I'd step into this world you've created
> And give you true love and tenderness
> And there'd be something new with every tomorrow
> To make this world better as days go by
>
> If I could build my whole world around you
> If I could build my whole world around you
> And that would be all right, oh, yeah
> *(repeat to fade)*

PRACTICAL ENGLISH
Episode 4 Boys' night out

Lesson plan

In the fourth episode the main functional focus is on expressions for making and responding to suggestions.

In the first scene, Rob and Paul are playing pool and reminiscing about old times. Paul thinks that Rob has changed a lot and is becoming very "American," which he believes is due to Jenny. In the next scene, Jenny joins them for a meal, and they then decide what they are going to do. They can't agree and in the end Paul and Rob decide to go to a concert Kerri (from Episode 2) is doing, and Jenny, pretty upset, calls Monica and goes to see her. The last scene takes places in the office. Jenny is at work and ready for a meeting with Don, but Rob calls to say that he doesn't feel well and isn't going to make it.

STUDY LINK
• **Workbook** Boys' night out

Testing Program CD-ROM
• **Quick Test 7**
• **File 7 Test**

Optional lead-in (books closed)

• Before starting Episode 4, elicit what Sts can remember about Episode 3, e.g., ask them *Who is Monica? What is her big news? Whose friend is Paul? What do Rob and Paul do at the end of the episode?*, etc.

• Alternatively, you could play the last scene of Episode 3.

1 ▶ ROB AND PAUL CATCH UP

a (4 26)) Books open. Tell Sts that this is the following day to the previous episode, after work. Focus on the photos and elicit what Sts think is happening. Elicit / teach *pool* (the game they are playing).

Now either tell Sts to close their books and write the question on the board, or get Sts to focus on the question and cover the rest of the page.

Play the DVD or audio once all the way through and then check the answer.

> He clearly doesn't like her and implies that she is bossy / controlling.

(4 26))
(script in Student Book on *page 128*)

P = Paul, R = Rob

P Bad luck, mate.
R Nice shot.
P I've had years of practice.
R You used to play pool a lot at university.
P You did, too.
R Yeah. I don't really have the time anymore.
P Or anybody to play with?... So what <u>do</u> you do in your free time?
R The magazine keeps me pretty busy. And when I'm free, I'm usually with Jenny...
P Tch. Your turn. Don't blow it.
R What is it?
P I was just thinking about you.
R What about me?
P Do you remember the great times we had at uni? You had such crazy hair – the last time I saw you it was blond!
R Don't remind me.
P Those were the days. But look at you now with your girlfriend and your nine-to-five job. If you don't come back to London soon, you'll become an all-American boy!
R Come off it.
P It's true! I mean, just look at that shirt.
R What's wrong with my shirt?
P You look like a businessman! Did you buy it?
R Me? No. It was... it was a present from Jenny.
P I thought so.
R What does that mean?
P Well, it's Jenny's taste.
R Yes, and I really like it.
P Jenny seems to know what she wants – and she probably gets it.
R That's one of the things I like about her... Terrible.
P You said it.
R Sorry, Paul. We've got to go.
P Oh come on, Rob. We haven't even finished the game.
R Another time. Jenny's waiting for us.
P Jenny. Right.

b Focus on sentences 1–6. Go through them with Sts and make sure they understand them.

Now play the DVD or audio again all the way through and get Sts to mark the sentences T (true) or F (false). Remind them to correct the false ones.

Get Sts to compare with a partner and then check answers.

> 1 T
> 2 F (He **doesn't** have time. / His job keeps him busy.)
> 3 T
> 4 T
> 5 F (**Jenny** gave Rob the shirt he's wearing.)
> 6 T

Extra support

• If there's time, you could get Sts to listen again with the script on *page 128*, so they can see exactly what they understood / didn't understand. Translate / explain any new words or phrases.

2 ▶ VIDEO MAKING SUGGESTIONS

a (4 27)» Focus on the photos and elicit what Sts think is happening.

Now either tell Sts to close their books and write the questions on the board, or get Sts to focus on the three questions and cover the rest of the page.

Before playing the DVD or audio, elicit / teach *a gig* (= a performance by musicians playing popular music or jazz in front of an audience).

Play the DVD or audio once all the way through and then check answers.

> Paul and Rob decide to go and see Kerri playing in a gig. Jenny says she has a busy day the next day. She ends up going to Monica's house.

(4 27)»

(script in Student Book on *page 128*)
P = Paul, R = Rob, J = Jenny, M = Monica

P Oh, yeah. That was good. So! What shall we do now?
R What do you want to do?
P Well... I haven't been on a dance floor for weeks now. I've got to move my body. Let's go dancing!
J I'm going running in the morning. Why don't you join me?
P No, thanks. I'm not very keen on running. But I've read about this place called Deep Space, where they play great music. We could go there.
J A club?
P Don't you feel like dancing?
J Not on a Wednesday night. How about going to the late show at MOMA?
P MOMA? What's that?
J MOMA. It's the Museum of Modern Art. There's a Kandinsky exhibition.
P That isn't exactly my idea of a great night out.
J What about staying in and watching a movie on TV?
P I'm in New York. I can watch TV anywhere.
J Who's that?
R It's a text from Kerri. She's doing a gig at the Bowery Ballroom.
P Kerri who?
R Kerri Johnson. I interviewed her last week.
P Kerri Johnson? I've seen her play live. She's cool. Do you like her, Jenny?
J I have to admit I'm not crazy about her music... or her for that matter.
P I didn't think so. So shall <u>we</u> go there?
R Why not? Actually Kerri's staying very near here and she doesn't know New York very well. We could meet her outside and go together.
P That's a great idea!
R I'll send her a text.
J I think I might have an early night. You two can go on your own.
R Are you sure you don't mind?
P Of course she doesn't mind!
J No, Rob, it's fine. I have another busy day tomorrow. You do too, actually.
R I know, we're meeting Don. I haven't forgotten... Oh, it's Kerri. She's on her way now.
P What are we waiting for? Let's go!
***
M Hello?
J Hi, Monica – it's not too late to call is it?
M Jenny! No, why? Are you OK?
J I need to talk.
M Can you come over? Why don't you take a cab?
J OK, thanks.

---

b Give Sts a minute to read questions 1–7 and to think who might have made each suggestion.

Now play the DVD or audio again and get Sts to write the correct initial.

Get Sts to compare with a partner and then check answers.

1 P	2 J	3 P	4 J	5 J	6 R	7 R

Extra support

- If there's time, you could get Sts to listen again with the script on *page 128*, so they can see exactly what they understood / didn't understand. Translate / explain any new words or phrases.

c (4 28)» Give Sts a minute to read through the extracts from the conversation and to think about what the missing words might be.

Now play the DVD or audio again and get Sts to fill in the blanks.

Get Sts to compare with a partner and then check answers.

See words in **bold** in script 4.28

(4 28)»

1
P What shall we **do** now?
R What do you want to do?
P Well... I haven't been on a dance floor for weeks now. I've got to move my body. **Let's** go dancing!
2
J I'm going running in the morning. Why **don't** you join me?
P No, thanks. I'm not very **keen** on running. But I've read about this place called Deep Space, where they play great music. We **could** go there.
3
J **How** about going to the late show at MOMA?
P MOMA? What's that?
4
J **What** about staying in and watching a movie on TV?
P I'm in New York. I can watch TV anywhere.
5
P I didn't think so. So **shall** we go there?
R **Why** not?
6
R We **could** meet her outside and go together.
P That's a great **idea**!

---

d Focus on the **Verb forms** box and go through it with the class.

Now focus on the instructions and make sure Sts understand the word *emphatic*.

Get Sts to compare with a partner and then check the answer.

> Let's go dancing.

e (4 29)» Tell Sts to focus on the highlighted phrases in the extracts. They should listen and repeat the phrases, copying the rhythm and intonation.

Play the DVD or audio, pausing for Sts to listen and repeat.

(4 29)»

See highlighted phrases in Student Book on *page 73*

Then repeat the activity, eliciting responses from individual Sts.

f Put Sts in pairs and tell them to practice the dialogues in **c**.

Monitor and help, encouraging Sts to pay attention to rhythm and intonation.

Make sure Sts change roles.

g Put Sts in small groups and tell them to organize their end-of-semester class party using the expressions for making suggestions.

Monitor and help.

Get some feedback from various groups.

3 ◼ THE MORNING AFTER THE NIGHT BEFORE

a (4 30)) Focus on the photos and ask Sts some questions, e.g., *Where are Rob and Jenny? What's happening?*, etc.

Now either tell Sts to close their books and write the question on the board, or get Sts to focus on the question and cover the rest of the page.

Play the DVD or audio once all the way through and then check the answer.

> Rob and Jenny have a meeting with Don, but Rob hasn't come in to work because he isn't feeling well.

> **(4 30))**
> (script in Student Book on *page 128*)
> **J = Jenny, R = Rob, D = Don**
>
> **J** Rob?
> **R** Hi, Jenny.
> **J** Are you OK? Where are you anyway?
> **R** I'm at home. I'm feeling terrible. We got back really late last night.
> **J** Now why doesn't that surprise me? You know, you're not a student anymore.
> **J** I know. There was a party after the gig – Kerri invited us and of course Paul said yes.
> **J** And this morning's meeting? In... ten minutes?
> **R** That's why I'm calling. I'm not going to make it. I'm really sorry.
> **J** Rob! It's a very important meeting! I'll cover for you this time, but I won't be able to do it again.
> **R** It *won't* happen again. I promise. Anyway, Paul's leaving.
> **J** He's leaving?
> **R** That's right. He's off to Boston this afternoon.
> **J** Maybe that's a good thing. I mean, it's not that I don't like Paul, but...
> **R** I know, I know....
> **J** I have to go. Talk to you later.
> **D** Jenny, have you seen Rob? I wanted to have a word with him before the meeting and he isn't even here.
> **J** I know. He just called to say he can't make it.
> **D** He what?
> **J** I was with him last night. He wasn't feeling very well. But it's OK, he told me everything I need to know for the meeting.
> **D** Oh. OK then.
> **J** You know Rob. He's such a professional.

b Focus on the instructions and give Sts time to read sentences 1–7. Make sure Sts realize they must use between one and three words only to complete each sentence.

Play the DVD or audio again, pausing if necessary to give Sts time to complete the sentences.

Get Sts to compare with a partner and then check answers.

1	terrible	5	it won't happen
2	a party	6	is leaving
3	the meeting	7	a professional
4	important meeting		

Extra support

- If there's time, you could get Sts to listen again with the script on *page 128*, so they can see exactly what they understood / didn't understand. Translate / explain any new words or phrases.

c Focus on the **Social English phrases**. In pairs, get Sts to think about what the missing words might be.

Extra challenge

- In pairs, get Sts to complete the phrases before they listen.

d (4 31)) Play the DVD or audio for Sts to listen and complete the phrases.

Check answers.

> See words in **bold** in script 4.31

> **(4 31))**
> **Jenny** Where are you **anyway**?
> **Rob** That's **why** I'm calling. I'm not going to make it.
> **Rob** It won't **happen** again.
> **Rob** He's **off** to Boston this afternoon.
> **Jenny** I mean, **it's** not that I don't like Paul, but...
> **Don** I wanted to have a **word** with him before the meeting.
> **Jenny** He's **such** a professional.

If you know your Sts' L1, you could get them to translate the phrases. If not, get Sts to look at the phrases again in context in the script on *page 128*.

e Now play the DVD or audio again, pausing after each phrase for Sts to listen and repeat.

Finally, focus on the **Can you...?** questions and ask Sts if they feel confident they can now do these things.

G reported speech: sentences and questions
V shopping, making nouns from verbs
P the letters *ai*

8A Sell and tell

Lesson plan

Shopping and complaining are the main themes for this lesson, which reviews and extends Sts' knowledge of reported speech.

The context for the presentation of reported speech at the beginning of the lesson is a website (*Never Liked it Anyway*) where people can sell things they no longer want, e.g., presents, after the breakup of a relationship. Sts then learn vocabulary related to shopping, which they put into practice in a questionnaire.

In the second half of the lesson, Sts read about "The King of Complainers," a man who has written more than 5,000 letters of complaint and who gives readers some advice on how to complain successfully. This is followed by a section on the different pronunciations of the letters *ai*. The Vocabulary then focuses on how to make nouns from verbs. In Listening and Speaking Sts listen to some people who have complained about bad service and then talk about their own experiences. Finally, in Writing Sts are shown how to write a letter of complaint.

STUDY LINK
• **Workbook** 8A

Extra photocopiable activities

• **Grammar** reported speech: sentences and questions *page 158*
• **Communicative** Ask and tell *page 188* (instructions *page 169*)

Optional lead-in (books closed)

• Write on the board:

WHO LIKES …?

   SHOPPING FOR CLOTHES

   SHOPPING FOR GADGETS

   SHOPPING FOR FOOD

• With a show of hands write down how many people in the class like each activity.

• Now write:

WHAT DO YOU PREFER…?

   SHOPPING IN STORES

   SHOPPING ONLINE

• And get another show of hands. Elicit some reasons why.

1 GRAMMAR

reported speech: sentences and questions

a Books open. Focus on the instructions and the image. Elicit ideas, but do <u>not</u> tell Sts if they are right yet.

b (4 32)) Tell Sts they are going to listen to part of a radio program about the website in **a**. The first time they listen they should just find the answer to **a**.

Play the audio once all the way through for Sts to listen.

Check the answer.

Extra support

• Before playing the audio, go through the listening script and decide if you need to preteach / check any lexis to help Sts when they listen.

> You can sell presents which you were given by an ex-partner and you no longer want. You can buy unwanted presents which other people are selling.

(4 32))
(script in Student Book on *page 128*)
H = host, J = Janice

H We're talking about great new shopping websites, and I think we have time for one more. Janice, can you tell us about it?

J Well, it's called "neverlikeditanyway.com." It's a very creative name for a website as you'll hear. This site was the idea of an American woman named Annabel Acton. She was living in New York City with her boyfriend, who was English. He had invited her to travel to London with him at Christmas to meet his family. But five days before Christmas, they broke up. Now, unlike some of us, Annabel didn't want to sit around crying and eating ice cream. She wanted to do something positive.

H So what gave her the idea for the website?

J Well, after the breakup, Annabel was left with a plane ticket to London that she didn't need. She also had jewelry that she didn't want anymore, and she had tickets to a concert that she didn't want to go to without her boyfriend. She also had paintings that they had bought together, that she didn't want on her wall anymore. She didn't want any of these things <u>herself</u>, but she thought someone somewhere would probably like to buy them, and that's what gave her the idea to set up the website.

H What exactly is it?

J Well, it's a website where people who have just broken up with a partner can sell presents and other things that they don't want anymore, maybe because they remind them of their ex; or maybe, as the name suggests because they never liked these things anyway! And the idea, which I think is genius, is that they also tell the personal story behind the thing they're selling. Annabel calls it "sell and tell"!

H What kinds of things do people sell on the website?

J Oh, everything – from something as small as a teddy bear to really expensive things like an engagement ring or a vacation. To give you an idea, today on the site one seller is offering a three-day honeymoon package at a luxury hotel in New York City and a woman is selling her ex-boyfriend's car. And they're selling all these things at very good prices. So on "neverlikeditanyway" you can get a bargain, and also help someone who is going through a breakup.

H Thanks, Janice, and that's all we have time for today…

Extra support

• If there's time, you could play the audio again while Sts read the script on *page 128*, so they can see what they understood / didn't understand. Translate / explain any new words or phrases.

c Tell Sts to read questions 1–3 and then to listen to the audio again.

Play the audio all the way through.

Play again if necessary and then check answers.

> 1 She set the website up because she had broken up with her boyfriend and she had a plane ticket she didn't need, and jewelry, concert tickets, and paintings she didn't want anymore, but she thought someone somewhere would probably like them.
> 2 Everything from something as small as a teddy bear to really expensive things like an engagement ring or a vacation.
> 3 They also tell the personal story behind the things they are selling.

d Tell Sts to look at the three objects being sold on the website and to read each story.

When Sts are ready, put them in pairs and get them to discuss the three questions.

Get some feedback from the class.

e Tell Sts to focus on the four sentences from the website and to decide, in pairs, what the people actually said. Look at the example together.

Check answers. Sts may say *Who has given it to you?* for question 4, but that is not right as she is asking about a specific moment in the past.

> 2 "I'll come and pick it up."
> 3 "Is it new?"
> 4 "Who gave it to you?"

f (4 33)⟫ (4 34)⟫ Tell Sts to go to **Grammar Bank 8A** on *page 146*. Focus on the example sentences and play the audio for Sts to listen to the sentence rhythm. You could also get Sts to repeat the sentences to practice getting the rhythm right. Then go through the rules with the class.

Additional grammar notes

Reported sentences

- This is a structure which may be new for some Sts and not for others (it was introduced in *American English File* 2 in File 12). The basic principle of reported speech is quite straightforward – when you report what someone else said you move the tenses / forms "backwards," i.e., present to past, *will* to *would*, etc. Making the link between a "reporter" who reports (i.e., tells other people what someone has said) and "reported speech" may help Sts understand both the grammatical term and concept.

- Point out that *that* after *say* and *tell* is optional.

- You should point out that when direct speech is reported at a later time or in a different place from when it was originally said, some time / place words may change as well, e.g., *tomorrow* may change to *the next day*, *this* to *that*, etc.

- ! In conversation people often do not change the simple past to the past perfect.

- Some typical mistakes include:
  - confusing *tell* and *say*, e.g., ~~He said me that he was sick.~~
  - forgetting to change the tenses, e.g., ~~The waiter said he will call the manager.~~

Reported questions

- These will probably be new to most Sts. The most important things to emphasize are the change in word order and the use of *if* / *whether* in *yes* / *no* questions.

- Some typical mistakes include:
  - forgetting to change the word order in reported questions, e.g., ~~She asked him what was his name.~~
  - using *did* in reported questions in the past, e.g., ~~They asked me where I did live.~~

Focus on the exercises and get Sts to do them individually or in pairs.

Check answers, getting Sts to read the full sentences.

> a
> 1 (that) he was selling all his books
> 2 (that) she had booked the flights
> 3 (that) my new dress didn't suit me
> 4 (that) he might not be able to go to the party
> 5 (that) she wouldn't wear those shoes again
> 6 (that) she hadn't bought me a present
> 7 (that) she had to get a dress for the party
> 8 (that) he hadn't been to the gym for a long time
> 9 (that) she had found a bargain at the sale
> 10 (that) he couldn't find anywhere to park
>
> b
> 1 when I was leaving
> 2 if / whether he had ever been engaged
> 3 if / whether he would be home early
> 4 where I usually bought my clothes
> 5 if / whether he had worn a suit to the job interview
> 6 if / whether she ever went to the theater
> 7 what time we would arrive
> 8 how much money she had spent at the sale
> 9 if / whether he could help her
> 10 what size I was

Tell Sts to go back to the main lesson **8A**.

Extra support

- If you think Sts need more practice, you may want to give them the Grammar photocopiable activity at this point or leave it for later as consolidation or review.

g (4 35)⟫ Focus on the task. Tell Sts to listen to the four questions and to write them down.

Play the audio, pausing after each question to give Sts time to write them down.

Play the audio again, then check answers and write the questions on the board.

> (4 35)⟫
> Do you usually go shopping on the weekend?
> What kinds of things do you buy?
> Did you go shopping last Saturday?
> What's the next thing you're going to buy?

Now give Sts some time to write their answers to the questions.

h Focus on the example and make sure Sts understand the task.

Put Sts in pairs and get them to tell their partner about their survey.

Get one or two Sts to tell the class.

Extra support

• You could get Sts to do this as a written exercise after they have done it orally.

2 VOCABULARY & SPEAKING shopping

a Focus on the task and then give Sts time to talk in pairs.

Check answers. Alternatively, you could give Sts a minute or so to discuss them one by one and elicit answers before moving on to the next pair of words.

> 1 the same
> 2 A **drug store** and a **pharmacy** are the same thing.
> 3 An **outlet store** is a store selling the goods of a particular wholesaler or manufacturer more cheaply because it is usually the previous season's stock.
>   A **department store** is a large store divided into departments, which sell a lot of different things.
> 4 A **shopping center** is the same as a **shopping mall**, but **shopping center** is British English.
> 5 A **library** is a place where you can borrow (but not buy) books to read.
>   A **bookstore** is a shop where you can buy books.
> 6 *to put on a shirt* is to wear it.
>   *to try on a shirt* is to see if it fits / suits you before buying it.
> 7 *It fits you* means it is the right size for you.
>   *It suits you* means it looks good on you.
> 8 **for sale** is when something is in a store and there's a price on it.
>   **on sale** means that something is in a store and it's original price has been reduced.

b In pairs, Sts look at the words in the list and explain their meaning.

Check answers. Model and drill pronunciation.

> a bargain = a thing bought for less than the usual price
> a discount = an amount of money that is taken off the usual cost of something
> a price tag = a label on something that shows how much you must pay
> a receipt = a piece of paper that shows that goods or services have been paid for
> a refund = a sum of money that is paid back to you because you returned goods to a store
> take something back = to return something that you bought to the store you bought it from (because it doesn't work or is the wrong size)

c Focus on the questionnaire and quickly go through the questions with the whole class.

Put Sts in new pairs. **A** (book open) asks **B** (book closed) the questions in the survey. When they change roles, tell **B** to ask the questions in a different order.

Monitor and help Sts with any more vocabulary they need.

When they have finished, get some feedback.

Extra idea

• Get the class to interview you first with some or all of the questions in the questionnaire.

3 READING

a Ask these questions to the whole class, making sure Sts know *to complain* and *service*. Elicit some opinions / experiences. Tell Sts what you usually do.

b Focus on the article on *page 76* and task. Then give Sts time to read it and answer the questions.

Elicit answers. They will vary depending on Sts' opinions.

Extra support

• Before Sts read the article, check it for words and phrases which your Sts might not know and be ready to help with these while they are answering the questions or afterwards.

c Focus on the task. Sts now read the article again and answer the questions.

Get Sts to compare with a partner, and then check answers.

> Clive thinks the best way to complain is to write a polite letter.
> 1 He got some free packages of cookies.
> 2 He got a Volkswagen Golf GTI (for his friend).
> 3 He got the cost of a vacation.
> 4 His daughters were invited to Heathrow Airport to inspect British Airways' catering facilities.

d Focus on the task and the title, *Clive's top tips*, making sure Sts can remember the meaning of *tip*.

Then focus on the **Glossary** and go through it with Sts.

Make sure Sts understand all the lexis in the headings.

Now give Sts a few minutes to insert the headings for each tip.

Get Sts to compare with a partner and then check answers.

> 1 Don't lose your temper   4 Threaten action
> 2 Write a letter   3 Know who you are writing to   5 Don't be too specific
> 6 Use flattery

Extra support

• Go through the article (reading it aloud or getting different Sts to read) paragraph by paragraph with the class making sure Sts understand it. If necessary, use Sts' L1 to clarify.

e Focus on the highlighted verbs and verb phrases. Get Sts, in pairs, to figure out their meaning. Tell them to read the whole sentence as the context will help them guess.

Check answers, either explaining in English, translating into Sts' L1, or getting Sts to check in their dictionaries.

Explain any other new vocabulary and encourage Sts to write down any useful new lexis from the text.

f Get Sts to vote on which two tips they think are the most important and why.

Finally, ask Sts which useful words and phrases from the article they want to try and remember and write them on the board.

4 PRONUNCIATION the letters *ai*

> **Pronunciation notes**
>
> • The letters *ai* between consonants are pronounced /eɪ/ when they are stressed, e.g., *main, complain*. Remind Sts that this sound is a diphthong. If you want to remind them what a diphthong is, refer them back to the information box on diphthongs in **Lesson 6B**, **3 Pronunciation** on *page 59*.
>
> • *Said* has an irregular pronunciation /ɛ/.
>
> • The letters *ai* between consonants but unstressed are pronounced /ə/, e.g., *bargain* /ˈbɑrgən/.
>
> • The letters *air* between consonants are pronounced /ɛr/.

a Focus on the three sound pictures and elicit the words and sounds: *train* /eɪ/, *chair* /ɛr/, and *computer* /ə/.

Now give Sts some time to put the words in the list in the correct column. Tell them also to underline the stress in the multisyllable words as this will help them to see when *ai* is /ə/, as it is always an unstressed syllable. Remind them that this kind of activity is easier if they say the words out loud to themselves.

b (4 36)) Play the audio for Sts to listen and check.

Check answers.

> (4 36))
>
> | | |
> |---|---|
> | train /eɪ/ | complain, email, obtain, paid, painting |
> | chair /ɛr/ | airline, fair, hairdresser, repair |
> | computer /ə/ | bargain, captain, villain |

Now elicit the answers to the questions.

> 1 The normal pronunciation of *ai* is:
>   a) /eɪ/ when stressed
>   b) /ə/ when unstressed.
> 2 *air* is usually pronounced /ɛr/.
> 3 *said* is pronounced /sɛd/.

Extra support

• Play the audio again for Sts to repeat after each group of words. Then get them to practice individually or in pairs.

c (4 37)) Tell Sts they are going to hear four sentences and they must write them down.

Play the audio all the way through for Sts just to listen.

> (4 37))
>
> 1 I'm going to write an email to the airline to complain.
> 2 She said that she had to pay for the repairs.
> 3 The captain found a bargain at the sale.
> 4 The villain in the story stole the painting from the old woman.

Play the audio, pausing after each sentence to give Sts time to write it down.

Then, if necessary, play the audio again for Sts to check.

Check answers by writing the sentences on the board.

> See sentences in script 4.37

Then get Sts to practice saying the sentences.

5 VOCABULARY making nouns from verbs

a Focus on the instructions and three nouns from the article. Elicit the verbs from the class.

> | complain | argue | compensate |
> |---|---|---|

b Tell Sts to go to **Vocabulary Bank** *Word building* on *page 163*.

Focus on **1 Making nouns from verbs** and get Sts to do **a** individually or in pairs. Before Sts start, check they know the meaning of all the verbs.

(4 38)) Now do **b**. Play the audio for Sts to check answers and to underline the stressed syllables.

Elicit the answers and write them on the board.

> (4 38))
>
> **Word building**
> **Making nouns from verbs**
> 1 compen<u>sa</u>tion, demon<u>stra</u>tion, expla<u>na</u>tion
> 2 a<u>chieve</u>ment, a<u>gree</u>ment, <u>ar</u>gument, at<u>tach</u>ment, <u>pay</u>ment
> 3 choice, com<u>plaint</u>, de<u>li</u>very, loss, re<u>sponse</u>, sale, su<u>ccess</u>

Play the audio again, pausing for Sts to repeat. Practice any words your Sts find difficult to pronounce, modeling and drilling as necessary.

For **c** put Sts in pairs, **A** and **B**. Make sure they change roles.

For **d** Sts complete each question with a noun from **a**. Tell Sts to be careful with singular and plural nouns.

(4 39)) Now do **e**. Play the audio for Sts to check answers.

> (4 39))
>
> 1 Have you ever opened an **attachment** on an email that contained a virus?
> 2 Do you often have **arguments** with your family? What about?
> 3 Do you prefer reading grammar **explanations** in your own language, or do you think it's better to read them in English?
> 4 Have you ever made a **complaint** to a company and gotten **compensation**?
> 5 Do you think that there's too much **choice** when you're shopping, for example, for a new phone?
> 6 Have you ever been in a **demonstration**? What were you protesting about?

Put Sts in pairs and get them to interview each other.

Get some feedback.

Tell Sts they will be doing **Part 2** in a later lesson (9A) and tell them to go back to the main lesson **8A**.

! The Vocabulary photocopiable activity for *Word building* includes part 2, so should be done in 9A.

6 LISTENING & SPEAKING

a (4 40)) Focus on the instructions and make sure Sts know what a consumer program is.

Play the audio once all the way through.

Check answers.

Extra support

• Before playing the audio, go through the listening script and decide if you need to preteach / check any lexis to help Sts when they listen.

1 The man complained that the taxi driver overcharged him.
2 The woman complained about the price of the Wi-Fi in her hotel room.
3 The woman complained that her food was cold.

---

4 40))

(script in Student Book on *page 129*)

1 I was at Sydney airport, in Australia, and I got a taxi to take me to the hotel. A few minutes after he'd left the airport, the taxi driver said that his meter was broken, but that he would charge me 50 dollars, which was what he said the trip usually cost. It was my first time in Sydney, and of course, I didn't have a clue what the usual fare was, so I just said OK. But later when I was checking in to the hotel I asked the receptionist what the usual taxi fare was from the airport, and she said about 35 dollars. I was really annoyed, and I sent an email to the taxi company, but I never got a reply.

2 I was traveling in the UK. It was a work trip, and I knew that I was going to have to answer a lot of emails during that time, so I booked a hotel in Liverpool where they advertised Wi-Fi in all the rooms. When I arrived it turned out the hotel charged 16 pounds for 24 hours of Wi-Fi, which is about the same as I pay for a month of Internet at home! I complained to the man at reception, but all he said was that I could use the Wi-Fi in the lobby, which was free. I wasn't very happy about it. Hotels used to make a lot of money from customers by charging a ridiculous amount for phone calls. Now that everybody uses their cell phones to make phone calls, some hotels now charge a ridiculous amount for Wi-Fi.

3 I was in an Italian restaurant in New York City recently, and I ordered *manicotti*, which is a kind of pasta a bit like cannelloni, and it's filled with cheese and served with tomato sauce. Well, when it arrived, the tomato sauce was really hot, but the pasta and the filling were cold–it was like they were still frozen. Anyway, I called the waitress, and she said that it couldn't be cold. So I said, "Sorry, it <u>is</u> cold. Do you want to try it?" So she took it back to the kitchen, and later the manager came out and apologized, and when I finally got the dish, it was good, hot all the way through. But I'd had to wait a long time for it. But later the manager came out again and offered me a free dessert. So I had a delicious tiramisu for free.

---

b Now give Sts time to quickly read questions 1 and 2.

Then play the audio and pause after the first story (the taxi). Give Sts time to answer the questions in pairs. Then play this story again if necessary.

Check answers and ask a few more comprehension questions, e.g., *Where was the speaker?*, etc.

The taxi
1 He complained to the taxi company.   2 Nothing.

Now repeat the process for the other two stories.

The hotel
1 She complained to the receptionist.
2 He said that the woman could use the Wi-Fi in the lobby as it was free.

The restaurant
1 She complained to the waitress.
2 The waitress took it back to the kitchen and gave the woman a new hot dish. She also told the manager, who apologized and later gave the woman a free dessert.

Extra support

• If there's time, you could play the audio again while Sts read the script on *page 129*, so they can see what they understood / didn't understand. Translate / explain any new words or phrases.

c Put Sts in pairs and focus on the task. Get Sts to discuss questions 1 and 2 for a few minutes.

Then get feedback from the class.

Extra idea

• Get Sts to ask you the questions first and tell them about any experiences you have had.

d Put Sts in pairs, **A** and **B**, preferably face-to-face. Tell them to go to **Communication** *I want to speak to the manager*, **A** on *page 107*, **B** on *page 111*.

Go through the instructions for the first role play and remind Sts that here student **A** is the customer and **B** is the salesperson. Tell **A**s to start by saying *Excuse me, I bought…*

When they have finished role-playing the first situation, tell them to read the instructions for the second situation. This time **A** is the restaurant manager and **B** is the customer. **B** starts *Good evening. Are you the manager?*

Get feedback to see whether different customers achieved their objectives or not.

Extra support

• You could write any new and useful words and phrases from **Communication** on the board for Sts to copy.

Tell Sts to go back to the main lesson **8A**.

7 WRITING a letter of complaint

Tell Sts to go to **Writing** *A letter of complaint* on *page 119*.

a Focus on the task and tell Sts to read the letter and then answer the five questions. Tell them not to worry about the blanks.

Check answers.

---

1 Sandra Adams, the Head of Department of John Leavis Customer Service.
2 A coffee machine. He ordered it two weeks ago and it still hasn't arrived, but payment has been charge to his credit card.
3 The customer service line.
4 The person he spoke to was rude and could not give him any information.
5 In the last paragraph. He says that he has bought a lot of things from John Leavis in the past and has always been very happy.

---

b Tell Sts to read the letter again and to fill in the blanks with a word or phrase from the list.

Get Sts to compare with a partner and then check answers.

---

2 number	4 delivered	6 unhelpful	8 forward
3 in stock	5 However	7 service	9 yours

---

c Focus on the **Useful language: a formal letter (or email)** box and go through it with Sts.

Now tell Sts they are going to write a similar letter or email of complaint for something they bought online. They should follow the model and use the **Useful language** to help them.

You may choose to get Sts to do the writing in class or you could assign it as homework. If you do it in class, set a time limit for Sts to write their description, e.g., 15–20 minutes.

d Sts should check their work for mistakes before turning it in.

G gerunds and infinitives
V work
P word stress

8B What's the right job for you?

Lesson plan

The topic of this lesson is work. In the first half of the lesson, Sts learn words and phrases related to work and these are recycled and practiced orally in Pronunciation and Speaking. The grammar focus is on when Sts have to use a gerund (or *-ing* form) or an infinitive and the context is a questionnaire which helps people to see what kind of job would most fit their personality. The grammar is practiced in a Communication activity.

In the second half of the lesson, Sts read about an American TV show called *Shark Tank* in which contestants try to convince a panel of business people to invest in a product or service that they want to commercialize. In Listening they hear about two products which were presented on *Shark Tank* and how successful they were. In Speaking Sts take part in a role play where they present a new product to the class as if they were appearing on the show. In Writing Sts learn how to write a cover email to send with their résumé to apply for a job. The lesson finishes with a song, *Piano Man*.

STUDY LINK
• **Workbook** 8B
• **iChecker**

Extra photocopiable activities

• **Grammar** gerunds and infinitives *page 159*
• **Communicative** Predict the story *pages 189–190* (instructions *page 169*)
• **Vocabulary** Work *page 212* (instructions *page 199*)
• **Song** *Piano Man page 224* (instructions *page 216*)
• **www.oup.com/elt/teacher/englishfile**

Optional lead-in (books closed)

• Jobs quiz. Put Sts in pairs or small groups. Then read the following quiz questions out loud or write them on the board.

  CAN YOU NAME…?

  – TWO JOBS WHICH PEOPLE DO IN A RESTAURANT

  – TWO JOBS CONNECTED WITH TRANSPORTATION

  – TWO JOBS THAT PEOPLE DO AT HOME

  – TWO JOBS WHERE YOU SPEND A LOT OF TIME OUTSIDE

  – TWO JOBS IN ENTERTAINMENT

• Check answers, making sure Sts can spell and pronounce the words correctly.

Possible answers
waiter, chef, etc.
taxi driver, pilot, bus driver, etc.
childcare provider, writer, etc.
police officer, farmer, soccer player, etc.
actor, singer, musician, etc.

1 VOCABULARY work

a Books open. Focus on the pictures and sentences. Give Sts, in pairs, a couple of minutes to match the sentences and pictures.

b (4 41))) Play the audio for Sts to listen and check. Model and drill pronunciation of the bold words and phrases.

2 I	3 G	4 D	5 C	6 F	7 H	8 A	9 B

Point out that:

– *set up* = start (a business)

– *fired* can be used with either *be* or *get*. If you are *fired*, you lose your job.

– we use *apply for* when you send a letter, a résumé, or a completed form to a company to ask for a job (usually in response to an advertisement).

– a résumé is a document which shows your qualifications, experience, and interests.

– *overtime* = extra hours that you work over and above your normal working hours

4 41)))		
E	1	Clare worked for a marketing company.
I	2	She had to work very hard and work overtime.
G	3	She made a good salary, but she didn't like her boss.
D	4	They had an argument, and Clare was fired.
C	5	She was unemployed and had to look for a job.
F	6	She applied for a lot of jobs, and sent in résumés.
H	7	She had some interviews, but didn't get the jobs.
A	8	She decided to set up an online business selling birthday cakes.
B	9	Her business is doing very well. Clare is a success!

Now get Sts to cover the sentences and look at the pictures. Then get them to retell the story in pairs from memory, **A** testing **B**, and then switching.

Then elicit the story from the class by asking individual Sts.

Extra support

• Before Sts work in pairs, you could elicit from the whole class the sentence for each picture.

c Now tell Sts to go to **Vocabulary Bank** *Work* on *page 164*.

Focus on **1 Verb phrases** and get Sts to do **a** individually or in pairs.

(4 42))) Now do **b**. Play the audio for Sts to check answers. Practice any words your Sts find difficult to pronounce, modeling and drilling as necessary. Point out the silent *g* in *resign*.

4 42)))
Work
Verb phrases
1 Dan has to **work** a lot of overtime. He has to work extra hours.
2 Matt **got promoted** last week. He was given a more important job.
3 Most nurses have to **work** shifts. Sometimes they work during the day and sometimes at night.
4 A man in our department **was fired** yesterday. He lost his job because of poor performance.
5 Colin **was** downsized last month. He lost his job because the company didn't need him anymore.
6 The politician is going to **resign**. He has decided to leave his job.
7 Lilian is going to **retire** next month. She's 65, and she's going to stop working.
8 Angela has **set up** a business to sell clothes online. She had the idea and has started doing it.
9 Everyone in the office has to **take** a training course. They need to learn how to use the new software.
10 She **applied for** a job. She replied to an advertisement and sent in her résumé.

Now get Sts to cover the sentences on the left and look at the second sentence on the right. Can they remember the verb or verb phrase used in each one?

Now focus on **2 Saying what you do** and get Sts to do **a** and **b** individually or in pairs.

4 43))) Now do **c**. Play the audio for Sts to check answers. Practice any words your Sts find difficult to pronounce, modeling and drilling as necessary.

4 43)))
Saying what you do
a
1 I'm **unemployed**.
2 He's **self-employed**.
3 She's **well-qualified**.
4 It's a **temporary** job.
5 It's a **part-time** job.

b
1 I work **for** a multinational company.
2 I'm **in** charge **of** the marketing department.
3 I'm responsible **for** customer loans.
4 I'm **in** school.
5 I'm **in** my third year.

Now focus on **3 Word building**. In pairs or individually, give Sts time to do **a** and **b**.

4 44))) Now do **c**. Play the audio for Sts to check answers.

Elicit the answers onto the board.

4 44)))
Word building
a
1 promote, **promotion**
2 apply, **application**
3 retire, **retirement**
4 employ, **employment**
5 qualify, **qualification**
6 resign, **resignation**

b
1 science, **scientist**
2 law, **lawyer**
3 music, **musician**
4 pharmacy, **pharmacist**
5 farm, **farmer**
6 translate, **translator**

Either get Sts to underline the stressed syllable in the new words before playing the audio again or play the audio again, pausing after each word for Sts to underline the stressed syllable.

Elicit which syllables are stressed and underline them on the board.

See script 4.44

Now play the audio again, pausing for Sts to repeat. Practice any words your Sts find difficult to pronounce, modeling and drilling as necessary.

For **d**, get Sts to cover the nouns and look at 1–6 in **a** and **b**. They can test each other or themselves on the nouns.

Now write the four endings -*er*, -*or*, -*ian*, and -*ist* on the board. Put Sts in pairs and get them to think of two more jobs for each ending.

Elicit answers onto the board.

Possible answers			
-er	*-or*	*-ian*	*-ist*
hairdresser	actor	electrician	pianist
banker	director	optician	receptionist

Extra idea
• If most of your Sts work, get them to tell you what they do.

Finally, focus on the *job or work?* box and go through it with Sts.

Tell Sts to go back to the main lesson **8B**.

Extra support
• If you think Sts need more practice, you may want to give them the Vocabulary photocopiable activity at this point or leave it for later as consolidation or review.

2 PRONUNCIATION & SPEAKING

word stress

a Focus on the words and phonetics and ask Sts if they can remember how the phonetics show them where the stress falls (the syllable after the apostrophe (') is the one which is stressed). Get them to underline the stressed syllable in each word.

b **4 45)))** Play the audio, pausing after each word to check answers. You could also ask Sts to tell you how each word is pronounced just before you play it.

4 45)))
1	apply	6	permanent
2	salary	7	qualifications
3	downsize	8	resign
4	experience	9	retire
5	overtime	10	temporary

Now give Sts a few minutes to practice saying the words. You could get them to practice saying them correctly by looking only at the phonetics and / or by repeating after the audio.

c Focus on the questions and give Sts a few minutes to read them and think whether they have a family member or friend who fits any of the categories. They should try and think of someone for as many of the questions as possible.

Put Sts in pairs and get them to tell their partner about anyone they know who fits one of the questions. Encourage them to give, and ask for, as many details as they can.

Get some feedback.

Extra support

- To help Sts with the task, tell them about real people you know for two or three of the questions.

d Focus on the instructions and give Sts time to think about their answers.

Extra support

- Elicit the eight questions from the class and write them on the board, e.g., WHAT DOES HE / SHE DO?

e Put Sts in pairs and focus on the instructions and example speech bubbles.

A should start by asking **B** the eight questions.

Make sure Sts change roles.

Get some feedback by asking one or two Sts who their partner told them about.

3 GRAMMAR gerunds and infinitives

a Focus on the instructions and the questionnaire. Quickly go through the questionnaire with Sts and make sure they understand all the vocabulary, e.g., *instincts, improvise*, etc.

Get Sts to complete it individually or in pairs.

Check answers. They should be able to do this reasonably well from what they already know and by instinct. If Sts ask for a reason why a particular verb takes the gerund or infinitive, tell them that they will see all the rules when they go to the **Grammar Bank** later in the lesson.

2	helping	10	to follow
3	not earning	11	to be
4	listening	12	improvising
5	making	13	Doing
6	Taking	14	solving
7	to work	15	to understand
8	managing	16	to calculate
9	expressing		

b Now tell Sts to read individually each sentence in the questionnaire carefully and check (✓) the sentences that they <u>strongly</u> agree with.

When they have finished, get them to compare their answers with a partner, explaining why they have checked certain statements.

c Focus on the instructions and tell Sts to go to **Communication** *The right job for you* on *page 107*.

Get Sts to read the "answer" paragraph corresponding to the section where they have most checks. Some Sts may have an equal number of checks in two sections in which case they should read both answer sections.

Get feedback from some Sts to find out what kind of job, according to the questionnaire, would suit them and if this is the kind of job that they would actually like to do.

Tell Sts to go back to the main lesson **8B**.

Extra support

- You could write any new and useful words and phrases from **Communication** on the board for Sts to copy.

d Now focus on the rules and give Sts a few minutes to complete them individually or in pairs.

Check answers.

1	the gerund	4	the gerund
2	the infinitive	5	the gerund
3	the infinitive		

e (4 46)) (4 47)) (4 48)) Tell Sts to go to **Grammar Bank 8B** on *page 147*. Focus on the example sentences and play the audio for Sts to listen to the sentence rhythm. You could also get Sts to repeat the sentences to practice getting the rhythm right. Then go through the rules with the class.

> **Additional grammar notes**
>
> - Sts who used *American English File 2* rules for using gerunds (or *-ing* forms) and the infinitive with *to* before, but separately. In this lesson they are brought together.
>
> - Sts will see in this lesson that there are three common verb forms in English: *to go* (infinitive), *go* (base form without *to*), and *going* (gerund or *-ing* form).
>
> - Verbs that can take either the gerund or infinitive, but with a different meaning, will be focused on in more detail in the next level of *American English File*.
>
> - Emphasize the importance of learning which verb form to use after a particular verb or construction and give Sts plenty of practice. After a while they will develop an instinctive feel for whether a gerund or infinitive is required.

Focus on the exercises and get Sts to do them individually or in pairs.

Check answers, getting Sts to read the full sentences.

a			
1	to spend	6	working
2	Applying	7	solving
3	not to say	8	not going
4	to start	9	modeling
5	not to ask	10	to learn
b			
1	to retire	6	leave
2	commuting	7	wear
3	not to worry	8	not to make
4	to lock	9	working
5	not to buy		

Tell Sts to go back to the main lesson **8B**.

Extra support

- If you think Sts need more practice, you may want to give them the Grammar photocopiable activity at this point or leave it for later as consolidation or review.

f Focus on the instructions. Then give Sts a few minutes to choose five topics and to write a couple of words and think about what they are going to say. Demonstrate the activity by talking about a couple of the topics yourself.

g Put Sts in groups of three or four and get them to tell the other people in the group what they have written. The others should listen and ask for more information when possible. Monitor to check that Sts are using the correct forms of the verbs.

Make sure Sts change roles.

Get feedback from a few different groups.

4 READING

a Focus on the instructions and on the four questions.

Give Sts time to read the first paragraph and to answer the questions.

Get Sts to compare with a partner and then check answers to 1–3. Elicit answers to 4 and find out if Sts like the show.

> 1 They are very successful business people.
> 2 The room where they meet the contestants.
> 3 The contestants make a presentation to the "Sharks," who then ask them questions and decide whether or not to invest in the contestants' business.

Help with any vocabulary problems (but not the highlighted phrases).

b Sts now look at the photos, read about three products that were presented on the show, and answer the six questions.

Get Sts to compare with a partner and then check answers.

Extra support

• Before Sts read the article, check it for words and phrases which your Sts might not know and be ready to help with these while they are answering the questions or afterwards. You may even want to preteach / check a few words / phrases to lighten the load (but not the highlighted words).

> 1 C   2 A   3 B   4 A   5 B   6 C

c In pairs, Sts tell each other which product they would or wouldn't be interested in buying and why.

Get feedback. Take a vote to find out if one product is more popular than another.

d Focus on the highlighted words and phrases. Get Sts, in pairs, to figure out their meaning. Tell them to read the whole sentence as the context will help them guess.

Check answers, either explaining in English, translating into Sts' L1, or getting Sts to check in their dictionaries.

Explain any other new vocabulary and encourage Sts to write down any useful new lexis from the text.

e Focus on the **Words with different meanings** box and go through it with Sts.

Now put Sts in pairs and get them to discuss the difference between the sentences in 1–4.

Check answers.

> 1 to run (a business) = to be in charge of (a business)
>   to run (a marathon) = to move using your legs, going faster than when you walk
> 2 to be fired = to lose your job
>   to fire = to shoot a bullet from a gun
> 3 a market for something = demand (a number of people who want to buy something)
>   a market = the open area or building where people sell vegetables, etc.
> 4 a company = a business organization that makes money by producing or selling goods or services
>   good company = pleasant to be with

Finally, ask Sts which words and phrases they want to try and remember from the article. Tell Sts to write them down.

5 LISTENING

a (4 49)) Focus on the photos of two more products from *Shark Tank*. Elicit from Sts why they think each product is special, but do **not** tell them yet if they are right. You could write their ideas on the board.

Play the audio once all the way through for Sts to listen and find out the answer.

Check answers.

Extra support

• Before playing the audio, go through the listening script and decide if you need to preteach / check any lexis to help Sts when they listen, e.g., *vanilla, anniversaries, production,* etc.

> The Man Candles have scents that men would like more than women.
> The Daisy Cakes are homemade from fresh ingredients, and they are perfect for people who want homemade dessert, but don't have time to make it.

(4 49))

(script in Student Book on *page 129*)

Johnson Bailey presented Man Candles. He argued that most candles smell like perfume and are designed for women. One day he was having some friends over to watch a football game, and his house smelled like old Chinese food and dirty clothes. The only candle he had at the time was a vanilla-scented one, and he didn't want his house to smell like perfume. That's why Bailey invented manly candles that smell like things men enjoy: basketballs, golf courses, the beach, popcorn, and barbecue sauce. He even has a horrible-smelling candle you can burn to get people you don't like–perhaps your mother-in-law–out of your house. He tried to convince the Sharks to invest by passing out his candles and asking them to smell them. The Sharks most wanted to smell the bad candle, which is Bailey's best-selling candle.

***

Kim Nelson's idea was a cake business that sells homemade cakes across the US. These cakes are made from all natural ingredients like fresh oranges in the "Oh! Oh! Orange" cake or one pound of grated carrots in "Daisy's Carrot Cake." Kim came up with the idea because many people don't have the time or the talent to bake a delicious, homemade cake for special occasions like birthdays, graduations, or anniversaries. Kim says that she has a talent for baking cakes, and more importantly, she feels it's her passion. Kim's products are currently sold online in her local area, but she would like to increase production and sell more cakes across the US. The cake business is called Daisy Cakes.

b Focus on the instructions and then play the audio again all the way through.

Get Sts to vote for **a** (the Sharks invested in both products), **b** (they didn't invest in either), or **c** (they invested in one of the products). For **c**, get Sts to vote again for the product they think the Sharks invested in.

c ④ **50**))) Now tell Sts to listen to what happened.

Play the audio the whole way through. Then play again if necessary.

Check answers.

> Only one Shark invested in Kim's cakes. Even though the male Sharks liked Kim's cake, and even went back for seconds, they didn't think her company would make much money. Barbara Corcoran thought there was a market for Kim's product and she invested $5,000.

---

④ **50**)))

(script in Student Book on *page 129*)
The Sharks asked Johnson a lot of questions, for example they asked him how much the candles sell for (10–12 dollars a candle) and how much money they made in sales the year before ($53,000). Johnson explained that currently, he and his wife had put over $40,000 of their own money into this product. The Sharks also asked how the candles were made, to which he answered that he poured them all into their containers by himself–he didn't have any help in his entire candle-making process.
In the end, they decided that they weren't interested. Their main reason was they thought the business just wasn't big enough or interesting enough, so they couldn't believe that it would ever make any money.

***

The Sharks were impressed by Kim's presentation, and they immediately asked to try her cakes. They really loved her cakes and complimented her on their fresh and delicious taste. Even though the male Sharks liked Kim's product, they were concerned that her company had reached its potential–making a respectable $27,000 in the last three months. In the end, Barbara Corcoran, the only female Shark decided to invest $50,000 in Kim's business because she thought there was a market for Kim's product.
And since then?
Kim's Daisy Cakes are now being sold online across the US. She was able to pay Barbara Corcoran back in only three weeks! And she has expanded her business by offering new products like lemon curd.
Although the Sharks thought Johnson's candles were funny, it's a good thing they didn't invest in his company. Johnson's website has been shut down and his candles have disappeared from store shelves.

Extra support

• If there's time, you could play the audio again while Sts read the scripts on *page 129*, so they can see what they understood / didn't understand. Translate / explain any new words or phrases.

d Do this as a whole-class activity.

6 SPEAKING

a Focus on the instructions and on the products and make sure Sts understand what they are. Put Sts in pairs and explain that they have to imagine they are about to appear in front of the Sharks in the Tank. They should look at the questions and think about their answers for their chosen products. Tell Sts that they will have three minutes to present their product (or give Sts longer if you think they need it).

Give Sts time to prepare their presentations. Monitor and help with any vocabulary.

b Focus on the **Presenting a product** box and go through it with Sts.

In pairs, Sts present their product to the class.

c Focus on the instructions and get Sts to invest in the products with a show of hands.

7 WRITING a cover email with your résumé

In this writing lesson Sts practice writing a formal cover email, i.e., the email you send with your résumé to a company or organization in response to a job advertisement. The layout and style apply both to emails and letters.

Tell Sts to go to **Writing *A cover email with your résumé*** on *page 120*.

a Focus on the job advertisement and make sure Sts understand all the lexis.

In pairs, Sts tell each other which area they could apply for a job in and why.

Get some feedback. You could have a vote for each to see if one is more popular than the others.

b Focus on the task and explain / elicit what a cover email (or letter) is (= an email / letter you send when you also attach / enclose something else, e.g., a résumé or a form, where you explain what you are sending and why). Get Sts to tell you what a résumé is. Remind Sts that the email is formal and that they should circle the expression that they think is more formal from each pair.

Get Sts to compare with a partner and then check answers. You might want to point out that *enclose* in 4 would be the correct verb if Ricardo were sending a letter, not an email. You could also remind Sts that they should always use *Dear Sir / Madam:* when they don't know the name of the person they are writing to.

> 1 I am writing
> 2 I have been working
> 3 I speak English fluently
> 4 I've attached
> 5 I look forward to hearing from you.
> 6 Sincerely yours,

c Tell Sts they are going to apply for one of the jobs in the next Olympics, so they need to write a cover email.

Sts should use Ricardo's email as their model to help them and the **Useful language** box on *page 119*. If Sts have not had any work experience, tell them to invent the details.

You may choose to get Sts to do the writing in class or you could assign it as homework. If you do it in class, set a time limit for Sts to write their cover email, e.g., 15–20 minutes.

d Sts should check their work for mistakes before turning it in.

Tell Sts to go back to the main lesson **8B**.

8 (4)(51)) **SONG** *Piano Man*

This song was originally made famous by American singer Billy Joel in 1973. For copyright reasons this is a cover version. If you want to do this song in class, use the photocopiable activity on *page 224*.

---

(4)(51))

Piano Man

It's nine o'clock on a Saturday
The regular crowd shuffles in
There's an old man sitting next to me
Making love to his tonic and gin

He says, "Son, can you play me a memory?
I'm not really sure how it goes
But it's sad and it's sweet and I knew it complete
When I wore a younger man's clothes"

La la la la di di da, la la di di da dum

> *Chorus*
> Sing us a song, you're the piano man
> Sing us a song tonight
> Well, we're all in the mood for a melody
> And you've got us feeling alright

Now John at the bar is a friend of mine
He gets me my drinks for free
And he's quick with a joke for the out-of-town folk
But there's someplace that he'd rather be

He says, "Bill, I believe this is killing me"
As the smile ran away from his face
"Well, I'm sure that I could be a movie star
If I could get out of this place"

Oh, la la la la di di da, la la di di da dum

Now Paul is a real estate novelist
Who never had time for a wife
And he's talking with Davy who's still in the Navy
And probably will be for life

And the waitress is practicing politics
As the businessmen talk to their phones
Yes, they're sharing a drink they call loneliness
But it's better than drinking alone

> *Chorus*

It's a pretty good crowd for a Saturday,
And the manager gives me a smile
'Cause he knows that it's me they've been coming to see
To forget about life for a while.

And the piano, it sounds like a carnival
And the microphone smells like a beer
And they sit at the bar and put bread in my jar
And say, "Man, what are you doing here?"

Oh, la la la da di da la la da di da dum

> *Chorus*

For instructions on how to use these pages see *page 40*.

Testing Program CD-ROM

- **Quick Test 8**
- **File 8 Test**

GRAMMAR

1	a	6	b	11	c
2	a	7	a	12	b
3	c	8	c	13	a
4	b	9	b	14	a
5	c	10	c	15	b

VOCABULARY

a 1 semesters
  2 nursery
  3 grades
  4 behave
  5 boarding

b 1 on
  2 ceiling
  3 gate
  4 on
  5 fireplace

c 1 choice
  2 agreement
  3 success
  4 complaint
  5 demonstration
  6 retirement
  7 qualifications
  8 translator
  9 scientists
  10 explanation

d 1 overtime
  2 shifts
  3 temporary
  4 set
  5 self-employed

PRONUNCIATION

a 1 uniform   3 kindergarten   5 educate
  2 wooden   4 said

b 1 sem**es**ter   3 de**li**very   5 a**chieve**ment
  2 unem**ployed**   4 a**pply**

CAN YOU UNDERSTAND THIS TEXT?

a Possible answer: It is better to do a job that **you love** than a job that you **hate**, but that **pays better**.

b 1 DS   2 T   3 F   4 DS   5 DS   6 T

CAN YOU UNDERSTAND THESE PEOPLE?

4 52)))
1 b   2 a   3 a   4 b   5 c

4 52)))
Amber
I = interviewer, A = Amber
I Do you think children learn better in mixed schools or single-sex schools?
A I think they learn better in mixed schools.
I Why?
A Because the real world is mixed so they learn how to interact with all kinds of people.
Max
I = interviewer, M = Max
I Do you prefer buying in stores or online?
M I think I prefer online. I tend to be a little bit introverted that way I suppose. If I can buy something online, then I can look at all these other things I can buy online. And it normally has a larger variety of wares available than at any specific store.
Simon
I = interviewer, S = Simon
I Have you ever sold anything online?
S Yes, I have sold on *eBay*.
I What was it?
S I sold a couple of things, I sold a computer scanner and a camera.
I Did you get what you wanted for it?
S Yes, I think so, I set a fairly, what I thought was a fairly realistic price for them, and I got what I expected.
Joe
I = interviewer, J = Joe
I If you could change one thing about your apartment, what would it be?
J Right now we don't have any artwork up on the walls, so I would definitely want to get some more pictures or maybe a couple of paintings to put up.
I Why would you change it?
J The walls are just really bare, so it doesn't feel very inviting when people come over, it just looks very, very plain.
Simone
I = interviewer, Si = Simone
I What's more important to you about a job, having a good salary or doing something you really enjoy?
Si Definitely doing something I really enjoy.
I Why?
Si Doing the course I study at university, I could become a banker, but I don't want to because I don't think I'd enjoy that even though I'd earn lots of money, so I want to do something I enjoy.

G third conditional
V making adjectives and adverbs
P sentence stress

9A Lucky encounters

Lesson plan

This lesson presents the third conditional in the context of two different aspects of luck. The lesson begins with reading and speaking activities based on three true stories about occasions in which a lucky meeting with a stranger changed people's lives. Extracts from the stories provide an introduction to the grammar, which is then further practiced in pronunciation, which focuses on the stress patterns in third conditionals.

The second half of the lesson opens with a speaking activity where Sts discuss various quotes about luck and how lucky or unlucky they consider themselves to be. They then read and listen to a review of a book by Malcolm Gladwell called *Outliers*, in which the author explains why certain people are successful, concluding that luck is an important factor. There is then a vocabulary focus on adjective and adverb formation, and this is consolidated through a writing game. The lesson ends with the song *Karma*.

STUDY LINK
• **Workbook** 9A

Extra photocopiable activities

• **Grammar** third conditional *page 160*
• **Communicative** Third conditional game *page 191* (instructions *pages 169–170*)
• **Vocabulary** Word building *page 213* (instructions *page 199*)
• **Song** *Karma page 225* (instructions *pages 216–217*)

Optional lead-in (books closed)

• Draw a horseshoe on the board with the open part at the top and ask Sts what it is. Tell them that in the US and UK, people believe that if you find a horseshoe, it will bring you good luck, and people often hang them up on the wall. Ask if a horseshoe also means good luck in your Sts' country.

• Then put Sts in pairs and ask them to think of things which in their country are considered either good luck or bad luck.

• Get feedback and write them in two columns GOOD LUCK / BAD LUCK on the board. Then ask Sts if they really believe in this.

1 READING & SPEAKING

a Books open. Focus on the questions and go through them. Put Sts in pairs and get them to discuss the four situations.

Get some feedback.

b Focus on the instructions and set a time limit for Sts to read *The ticket inspector*. You might want to tell Sts that Bernard Hare was born in 1958 in Leeds, in the north of England, into a mining family.

Then put Sts in pairs and tell them to discuss what they think happened next.

Elicit some ideas, but do <u>not</u> tell Sts if they are right yet.

c **5 2))** Now tell Sts they are going to listen to the end of the story. Play the audio once all the way through.

! The script for audio 5.2 has not been included in the Listening section of the Student Book so that Sts find out together in class what happens in the end.

Elicit what happened.

Extra support

• Before playing the audio, go through the listening script and decide if you need to preteach / check any lexis to help Sts when they listen, e.g., *connection*, *desperate*, *hitchhike*, etc.

> The ticket inspector radioed Peterborough station and told them to make the train to Leeds wait for Bernard.

5 2))
The ticket inspector touched my arm. "Listen," he said "when we get to Peterborough station, run as fast as you can to Platform 1. The Leeds train will be there." I looked at him, without really understanding what he had said. "What do you mean?" I said. "Is the train late or something?" "No, it's not late," the ticket inspector said. "I've just radioed Peterborough station. The train is going to wait for you. As soon as you get on, it'll leave. The passengers will complain, but let's not worry about that. You'll get home, and that's the main thing." And he walked away.
I suddenly realized what an amazing thing he had done. I got up and went after him. I wanted to give him everything I had, all the money in my wallet – but I knew he would be offended. I grabbed his arm. "I... uh... just wanted to...," but I couldn't continue.
"It's OK," he said. "No problem." "I wish I had a way to thank you," I said. "I really appreciate what you've done." "No problem," he said again. "Listen, if you want to thank me, the next time you see someone in trouble, help them. That will pay me back. And tell them to do the same to someone else. It'll make the world a better place."
When the train stopped, I rushed to Platform 1 and sure enough the Leeds train was there waiting, and a few hours later I was with my mom in hospital.
Even now, years later, whenever I think of her, I remember the Good Ticket Inspector on that late-night train to Peterborough. It changed me from a young man who was nearly a criminal into a decent human being. I've been trying to pay him back ever since then.

d Now tell Sts to read the three questions and play the audio again.

Get Sts to compare with a partner and then check answers.

> 1 He had to run to Platform 1.
> 2 He was very happy and wished he had a way to thank the ticket inspector.
> 3 He asked Bernard to help the next person he sees who is in trouble and then to tell them to do the same to someone else.

e Put Sts in pairs, **A** and **B**, and focus on the instructions. The **A**s read *The students* and the **B**s read *The angel*. Make sure Sts know what an angel is. Model and drill its pronunciation.

f Focus on the three prompts and tell Sts to now tell their partner about their story using the prompts to help them. You could write the three prompts on the board and ask Sts to close their books.

Sts tell their partner about their story.

g In pairs, get Sts to answer the questions. Check Sts understand the meaning of the adjective *moving* (= causing you to have deep feelings of sadness or sympathy).

Extra support
- Do these as open-class questions.

Get some feedback if Sts answered the questions in pairs.

h In pairs, small groups, or as a whole-class activity. Sts answer the questions.

Get some feedback.

2 GRAMMAR third conditional

a Focus on the instructions and get Sts to match the sentence halves.

Check answers.

1 C	2 A	3 B

b Focus on the questions and the two sentences. Then either get Sts to answer the questions in pairs or elicit the answers from the class.

Check answers.

> 1 describes how the situation might have been different.
> 2 describes what really happened.

c (5 3)) Tell Sts to go to **Grammar Bank 9A** on *page 148*. Focus on the example sentences and play the audio for Sts to listen to the sentence rhythm. You could also get Sts to repeat the sentences to practice getting the rhythm right. Then go through the rules with the class.

> **Additional grammar notes**
> - If Sts have a similar structure in their own language, they may not have too many problems with the concept of the third conditional, but most Sts will have problems with the "mechanics" of the structure, i.e., remembering which verb form goes in each part of the sentence and also in understanding and producing contracted forms.
> - Some typical mistakes include:
>   – using *would have* in the *if*-clause, e.g., ~~If I would have known, I would have done something about it.~~
>   – using the past perfect in both clauses, e.g., ~~If I had known, I had done something about it.~~

Focus on the exercises and get Sts to do them individually or in pairs.

Check answers, getting Sts to read the full sentences.

> **a**
> | 1 | I | 4 | E | 7 | B |
> |---|---|---|---|---|---|
> | 2 | F | 5 | A | 8 | G |
> | 3 | H | 6 | J | 9 | C |
>
> **c**
> 1 hadn't taken, would have missed
> 2 wouldn't have won, hadn't given
> 3 would have enjoyed, had come
> 4 hadn't bought, would have been
> 5 would have forgotten, hadn't reminded
> 6 had arrived, wouldn't have caught
> 7 hadn't lent, wouldn't have been able
> 8 would have hurt, had fallen
> 9 wouldn't have found, hadn't seen
> 10 had known, would have applied

Tell Sts to go back to the main lesson **9A**.

Extra support
- If you think Sts need more practice, you may want to give them the Grammar photocopiable activity at this point or leave it for later as consolidation or review.

3 PRONUNCIATION sentence stress

> **Pronunciation notes**
> - The main focus here is on getting Sts to say third conditional sentences with good rhythm, by stressing the information words. You may also want to highlight the weak form of *would have* (/wədəv/) and the contraction of *had* in these kinds of sentences. These forms are commonly used by native speakers, but at this level it is more important for Sts to be able to understand them rather than produce them themselves.

a (5 4)) Focus on the instructions and give Sts a minute to read the sentences.

Play the audio once all the way through for Sts to listen.

> (5 4))
> See sentences in Student Book on *page 85*

Now play the audio again, pausing after each sentence for Sts to repeat.

Then repeat the activity, eliciting the sentences from individual Sts.

b (5 5)) Focus on the task and tell Sts that they are going to hear five more third conditional sentences which they have to try to write down.

Play the audio once all the way through for Sts just to listen.

Now play the audio again, pausing after each sentence to give Sts time to write. Repeat if necessary.

> (5 5))
> 1 It would have been much quicker if we'd taken a taxi.
> 2 She wouldn't have found out if you hadn't told her.
> 3 The tickets would have been cheaper if we'd booked them earlier.
> 4 If you hadn't done your homework so quickly, you wouldn't have made so many mistakes.
> 5 I would have lent you some money if you'd asked me.

Check answers and write the correct sentences on the board.

Extra idea

- Play the audio again, pausing for Sts to repeat and copy the rhythm. Put Sts in pairs and get them to practice saying the sentences.

c Put Sts in pairs, **A** and **B**, and tell them to go to **Communication** *Guess the conditional*, **A** on *page 108*, **B** on *page 111*.

Demonstrate the activity by writing in large letters on a piece of paper the following sentence:

IF I HAD KNOWN IT WAS YOUR BIRTHDAY, I WOULD HAVE BOUGHT YOU A PRESENT.

Don't show the sentence to your Sts.

Then write on the board:

IF I HAD KNOWN IT WAS YOUR BIRTHDAY, I _____ YOU A PRESENT (+).

Tell Sts that you have this sentence completed on a piece of paper and they have to try to guess what it is.

Elicit possible completions with a positive (+) verb phrase (e.g., *would have gotten / would have given*). Say *Try again* if they say a different phrase from the one you have written, until someone says *I would have bought you a present*. Then say *That's right*.

Now go through the instructions. Emphasize that Sts should write their ideas next to the sentence, but not in the blank, and only fill in the blank when their partner says *That's right*.

Sts continue in pairs. Monitor and help.

Extra support

- You could write any useful words and phrases from **Communication** on the board for Sts to copy.

Tell Sts to go back to the main lesson **9A**.

4 SPEAKING

a Focus on the instructions and help Sts with new vocabulary like the expression *a stroke of luck*.

Then give Sts a few minutes to think about their answers to the four questions.

b Put Sts in groups of three or four and get them to discuss their answers, giving as much information as possible.

Get feedback from the class for each question if possible.

Extra support

- You could discuss what the quotes mean and whether Sts think they are true or not with the whole class, and then get Sts to answer 2–4 with a partner.

5 READING & LISTENING

a Do this in pairs or as a whole-class activity. Make sure Sts know what *talent* means.

With a show of hands find out what Sts think is behind success.

b Tell Sts that they are going to read an article on success.

Now set a time limit for Sts to read the article and answer questions 1–3.

Get Sts to compare with a partner and then check answers.

Extra support

- Before Sts read the article, check it for words and phrases which your Sts might not know and be ready to help with these while they are answering the questions or afterwards. You may even want to preteach / check a few words / phrases to lighten the load, e.g., *elite*, *come to light*, etc.

1 Talent, luck, and practice.
2 Because they will probably be bigger, stronger, and more coordinated than other sports players in their school year, and will be chosen for sports teams.
3 It is a theory that says that in order to get to the very top you need to put in 10,000 hours of practice.

c (5 6)) Focus on the instructions and the task. Elicit some information from the class about The Beatles and Bill Gates.

Play the audio once all the way through.

Check the answer.

Extra support

- Before playing the audio, go through the listening script and decide if you need to preteach / check any lexis to help Sts when they listen.

Luck and hard work / practice.

(5 6))
(script in Student Book on *page 129*)
Apart from the hockey players, he also gives the examples of The Beatles, the most famous rock band of all time, and Bill Gates, the founder of Microsoft. The Beatles were really lucky to be invited to play in Hamburg in 1960. The club owner who invited them usually only invited bands from London, but on one trip to the UK he met an entrepreneur from Liverpool who told him that there were some really good bands in that city. When The Beatles arrived in Hamburg, they had to work incredibly hard. They had to play for up to eight hours a night in the club seven nights a week. As John Lennon said later, "We got better and we got more confidence. We couldn't help it, with all the experience we got from playing all night long in the club." By 1964, when they became really successful, The Beatles had been to Hamburg four times, and had already performed live an estimated 1,200 times, far more than many bands today perform in their entire careers.
Bill Gates's huge stroke of good luck came in 1968, when the high school he was attending decided to spend some money they'd been given on a computer. This computer was kept in a little room that then became the computer club. In 1968, most *colleges* didn't have a computer club, let alone schools. From that time on, Gates spent most of his time in the computer room, because he and his friends taught themselves how to use it. "It was my obsession," Gates says of those early high school years. "I skipped sports. I went up there at night. We were programming on weekends. It would be a rare week that we wouldn't get 20 or 30 hours in." So Gates was unbelievably lucky to have access to a computer, but of course he also put in all those hours of practice, too.
Talent, Gladwell concludes, is obviously important, but there are many talented people out there. What makes just a few of them special is that they are lucky and that they put in far more hours of practice than the rest.

d Before playing the audio again, give Sts time to read questions 1–8.

Play the first part of the audio about The Beatles, and then give Sts time to answer questions 1–4. If necessary, play that section again.

Get Sts to compare with a partner and then check answers.

Repeat for the second part about Bill Gates.

1 They played in Hamburg / Germany between 1960 and 1964.
2 London
3 They had to play for up to eight hours a night seven nights a week.
4 They had performed live about 1,200 times.
5 In 1968.
6 Because in those days most colleges, let alone schools didn't have a computer.
7 They spent time at the computer club programming.
8 Between 20 and 30 hours.

! The noun *computer program* is spelled the same in both American and British English. The verb is *to program*, but in American English we double the *m* in the continuous form and the participle (*programming*, *programmed*).

Extra support

• If there's time, you could play the audio again while Sts read the script on *page 129*, so they can see what they understood / didn't understand. Translate / explain any new words or phrases.

e In pairs, Sts discuss the two questions.

Get some feedback from various pairs.

Extra support

• You could do question 1 with the whole class and then elicit answers to 2 from any Sts who feel that there is something they are good at.

6 VOCABULARY

making adjectives and adverbs

a Focus on the sentence from the article, and elicit that *lucky* is an adjective and *luck* is a noun.

! The phrase *be lucky* may be a problem for some Sts who express the same concept in their L1 as *have luck*.

Now focus on questions 1–3 and get Sts either in pairs or individually to answer them.

Check answers.

1 unlucky
2 luckily
3 unluckily

b Tell Sts to go to **Vocabulary Bank** *Word building* on *page 163*.

Focus on **2 Making adjectives and adverbs** and get Sts to do **a** in pairs.

(5 7)) Now do **b**. Play the audio for Sts to check answers. Play the audio again, pausing for Sts to repeat. Practice any words your Sts find difficult to pronounce, modeling and drilling as necessary. You could use the audio to do this.

(5 7))
Word building
Making adjectives and adverbs
luck	lucky, unlucky, luckily, unluckily
fortune	fortunate, unfortunate, fortunately, unfortunately
comfort	comfortable, uncomfortable, comfortably, uncomfortably
patience	patient, impatient, patiently, impatiently
care	careful, careless, carefully, carelessly

Point out that:

– *-y* and *-able* are both typical adjective endings.

– *un-* and *im-* are common prefixes to make an adjective negative, but adjectives formed with the suffix *-ful*, e.g., *careful*, usually (but not always) form the opposite adjective with *-less*, e.g., *useful*, *useless*.

– the suffix *-ful* = *full of* or *with*, *-less* = *without*.

– sometimes there are spelling changes, e.g., the final *e* is dropped before an *-ly* suffix, e.g., *comfortably*, *possibly*, etc. With adjectives ending in consonant + *y*, the *y* changes to *i* before adding the suffix, e.g., *lucky–luckily*, *healthy–healthily*, etc.

Extra support

• Get Sts to underline the stressed syllable in all the words in the chart.

For **c**, get Sts to fill in each blank with the adjective or adverb made from the noun in bold. Tell them to be careful as some are positive and some negative.

(5 8)) Now do **d**. Play the audio for Sts to listen and check answers.

(5 8))
1 The beach was beautiful, but **unfortunately** it rained almost every day.
2 My new shoes are very **comfortable**. I wore them for the first time yesterday, and they didn't hurt at all.
3 He took the exam quickly and **carelessly**, and so he made a lot of mistakes.
4 We were really **unlucky**. We missed the flight by just five minutes.
5 Jack is a very **impatient** driver! He can't stand being behind someone who is driving slowly.
6 It was a bad accident, but **luckily** nobody was seriously hurt.
7 It was raining, but fans waited **patiently** in line to buy tickets for tomorrow's concert.
8 The roads will be very icy tonight, so drive **carefully**.
9 The temperature dropped to 20 degrees, but **fortunately** we were all wearing warm coats and jackets.
10 The bed in the hotel was incredibly **uncomfortable**. I hardly slept at all.

Tell Sts to go back to the main lesson 9A.

Extra support

• If you think Sts need more practice, you may want to give them the Vocabulary photocopiable activity at this point or leave it for later as consolidation or review.

7 WRITING

a Tell Sts they are going to play *The sentence game* and read the rules together as a class. Make sure everything is clear. You could demonstrate the activity by writing on the board FRIEND (7 WORDS) and then PEOPLE IN MY COUNTRY ARE VERY FRIENDLY.

b Put Sts in teams of three or four and give them five minutes to write five sentences. If they need more time, just extend the limit.

c When the time is up, get each team to read their sentences aloud. The teams with five correct sentences are the winners.

Extra support
- You could write each team's sentences on the board and get the other teams to say if they are correct or not.

8 **SONG** *Karma* ♫

This song was originally made famous by American singer Alicia Keys in 2004. For copyright reasons this is a cover version. If you want to do this song in class, use the photocopiable activity on *page 225*.

(5 9)))

Karma

Come on
Come on
Come on
Weren't you the one who said
That you don't want me anymore
And how you need your space
And give the keys back to your door
And how I cried and tried
And tried to make you stay with me
But still you said your love was gone
And that I had to leave

> **Chorus**
> (Now you) talking 'bout a family
> (Now you) saying I complete your dream
> (Now you) saying I'm your everything
> You're confusing me, what you say to me
> Don't play with me, don't play with me, 'cause...
> What goes around, comes around
> What goes up, must come down
> Now who's crying, desiring to come back to me?
> What goes around, comes around
> What goes up, must come down
> Now who's crying, desiring, to come back?
> I remember when I was sitting home alone
> Waiting for you 'til three o'clock in the morn

And when you came home
You'd always have some sorry excuse
Half explaining to me
Like I'm just some kind of a fool
I sacrificed the things I want
Just to do things for you
But when it's time to do for me
You never come through

> **Chorus**

Night after night knowing something going on
Wasn't long before I be g-g-g-gone
Lord knows it wasn't easy, believe me
Never thought you'd be the one that would deceive me
And never knew what you supposed to do
No need to approach me fool, 'cause I'm over you

What goes around, comes around
What goes up, must come down
Now who's crying, desiring to come back to me
What goes around, comes around
What goes up, must come down
It's called karma baby and it goes around
(Repeat to fade)

G quantifiers, 🔍separable phrasal verbs
V electronic devices, phrasal verbs
P *ough* and *augh*, linking

9B Too much information!

Lesson plan

This lesson reviews and extends Sts' knowledge of quantifiers, e.g., *a lot | plenty of, too much, not enough*, etc. through the topic of information overload. First, the grammar is presented through sentences related to the Internet and electronic devices. There is then a pronunciation focus on the frequently problematic combinations *-ough* and *-augh*. Sts then read and discuss an article about information overload, i.e., how nowadays we are bombarded with far more information than we need.

The vocabulary focus is on electronic devices and their accessories, and phrasal verbs associated with these devices. This is followed with more pronunciation practice on linking words. The main topic of this second half is a radio show about a book called *The Winter of Our Disconnect*, which describes the experiment that a journalist did where she and her family had to live without the Internet and screen-based devices for six months. The lesson ends with a writing focus where Sts write a magazine article analyzing the advantages and disadvantages of smartphones.

STUDY LINK
- **Workbook** 9B
- **iChecker**

Extra photocopiable activities

- **Grammar** quantifiers *page* 161
- **Communicative** Lifestyle survey *page* 192 (instructions *page* 170)
- **Vocabulary** Phrasal verbs *page* 214 (instructions *page* 199)

Optional lead-in (books closed)

- Tell Sts to imagine they have just boarded a plane and are in their seats. Ask them to think of all the announcements they will hear between now and takeoff.

- Try to elicit *Please turn off all electronic devices*, and write it on the board. Elicit / explain that *electronic devices* are gadgets like phones, iPads or other tablets, laptops, etc.

1 GRAMMAR quantifiers

a Books open. Focus on the instructions and the illustration. If you didn't do the **Optional lead-in**, elicit the meaning of *devices*. Model and drill the pronunciation of *device* /dɪˈvaɪs/ and the plural *devices* /dɪˈvaɪsɪz/.

Elicit what Sts can see in the picture, e.g., a cell phone, a laptop, a tablet (iPad), a smartphone (iPhone), an iPod, and a webcam.

Now get Sts to answer the questions in pairs.

Get feedback from the class.

b Focus on the task and get Sts to circle the correct phrase in 1–6.

Get Sts to compare with a partner and then check answers. Drill the pronunciation where necessary, e.g., *enough* /ɪˈnʌf/.

1	a lot of	4	a few, none
2	enough money	5	big enough
3	too much	6	too

c (5 10)) (5 11)) (5 12)) (5 13)) Tell Sts to go to **Grammar Bank 9B** on *page 149*. Focus on the example sentences and play the audio for Sts to listen to the sentence rhythm. You could also get Sts to repeat the sentences to practice getting the rhythm right. Then go through the rules with the class.

Additional grammar notes

Quantifiers

- Sts should have seen most or all of these forms previously, but here they are brought together.

large quantities

- *Lots of* is a colloquial equivalent of *a lot of*. Be careful Sts don't say *a lots of*.

- Some nationalities confuse *plenty of* and *full of* because of L1 interference.

small quantities

- *A little* and *very little* are quite different in meaning (the second is more negative). The same applies to *a few* and *very few*.

more or less than you need or want

- Some typical mistakes include:

  – using *too much* + an adjective, e.g., ~~I'm too much busy~~.

  – the position of *enough*, e.g., ~~I'm not enough tall to open the cupboard~~.

  – mispronouncing *enough*.

zero quantity

- You may want to point out that *no* is an adjective and must be used with a noun, e.g., *I have no time, no brothers and sisters*, etc. *None* is a pronoun, so it is used on its own, e.g., *Is there any milk? No, I'm afraid there's none left*.

Focus on the exercises and get Sts to do them individually or in pairs.

Check answers, getting Sts to read the full sentences.

```
a
1   a few            6   a lot
2   much             7   too
3   ✓                8   ✓
4   very few         9   old enough
5   ✓               10   ✓
b
1   A lot
2   ✓
3   I don't use any social networks
4   too loud / much too loud
5   ✓
6   isn't fast enough
7   too many phone calls
8   None
9   only a few websites
10  ✓
```

Tell Sts to go back to the main lesson **9B**.

Extra support
* If you think Sts need more practice, you may want to give them the Grammar photocopiable activity at this point or leave it for later as consolidation or review.

d Put Sts in pairs and get them to discuss whether sentences 1–6 in **b** are true for them. Tell them to give as much information as possible.

Get some feedback.

2   PRONUNCIATION   *ough* and *augh*

> **Pronunciation notes**
> * The aim of these exercises is to help Sts remember the pronunciation of a group of high frequency words which all contain -*ough* / -*augh* – a combination of letters which has a relatively complex spelling / pronunciation relationship.

a Focus on the ***ough* and *augh*** box and go through it with Sts.

Then focus on the five columns and elicit the sound word for each.

Now get Sts to put the words in the right column. They could do this in pairs. Encourage them to say the words out loud and to use their instinct to help them decide.

b **5 14))** Play the audio once for Sts to listen and check.

Check answers.

```
5 14))
up /ʌ/        enough, tough
saw /ɔ/       bought, brought, caught, cough, daughter, thought
phone /oʊ/    although
cat /æ/       laugh
boot /u/      through
```

Then ask Sts *Which is the most common sound?*

/ɔ/ is the most common sound.

Point out to Sts that this is true especially when there is a *t* after -*ough* or -*augh*. This includes the simple past / past participle forms (*bought, brought, caught, taught,* and *thought*).

Now ask Sts *Which four words end with the sound /f/?*

enough, tough, laugh, cough

Emphasize that this is a small group of very common (but slightly irregular) words, and it is worthwhile for Sts to memorize their pronunciation.

Finally, play the audio again, pausing after each group of words for Sts to listen and repeat.

c **5 15))** Focus on the sentences, which all contain the target sounds. Play the audio all the way through for Sts just to listen.

> **5 15))**
> See sentences in Student Book on *page 88*

Give Sts time to practice saying them in pairs.

Finally, elicit the sentences from individual Sts.

Extra support
* Play the audio first, pausing for Sts to repeat. Then let Sts practice saying them again.

3   READING & SPEAKING

a Focus on the article and the question. Give Sts time to read the first paragraph.

Get Sts to compare with a partner and then check the answer.

"Information overload" means getting too much information.

b Focus on the task and give Sts time to read the three multiple-choice questions. Then set a time limit for them to read the article and choose the right answers.

Get Sts to compare with a partner and then check answers.

Extra support
* Before Sts read the article, check it for words and phrases that your Sts might not know and be ready to help with these while they are answering the questions or afterwards. You may even want to preteach / check a few words / phrases to lighten the load, e.g., *obscure, irritation,* etc. (but not the highlighted words).

1 b   2 c   3 b

c Focus on the highlighted words and phrases related to the Internet and technology. Get Sts, in pairs, to read the article again and figure out their meaning.

Check answers, either explaining in English, translating into Sts' L1, or getting Sts to check in their dictionaries.

Help with any other new vocabulary.

d In pairs, Sts discuss the questions. Monitor and help, correcting any mistakes with quantifiers.

Get some feedback from the class.

4 VOCABULARY & PRONUNCIATION

electronic devices, phrasal verbs, linking

a Focus on the instructions and the words in the list.

Give Sts time, individually or in pairs, to match the words and pictures.

b **5 16))** Play the audio once for Sts to listen and check.

5 16))		
1	a switch	7	a mouse
2	a plug	8	a speaker
3	headphones	9	a flash drive
4	a remote control	10	an adaptor
5	a screen	11	a USB cable
6	a keyboard	12	an outlet

Then play it again, pausing after each word for Sts to listen and repeat.

Now put Sts in pairs and tell them to test each other by covering the words and looking at the pictures.

c Tell Sts that all the sentences refer to electronic devices and the verbs or phrases we commonly use to talk about them.

Now give Sts time to match 1–7 and A–G according to their meaning.

Get Sts to compare with a partner.

d **5 17))** Play the audio once for Sts to listen and check.

Check answers.

See **bold** in script 5.17

5 17))

1 C I changed the heat from 70 degrees to 62 degrees. I **turned it down**.
2 F I disconnected my iPod from the computer. I **unplugged it**.
3 D I increased the volume on the TV. I **turned it up**.
4 A I pressed the "off" button on the TV. I **switched it off**.
5 G I programmed the alarm on my phone. I **set it for 7:30**.
6 E I put my phone charger into an outlet. I **plugged it in**.
7 B I pressed the "on" button on my laptop. I **switched it on**.

Focus on the **Separable phrasal verbs** box and go through it with Sts.

e **5 18))** Play the audio for Sts to listen and notice how the words are linked.

Then play it again, pausing after each sentence for Sts to repeat.

5 18))

A	I switched it off.	E	I plugged it in.
B	I switched it on.	F	I unplugged it.
C	I turned it down.	G	I set it for 7:30.
D	I turned it up.		

Now get individual Sts to say the sentences.

Finally, tell Sts to cover sentences A–G, look at 1–7, and say A–G from memory.

Extra support

- If you think Sts need more practice, you may want to give them the Vocabulary photocopiable activity at this point or leave it for later as consolidation or review.

f Quickly go through questions 1–6, making sure Sts understand them.

Put Sts in pairs and get them to ask and answer the questions. Encourage them to give reasons for their answers.

Get some feedback.

5 LISTENING & SPEAKING

a Focus on the task. Make sure Sts understand the book review information and highlight the note on the title of the book.

Get Sts to answer the questions in pairs or do it as a whole class. Do <u>not</u> tell Sts if they are right yet.

b **5 19))** Focus on the instructions and give Sts time to read the six questions.

Play the audio once all the way through. Play it again, pausing if necessary after each answer is given to give Sts time to write.

Get Sts to compare with a partner and then check answers.

Extra support

- Before playing the audio, go through the listening script and decide if you need to preteach / check any lexis to help Sts when they listen.

1 Because the whole family, especially the children, were always plugged into a device, e.g., their laptops, their iPods, etc. and weren't relating to the other people in the family.
2 No, it was the whole family.
3 "Digital immigrants" are people who did not grow up with digital technology (anyone born before 1980). "Digital natives" are people who were born <u>after</u> computers and the Internet already existed.
4 At home they had to switch off any electrical gadgets with a screen (smartphones, TVs, laptops or computers, gameboxes and iPods).
5 They were allowed to use technology in school or at friends' houses, or in Internet cafes, and they were allowed to use landline phones.
6 She told them she was going to write a book about the experiment and that they would share in any profits that she made from the book.

5 19))

(script in Student Book on *page 129*)
H= host, J = Jeremy, A = Andrew, C = Chloe, S = Sally

Part 1

H And now it's time for our book of the week, which is *The Winter of our Disconnect* by Susan Maushart. Jeremy, to start with, it's a good title, isn't it?
J Yes, amazing. And it was a fascinating experiment and a good read.
H Tell us about it.
J Well, Susan Maushart is a journalist who's raising three teenage children. She decided to do the experiment after reaching a point where she felt that the whole family, especially her children, were all living in their own little worlds, with headphones on, plugged into their laptops or their iPods or their smartphones, and that they weren't relating to the other people in the family.

A So it wasn't just her children who were permanently plugged into an electrical device?

J Well, she admits that she herself was addicted to her phone and to her iPod and her laptop and that she was constantly reading news sites and googling information, but it was really her children who were totally dependent on new technology. In the book she makes the interesting distinction between "digital immigrants" and "digital natives".

C What does that mean?

J She describes herself is a digital immigrant, that's to say someone who didn't grow up with digital technology, which is really anyone who was born before 1980. Her children are digital natives, which means that they were born <u>after</u> computers and the Internet were already part of life.

C Well, that's me then.

J Yes, well, the main difference, she says, is that digital immigrants <u>use</u> the technology, to find information or to listen to music, but digital natives live and breathe the technology. So for them living without it is like living without water, without electricity... in the dark ages.

C What were the rules of the experiment?

J The family had to live for six months without using any electrical gadgets in the house with a screen. So no smartphones, no TVs, no laptops or computers, no video consoles and no iPods. They <u>were</u> allowed to use technology at school or at friends' houses, or in Internet cafes, and they were allowed to use landline phones. But everything else was switched off for the whole six months.

S Six months? How on earth did she get the children to agree?

J She bribed them. She told them that she was going to write a book about the experiment and that they would share in any profits that she made from the book!

S Wow, that was very smart of her...

c (5 20)) Focus on the question and tell Sts to listen for the answer.

Play the audio once all the way through.

Get Sts to compare with a partner and play the audio again if necessary.

Check the answer.

> In general, the experiment was positive because Susan's family talked more to each other, they did more activities alone and together, they slept better, and the children's school work improved.

(5 20))

(script in Student Book on *pages 129–130*)

Part 2

H So what were the results? Was it a positive experience?

J At the end of the book, Susan says that it was a positive experience in every way. At first, of course, the kids complained bitterly, they kept saying they were bored. But then they started to talk to each other again, to go and sit in each other's rooms and talk. They got interested in cooking and reading, they went to the movies together. They played CDs on the CD player and they actually sat and listened to the music instead of just having music on their headphones all the time as background music. And Susan's 15-year-old son started playing the saxophone again. He'd stopped playing a few years before, but then he started taking lessons again and even started giving concerts... Oh and the children said that they slept better!

S Oh, well that's good, yeah. What about the children's schoolwork? I mean nowadays we sort of assume that everyone needs the Internet to do research for homework and so on.

J In fact, the children's report cards showed that they all improved. When they needed the Internet, they used the computers at school or at college (the eldest daughter was in college), or they went to friends' houses. But when they did their homework, they did it better than before because they weren't multitasking – they weren't doing homework <u>and</u> listening to music <u>and</u> sending messages all at the same time. So they concentrated better, and their schoolwork improved.

A What about Susan, the mother? Did she find it difficult to live without modern technology?

J What she found most difficult was writing her weekly article for the newspaper because she had to do it by hand, and not on her laptop. She says that at the beginning her hand used to really ache, she just wasn't used to writing by hand anymore. But that was just a small problem.

C Any other negatives?

J Well, of course the phone bill for their landline was huge!

C Has the experiment had a lasting effect?

J Susan says that it has. She thinks that they all get along much better as a family, her son is still playing the saxophone, and he sold his video console. They've all realized that we live in a digital world, but that we need to disconnect from time to time and to reconnect with the people around us. So they have new rules in the house, like no TVs in bedrooms and no TV in the kitchen where they eat. And no wasted hours on the Internet.

S Sounds great. That would be a good rule for me too!

d Give Sts time to read the beginning of six sentences, which they have to complete.

Play the audio again, pausing if necessary after each answer is given to give Sts time to write.

Get Sts to compare with a partner and play the audio again if necessary.

Check answers.

> **Possible answers**
> 1 they were bored.
> 2 talk to each other again.
> 3 play the saxophone again.
> 4 write her weekly article for the newspaper.
> 5 the phone bill for their landline was huge.
> 6 no TVs in bedrooms or in the kitchen and no wasted hours on the Internet.

e (5 21)) Focus on the instructions and the chart and tell Sts they will hear each of the people on the program saying what they would miss the most if they had to do the experiment.

Play the audio once all the way through.

Get Sts to compare with a partner. Then play the audio again, pausing after each person, and check answers.

Sally	the Internet
Andrew	a computer or laptop
Jeremy	nothing
Chloe	her phone (she wouldn't do the experiment)

(5 21))

(script in Student Book on *page 130*)

Part 3

H OK, so imagine you all did the experiment. What would you miss the most? Sally?

S Well, I already live without the Internet many weekends because we have a house in the country in the middle of nowhere where there's no Internet service. So I know that what I would miss most is being able to google information, like the phone number of a restaurant, or what time a movie starts. Or even, dare I say it, the sports scores. I don't have a TV, so I wouldn't miss that, but I would miss not having the Internet.

H Andrew?

A Well, I just couldn't live without a computer or a laptop because I work from home, so I don't have an office to go to, and I absolutely need the Internet too. I couldn't do the experiment – I just wouldn't be prepared to go to an Internet cafe all day to work. Susan, the journalist who did the experiment, only had to write one column a week, but I work from home eight hours a day.

H Jeremy.

J I think I could do it, I think I could easily live without any of these electrical gadgets at home. I mean, I have my office, so I could use the Internet there. I don't use an iPod, I still prefer to listen to CDs...

C You old dinosaur!

J Yes, yes I know, and I don't watch much TV. I am very attached to my Blackberry, but I wouldn't mind using a regualr phone for six months. I don't think there's anything I'd miss too much.

H And finally Chloe, our only digital native.

C Well, I'm sorry, but I just wouldn't be prepared to even try the experiment, not even for a week let alone six months. I wouldn't be prepared to live without my phone. I use it for everything, calling, music, the Internet. So, no I wouldn't do it.

H Not even if you were offered money?

C It would have to be a huge amount of money. No, I'm definitely not going to do it!

Extra support

- If there's time, you could play the audio again while Sts read the scripts on *pages 129–130*, so they can see what they understood / didn't understand. Translate / explain any new words or phrases.

f Focus on the **Useful language** box and go through it with Sts.

Put Sts in pairs and get them to discuss the three questions.

Get some feedback. For question 3, you could see if there is one device that the majority of the class would miss the most.

6 **WRITING** a magazine article – advantages and disadvantages

Tell Sts to go to **Writing** *A magazine article – advantages and disadvantages* on *page 120*.

a Focus on the instructions and give Sts time to read the article and correct the mistakes.

Get Sts to compare with a partner and then check answers. Elicit the answers onto the board.

1	has	6	shows
2	talking	7	documentaries
3	better	8	what's
4	different	9	although
5	their	10	off

Extra challenge

- Before Sts read the article, write on the board ADVANTAGES AND DISADVANTAGES OF LIVING WITHOUT A TV. Put Sts in pairs or small groups and tell them to think of three advantages and three disadvantages. Then get them to read the article to see if their ideas are there.

b Focus on the instructions and the task.

Give Sts time to read the article again.

Now get them to cover it and, in pairs, answer the three questions.

Check answers.

> 1 Families spend more time talking to each other.
> They spend more time doing more creative things like reading or painting.
> They spend more time outdoors and are usually in better shape.
> 2 Children who don't have a TV may feel different from their school friends and often won't know what they are talking about.
> People who live without a TV may know less about what's happening in the world.
> 3 The writer is for having a TV.

c Now tell Sts they are going to write a similar article about smartphones.

Put Sts in pairs and give them time to write a list of three advantages and three disadvantages for living without a smartphone.

d Individually Sts now number their advantages and disadvantages from 1 to 3 with 1 being the most important advantage and disadvantage.

Focus on the **Useful language: writing about advantages and disadvantages** box and go through it with Sts.

e Write the title of the article on the board: SMARTPHONES – A GREAT INVENTION?

Go through the introduction with Sts and tell them to write three more paragraphs as in the model, and to use the **Useful language** box to help them.

You may choose to get Sts to do the writing in class or you could assign it as homework. If you do it in class, set a time limit for Sts to write their article, e.g., 15–20 minutes.

f Sts should check their work for mistakes before turning it in.

PRACTICAL ENGLISH
Episode 5 Unexpected events

Lesson plan

In this final episode Sts learn how to ask questions in an indirect way, e.g., beginning with *Could you tell me…?* or *Do you know…?*

In the first scene Jenny arrives at Rob's apartment and is surprised to find Paul still there, since Rob had said he was leaving. Paul then tells Jenny that Rob is planning to go back to the UK. Jenny is upset and leaves just as Rob arrives. Rob is furious with Paul for telling Jenny something that simply isn't true, and makes it clear to Paul how serious he is about Jenny. In the next scene Rob attempts to explain and make things right, but Jenny is not convinced that he is serious about their relationship. However, in the final scene Rob does his best to prove that he is.

STUDY LINK
• **Workbook** Unexpected events

Testing Program CD-ROM

• Quick Test 9
• File 9 Test

Optional lead-in (books closed)

• Elicit from the class what happened in the previous episode. Ask some questions, e.g., *Where did Rob and Paul go? Where did Jenny go? Why didn't she go with them?*

• Alternatively, you could play the last scene of Episode 4.

1 ◄ JENNY GETS A SURPRISE
VIDEO

a (5 22)») Books open. Focus on the photos and ask Sts *Where is Jenny in the first photo?* (Outside Rob's apartment building), *What do you think Rob is saying?*, etc.

Now either tell Sts to close their books and write the question on the board, or get Sts to focus on the question and cover the rest of the page.

Play the DVD or audio once all the way through and then check the answer.

> Jenny is upset and Rob is furious.

(5 22)»)
(script in Student Book on *page 130*)
P = Paul, J = Jenny, R = Rob

P Yeah?
J Hi, there. It's me. Should I come up?
***
J Paul!
P That's right.
J Uh... hi.
P Hi... Are you OK?
J Yes, fine. Thanks. It's just that I um...
P What?
J I wasn't expecting to see you.

P Really? Well, as you can see, I'm still here. It seems Rob just can't live without me. Yeah, he's going to miss me when I'm gone. But not for long. We'll meet up again when he goes back to London.
J Goes back...?
P Yeah, he told me last night that he was planning to leave New York pretty soon.
J He what?
R Hi, Jenny. Do you want some breakfast? I've got bagels.
J No, thank you, Rob. Why don't you two enjoy them?
R What's wrong?
P No idea. I just said you were planning to leave New York soon and she...
R You what? I didn't say that!
P You didn't have to. This New York life isn't you, Rob, and you know it.
R No, I don't! I like New York and Jenny's here.
P Oh, come on! What's the big deal? It's not like you want to marry her.
R Well...
P What? You do?
R Look, Paul. I'm serious about New York and I'm serious about Jenny. And I want you to leave. Today.
P You're joking, mate.
R No, I'm not. I'll even buy the ticket.

b Focus on sentences 1–6. Go through them with Sts and make sure they understand them.

Now play the DVD or audio again all the way through, and get Sts to mark the sentences T (true) or F (false). Remind them to correct the false ones.

Get Sts to compare with a partner and then check answers.

> 1 T
> 2 F (Paul tells Jenny that Rob is planning **to go back to London.**)
> 3 F (Rob arrives with **bagels** for breakfast.)
> 4 T
> 5 T
> 6 F (Rob says he will **buy Paul's ticket** to Boston.)

Extra support

• If there's time, you could get Sts to listen again with the script on *page 130*, so they can see exactly what they understood / didn't understand. Translate / explain any new words or phrases.

2 ◄ INDIRECT QUESTIONS
VIDEO

a (5 23)») Focus on the photo and the instructions and make sure Sts understand the question.

Now either tell Sts to close their books and write the question on the board, or get Sts to focus on the question and cover the rest of the page.

Play the DVD or audio once all the way through and then check the answer.

> No, they don't.

---

5 23))

(script in Student Book on *page 130*)

R = Rob, J = Jenny, D = Don

R   Hi, Jenny.
J   Rob.
R   Paul told me what he said to you and it's not true. I'm not planning to leave New York.
J   Oh, really? Could you tell me why Paul is still in your apartment?
R   Well, he couldn't get a ticket to Boston…
J   But you told me he was going a few days ago. Or was that another lie?
R   No, of course it wasn't! He couldn't get a ticket. The buses to Boston were all full.
J   So do you know if he's got one now?
R   I bought it! He's leaving this evening. But that isn't really the issue here, is it? You have to believe me – I don't want to leave New York!
J   How can I believe you? I know you're missing London because you said the same thing to Kerri at the restaurant. Look Rob, I'd like to know what you really want.
R   What do you mean?
J   When you and Paul were together, it was like you were a different person.
R   You know what Paul's like. What was I meant to do? But that isn't the kind of life I want anymore. I'm not like that.
J   I know you're not, but I wonder if you really want to be here. I wonder if…
R   Jenny, what is it?
J   Forget it.
R   Jenny… what are you worrying about?
J   I don't know if this is going to work out.
R   You're not serious.
J   I'm just not sure if we want the same things anymore.
R   That's crazy…
D   Jenny – oh, good morning, Rob.
R   Don.
D   I need a word. Can you tell me what you decided at the last meeting?
J   Right away, Don. Rob was just leaving.

---

b Give Sts time to read questions 1–5.

Play the DVD or audio again, pausing if necessary to give Sts time to answer the questions.

Get Sts to compare with a partner and then check answers.

1   Paul couldn't get a ticket to Boston because all the buses were full.
2   Rob bought Paul's ticket to Boston.
3   Because he told Kerri that he misses London.
4   He behaved like a different person.
5   That she doesn't know if it is going to work out.

Extra support

• If there's time, you could get Sts to listen again with the script on *page 130*, so they can see exactly what they understood / didn't understand. Translate / explain any new words or phrases.

c **5 24**)) Give Sts a minute to read through the extracts from the conversation and to think about what the missing words might be.

Now play the DVD or audio again and get Sts to fill in the blanks.

Get Sts to compare with a partner and then check answers.

See words in **bold** in script 5.24

---

5 24))

1
J   Could you **tell** me why Paul is still in your apartment?
R   Well, he couldn't get a ticket to Boston…
2
J   Do you **know** if he's got one now?
R   I bought it! He's leaving this evening.
3
J   Look Rob, I'd **like** to know what you really want.
R   What do you mean?
4
J   I **wonder** if you really want to be here. I wonder if…
R   Jenny, what is it?
5
D   I need a word. **Can** you tell me what you decided at the last meeting?
J   Right away, Don. Rob was just leaving.

---

d **5 25**)) Tell Sts to focus on the highlighted phrases in the extracts. They should listen and repeat the phrases, copying the rhythm and intonation.

Play the DVD or audio, pausing for Sts to listen and repeat.

5 25))

See highlighted phrases in Student Book on *page 92*

Then repeat the activity, eliciting responses from individual Sts.

e Put Sts in pairs and tell them to practice the dialogues in **c**.

Monitor and help, encouraging Sts to pay attention to rhythm and intonation.

Make sure Sts change roles.

f Focus on the **Indirect questions** box and go through it with the class.

Now focus on the instructions and give Sts time to complete indirect questions 1–5.

Get Sts to compare with a partner and then check answers.

1   where the station is
2   what he said
3   if / whether she likes me
4   if / whether your brother is coming tonight
5   what time the store closes

g Put Sts in pairs, **A** and **B**, and tell them to go to **Communication** *Asking politely for information*, **A** on *page 106*, **B** on *page 110*.

Go through the instructions with them carefully. Tell Sts to focus on instruction **a** and give them some time to write the indirect questions. When they are ready, tell the **A**s they are the tourists and they should turn to the **B**s and start by saying *Excuse me*.

Monitor and help.

Make sure they change roles.

When they have finished, get feedback.

Extra support

• You could write any new and useful words and phrases from **Communication** on the board for Sts to copy.

Tell Sts to go back to the main lesson.

3 ROB GETS SERIOUS

a (5 26)》) Focus on the photos and ask Sts some questions, e.g., *What's happening?*, *How do they look?*, etc.

Now either tell Sts to close their books and write the question on the board, or get Sts to focus on the question and cover the rest of the page.

Elicit Sts' predictions.

Play the DVD or audio once all the way through, and then check the answer.

Sts' own answers

(5 26)》)

(script in Student Book on *page 130*)

R = Rob, J = Jenny

R But what can I do, Jenny? What can I say to convince you? I'm serious.
J I don't know, Rob.
R Wait! What Paul said just isn't true.
J It isn't just what Paul said. It's obvious you want to go back.
R Of course I miss London, but I love my life here. What proof do you want of my commitment to New York, to you, to everything?
J I don't know.
R There must be something I can do.
J Look, we're going to see my parents later. I don't want us to be late.
R We won't be late. And I won't forget the chocolates this time either.
J Well, that's a start, I guess.
R But Jenny – we need to talk about this.
J We don't have time to discuss it now.
R Jenny!
J What is it?
R What if I proposed to you?
J "Proposed"?
R That's right. Proposed.
J Like, "Will you marry me?"
R Exactly.
J On one knee?
R I can do that… So what would you say?
J Rob, stop it. It's embarrassing.
R Tell me.
J Are you for real?
R Yes, I am actually. What about you?
J Yes!

b Focus on the instructions and give Sts time to read sentences 1–6. Make sure Sts realize they must use between two and four words only to complete each sentence.

Play the DVD or audio again, pausing if necessary to give Sts time to complete the sentences.

Get Sts to compare with a partner and then check answers.

Extra support

• Before playing the audio, go through the listening script and decide if you need to preteach / check any lexis to help Sts when they listen.

1 is serious
2 go back to London
3 life in New York City
4 Jenny's parents
5 the chocolates
6 marry him

Extra support

• If there's time, you could get Sts to listen again with the script on *page 130*, so they can see exactly what they understood / didn't understand. Translate / explain any new words or phrases.

c Focus on the **Social English phrases**. In pairs, get Sts to think about what the missing words could be.

Extra challenge

• In pairs, get Sts to complete the phrases before they listen.

d (5 27)》) Play the DVD or audio for Sts to listen and complete the phrases.

Check answers.

See words in **bold** in script 5.27

(5 27)》)

Jenny	It's **obvious** you want to go back.
Rob	Of **course** I miss London, but I love my life here.
Rob	And I won't forget the chocolates this time **either**.
Jenny	Well, that's a start, I **guess**.
Rob	**What** if I proposed to you?
Jenny	Rob, **stop** it. It's embarrassing.

If you know your Sts' L1, you could get them to translate the phrases. If not, get Sts to look at the phrases again in context in the script on *page 130*.

e Now play the DVD or audio again, pausing after each phrase for Sts to listen and repeat.

Finally, focus on the **Can you…?** questions and ask Sts if they feel confident they can now do these things.

G relative clauses: defining and nondefining
V compound nouns
P word stress

10A Modern icons

Lesson plan

The theme of this lesson is modern icons, both people and objects. The first half of the lesson focuses on Steve Jobs, the cofounder of Apple, the computer company. This context is used to review and extend Sts' knowledge of relative clauses. The new grammar (nondefining clauses) is consolidated in a writing activity about Mark Zuckerberg, the creator of *Facebook*.

The second half of the lesson focuses on great American design icons such as the Chrysler Building in New York City. Sts listen to information about several of these icons and how they were invented. They then talk about iconic people and objects they admire. The lexical and pronunciation focus is on compound nouns and is followed by a vocabulary race reviewing compounds nouns that were learned earlier in the book. The lesson finishes with a song, *Greatest Love of All*.

STUDY **LINK**
• **Workbook** 10A

Extra photocopiable activities

• **Grammar** relative clauses *page 162*
• **Communicative** Relative clauses quiz *page 193* (instructions *page 170*)
• **Song** *Greatest Love of All page 226* (instructions *page 217*)

Optional lead-in (books closed)

• Write APPLE INC. on the board and ask Sts to tell you what products (apart from computers) they are famous for. Write these on the board, e.g., iPhone, iPod, iPad, iTunes, etc.

• Find out how many Sts in the class own an Apple product.

• Then ask Sts if they can name the man who cofounded Apple and who is considered to be the "father of the digital revolution," and elicit Steve Jobs.

1 READING

a Books open. Focus on the quiz and put Sts in pairs to answer the questions. Set a time limit.

b (5 28)》 Put two pairs together and get them to compare their answers.

Now play the audio for Sts to listen and check their answers.

1 b	2 b	3 a	4 a	5 a	6 b	7 b

(5 28)》
1 Steve Jobs was born in San Francisco in 1955.
2 He dropped out of Reed College in Oregon after just six months.
3 His first job was with Atari, the video game company.
4 The Apple Macintosh was the first successful computer to use a mouse.
5 He cofounded Pixar in 1986, the company that produced *Toy Story*.
6 He died of cancer of the pancreas in 2011.
7 He was only 56 years old when he died.

c Get Sts to cover paragraphs 1–5 and to focus on the photos. Tell Sts to try and guess what the connection is between the photos and Steve Jobs. Elicit ideas from Sts (e.g., *I think …*, etc.), but do <u>not</u> tell them if they are right or wrong yet.

d Now get Sts to read paragraphs 1–5 to find out the connection between the photos and Steve Jobs.

Check answers.

1 It was the first commercially successful computer made by Apple.
2 He founded Apple computers (now Apple Inc.) with Steve Jobs.
3 She's Steve Jobs's sister.
4 It's the city in the US where Steve Jobs grew up.
5 It's the logo which was designed as a tribute to Steve Jobs when he died.

Help with any vocabulary problems.

2 GRAMMAR relative clauses

a Tell Sts to cover the text and look at sentences 1–5 (which are all taken from the text). They should fill in the blanks with a relative pronoun from the list.

Check answers.

1 that	3 that / which	5 which
2 who, whose	4 where	

b Now tell Sts, in pairs, to answer questions 1 and 2.

Check answers. For question 2, point out to Sts that the relative clause can be left out as it gives extra information and that this extra information is between commas.

1 phrase 3
2 sentence 5

Tell Sts that they will learn the rules in the **Grammar Bank** for when they can leave out the relative pronoun.

c (5 29)》 (5 30)》 Tell Sts to go to **Grammar Bank 10A** on *page 150*. Focus on the example sentences and play the audio for Sts to listen to the sentence rhythm. You could also get Sts to repeat the sentences to practice getting the rhythm right. Then go through the rules with the class.

Additional grammar notes

- Sts who used *American English File* 2 have already had an introduction to defining relative clauses, but not to nondefining ones. Highlight that while defining clauses give important information which can't be left out (e.g., *Steve Jobs is the man who cofounded Apple Inc.*), nondefining clauses give extra information which <u>can</u> be left out and the sentence will still make grammatical sense (e.g., *Steve Jobs, who was born in 1955, is the man who cofounded Apple Inc.*). Nondefining clauses appear between commas in written English.

- Although *that* is a common alternative to *who* / *which* in defining relative clauses, it cannot be used in nondefining clauses. For this reason, it may be advisable to train your Sts to always use *who* / *which* in both kinds of clauses to avoid error.

- *Whom* is also sometimes used as a relative pronoun instead of *who* to refer to the object of the verb in the relative clause, or after prepositions, e.g., *She's the woman whom I met yesterday. He's the man to whom I spoke yesterday.* It is much less common and more formal than *who*. You may wish to point out its use to Sts.

- Some typical mistakes include:

  – confusing *who* and *which*, e.g., ~~She's a friend which lives near her.~~

  – using a personal pronoun, e.g., ~~He is the man who he works with my father.~~

  – using *that* in nondefining relative clauses, e.g., ~~This film, that won an Oscar in 1999, will be shown on TV tonight for the first time.~~

Focus on the exercises and get Sts to do them individually or in pairs.

Check answers, getting Sts to read the full sentences.

a
1	who	5	whose	9	where
2	where	6	that / which	10	who
3	that / which	7	which	11	who
4	who	8	whose	12	where

b
Check the following items: 3, 6, 11, 12

c
3 Beijing, which is one of the world's biggest cities, hosted the 2008 Olympic Games.
4 Michael Jackson's *Thriller*, which was released in 1982, was one of the best-selling albums of the 80s.
6 Sally and Joe, who got married last year, are expecting their first baby.

Tell Sts to go back to the main lesson **10A**.

Extra support

- If you think Sts need more practice, you may want to give them the Grammar photocopiable activity at this point or leave it for later as consolidation or review.

d Now get Sts to cover the text and look only at the photos. Ask them if they can remember what the connection was between each photo and Steve Jobs. Encourage Sts to try to use a relative clause in their answers, e.g., *It's the city where Steve Jobs grew up. It's the computer that was made by Apple in 1990.*

Extra idea

- Put Sts in pairs, **A** and **B**. **A** (text covered) tells **B** what he / she can remember for 1, 2, and 3. **B** (text uncovered) helps. Then they change roles for 4 and 5.

Extra idea

- You could now ask the class what they think of Steve Jobs, if they have (or have ever had) any Apple devices, e.g., an iPad, iPhone, etc. and what they think of them.

3 WRITING a biography

a Tell Sts to go to **Writing A biography** on *page 121*.

Focus on **a** and find out if Sts know who Mark Zuckerberg is.

Now focus on the first paragraph of the text, sentence A in the chart, and the example under the chart.

Tell Sts to read the text carefully and rewrite it using the extra information in sentences B–F.

Check answers.

In his teens he began to write software programs as a hobby. After high school he went to Harvard, **where he studied computer science and sociology**. While he was there he created a website called *Facemash*, **which allowed students to share photos**. It was shut down by the university, but it inspired him to create *Facebook*, **which he launched from his room in 2004**.
He left Harvard and moved to California with Dustin Moskovitz, **who had been his roommate**. Together they made *Facebook* an international success.
In 2012 Zuckerberg married Priscilla Chan, **who he had dated for nine years**.

Tell Sts to do **b** and cover phrases A–F and read the text to see if they can remember the extra information.

Now focus on **c** and tell Sts they are going to write a biography. They should write four paragraphs as in the model and try to use relative clauses.

You may choose to get Sts to do the writing in class or you could assign it as homework. If you do it in class, set a time limit for Sts to write their biography, e.g., 15–20 minutes.

In **d** Sts should check their work for mistakes before turning it in.

Tell Sts to go back to the main lesson **10A**.

b Put Sts in pairs, **A** and **B**, preferably face-to-face. Tell Sts to go to **Communication Relatives quiz**, **A** on *page 108*, **B** on *page 112*.

Go through their instructions and make sure Sts understand what they have to do. You could demonstrate the activity by doing number 1 (for **A** and **B**) with the whole class, before getting them to write their questions.

Monitor to make sure Sts are writing sensible questions.

Sts then take turns asking their questions to their partner.

Extra challenge

- Encourage Sts to make their clues a little cryptic, so that they are more difficult to get, e.g., if the word was *generous*, instead of defining it as *a person who likes giving presents*, they could define it as, e.g., *a person who is always the first to take out his wallet in a restaurant when the waiter brings the check*.

Extra support

- You could write any new and useful words and phrases from **Communication** on the board for Sts to copy.

Tell Sts to go back to the main lesson **10A**.

4 LISTENING

a Focus on the instructions and elicit some opinions / ideas from the class. Do <u>not</u> tell Sts if they are right or not.

b (5 31))) Focus on the task and explain / elicit the meaning of *icon* (= a famous person or thing that people see as a symbol of a particular idea, way of life, etc.). Explain that Sts are going to listen to a professor talking about some great American icons and they must complete sentences 1–4.

Play the audio once all the way through for Sts to listen. Play the audio again, pausing if necessary after each icon, and give Sts time to discuss with a partner how to complete the relevant sentence.

Check answers.

Extra support

- Before playing the audio, go through the listening script and decide if you need to preteach / check any lexis to help Sts when they listen.

1 Ruth Handler was the woman who **designed the Barbie Doll**.
2 William Van Alen was the man who **designed the Chrylser Building**.
3 Robert Indiana is the man who **designed the Love sculpture**.
4 Peter Moore and Tinker Hatfield are the men who **designed the Nike Air Jordan**.

---

5 31))
(script in Student Book on *pages 130–131*)
Barbie
Until the late 1950s, most American girls played with baby dolls, which often limited their imaginations to mother or caregiver roles. At around the same time, Ruth Handler noticed that her pre-teen daughter was playing with paper dolls, giving them adult roles such as actresses or secretaries. On a trip to Europe, Ruth saw an adult-figured doll in Germany and brought several of them back to the US. Handler had the idea that girls could expand their imagination and play-acting roles with a doll that looked like an adult. So she and engineer Jack Ryan redesigned the doll for the US market and called her Barbie after Ruth's daughter, Barbara. The first Barbie dolls were produced in 1959 and sold over 350,000 in the first year.
Barbie is still popular today, and billions have been sold around the world since 1959. Mattel, Inc. the company that produces Barbie, reports that 90 percent of American girls between the ages of three and ten have a Barbie doll.

The Chrysler Building
The Chrysler Building has been one of the most iconic New York City landmarks since it was completed in 1930. Architect William Van Alen designed the Art Deco building for Walter P. Chrysler, who owned the automobile company Chrysler Corporation. In fact, Van Alen modeled many of the building's decorative features using Chrysler car parts as inspiration. For example, the decorations on the outside of the building for the thirty-first floor are fashioned after engine parts from a 1929 Chrysler car.
Today, the Chrysler Building is still considered one of the best examples of Art Deco architecture in the US. In fact, it was voted New York City's favorite building in 2005 by Skyscraper Museum. In addition, the building appears regularly in movies and TV shows that film in New York City.

The "LOVE" Sculpture
In 1965, artist Robert Indiana had an idea for a painting with the word "LOVE" as the main focus. He decided to break the word up into two lines, putting the "LO" on top of the "VE." He then tilted the "O" a little, and an iconic American design was born. In fact, it became so popular that the Museum of Modern Art and the United States Postal Service asked Indiana to create versions of his "LOVE" painting for cards and stamps. In the early 1970s, Indiana made a series of "LOVE" sculptures for display in public parks. The first of these "LOVE" sculptures was placed in New York City, on the corner of Sixth Avenue and Fifty-fifth Street. Additional "LOVE" sculptures were placed in New Orleans, Philadelphia, Vancouver, Tokyo, and Singapore, as well as many other cities.
Unfortunately, Indiana didn't make much money from his "LOVE" paintings and sculptures. He never signed his paintings or applied for copyright, so he didn't have legal protection against the many imitations of his work.

Air Jordan Sneakers
When Michael Jordon started playing basketball for the Chicago Bulls in 1984, he had special Nike sneakers designed for him by Peter Moore. These sneakers were called the Air Jordan 1, or more simply --Air Jordans. They were red and black --the Chicago Bulls colors. Because the sneakers did not have any white on them, Jordan was fined $5,000 by the National Basketball Association each time he wore them for a game. Every year since then, Nike has created a new pair of Air Jordans to sell. In 1987, Tinker Hatfield took over the design responsibilities for these sneakers, and he has been associated with them ever since. Hatfield introduced the Jumpman logo on the sneakers, which is a silhouette of Michael Jordan dunking a basketball with his legs spread wide. In 2010, Hatfield designed the Jordan 2010s to celebrate the sneakers' twenty-fifth anniversary.

c Give Sts time to read questions 1–8.

Now play the audio again all the way through.

Get Sts to compare with a partner and then if necessary play again.

Check answers.

1	Air Jordan sneakers	5	"LOVE"
2	Chrysler Building	6	Air Jordan sneakers
3	"LOVE"	7	Barbie
4	Barbie	8	Chrysler Building

Extra challenge

- Put Sts in pairs and get them to see if they can answer any of the questions before you play the audio again.

Extra support

- If there's time, you could play the audio again while Sts read the script on *pages 130–131*, so they can see what they understood / didn't understand. Translate / explain any new words or phrases.

d In pairs, small groups, or as a class, discuss the questions.

Get some feedback from the class.

5 SPEAKING

a This is a free-speaking activity which gives Sts a chance to talk about their own icons.

Give Sts time to write a name of a person, thing, or place in as many of the seven categories as possible and give them a few minutes to prepare to talk about them (who they are, what they have done, and why they admire them, why they like the landmark / object, etc.). Monitor and help Sts with any vocabulary they may need.

b Put Sts into small groups of three (or if this is impractical, in pairs).

Sts take turns talking about one of the categories they have chosen (i.e., each student talks about one category, then the next student speaks about the same one or another, etc.).

Get some feedback.

Extra idea
- Begin by telling Sts about a couple of categories that you have chosen and explain why.

6 VOCABULARY & PRONUNCIATION

compound nouns, word stress

> **Pronunciation notes**
> - Compound noun phrases, e.g., *bus stop*, have more stress on the first word, e.g., <u>bus</u> stop. Depending on their L1, some Sts may tend to stress the second word, i.e., bus <u>stop</u>. This rule applies whether the compound noun is one word, e.g., *sunglasses*, or two, e.g., *traffic jam*.

a Focus on the **Compound nouns** box and go through it with Sts.

Now focus on the two columns and tell Sts to match a noun from **A** with one from **B** to form a compound noun.

Get Sts to compare with a partner.

b (5 32))) Play the audio once for Sts to listen and check.

Check answers, getting Sts to tell you if the compound nouns are one word or two.

> The three written as one word are *sunglasses*, *bookcase*, and *classmate*.

> (5 32)))
> soccer field
> speed camera
> sunglasses
> town hall
> bookcase
> classmate
> profile picture

Ask Sts which word is usually stressed more in compound nouns.

> The strong stress usually falls on the first word.

Put Sts in pairs and get them to practice saying the words, paying particular attention to stress.

c Tell Sts that questions 1–12 are from Files 1–10 and that each one has a compound noun as an answer. They have three minutes, in pairs, to answer as many as possible.

When time is up, check answers.

1	part-time	7	a sports arena
2	a boarding pass	8	a ringtone
3	a parking fine	9	science fiction
4	a seat belt	10	a public school
5	a traffic jam	11	the second floor
6	a tennis court	12	a flash drive

The pair with the most correct answers wins.

Extra idea
- Get Sts to write their names on a piece of paper and then the answers to the questions. When time is up, collect all the pieces of paper and redistribute them. Sts correct each other's answers.

7 (5 33))) SONG *Greatest Love of All* ♫

This song was originally made famous by American singer Whitney Houston in 1986. For copyright reasons this is a cover version. If you want to do this song in class, use the photocopiable activity on *page 226*.

> (5 33)))
>
> *Greatest Love of All*
>
> I believe the children are our future
> Teach them well and let them lead the way
> Show them all the beauty they possess inside
> Give them a sense of pride to make it easier
> Let the children's laughter remind us how we used to be
>
> Everybody's searching for a hero
> People need someone to look up to
> I never found anyone who fulfilled my needs
> A lonely place to be
> And so I learned to depend on me
>
> *Chorus*
> I decided long ago, never to walk in anyone's shadows
> If I fail, if I succeed
> At least I'll live as I believe
> No matter what they take from me
> They can't take away my dignity
> Because the greatest love of all
> Is happening to me
> I found the greatest love of all
> Inside of me
> The greatest love of all
> Is easy to achieve
> Learning to love yourself
> It is the greatest love of all
>
> I believe the children are our future
> Teach them well and let them lead the way
> Show them all the beauty they possess inside
> Give them a sense of pride to make it easier
> Let the children's laughter remind us how we used to be
>
> *Chorus*
>
> And if, by chance, that special place
> That you've been dreaming of
> Leads you to a lonely place
> Find your strength in love

G tag questions
V crime
P intonation in tag questions

10B Two murder mysteries

Lesson plan

The topic of this lesson is murder mysteries; first, the true story of the death of Natalie Wood and a crime writer's theory as to who he was, and then a well-known short story by Graham Greene.

The lesson begins with a vocabulary focus on words and phrases related to crime. Then Sts activate the new vocabulary by filling in the blanks in an article about the mysterious death of Natalie Wood and the story of the people with her the night she died. In Listening Sts listen to an expert on the Natalie Wood mystery talking about the events of that night. Grammar focuses on tag questions, which are further practiced in Pronunciation and Speaking.

In the second half of the lesson, Sts read and are questioned on the first part of the Graham Greene short story *The Case for the Defense* and then listen and answer questions on the second part.

If you would like to end the last lesson without the book, there is a Communicative review photocopiable activity on *page 195* (instructions *page 170*).

STUDY LINK
- **Workbook** 10B
- **iChecker**

Extra photocopiable activities

- **Grammar** tag questions *page 163*
- **Communicative** Memory game: tag questions *page 194* (instructions *page 170*)
  Review *page 195* (instructions *page 171*)

Optional lead-in (books closed)

- Write the word MURDER on the board and elicit what it means and how it's pronounced /ˈmɜrdər/. Then give Sts, in pairs, three minutes to brainstorm ten words connected with murder.
- Write their suggestions on the board.

Possible words
murderer, kill, victim, detective, knife, gun, police, police station, body, blood, suspect, crime, witness, etc.

1 VOCABULARY crime

a Books open. If you didn't do the **Optional lead-in**, then do this as a class.

Elicit answers to the questions. You could write down anything they know about Natalie Wood on the board, but don't say whether any of the information is right. Tell Sts that they will find out later.

b Tell Sts to read definitions 1–9 and then to match them with words in the list.

Get Sts to compare with a partner.

c (5 34)) Play the audio for Sts to listen and check.

Check answers. Model and drill any difficult words for your Sts. You can use the audio to do this.

> **(5 34))**
> | | | | |
> |---|---|---|---|
> | 1 | de**tec**tives | 6 | **ev**idence |
> | 2 | **wit**nesses | 7 | **sus**pects |
> | 3 | **vic**tim | 8 | solve |
> | 4 | **mur**derer | 9 | prove |
> | 5 | **mur**der | | |

Extra idea

- Play the audio again and get Sts to underline the stressed syllable in each word. See script 5.34 for answers.

In pairs, Sts practice saying the words.

d Tell Sts they are now going to read about the mysterious death of Natalie Wood. They need to fill in each blank with a word from **b**.

Give Sts time to do the task and get them to compare with a partner, and then check answers.

> | | | | | | |
> |---|---|---|---|---|---|
> | 2 | solve | 5 | detectives | 8 | murderer |
> | 3 | witnesses | 6 | evidence | 9 | suspects |
> | 4 | murder | 7 | prove | | |

e Focus on the instructions and the questions, making sure Sts understand all the lexis.

Now set a time limit for Sts to read the article again and answer the questions.

Get Sts to compare with a partner and then check answers.

> | | |
> |---|---|
> | 1 | November 29, 1981 |
> | 2 | It was cold and rainy |
> | 3 | floating in the water, far from *The Splendour* |
> | 4 | Her husband, her friend, and the captain |
> | 5 | her husband |
> | 6 | more than thirty years later |

Extra idea

- Alternatively, you could read the article paragraph by paragraph together with the class, asking Sts to guess the meaning of new words as you go and explaining / translating the meaning of any that they can't guess.

2 LISTENING

a (5 35)) Focus on the three photos of the people on the boat with Natalie Wood that night.

Then play the audio once all the way through.

Get Sts to compare their answers with a partner and play the audio again, pausing after each person if necessary.

Check answers.

Extra support

• Before playing the audio, go through the listening script and decide if you need to preteach / check any lexis to help Sts when they listen.

Robert Wagner, Natalie Woods' **husband**
Christopher Walken, Natalie Wood's **friend** and movie actor
Dennis Davern, **boat** captain

---

⑤ 35))

(script in Student Book on *page 131*)
I = interviewer, R = Detective Ryan

I Good morning and thank you for coming, Mr. Ryan – or should it be Detective Ryan? You were a detective with the Los Angeles Police Department, weren't you?

R Yes, that's right. For 25 years. I retired last year.

I People today are still fascinated by Natalie Wood's death even though it was more than 30 years ago. That's incredible, isn't it?

R Well, it's not really that surprising. People are always interested in unsolved mysteries – and Natalie Wood was a well-known and talented actress.

I Now, to be clear, none of the people on the boat the night Ms. Wood died were or are suspects. But – can you tell us *who* was on the boat that night?

R That is correct – none of them were or are suspects. But in order to get a better understanding about what happened that night, it *is* important to know who was on the boat. So, the people were her husband, movie and TV actor Robert Wagner; her friend and movie actor Christopher Walken; and the captain of the boat, Dennis Davern.

---

b ⑤ 36)) Focus on the instructions and give Sts time to read sentences 1–10 first. Make sure they understand *Coroner's Office* and *cause of death*.

Then play the audio once all the way through. Tell Sts they need to mark the sentences T (true) or F (false). Tell them **not** to try to correct the F ones at this stage.

Extra support

• Before doing **c**, check answers.

---

⑤ 36))

(script in Student Book on *page 131*)

I Recently, the LA County Coroner's Office re-examined Ms. Wood's cause of death because of some new information about the bruises and scratches that were found on her body the night she died.

R Yes, that's correct. This new information suggests that Ms. Wood may have been hit or beaten right before she died. And the Coroner changed Ms. Wood's original cause of death from "accidental drowning" to "drowning and other undetermined factors."

I So what does this mean for the other people on the boat?

R Officially, it doesn't mean anything for them. They still aren't suspects.

I And you don't think they're suspects, do you?

R No, I don't. I don't think any of them can be considered suspects without some kind of convincing evidence.

I What about Robert Wagner? There are reports that he was jealous of his wife's friendship with Mr. Walken.

R Well, yes, Mr. Wagner wrote in his book Pieces of *My Heart* that he was jealous of the relationship, and that he and Mr. Walken argued that night on the boat. But that doesn't make him a suspect.

I And Christopher Walken, Ms. Wood's friend and co-star?

R Mr. Walken has remained mostly silent about what happened that night, but he has talked to the police.

I The boat captain changed his story about what happened that night, didn't he? That he originally lied to police the night Natalie died.

R Yes. Mr. Davern told a TV news program that he lied about the events of that night. He now says that Mr. Wagner and Ms. Wood had an argument, and that Ms. Wood went missing shortly after. Mr. Davern also claims that Mr. Wagner delayed contacting the police, implying that Mr. Wagner was responsible for Ms. Wood's death.

I Do you believe the captain's new story?

R Well, no. I think the timing of his new story is suspicious since he released it so close to the thirty-year anniversary of her death. I think he was looking to make some money by bringing this sad story back into the news.

I So, what do *you* think happened that night?

R I can't tell you because I don't know.

I So you don't think we'll ever solve the mystery?

R No, I wouldn't say that. I think one day the mystery *will* be solved. Some new evidence will appear, and we'll be able to say that Natalie Wood's mysterious death is finally solved. But right now, it's still a mystery, and people like a good mystery.

---

c Now play the audio again, so Sts can find out why the F statements are false.

Get Sts to compare with a partner, explaining why they think they are false.

Check answers, getting Sts to say why the F sentences are false.

1 T
2 F new evidence found on her body
3 F Mr. Wagner was jealous of Ms. Wood and Mr. Walken's friendship
4 T
5 T
6 F Mr. Walken hasn't spoken to many people about that night.
7 Mr. Wagner and Mr. Walken had an argument
8 T
9 T
10 F He thinks it will be solved one day.

Extra support

• If there's time, you could play the audio again while Sts read the scripts on *page 131*, so they can see what they understood / didn't understand. Translate / explain any new words or phrases.

d Do this as an open-class activity.

3 **GRAMMAR** tag questions

a Focus on the instructions and questions 1–4. Give Sts time to complete them.

b **⑤ 37))** Play the audio for Sts to listen and check.

Check answers.

1	weren't you	3	do you
2	isn't it	4	didn't he

Extra challenge

• You could elicit ideas first for what the two missing words are.

---

⑤ 37))

1 "You were a detective with the Los Angeles Police Department, weren't you?"
2 "That's incredible, isn't it?"
3 "And you don't think they're suspects, do you?"
4 "The boat captain changed his story about what happened that night, didn't he?"

10B

Now ask Sts what the difference is between this kind of question and a direct question.

> This kind of question is used to check that a statement is correct.

c (5 38))) Tell Sts to go to **Grammar Bank 10B** on *page 151*. Focus on the example sentences and play the audio for Sts to listen to the sentence rhythm. You could also get Sts to repeat the sentences to practice getting the rhythm right. Then go through the rules with the class.

Additional grammar notes

- Tag questions are difficult for Sts to use with any fluency because they need to use the correct auxiliary each time depending on the tense or modal verb they are using. Getting the right intonation can also be challenging. This lesson provides Sts with a gentle introduction and focuses on their most common use, which is to check information.

Focus on the exercises and get Sts to do them individually or in pairs.

Check answers, getting Sts to read the full sentences.

```
a
1 I    3 A   5 C   7 K   9 B
2 E    4 F   6 H   8 D   10 J
b
1 doesn't he       6 was she
2 do they          7 didn't she
3 is he            8 will he
4 weren't you      9 have you
5 haven't they     10 did they
```

Tell Sts to go back to the main lesson **10B**.

Extra support

- If you think Sts need more practice, you may want to give them the Grammar photocopiable activity at this point or leave it for later as consolidation or review.

4 PRONUNCIATION & SPEAKING

intonation in tag questions

Pronunciation notes

- The usual intonation for a tag question when we say something that we think is right or true and that we expect the other person to agree with, is a falling tone. Examples would include *It's hot today, isn't it? You're French, aren't you?* (= I'm almost sure you're French). This is what is modeled on the audio in these exercises.

! Tag questions can sometimes be used as real questions with rising intonation, usually to express surprise, or to check information that we are not very sure about. This use is not focused on here.

a (5 39))) Focus on the task and the dialogue, and elicit that the police inspector probably already has the information and is just checking what he knows.

Now play the dialogue once all the way through for Sts to listen.

Give Sts a few minutes to complete the tag questions and then play the audio again for them to check.

Check answers.

> See words in **bold** in script 5.39

```
(5 39)))
I = inspector, S = suspect
I  Your last name's Jones, isn't it?
S  Yes, it is.
I  And you're 27, aren't you?
S  Yes, that's right.
I  You weren't at home last night at 8:00, were you?
S  No, I wasn't. I was at the movie theater.
I  But you don't have any witnesses, do you?
S  Yes, I do. My wife was with me.
I  Your wife wasn't with you, was she?
S  How do you know?
I  Because she was with me. At the police station. We arrested her yesterday.
```

b (5 40))) Ask Sts if they think the intonation of the tag questions went up or down (demonstrate both ways), and elicit that it goes down. Point out that this is the usual intonation when you are checking information, not asking a new question.

Play the audio, pausing for Sts to listen and repeat the police inspector's questions.

```
(5 40)))
1  Your last name's Jones, isn't it?
2  And you're 27, aren't you?
3  You weren't at home last night at eight o'clock, were you?
4  But you don't have any witnesses, do you?
5  Your wife wasn't with you, was she?
```

Then repeat the activity, eliciting responses from individual Sts.

Extra support

- Give Sts extra practice by getting them to read the dialogue in pairs.

c Put Sts in pairs, **A** and **B**, preferably face-to-face. Tell them to go to **Communication** *Just checking*, **A** on *page 108*, **B** on *page 112*. If there is an odd number of Sts, you should take part in the activity yourself.

Go through the instructions. Make sure Sts are clear that first **A** (as police inspector) will ask **B** some questions and try to remember the answers, and then he / she will check them with tag questions. Then they change roles. Demonstrate the activity by taking **A**'s role and asking one student the questions and then checking.

Monitor and help Sts to form the tag questions correctly.

When both have done their interviews, get feedback to find which "police inspectors" had the best memory.

Extra support

- You could write any new and useful words and phrases from **Communication** on the board for Sts to copy.

Tell Sts to go back to the main lesson **10B**.

d Put Sts in pairs and get them to ask and answer the questions, giving as much information as possible.

Get some feedback.

5 READING & LISTENING

a Get Sts to do this in pairs or as a whole-class activity.

b (5 41)) Tell Sts they are going to read and listen to a story by Graham Greene (1904–1991), a famous English author. You might want to tell them that many of his novels have been made into films, e.g., *Brighton Rock*, *The Third Man*, *The Quiet American*, *Our Man in Havana*, etc.

Focus on the information about the short story and read it with Sts, making sure they understand the title and all the lexis, e.g., *death penalty* and *abolish*.

Now focus on **Glossary 1** and go through it with Sts.

Give Sts time to read questions 1–6.

Now play the audio and tell Sts to follow in their books.

In pairs, Sts answer the questions.

Check answers.

Extra support

- Before playing the audio, go through the text and decide if you need to preteach / check any lexis to help Sts when they listen.

1 Northwood Street
2 He was well-built and had bloodshot eyes. He was ugly.
3 four
4 Because she heard a door shut.
5 When he was driving home.
6 yes

(5 41))
See text in Student Book on *page 100*.

---

c (5 42)) Tell Sts they are going to read and listen to **Part 2** of the story.

Now focus on **Glossary 2** and go through it with Sts.

Give Sts time to read questions 1–4.

Now play the audio once all the way through.

In pairs, Sts answer the questions.

Check answers.

1 It means people think they saw Adams, but in fact it wasn't him.
2 He said he was at home with his wife.
3 If she saw the man in court.
4 She has good eyesight (she has never had to wear glasses), there was moonlight, there was lamplight on his face, and his face is unforgettable.

(5 42))
See text in Student Book on *page 101*.

---

d (5 43)) Tell Sts they are going to hear **Part 3** of the story.

Now focus on **Glossary 3** and go through it with Sts.

Give Sts time to read questions 1–9.

Now play the audio once all the way through.

! The script for audio 5.43 has not been included in the Listening section of the Student Book so that Sts find out together in class what happens in the end.

Get Sts to compare their answers with a partner and then play the audio again, pausing if necessary for them to complete and check their answers.

Play the audio again if necessary.

Check answers.

1 Mr. Adams's twin brother
2 He was wearing a tight blue suit and a striped tie – exactly the same as his brother.
3 He asked Mrs. Salmon if she could still swear that the man she saw in Mr. Parker's garden was the prisoner and not his twin brother.
4 He had been with his wife.
5 Because none of the witnesses were prepared to swear that it was the prisoner they'd seen.
6 They were waiting to see the twins.
7 Because the accused twin said that he had been acquitted.
8 He was accidentally pushed in front of a bus and run over.
9 Because the surviving twin brother might want revenge, especially if he was the murderer.

(5 43))
Part 3

The lawyer for the defense took a look round the court for a moment. Then he said, "Do you mind, Mrs. Salmon, examining again the people in court? Stand up, please, Mr. Adams." There at the back of the court, with a well-built body and a pair of bloodshot eyes, was a man who looked exactly like the prisoner. He was even dressed the same – a tight blue suit and a striped tie.

"Now think very carefully, Mrs. Salmon. Can you still swear that the man you saw in Mrs. Parker's garden was the prisoner – and not this man, who is his twin brother? You can't be sure, can you?" Of course, she couldn't. She looked from one to the other and didn't say a word. The prisoner sat in the dock, and the other man stood at the back of the court and they both stared at Mrs. Salmon. She shook her head.

That was the end of the case. None of the witnesses were prepared to swear that it was the prisoner he'd seen. The brother had his alibi, too; he had been with his wife. And so the man was acquitted because there was no evidence. But whether he committed the murder, or whether it was his brother, I don't know.

That extraordinary day had an extraordinary end. I followed Mrs. Salmon out of the court. There was a big crowd of people outside the courtroom who were waiting, of course, for the twins. The police tried to make the crowd go away, but all they could do was keep the road clear for traffic. The police tried to get the twins to leave by a back door, but they refused. One of them – no one knew which – said, "Why by the back door? I've been acquitted, haven't I?" and they walked out of the front entrance. Then it happened. I don't know how; though I was only six feet away. The crowd moved and somehow one of the twins was pushed onto the road right in front of a bus. He gave a scream and that was all; he was dead. His brother looked straight at Mrs. Salmon. He was crying, but whether he was the murderer or the innocent man, nobody will ever know. But if you were Mrs. Salmon, could you sleep at night?

Extra support

- If you would like your Sts to read and listen to the end of the story, we suggest you photocopy script 5.43 from the Teacher's Book.

Extra support

- You could write any new and useful words and phrases from the text and audio on the board for Sts to copy.

e Do this as an open-class activity.

Extra support

- If you would like to end the last lesson without the book, there is a Communicative review photocopiable activity on *page 195* (instructions *page 171*).

For instructions on how to use these pages see *page 40*.

Testing Program CD-ROM

- Quick Test 10
- File 10 Test
- End-of-course Test

GRAMMAR

1 b	6 a	11 a
2 c	7 b	12 a
3 c	8 b	13 b
4 b	9 a	14 c
5 a	10 c	15 a

VOCABULARY

a 1 luckily
2 careless
3 uncomfortable
4 unfortunately
5 impatient

b 1 turned
2 set
3 unplug
4 turn
5 turn / switch

c 1 remote control
2 keyboard
3 flash drive
4 headphones
5 mouse

d 1 soccer field
2 profile picture
3 first floor
4 gas station
5 speed camera

e 1 detective
2 prove
3 victim
4 solve
5 suspect

PRONUNCIATION

a 1 through   2 charge   5 careful
2 although   4 headphones

b 1 comfortable   3 cable   5 evidence
2 adaptor   4 witness

CAN YOU UNDERSTAND THIS TEXT?

a 1 F   2 T   3 DS   4 DS   5 T   6 T   7 F

CAN YOU UNDERSTAND THESE PEOPLE?

5 44))
1 a   2 c   3 c   4 b   5 b

5 44))

Ryder
I = interviewer, R = Ryder
I   Have you ever helped a stranger or been helped by a stranger?
R   Yes, one time I saw somebody have their phone stolen, and I ran after the guy and retrieved the cell phone.

Elizabeth
I = interviewer, E = Elizabeth
I   Do you think we rely too much on technology?
E   Yes.
I   Why?
E   Because technology often breaks and then you don't have the skills that you need to deal with the situation.
I   Are there any gadgets you just couldn't live without?
E   I couldn't live without my hairdryer.

Sean
I = interviewer, S = Sean
I   Do you like detective or mystery novels or TV series?
S   I do, yes.
I   Do you have a favorite author or detective?
S   I do like Raymond Chandler and the Philip Marlowe character.
I   Do you usually guess who the murderer is?
S   I don't, but I don't usually try to. I think I quite like just to wait, and find out what happens.

Isobel
I = interviewer, Is = Isobel
I   Do you have a favorite designer?
Is I think my favorite designer is Alexander McQueen, who's a clothing designer, though it's too expensive, so I can't buy any of the clothes, but I like looking at pictures of them.
I   Why do you like his clothes?
Is Because they are very very unusual and very, they use lots of very interesting materials and they are different designs, they're not just using designs from the past.

Giles
I = interviewer, G = Giles
I   Do you think you are generally a lucky person?
G   Yes, I suppose I think I possibly am a lucky person, I certainly wouldn't count myself as unlucky, but I haven't won the lottery yet, but I'm enjoying life and I think that's possibly as lucky as you can hope to be.
I   Can you think of a time when you've been really lucky?
G   Yes, I was very lucky when I was on holiday in Australia, and I was due to catch my flight back to England, but I turned up a day late and I'd missed it, but luckily there was one spare space on the plane leaving that day and they were able to put me on it.

Photocopiable activities

Contents

Photocopiable material

- There is a **Grammar activity** for each main (A and B) lesson of the Student Book.
- There is a **Communicative activity** for each main (A and B) lesson of the Student Book.
- There is a **Vocabulary activity** for each section of the Vocabulary Bank in the Student Book.
- There is a **Songs activity** for every File of the Student Book, in either lesson A or B. The recording of the song can be found in the relevant lesson of the Class CD.

Using extra activities in mixed ability classes

Some teachers have classes with a very wide range of levels, where some students finish Student Book activities much more quickly than others. You could give these fast-finishers a photocopiable activity (Grammar, Vocabulary, or Communicative) while you help the slower students. Alternatively some teachers might want to give faster students extra oral practice with a communicative activity while slower students consolidate their knowledge with an extra grammar activity.

Tips for using Grammar activities

The Grammar activities are designed to give students extra practice in the main grammar point from each lesson. How you use these activities depends on the needs of your students and the time you have available. They can be used in the lesson if you think all of your class would benefit from the extra practice, or you could assign them as homework for some or all of your students.

- All of the activities start with a writing stage. If you use the activities in class, get students to work individually or in pairs. Allow students to compare before checking the answers.

- The activities have an **Activation** section that gets students to cover the sentences and to test their memories. If you are using the activities in class, students can work in pairs and test their partner. If you assign them for homework, encourage students to use this stage to test themselves.

- If students are having trouble with any of the activities, make sure they refer to the relevant Grammar Bank in the Student Book.

- Make sure that students keep their copies of the activities and that they review any difficult areas regularly. Encourage them to go back to activities and cover and test themselves. This will help with their review.

Grammar activity answers

Introduction a

2 a   3 b   4 c   5 c   6 a   7 b   8 c   9 a   10 a
11 a   12 b   13 a   14 b   15 a   16 c   17 c   18 b
19 b   20 a

Introduction b

3 've lived   4 wife's name's Emilia   5 We don't
have any children   6 ✓   7 we'd like to have
8 ✓   9 ✓   10 Emilia is a translator   11 work very hard
12 don't have to do   13 they take care of the house
14 much free time   15 ✓   16 ✓   17 I don't have
enough time   18 I want to get   19 ✓
20 I often make mistakes   21 ✓   22 to take

1A simple present and continuous

a   2 I'm studying   3 are you   4 do you have
5 It depends   6 Do you know   7 Do you mean
8 I'm getting ready   9 are you living   10 I'm staying
11 are you doing   12 want

b   2 'm buying   3 don't like   4 depends   5 gets
6 do   7 sounds   8 Do (you) have to   9 have
10 doesn't work   11 meet   12 Do (you) want
13 need   14 is staying

1B future forms

2 're getting married ("re going to get married" also
possible but less common)   3 'm going to look for
4 'm having / 'm going to have   5 'm going to be / 'll be
6 's going to fall / 'll fall   7 won't tell   8 'll check
9 's going to pass / 'll pass   10 're going ("re going to
go skiing" also possible but less common)   11 'll turn
12 won't take   13 'm introducing / 'm going to introduce
14 'm going ("'m going to go shopping" also possible but
less common)   15 'll work / 're going to work

2A present perfect and simple past

a   2 I've been   3 did you go   4 graduated   5 I've been
6 did you go   7 went

b   1 2 had   3 did you meet   4 was   5 went   6 've known
7 got   8 were you   9 just met

2 1 Have you taught   2 taught   3 just came
4 have you been   5 was   6 started
7 haven't finished

2B present perfect + *for* / *since*, present
perfect continuous

a   2 's been playing   3 hasn't been feeling / hasn't been
4 've been looking   5 have you been doing
6 's been reading

b   2 A have you been working
B 've been working; for
3 A have you been going out
B 've been going out; since
4 A has Pam been
B 's been single; since

5 A have you had
B 've had; for
6 A has Pete been trying
B 's been trying; since
7 A has your sister wanted
B 's wanted; since
8 A have you known
B 've known; for

3A comparatives and superlatives:
adjectives and adverbs

3 less   4 more comfortable than   5 younger than
6 ✓   7 ✓   8 more modern than   9 much better
10 ✓   11 the most beautiful beach I've ever been
12 the worst actor   13 ✓   14 the best in the world
15 nicer   16 ✓   17 hotter   18 the same school as
19 as much food as   20 ✓

3B articles: *a* / *an*, *the*, no article

3 the   4 –   5 –   6 the   7 –   8 The   9 –   10 an
11 –   12 an   13 –   14 – / –   15 the / –   16 a / –
17 – / –   18 an / the   19 a / a / The / the   20 – / –

4A *can*, *could*, *be able to*

a   2 both possible   3 be able to   4 both possible
5 not being able to   6 be able to   7 both possible
8 be able to   9 both possible   10 both possible
11 being able to   12 both possible

b   2 couldn't   3 be able to   4 can   5 been able to
6 couldn't   7 being able to   8 can't   9 Being able to
10 be able to   11 be able to   12 can't

4B modals of obligation: *must, have to, should*

a   2 must not   3 don't have to   4 both possible   5 should
6 doesn't have to   7 have to   8 must not   9 should

b   2 must not   3 don't have to   4 must / have to
5 don't have to   6 must / have to   7 must not
8 must / have to

5A past tenses

3 was still feeling   4 didn't have   5 didn't matter
6 knew   7 had always wanted   8 called   9 told
10 was shining   11 was driving   12 were talking
13 saw   14 had flown   15 tried   16 was buzzing
17 disappeared   18 felt   19 had stung
20 was driving   21 crashed

5B *usually* and *used to*

2 works   3 don't live   4 used to dream   5 didn't use
to eat   6 (usually) cook   7 used to live   8 (usually)
stay   9 didn't use to play   10 doesn't ride
11 (usually) wear   12 used to be   13 (usually) stay in
14 used to have

6A the passive be + past participle

a 2 are stolen 3 disappear 4 is sent 5 is bitten
6 fights 7 falls 8 were made 9 have been bought

b 2 will be accepted 3 be washed 4 was being
followed 5 Has (the thief) been caught
6 Have (you ever) been told 7 has been robbed
8 had already been made 9 is being painted
10 wasn't offered 11 be returned 12 had been stolen

6B modals of deduction: might / may, can't, must

a 2 might 3 must 4 can't 5 can't 6 may

b 1 can't; must 2 can't; might; might; might
3 can't; must / might / may; might / may 4 can't; must

7A first conditional and future time clauses

2 get 3 'll send 4 finishes 5 Come
6 can 7 don't call 8 get 9 're 10 are
11 won't be able to 12 pass 13 see 14 don't study
15 won't have

7B first and second conditionals

a 2 'd buy; won 3 painted; would be 4 would do; had
5 wouldn't be; didn't spend 6 shared; could / would
get along 7 would be able to / could; had 8 would
move; found 9 didn't have to; would be able to / could
10 went; wouldn't be

b 2 would buy 3 goes 4 reduce 5 would take
6 gets 7 weren't / wasn't 8 found
9 'll never finish 10 will be

8A reported speech: sentences and questions

a 2 was 3 had been 4 hadn't been 5 had started
6 had enjoyed 7 had loved 8 had been able to
9 was going to be 10 depended 11 would be
12 had to

b 2 if there was too much violence in movies
3 who the most difficult actor he had ever worked
with was / who was the most difficult actor he had
ever worked with
4 what a young person who wanted to go into acting
should do
5 when he was going to retire

8B gerunds and infinitives

2 calling 3 to speak 4 not to buy 5 going
6 to watch 7 using 8 Waiting 9 to consider
10 drawing 11 to work 12 to go 13 doing
14 to hear 15 studying 16 to think 17 cooking
18 to like 19 Eating; feel 20 to give

9A third conditional

a 2 have missed the movie if you'd been here on time
3 'd offered you the job, would you have taken it
4 have finished the race if she hadn't fallen
5 told me you were taking a picture, I'd have smiled
6 have eaten that if you'd known what was in it

b 2 'd known; 'd have taken
3 'd have enjoyed; 'd gone
4 would have called; hadn't left
5 wouldn't have deleted; 'd realized
6 Would you have married; 'd asked

9B quantifiers

2 too much 3 enough 4 no 5 very little
6 How many 7 Very few 8 a lot of 9 enough time
10 any 11 plenty 12 very few 13 A few
14 very little 15 too 16 too much 17 enough
18 no

10A relative clauses

a 2 that / which 3 that / which 4 that / which
5 that / which 6 who 7 that / which 8 whose
9 who 10 that / which 11 where 12 that / which

b 2, 3, 4, 5, 10

c 2 whose best known painting is *Guernica*
3 which is the capital of Australia
4 where I used to work
5 who was born in Rosario in Argentina
6 which was the worst for over 75 years

10B tag questions

2 do you 3 weren't we 4 was it 5 is he 6 do they
7 aren't we 8 do you 9 won't she 10 isn't it
11 isn't it 12 wasn't it 13 are you 14 have you
15 wouldn't you

● Circle the correct answer, a, b, or c.

1 My sister _____ a car.
   a hasn't   **b** don't have   **c** doesn't have

2 _____ Mr. S. Roberts live here?
   a Does   **b** Is   **c** Do

3 My dad _____ at the university.
   a teachs   **b** teaches   **c** teach

4 I _____ to the movies with Katie tonight. I bought the tickets.
   a go   **b** 'm going go   **c** 'm going

5 I _____ back from New York City this morning.
   a flied   **b** flown   **c** flew

6 He didn't _____ his vacation very much.
   a enjoy   **b** enjoyed   **c** enjoys

7 I _____ a shower when the water stopped working.
   a had   **b** was taking   **c** were taking

8 **A** I'm thirsty.
   B _____ get you a drink?
   a Will I   **b** Am I going to   **c** Can I

9 **A** I have a new phone.
   B I'm sure you _____ it, just like your last one.
   a 'll lose   **b** 're losing   **c** lose

10 **A** Would you like something to eat?
   B No, thanks, _____ lunch.
   a I've already had   **b** I already have had   **c** I've had already

11 Have you ever _____ to Paris?
   a been   **b** go   **c** went

12 The traffic is _____ than it used to be.
   a badder   **b** worse   **c** more bad

13 Riding a bike isn't as dangerous _____ skiing.
   a as   **b** than   **c** that

14 What _____ you do if there was a snake in your room?
   a will   **b** would   **c** did

15 I'll come to your party if I _____ work early enough.
   a finish   **b** will finish   **c** finished

16 You drive much _____ than me.
   a slowly   **b** slowlier   **c** more slowly

17 If I _____ you, I'd look for a new job.
   a was   **b** am   **c** were

18 My bike _____ last week.
   a is stolen   **b** was stolen   **c** stole

19 We were too late. When we arrived at the station, the train _____.
   a already left   **b** had already left   **c** has already left

20 He said he _____ her.
   a loved   **b** love   **c** is loving

 American English File 2nd edition **Teacher's Book 3** Photocopiable © Oxford University Press 2014

INTRODUCTION GRAMMAR b

a Read about Roberto. Then look at the **bold** phrases. Check (✓) the phrases that are right and correct the wrong ones. Use contractions where possible.

My name's Roberto. [1]**I'm 32**, and I'm from Chile.
[2]**I'm born** in Santiago, and [3]**I live** there all my life.
I'm married. My [4]**wife name's Emilia**. She's from Santiago
too. [5]**We don't have some children**. We live with Emilia's
parents in their apartment, and I [6]**get along with them** very well, but
[7]**we'd like having** our own place. [8]**We're looking for an apartment**
right now. [9]**I work for** a pharmaceutical company,
and [10]**Emilia is translator**. We both [11]**work very hardly**,
but luckily we [12]**don't have do** any housework.
Emilia's parents are retired, so [13]**they take care the house**.
I don't have [14]**many free time**, but when I have the chance
I [15]**enjoy playing** sports. [16]**I used to play** tennis, but now
[17]**I don't have time enough**. I'm learning English because
I need it for my job. My writing is OK, but [18]**I want get**
better at speaking. [19]**I have to speak** to many clients in
English, and [20]**I make often mistakes**. Next summer,
[21]**I'm going to go to** the US [22]**for take** a business English course.

1	✓
2 *I was born*	3 _____
	4 _____
	5 _____
	6 _____
7 _____	8 _____
	9 _____
10 _____	11 _____
	12 _____
	13 _____
	14 _____
15 _____	16 _____
	17 _____
	18 _____
	19 _____
	20 _____
21 _____	22 _____

activation

b Write a similar paragraph about yourself, where you live, your work and / or studies, your hobbies, and why you are learning English.

1A GRAMMAR simple present and continuous, action and nonaction verbs

a (Circle) the correct form of the verbs.

Jason What ¹**do you study / are you studying?**

Elena Humanities.

Jason ²**I study / I'm studying** Fine Arts. Where ³**are you / are you coming** from?

Elena I'm from Madrid, in Spain.

Jason And how many hours of classes ⁴**do you have / are you having** a week?

Elena ⁵**It depends / It's depending** on the week, but usually about 20 hours. ⁶**Do you know / Are you knowing** about the party tonight?

Jason ⁷**Do you mean / Are you meaning** the one for new students? I can't go, because ⁸**I get ready / I'm getting ready** to move into my apartment tomorrow.

Elena Where ⁹**do you live / are you living** right now?

Jason ¹⁰**I stay / I'm staying** in a student dorm.

Elena What ¹¹**do you do / are you doing** on Sunday afternoon? If you ¹²**want / are wanting**, we could meet and look around the city.

Jason I'm busy in the afternoon, but what about Sunday morning?

Elena Fine. Where should we meet?

b Complete the dialogue with the correct form of the verbs: simple present or present continuous.

Maggie Hello, Jo, what a surprise! What ¹ _are you doing_ (do) here?

Jo The same as you probably! ²I _____ (buy) a few things for dinner.

Maggie How are things? Are you still working at the same place?

Jo Yes, but I ³_____ (not like) it very much. My boss ⁴_____ (depend) on me for everything. The worst thing is that she always ⁵_____ (get) the credit, and I ⁶_____ (do) all the work!

Maggie That ⁷_____ (sound) terrible. ⁸_____ you _____ (have to) go back to work this afternoon?

Jo No, I only work until lunchtime on Fridays because I always ⁹_____ (have) lunch with my friend Paula. She ¹⁰_____ (not work) on Fridays, so we usually ¹¹_____ (meet) at that nice little Italian restaurant in town. ¹²_____ you _____ (want) to come?

Maggie I'd love to but I ¹³_____ (need) to get home. My sister ¹⁴_____ (stay) with us for a few days. Some other time!

activation

c Practice the dialogues in **a** with a partner.

1B GRAMMAR future forms

a Complete the sentences using the verb in parentheses plus *will* or *going to*, or use the verb in the present continuous. Write the answers in the column on the right and use contractions where possible. Sometimes two answers are possible.

1 **A** I can hardly lift this suitcase.

   B Wait. I ▓ you with it! (help)   *'ll help*

2 We ▓ on June 3rd at 5:30 p.m. We hope you can come! (get married)   _____

3 I decided that I ▓ a new job. (look for)   _____

4 **A** Do you want to come to Dave's on Thursday?

   B I can't. I ▓ dinner with Sam. (have)   _____

5 My brother's having a baby so I ▓ an aunt in a couple of weeks. (be)   _____

6 That little boy's riding his bike too fast. He ▓ off. (fall)   _____

7 **A** Can I tell you a secret?

   B Of course. I ▓ anyone. (not tell)   _____

8 **A** What time is their flight arriving?

   B I'm not sure. I ▓ online. (check)   _____

9 Meg didn't study for the exam so she doesn't think she ▓ it. (pass)   _____

10 Did I tell you that we ▓ skiing in the Alps next week? (go)   _____

11 **A** Is the air conditioner on? I'm freezing.

   B Yes, I think so. I ▓ it off. (turn)   _____

12 I hate it when people take pictures of me without telling me. Please promise
   you ▓ anymore! (not take)   _____

13 **A** Your girlfriend's really nice.

   B Yes, she is. I ▓ her to my parents next week. (introduce)   _____

14 Sorry, but I can't help you now. I ▓ shopping. (go)   _____

15 Do you think you ▓ late tonight? (work)   _____

13–15 Excellent. You can use different future forms very well.

9–12 Good, but check the rules in the Grammar Bank for any questions that you got wrong.

1–8   This is difficult for you. Read the rules in the Grammar Bank. Then ask your teacher for another photocopy and do the exercise again at home.

---

activation

b Cover the column on the right and look at the sentences. Read the sentences aloud with the verbs in the correct form.

2A GRAMMAR present perfect and simple past

a (Circle) the correct verb.

Mike So, where should we go for our honeymoon?

Gina I don't know. Maybe somewhere in North Africa. Have you ever [1](**been**)/ **gone** to Morocco?

Mike Yes, [2]**I've been** / **I went** there.

Gina I didn't know that. When [3]**have you been** / **did you go** there?

Mike The year after I [4]**have graduated** / **graduated** from college.

Gina What about Egypt?

Mike [5]**I've been** / **I went** there, too.

Gina Who [6]**have you been** / **did you go** with?

Mike With an ex-girlfriend. But we only [7]**have been** / **went** to Cairo. Let's go there.

Gina No, let's go somewhere else.

b Complete the dialogues with the correct form of the verbs in parentheses: simple past or present perfect. Use contractions where possible.

1 **A** How long _____*have you been*_____ (you / be) married, Glenn?

B Twenty-two years! Maxine and I [2]_____ (have) our wedding anniversary three weeks ago.

A Where [3]_____ (you / meet)? In college?

B No, it [4]_____ (be) long before that. Actually, we [5]_____ (go) to the same elementary school. We [6]_____ (know) each other for a long time. What about you?

A I'm divorced. I [7]_____ (get) divorced a year ago.

B How long [8]_____ (you / be) married?

A Just a couple of years.

B So, you're on your own now?

A Yes, but I [9]_____ (just / meet) someone new and I really like her.

2 **A** [1]_____ (you / teach) English abroad before, Ms. Jenkins?

B Yes, I [2]_____ (teach) from 2009-2011 in Bolivia, and I [3]_____ (just / come) back from a four-month job in Columbia.

A How long [4]_____ (you / be) a language teacher?

B Exactly six years. Before that I [5]_____ (be) an elementary school teacher.

A Do you have any post-graduate qualifications?

B I [6]_____ (start) an MA in Linguistics with the Open University last year, but I [7]_____ (not finish) it yet.

activation

c Practice the dialogues in **a** and **b** with a partner.

American English File 2nd edition Teacher's Book 3 Photocopiable © Oxford University Press 2014

2B GRAMMAR present perfect + *for / since*
present perfect continuous

a Look at the pictures. What have they been doing? Use the present perfect continuous. Use contractions where possible.

1 He _'s been cooking_____.

2 She _____ the violin since she got up this morning.

3 Melanie _____ well since last week. She has the flu.

4 You _____ at her for hours. Go and talk to her!

5 Your face looks like a tomato! What _____?

6 Tim _____ the instructions for hours.

b Complete the questions and answers with the present perfect or the present perfect continuous and *for* or *since*. Use contractions where possible.

1 **A** How long _has he been waiting_ to speak to someone? (he / wait)

  B He _'s been waiting_____ ___for___ half an hour.

2 **A** How long _____ here? (you / work)

  B I _____ here _____ three months now.

3 **A** How long _____ with Rob? (you / go out)

  B We _____ _____ we left school.

4 **A** How long _____ single? (Pam / be)

  B I think she _____ _____ she broke up with Paul.

5 **A** How long _____ your driver's license? (you / have)

  B I _____ it _____ ten years.

6 **A** How long _____ to find a job? (Pete / try)

  B He _____ _____ he graduated from college last year, but no luck!

7 **A** How long _____ to be a doctor? (your sister / want)

  B She _____ to be a doctor _____ she was seven years old.

8 **A** How long _____ Dave? (you / know)

  B I _____ him _____ years. He's an old friend of the family.

activation

c Cover the sentences in **b**. Look at the pictures and remember the sentences.

3A GRAMMAR comparatives and superlatives

a Check (✓) the sentences that are right and correct the wrong ones. Write the answers in the column on the right.

1 Riding a bike to work is **more quickly** than walking. _____quicker_____

2 Olga drives **more carefully** than Bill. _____✓_____

3 My dad has **least** hair now than he had five years ago. _____

4 Now that I've tried them on, these shoes are **more comfortable that** I thought they were going to be. _____

5 In this photo you look **more young than** your sister. _____

6 Taxis are **much more expensive than** buses or the subway. _____

7 Anne's **not as tall as** Susie, but she's thinner. _____

8 My phone is **moderner than** yours. It's got a better camera. _____

9 I love riding my scooter, it's **much more better** than driving a car. _____

10 Can you say that again **more slowly**, please? I didn't understand a word! _____

11 It's **the most beautiful beach I've never been** to. The ocean looks amazing. _____

12 Sean's **the worse actor** in the group, but he's the best singer. _____

13 What's **the nicest thing anyone's ever said** to you? _____

14 Everyone thinks their mom's cooking is **the best of the world**. _____

15 Which sofa looks **the more nice** do you think? The blue one or the red one? _____

16 I think we should take this case. It's **the biggest** one that we have. _____

17 It's usually **hoter** here in June than it is in May. _____

18 Did you go to **the same school than** your brother? _____

19 That restaurant over there is fantastic. It's cheap, and you can eat **as many food as** you like. _____

20 I read **a lot faster than** my brother. I finished the book, and he's still on page 30. _____

activation

b Cover the column on the right and look at the sentences. Read the correct sentences aloud.

American English File 2nd edition **Teacher's Book 3** Photocopiable © Oxford University Press 2014

3B GRAMMAR articles: *a / an, the*, no article

a Complete the sentences with *a, an, the*, or – (= no article). Write the answers in the column on the right.

1 Did you remember to lock [___] kitchen door before we left?   *the*

2 I shouldn't drink [___] coffee. It keeps me awake at night.   _–_

3 Can you turn on [___] air conditioner? It's boiling in here!   _____

4 Jane is allergic to [___] cats. She starts sneezing when one comes near her.   _____

5 Eric and Charlotte are going away [___] next weekend.   _____

6 Are these [___] keys you were looking for?   _____

7 I wasn't feeling very well yesterday so I didn't go to [___] work.   _____

8 [___] river that runs through Paris is called the Seine.   _____

9 I'm seeing Katie tomorrow. We haven't seen each other since [___] last year.   _____

10 It looks as if it's going to rain. Take [___] umbrella!   _____

11 Hurry up! You're going to be late for [___] school.   _____

12 I have a friend who is [___] electrician. Do you want his phone number?   _____

13 It's cheaper to buy [___] books online than in a store.   _____

14 I don't like [___] people who talk about [___] sports all the time.   _____ / _____

15 Luckily [___] people who work in my office don't talk about [___] sports at all.   _____ / _____

16 My sister works in [___] restaurant. She gets home from [___] work late every evening.   _____ / _____

17 What's your favorite meal of the day? [___] breakfast or [___] dinner?   _____ / _____

18 That's [___] easy question. I think I know [___] answer.   _____ / _____

19 Audrey has two children, [___] boy and [___] girl.   _____ / _____
    [___] boy's ten and [___] girl's two years younger.   _____ / _____

20 [___] good health is more important than [___] money.   _____ / _____

activation

b Cover the column on the right and look at the sentences. Read the sentences aloud with the correct article.

4A GRAMMAR *can, could, be able to* (ability and possession)

a Circle the correct verb. Sometimes both verbs are possible.

Anyone for tennis?

I love all sports and have always wanted to ¹**be able to** / **can** play tennis. So, last year, at the age of 45, I decided to learn. I was really happy when I found a teacher who ²**was able to** / **could** give me lessons and so I started. Unfortunately, after the first few lessons, I realized that I'd never ³**can** / **be able to** play this game. One of the problems was that I ⁴**couldn't** / **wasn't able to** move fast enough because I am not in good shape. The other problem is that tennis is not an easy sport to learn quickly. I hated ⁵**not can** / **not being able to** hit the ball over the net. It was really frustrating! Did I learn anything? Yes, I did… that I'll never ⁶**be able to** / **can** play tennis!

It's never too late

My 78-year-old grandfather ⁷**couldn't** / **wasn't able to** even turn on a computer until about two years ago. All that changed when he decided that he wanted to ⁸**can** / **be able to** use the Internet, and he did a course at his local adult education center. Although he really enjoyed the course, he ⁹**couldn't** / **wasn't able to** put what he learned in his classes into practice because he didn't have a computer. So, for his birthday, I bought him his own laptop, and that's when he really started learning! Now, he ¹⁰**'s able to** / **can** use the Internet really well and send emails. What he loves most is ¹¹**can** / **being able to** speak and see his grandchildren on Skype at least once a week. They live in Australia, and if he didn't have a computer, he ¹²**couldn't** / **wouldn't be able to** keep in touch with them so much.

b Complete the sentences with *can* / *can't* or *could* / *couldn't*. If a form of *can* / *could* isn't possible, complete the sentence with a form of *be able to*.

1 At the end of the six-week course, you'll ___be able to___ design your own website.

2 Melissa called me yesterday because she _____ remember how to get to my house.

3 Josh isn't going to _____ finish the report by the end of the day.

4 Scott has passed his driving test so now he _____ drive his father's car.

5 I haven't _____ speak to Harry for over three weeks. He never answers his phone.

6 The train was late so I _____ get to the meeting on time.

7 Miriam hates not _____ play chess as well as Luke. He always beats her, and she's a really bad loser!

8 Sometimes when you're on Skype you _____ hear the other person very well.

9 _____ do what you want is the best thing about a vacation.

10 I'm afraid I won't _____ go away this weekend. I'm too busy.

11 You should _____ do this exercise without any help. It's very easy.

12 We _____ park here: there are no spaces.

activation

c Cover the stories in **a**. In pairs, tell each other the stories from memory.

4B GRAMMAR modals of obligation: *must, have to, should*

a Circle the correct verb. Sometimes both verbs are possible.

1 No, thanks. I **must not / shouldn't** eat anymore cake. I'm on a diet.

2 You **must not / don't have to** tell anyone what I just told you. It's a secret.

3 Living at home is great. I **must not / don't have to** do anything because my mom does it all for me!

4 You **must / have to** get a visa if you want to go to Cuba.

5 You **should / have to** do your homework on Saturday morning. That way you'll have the rest of the weekend free.

6 Jerry **doesn't have to / must not** get up early this morning. He isn't going to work.

7 It's Meg's birthday tomorrow. I **have to / should** remember to call her.

8 You **must not / don't have to** touch electrical things when your hands are wet. It's very dangerous.

9 I think you **should / must** go to bed early tonight. You look really tired.

b Complete the sentences with *must, must not, have to*, or *don't have to*. Sometimes two answers are possible.

1 You ___*have to pay*___ for food and drinks separately.

2 You _____ drive at more than 65 mph.

3 Service is included so you _____ leave a tip.

4 You _____ wait here before showing your passport.

5 You _____ pay on Sundays.

6 You _____ fasten your seatbelt now.

7 You _____ leave your bags unattended.

8 You _____ leave your hotel room before 12 o'clock.

activation

c Cover the sentences in **b**. Look at the pictures and remember the sentences.

5A GRAMMAR past tenses

a Complete the text with the correct form of the verbs in parentheses: simple past, past continuous, or past perfect.

My first car nightmare

This story [1] _____happened_____ (happen) to me about five years ago, and it's probably the worst thing that's ever happened to me while driving a car.

I [2] _____had bought_____ (buy) my car the week before, and I [3] _____ (still feel) very excited about it. It [4] _____ (not have) air conditioning but that [5] _____ (not matter) to me because it was my first ever car! I [6] _____ (know) that my best friend Penny [7] _____ (always want) to visit a picturesque little village in the mountains about 100 miles from where we live, so I [8] _____ (call) her and [9] _____ (tell) her that I would take her there the following day.

It was a perfect, warm spring day. The sun [10] _____ (shine) and the sky was blue. While I [11] _____ (drive) and we [12] _____ (talk), I [13] _____ (see) something out of the corner of my eye. It was a wasp that [14] _____ (fly) into the car! Penny and I both [15] _____ (try) to kill the wasp that [16] _____ (buzz) around inside the car. But the wasp suddenly [17] _____ (disappear). Then I [18] _____ (feel) a pain in my arm: the wasp [19] _____ (sting) me! I forgot that I [20] _____ (drive), and... BANG! I [21] _____ (crash) into the car in front of us. Nobody was hurt, but that was the end of our day out and of my car.

activation

b Cover the text. Look at the picture and try to remember the story.

5B GRAMMAR *usually* and *used to*

	then	now
Occupation	college students	Pierre: photographer, Lucie: journalist
Residence	Paris, France	Chicago, US
Hopes and dreams	be rich	be healthy and happy together
Eating habits	ate prepared food	mostly homemade food
House	lived with their parents	penthouse apartment with their dog
Holidays	camping	normally stay in 4- or 5-star hotels
Sport	didn't play sports	both ride bikes on the weekend. Pierre often plays golf to network
Vehicle	both rode bikes; Pierre: an old scooter	a Mercedes. Pierre sometimes rides his Harley Davidson
Clothes	secondhand	often designer clothes, but not always
Body type	slim	Pierre: putting on weight
Weekends	got up late, went out at night with friends	normally stay in, cook, and watch TV
Friends	lots of friends	just a few close ones

a Look at the table and complete the sentences with *used to*, *didn't use to*, or the simple present. Use *usually* where appropriate, although it is not always possible.

1 Pierre and Lucie _usually ride bikes_ on the weekend.   **ride bikes**
2 Pierre _____ as a photographer.   **work**
3 They _____ in Paris anymore.   **not live**
4 They _____ of being rich.   **dream**
5 They _____ homemade food when they were students.   **not eat**
6 They _____ their meals at home now.   **cook**
7 They _____ with their parents.   **live**
8 They _____ in expensive hotels these days.   **stay**
9 Pierre _____ golf when he was a student.   **not play**
10 Pierre _____ his old scooter anymore; he has a Harley Davidson.   **not ride**
11 They _____ designer clothes, but not all the time.   **wear**
12 He _____ very slim.   **be**
13 They _____ on the weekend and watch TV.   **stay in**
14 They _____ lots of friends.   **have**

activation

b Cover the sentences and look at the table. Make three sentences about Pierre and Lucie using *used to* and three sentences using *usually*.

6A GRAMMAR the passive *be* + past participle

a Circle the correct form, active or passive.

My favorite film: *Spider-Man*

The Spider-Man movies [1]**based** / **are based** on the Marvel Comics character Spider-Man, who is the alter ego of Peter Parker, a photographer who works for a local newspaper, the *Daily Bugle*.

When he is young, some important documents [2]**steal** / **are stolen** from Peter's home, and his parents then mysteriously [3]**disappear** / **are disappeared.** Peter [4]**sends** / **is sent** to live with his aunt and uncle. Here, he starts a new school, a new life, and becomes interested in science.

One day, he's in the school laboratory doing some experiments and he [5]**bites** / **is bitten** by a genetically modified spider. From that moment, he has the same abilities as a spider. During the movies he [6]**fights** / **is fought** against criminals and [7]**falls** / **is fallen** in love with his classmate, Gwen Stacey.

The special effects for the latest Spider-Man movie [8]**made** / **were made** with a special 3D-camera. The fantastic soundtrack was partly written by the British group Coldplay, and thousands of copies of the track [9]**have bought** / **have been bought** all over the world.

b Complete the sentences with the correct passive form of the verbs in parentheses. Write the answers in the column on the right.

1 I ▮▮▮ (give) a book for my birthday that I'd already read. *was given*

2 If you take a credit card with you on vacation, I'm sure it ▮▮▮ (accept) in most places. _____

3 This dress is silk. It has to ▮▮▮ (wash) in cold water or it will shrink. _____

4 The actress realized that she ▮▮▮ (follow) by the paparazzi, so she drove home again. _____

5 **A** ▮▮▮ the thief ▮▮▮ (catch) yet? _____
   B I don't think so. The police are still looking for him.

6 ▮▮▮ you ever ▮▮▮ (tell) a secret that you couldn't keep? _____

7 This bank ▮▮▮ (rob) twice since it opened last year. _____

8 When Jack arrived at the meeting, the decision ▮▮▮ (already make). _____

9 Our apartment ▮▮▮ (paint) right now. Everything's a real mess! _____

10 Although Pete thought the interview had gone really well, he ▮▮▮ (not offer) the job. _____

11 When does this book have to ▮▮▮ (return) to the library? _____

12 When we got to the parking garage we saw to our horror that our car ▮▮▮ (steal). _____

activation

c Cover the column on the right in **b** and look at the sentences. Read the sentences aloud with the passive in the correct form.

6B GRAMMAR modals of deduction: *might / may, can't, must*

a Circle the correct verb.

A Don't look now but isn't that Jane Marshall over there?

B Where?

A At that table by the window.

B No, it ¹**must** / **can't** be. She went to live in Chicago.

A But I'm sure it's Jane.

B Mmm, I suppose it ²**can't** / **might** be her. But if it is, she looks much thinner than she used to.

A Well it ³**must** / **can't** be five years since we last saw her. Someone can change a lot in five years!

B You're right, it is Jane. But who do you think the man is? He ⁴**can't** / **might not** be her husband, can he?

A No, he ⁵**can't** / **might not** be. They broke up years ago and haven't spoken to each other since.

B He ⁶**can** / **may** be her new boyfriend – or her son!

A Should we go over and find out?

b Complete the dialogues with *must, might, might not,* or *can't.*

1 A That's the second laptop that Jack's bought this year.

B He ___*must*___ have a lot of money then!

A He's a student so he _____ be that rich.

B He _____ have generous parents then.

2 A Do you know where Charlie is?

B Well, he _____ be far away. His phone's on the table.

A Any idea where he _____ be?

B He _____ be talking to the boss or he _____ be in the photocopying room. Do you want me to look for him?

3 A I have a missed call and I don't recognize the number.

B So, it _____ be from anyone you know.

A Ah, I know! It's that company who interviewed me last week. They _____ be calling to offer me the job. I'm not surprised: I had a really good interview.

B Well, don't be too confident because they _____ be calling to say you didn't get the job.

A There's only one way to find out!

4 A This steak _____ be for me. It looks like it's medium-rare, and I asked for a well-done steak.

B It _____ be mine, then. I ordered a medium-rare steak.

activation

c Cover the dialogues in **b**. Look at the pictures and try to remember the dialogues.

7A GRAMMAR first conditional and future time clauses

a Complete the messages with the verbs in the correct form: simple present, imperative, or *will* + infinitive. Use contractions where possible.

Annie   8:05

Katie!
How's it going? I'm studying so hard, but I need a break. Do you want to meet tomorrow evening? We could get a pizza and catch up.
I ¹ *'ll call*_____ (call) you when I ²_____ (get) home, OK? xx

Katie   8:08

Hi, Annie! I'm studying too!!! My history final is tomorrow afternoon. I'm really worried about it. OK for tomorrow evening, but not too early. I ³_____ (send) you a message when the exam ⁴_____ (finish). xx

Annie   8:09

OK. ⁵_____ (come) to my place as soon as you ⁶_____ (can). We can order pizza :)

Katie   8:10

OK. But ⁷_____ (not call) the pizza place until I ⁸_____ (get) there. I might be late.
I've been thinking, if you ⁹_____ (be) free when all our finals ¹⁰_____ (be) over in a couple of weeks, why don't we go away somewhere to celebrate?

Annie   8:11

Great idea! We could go away for a few days to relax!!
But I ¹¹_____ (not able to) go away unless I ¹²_____ (pass) all the exams :(
We can talk about it when we ¹³_____ (see) each other tomorrow night. xx

Katie   8:13

OK. Time to get back to work. If I ¹⁴_____ (not study) a little more tonight, I ¹⁵_____ (not have) any chance of passing history tomorrow. Wish me luck!! xx

activation

b Practice the messages in **a** with a partner.

7B GRAMMAR first and second conditionals

a Complete the sentences with the correct form of the verbs in parentheses to make second conditional sentences. Use contractions where possible.

1 If we ___*rented*___ (rent) that big apartment, we ___*'d have*___ (have) enough room for the dog.
2 I _____ (buy) a huge house with a yard if I _____ (win) the lottery.
3 If you _____ (paint) this room white it _____ (be) much lighter.
4 I _____ (do) it myself if I _____ (have) more time.
5 I _____ (not be) so broke if I _____ (spend) so much on going out.
6 Maybe if I _____ (share) an apartment with friends, I _____ (get along) better with my parents.
7 I _____ (can) travel next summer if I _____ (have) more money.
8 Carla _____ (move) out of her shared apartment if she _____ (find) a job.
9 If my girlfriend _____ (not have to) work so hard, we _____ (can) see each other more often.
10 If I _____ (go) to bed earlier, I _____ (not be) so tired all the time.

b Complete the sentences with a verb from the list in the first or second conditional. Write your answers in the column on the right. Use contractions where possible.

be   buy   find   get   go   never finish   not be   ~~not hurry~~   reduce   take

1 If they ▮▮▮, they'll miss the bus.   ___*don't hurry*___
2 If we had the money, we ▮▮▮ a beautiful house in the country.   _____
3 Lisa will have a lot of fun when she ▮▮▮ to Germany to study next year. _____
4 Unless they ▮▮▮ the price, they'll never sell their house.   _____
5 If I were you, I ▮▮▮ the dress back to the store: it just doesn't suit you. _____
6 Annabel will look for a job as soon as she ▮▮▮ her degree.   _____
7 If it ▮▮▮ so windy, we could go for a walk on the beach.   _____
8 If you ▮▮▮ some extra money in your bank account, would you spend it? _____
9 You ▮▮▮ your homework if you keep chatting with your friends on Facebook. _____
10 Sarah ▮▮▮ upset if she doesn't find her necklace. We have to help her look for it. _____

activation

c Cover the column on the right in **b** and look at the sentences. Read the sentences aloud with the verbs in the correct form.

8A GRAMMAR reported speech: sentences and questions

a Read the interview. Then complete the journalist's report below with the **bold** verbs from the interview in the correct tense.

Journalist	Mike, thank you very much for agreeing to this interview. I know you're a busy man. You have the leading role in the latest Kathryn Bigelow film. What is it like working with her?
Mike	You [1]**can't** begin to imagine what a fantastic experience it [2]**is**. In fact, it [3]**has been** an honor to work with her. However, I have to say that it [4]**wasn't** easy at first, because filming [5]**started** at 7:00 a.m. every day for the first three weeks. I'm not a person who likes to get up early!
Journalist	Yes, I had heard that! What [6]**did you enjoy** most about working with her?
Mike	I [7]**loved** the way that she [8]**could** get all the actors, including me, to do exactly what she wanted us to do.
Journalist	Are you [9]**going to be** in anymore of her movies in the near future?
Mike	It [10]**depends** on Kathryn, but I hope I [11]**will be**. I'm really sorry, but we [12]**must** stop the interview now as I have a photo shoot with *Vogue* magazine.

Mike told me that I [1] _couldn't_ begin to imagine what a fantastic experience working with Kathryn Bigelow [2]_____. He also said that working with her [3]_____ an honor. However, it [4]_____ easy at first because filming [5]_____ every day at 7:00 a.m. for the first three weeks. When I asked him what he [6]_____ most about working with Kathryn Bigelow, he told me that he [7]_____ the way that she [8]_____ get the actors to do what she wanted. Finally, I asked Mike if he [9]_____ in anymore of her movies in the future. He said that it [10]_____ on Kathryn, but he hoped he [11]_____. We then finished the interview because Mike said that he [12]_____ go to a photo shoot with *Vogue* magazine.

b Write the other questions journalists asked Mike in reported speech.

> What's the most interesting role that you've played?

1 The radio host asked Mike _what the most interesting role_ _he had played was_ .

> Is there too much violence in movies?

2 The TV interviewer asked him _____ _____ .

> Who's the most difficult actor that you've ever worked with?

3 The magazine writer asked him _____ _____ .

> What should a young person who wants to go into acting do?

4 The blogger asked him _____ _____ .

> When are you going to retire?

5 The newspaper reporter asked him _____ _____ .

activation

c Cover **b** and the journalist's report in **a**. Look at the interview in **a** and try to remember the journalist's report.

8B GRAMMAR gerunds and infinitives

a Complete the sentences with the correct form of the verbs in parentheses. Use the gerund, the infinitive with *to*, or the infinitive without *to*.

1   Emily's parents aren't strict enough with her. They let her ▮▮ whatever
    she wants. (do)   *do*

2   I'm really busy right now. Would you mind ▮▮ me back in about
    five minutes? (call)   _____

3   My boss told me she wanted ▮▮ to me in her office. (speak)   _____

4   We decided ▮▮ her a birthday present because we weren't sure what
    she wanted. (not buy)   _____

5   Have you ever thought of ▮▮ back to live in Chicago or are you
    happy in New York City? (go)   _____

6   My neighbor offered ▮▮ my children while I went to do some
    shopping. (watch)   _____

7   Have you finished ▮▮ the computer yet? I need it. (use)   _____

8   ▮▮ for people who are late makes me really angry. (wait)   _____

9   My parents would like me ▮▮ medicine as a career. (consider)   _____

10 I think Ben should study architecture. He's very good at ▮▮. (draw)   _____

11 Do you think you'd like ▮▮ with children or would you find it too
    stressful? (work)   _____

12 If they can save enough money, they're hoping ▮▮ to Miami for
    their honeymoon. (go)   _____

13 Have you ever thought about ▮▮ yoga or Pilates? They're very good
    if you have problems with your back. (do)   _____

14 I was really surprised ▮▮ that he'd failed the exam. I thought he was
    going to pass. (hear)   _____

15 Are you going to continue ▮▮ English here next year? (study)   _____

16 I want you ▮▮ very seriously about what you're going to do after you
    graduate. (think)   _____

17 I don't really feel like ▮▮ tonight. Let's go out for dinner. (cook)   _____

18 Don't pretend ▮▮ the present if you don't. We can always exchange it
    for something else since I still have the receipt. (like)   _____

19 ▮▮ late at night always makes me ▮▮ a little uncomfortable. I just can't
    go to bed on a full stomach. (eat / feel)   _____

20 Angela asked her brother ▮▮ her a ride into town. (give)   _____

activation

b Cover the column on the right and look at the sentences. Read the sentences aloud with the
   verbs in the correct form.

9A GRAMMAR third conditional

a Put the words in the correct order to complete the conditional sentences.

1 would / scored / 'd / the / they / have / won / game
   If he *'d scored, they would have won the game* _____
   _____.

2 missed / here / on time / if / the movie / have / been / you'd
   We wouldn't _____
   _____.

3 offered / you / 'd / have / it / the job / you / would / taken
   If they _____
   _____?

4 finished / if / fallen / she / the race / have / hadn't
   Ella would _____
   _____.

5 me / smiled / have / told / a picture / were taking / 'd / you / I
   If you'd _____
   _____.

6 known / that / eaten / you / was / what / have / in it / if / 'd
   You wouldn't _____
   _____.

b Put the verbs in parentheses in the correct tense to make third conditional sentences. Use contractions where possible.

1 We _*wouldn't have met*_ (not meet) if you _*hadn't invited*_ (not invite) us both to dinner that night.
2 If I _____ (know) how cold it was going to be in San Francisco, I _____ (take) warmer clothes.
3 You _____ (enjoy) the party if you _____ (go).
4 Dora _____ (call) you this morning if she _____ (not leave) her cell phone on the train.
5 I _____ (not delete) the email if I _____ (realize) it was important.
6 _____ (you / marry) him if he _____ (ask) you?

activation

c Cover the sentences in **a**. Look at the pictures and try to remember the sentences.

9B GRAMMAR quantifiers

LIVE The two leading candidates are having a debate on live television.

a Circle the correct answer for each blank.

A After four years of your party in power, it's time for a change.
We're the party to do that. The country has ▮ of problems,   [1](a lot)/ many
and we know how to solve them. First, there's ▮ unemployment.   [2] too many / too much
Second, there aren't ▮ teachers in our schools and third,   [3] no / enough
there's ▮ money left for our seniors!   [4] any / no

B What you have to remember is that this situation is a direct result
of your party's policies when you were in power.
We've had ▮ time to repair the damage you caused.   [5] very little / very few
▮ people voted for you in the last election?   [6] How many / How much
▮! And do you know why? Because the voters were fed up and   [7] Very few / Very little
so were ▮ members of your own party!   [8] much / a lot of

A My dear friend, you really don't have any idea what you're
talking about! You say you haven't had ▮ . I say you don't have   [9] enough time / time enough
▮ original ideas!   [10] no / any

B I can assure you we have ▮ of ideas   [11] many / plenty
and that ▮ of them aren't original or effective.   [12] very few / very little

A Nonsense! ▮ years ago when we were in power, our economy was   [13] A little / A few
stronger and we had ▮ unemployment. How do you explain that?   [14] very few / very little

B You know that's not true and so do the voters.
The people of this country are ▮ intelligent to believe your lies.   [15] too / enough

A The problem is that your party spends ▮ time insulting the   [16] too / too much
opposition, and not ▮ time thinking of new ideas.   [17] enough / many

C Thank you very much, ladies and gentlemen.
I'm afraid we have ▮ more time today…   [18] any / no

activation

b Cover the column on the right. Look at the debate and try to remember the missing words.

10A GRAMMAR relative clauses

a Complete the text with *who*, *that*, *which*, *where*, or *whose*.

| a place | a song | a number | a photo | a person | an animal | a store | an object |

We asked students to tell us about their favorite things in life:

This week Ana, a student from Brazil, tells us about hers.

I have to say that my favorite place in the world is the village
¹___*where*___ I was born. I've traveled all over the world, but it's still
the place ²_____ I love the most. A song… that's an easy one!
It's *Lady in Red* by Chris de Burgh, for two reasons. First, it was the
color of the dress ³_____ I was wearing the night I met my
husband. Second, it was the song ⁴_____ the DJ played as we
danced. The number ⁵_____ I chose is the number nine. My
grandmother, ⁶_____ used to live with us when I was little,
always asked me to get her a lottery ticket with this number. I think that's
why I like it so much. For a photo, I chose a black and white photo of my
parents ⁷_____ I've had for about 20 years. Every time I look
at it, I can see two happy people in their early twenties ⁸_____
lives were about to change forever. Why? Well because my mom was
pregnant with me in the photo! My English teacher at school was the
woman ⁹_____ inspired me to love languages. So, I chose her
to be my favorite person. Animals? No question about it! The animals ¹⁰
_____ I like most are dogs. The store ¹¹_____ I could
spend all day would be one selling perfumes and cosmetics. Finally, an
object ¹²_____ is very special to me is my engagement ring,
because it used to belong to my husband's grandmother. It's beautiful.

b In which sentences could you leave out *who*, *that*, or *which*?

c Combine the two sentences using a non-defining relative clause.

1 Our neighbors are both teachers. They work at the same school.

   Our neighbors, ___*who are both teachers*___, work at the same school.

2 Pablo Picasso's best known painting is *Guernica*. He was born in Malaga in 1881.

   Pablo Picasso, _____, was born in Malaga in 1881.

3 Canberra is the capital of Australia. It's smaller than Sydney and Melbourne.

   Canberra, _____, is smaller than Sydney and Melbourne.

4 Our local post office has closed down. I used to work there.

   Our local post office, _____, has closed down.

5 Lionel Messi is possibly the most talented soccer player of his generation. He was born in Rosario in Argentina.

   Lionel Messi, _____, is possibly the most talented soccer player of his generation.

6 The hurricane caused millions of dollars' worth of damage. It was the worst for over 75 years.

   The hurricane, _____, caused millions of dollars' worth of damage.

activation

e Read **a** again. Write a paragraph about your favorite things in life.

10B GRAMMAR tag questions

a Complete the dialogues with a tag question.

1 **A** Hi. Your name's Angela, [1]___*isn't it*___?

   B Yes, it is. Do we know each other?

   A You really don't remember me, [2]_____?

   B I'm afraid I don't.

   A It's Jeff. Jeff Dawson.

   B Oh, my goodness! We were in school together, [3]_____?

   A That's right!

2 **A** Guess who called me this morning?

   B It wasn't your ex, [4]_____?

   A Uh huh.

   B He isn't still calling you, [5]_____? What did he want?

   A Just to talk, I think.

   B But ex-boyfriends don't just call to talk, [6]_____?

3 **A** We're still going to the music festival, [7]_____?

   B Well, it depends.

   A On what exactly? You don't have enough money, [8]_____?

   B Well, not really.

   A Your mom will lend you some, [9]_____? She always does.

4 **A** It's cold today, [10]_____?

   B Well it's January, [11]_____?

   A It was much colder this time last year, [12]_____?

   B I suppose so. Oh look, here's my bus!

5 **A** What's wrong, honey?

   B Nothing.

   A You're not having problems with the other children at school, [13]_____?

   B No, I'm not. Everything's fine.

   A And you haven't had an argument with one of your friends, [14]_____?

   B Of course not.

   A You'd tell me if there was a problems, [15]_____?

   B Yes, mom. Now will you please leave me alone?

activation

b Practice the dialogues in **a** with a partner.

Communicative Activity Instructions

Tips for using Communicative activities

- We have suggested the ideal number of copies for each activity. However, you can often manage with fewer, e.g., one copy per pair instead of one per student.
- When Sts are working in pairs, if possible get them to sit face to face. This will encourage them to really talk to each other and also means they can't see each other's sheet.
- If your class doesn't divide into pairs or groups, get two Sts to share one role, or get one student to monitor, help, and correct.

Extra idea

- If some Sts finish early, they can change roles and do the activity again, or you could get them to write some of the sentences from the activity.

Getting to know you

A pairwork activity

This photocopiable "getting to know you" activity can be used together with the introductory Grammar activities as a first-day class, especially if your Sts do not yet have the Student Book.

- Sts write the information about themselves. They then switch with a partner and ask each other to explain the information.
- Copy one **A** sheet and one **B** sheet per student.

> **Language**
> general review of *American English File 2* grammar and vocabulary

- Put Sts in pairs and give each student instructions and a chart (**A** or **B**)
- Give Sts five minutes to write answers in the appropriate place in the chart.
- Now get Sts to exchange charts. Demonstrate the activity by taking a chart from a student and asking him / her *Why did you write…?* Ask follow-up questions to continue the conversation.
- Sts now do the activity in pairs. Make it clear to them that they had different instructions, and stress that they can ask about the information in any order. Monitor and help where necessary. Stop the activity when most Sts have asked about all their partner's information.

1A Spot the difference

A pairwork information gap activity

Sts describe their pictures to each other and find ten differences between them. Copy one sheet per pair and cut into A and B.

> **Language**
> simple present and continuous, food vocabulary
> *In the restaurant, a man and a woman are sitting at a table. They're talking.*

- Review any food and cooking words that you think Sts may have forgotten and which they will need for the activity.
- Put Sts into pairs, ideally face to face, and give out the sheets. Make sure Sts can't see each other's sheets.
- Explain that they both have the same picture, but it has been changed so that there are ten differences.
- Student A begins by describing the scene in the restaurant, and B listens to find differences. Then Student B describes the scene in the kitchen.
- They should ask their partner questions if necessary to identify the differences.
- When they have found the differences they can show each other the pictures to make sure they have identified them correctly.
- Check the differences orally with the class.

Extra support

- You could tell Sts that there are five differences in the restaurant scene and five in the kitchen.

Differences in restaurant pictures

1. A The waiter is going into the kitchen.
   B The waiter is coming out of the kitchen.
2. A The waiter is carrying a cake on a plate.
   B The waiter is carrying a roast chicken on a plate.
3. A The man and the woman at table 2 are sitting opposite each other and look happy.
   B The man and the woman at table 2 are sitting next to each other and look unhappy.
4. A The businessman at table 1 is talking on his phone.
   B The businessman at table 1 is typing into his cell phone.
5. A The woman at table 3 is eating with a fork in her left hand and an iPad or e-reader in her right hand.
   B The woman at table 3 is holding a book in her left hand, and a glass in her right hand.

Differences in kitchen pictures

1. A There is a no smoking sign on the wall.
   B The sign on the wall asks people to wash their hands.
2. A The male cook is trying the food.
   B The male cook is adding salt to the food.
3. A The male cook with a large hat is stirring something in a pot.
   B The male cook with a large hat is frying a steak in a pan.
4. A The female cook is looking in the refrigerator.
   B The female cook is standing with her back to the refrigerator and looking at the cooks.
5. A The man at the sink is starting to wash the dishes.
   B The man at the sink is finishing washing the dishes.

1B Who is it?

A pairwork interview activity

Sts use question prompts to interview each other about somebody they know. Copy one sheet per student.

> **Language**
> question forms in the present and future
> *What does she do? When are you going to see her next?*

Extra support

- Give Sts, working alone, a few minutes to write the complete form of each question in the space provided. Remind Sts that "/" means there is a word missing or a change needs to be made to the verb. Check answers.

- Give each student a sheet, and focus on rubric **a**. Give Sts a few minutes to think of someone they know well. They can use the words at the top of the sheet for ideas. They shouldn't tell their partner anything about the person they are thinking about yet, except whether the person is male or female.

- Now focus on the question prompts and give Sts time to think about how to make the questions.

- Now tell the Sts that they're going to ask each other about their mystery person to discover their identity. Demonstrate the activity by thinking of a person yourself. First tell them if it's a man or a woman and then get Sts to ask you the questions until they guess who the person is. Insist on correct question forms.

- In pairs, **A** interviews **B** and then tries to guess what the relationship is between **B** and the person they are describing.

- Sts change roles.

- When they've finished, get feedback by asking who each student described, and if their partner was able to guess the relationship.

> **1 Family**
> Where was he / she born? Where does he / she live? Who does he / she live with?
> **2 Occupation / School**
> What does he / she do? Where does he / she work / go to school? Does he / she like his / her job / what he / she is studying? Is he / she going to change jobs or schools in the future?
> **3 Appearance and personality**
> What does he / she look like? What kind of clothes does he / she wear? What is he / she like? What is his / her best and worst quality?
> **4 Interests**
> What does he / she like doing in his / her free time? Does he / she play any sports or exercise? Which? What kind of music does he / she like? Does he / she speak foreign languages?
> **5 Your relationship with this person in the present**
> How often do you see each other? Do you get along well? What do you have in common? What do you do together?
> **6 Your relationship with this person in the future**
> When are you seeing him / her next? What do you do together? Are you going on vacation together this year? Do you think you'll know him / her ten years' from now?

2A Money, money, money...

A pairwork speaking activity

Sts interview each other about questions related to money. Copy one sheet per pair and cut into a and b.

> **Language**
> question forms in the simple present and the present perfect
> *What's the most expensive thing you've ever bought? How much money have you spent today?*

- Be sensitive to any concerns Sts may have about money.

- Put Sts in pairs and give out the sheets. Make sure that they can't see each other's questions. Give them a few minutes to read their questions.

- Sts take turns asking each other the questions on their sheet. Remind them to always ask for more information.

- When Sts have finished the questions get some feedback from individual pairs.

2B How long have you...?

A class mingle

Sts have a question which they use to survey the rest of the class. Copy and cut up one sheet per 12 Sts.

> **Language**
> Present perfect and present perfect continuous
> *How long have you known him? How long have you been living there?*

- If you have more than 12 Sts, divide the class into two groups and make them move to different sides of the room. Give each student a different question card. Tell Sts to work out what the second question is (they must use either the present perfect or continuous), but not to write it. Elicit and check the questions before Sts start the activity.

> **Occupation** How long have you been working / worked there?
> **House** How long have you been living / lived there?
> **Interests** How long have you been doing it?
> **Gadgets** How long have you had it / them?
> **Sports** How long have you been doing it?
> **Vacations** How long have you been going there?
> **Social networks** How long have you had an account?
> **Giving** How long have you been helping them?
> **TV** How long have you been watching it?
> **Friends** How long have you known him or her?
> **Learning** How long have you been learning it?
> **Gym** How long have you been a member?

Extra support

- You could let Sts write down their second question on the back of their card.

- Now tell Sts they have to ask their question to all the other Sts in the class or group and make a note of their answers.

- Sts stand up and mingle, asking their questions. If you have two groups, get them to mingle in different halves of the classroom. Take part in the mingle yourself, and monitor.

- When Sts have asked everyone their questions, get them to sit down.

- Get feedback for each card to find out who has been doing each activity the longest.

Non-cut alternative

- Copy one sheet per pair of Sts, and cut in half. Put Sts in pairs (preferably sitting face to face) and give them one half of the sheet each. **A** asks **B** his / her first and second questions. **B** answers, and then returns the questions, asking *What about you?* Then **B** asks **A** his / her first and second questions. They find out between the two of them who has been doing each thing the longest.

3A Questionnaire

A pairwork questionnaire

Sts review comparatives and superlatives by completing a questionnaire with comparatives or superlatives and then asking and answering the questions. Copy one sheet per pair and cut into a and b.

> **Language**
> comparatives and superlatives
> *Are you taller than your sister?*
> *Where's the best place to park?*

- Put Sts in pairs and give out the questionnaires.
- Focus on the adjectives / adverbs and tell Sts to complete each question with a comparative or superlative of the adjective / adverb.
- Tell Sts that there may be two comparatives or two superlatives in each pair of questions – it's not always one of each.
- Check answers. You could copy the key onto the board.
- Now focus on **b**. Get Sts sitting face to face if possible to ask and answer the questions. They can either ask alternate questions, or **A** can interview **B** and they then change roles. If there's time, they could also return the questions asking *What about you?*

> A **English** 1 harder, 2 the most difficult; **Traveling** 1 the worst, 2 more often; **Your life** 1 more active, 2 unhealthiest; **Friends and family** 1 the best-looking (the most good-looking), 2 closest; **Technology** 1 the best, 2 more practical
> B **English** 1 the most useful, 2 easier; **Traveling** 1 the longest, 2 more enjoyable; **Your life** 1 the most relaxing, 2 more healthily; **Friends and family** 1 best, 2 the most fluent; **Technology** 1 cheaper, 2 the most expensive

3B Generally speaking

A group discussion

Sts practice generalizing by discussing topics in small groups. Copy one sheet per group of three or four Sts and cut into cards.

> **Language**
> not using *the* for generalizing
> *I think cats make the best pets because...*

- Put Sts in groups of three or four. Try to have a diverse group where possible, as this will help to promote disagreement. Give out one set of cards to each group and put face down.

- Pick up the top card from one group and read it aloud. Say whether you agree or disagree and give a reason.
- Sts continue in groups. One student picks up a card and reads it aloud, says whether he / she agrees or not, giving reasons, and the others then say what they think. Monitor and correct any misuse of the definite article.
- Get some feedback to see whether, generally speaking, Sts agree or disagree with the sentences.

Extra support

- You could write some useful expressions on the board for Sts to use, e.g., *I agree / don't agree, (Personally,) I think…, In my opinion…, For example,…* Remind Sts not to use the definite article when they generalize.

Non-cut alternative

- Give one sheet to each pair or group and get them to discuss the statements one by one.

4A Language learning

A pairwork speaking activity

Sts compare their opinions on language learning. Copy one sheet per student.

> **Language**
> Different forms of *can / be able to*
> *The Internet can help you when you're learning a language.*

- Give out the sheets and tell Sts to spend five minutes reading through the sentences. Explain that they have to put a check mark in the column after each statement if they agree with it and an ✗ if they disagree.
- Put the Sts in pairs. Tell them to compare their answers and explain the reasons for their choices. Monitor, correcting especially any mistakes which relate to grammar in 4A.
- Get feedback from individual pairs.

4B Tell us about...

A group board game

Sts move around the board making sentences using *have to, must, should*. Copy one sheet per group of three or four Sts.

> **Language**
> *have to, must, should*
> *You must not text when you're driving.*

- Put Sts in groups of three or four and give each group a copy of the board game pieces. They will also need counters (or pieces of paper) and a coin.
- Each player puts a counter on a START triangle.
- Explain the rules of the game. Sts take turns throwing the coin and moving one circle for heads and two for tails. When they land on a circle, they must make a sentence following the instruction. The rest of the group has to decide if the sentence is correct and makes sense. Be the final judge in case of dispute.
- If the sentence is wrong, Sts move back a circle. If it's correct, they stay on the circle.

- When Sts reach their own "Finish," they take another turn and continue around the board.
- The first student to reach the next "Finish" wins.
- Alternatively, if there is time, tell Sts to continue around the whole board. The first student to reach the final "Finish" before his or her "Start" triangle then wins.

Extra idea
- If Sts need more written practice using the verbs, you could do this as a written race. After you say "Go!" Sts, in pairs, have ten minutes to complete as many of the sentences as possible, starting with number one. Get the pair who has completed most to read out their sentences. Other pairs should read theirs, too, if they're different. The pair with the most grammatically correct answers wins.

Example answers
1 You shouldn't drink coffee / play on your computer / have a big dinner.
2 I have to go to the library / review for the test / do my homework / practice speaking English.
3 You must print your boarding pass / pack / check in / show your passport.
4 You don't have to work / go to classes / get up early / do anything.
5 You shouldn't go to bed late / worry / review too much / eat a lot.
6 You don't have to pay cash / go to the store / try things on / carry bags home with you.
7 You must fasten your seat belt / follow traffic rules / keep your eyes on the road. You must not lose your concentration / text / eat / drink.
8 You should think about the price / why you need one / if you need a new one / any special offers and contracts.
9 I had to do my homework on time / speak in English / write compositions / give a presentation.
10 You have to learn English / find somewhere to live / get a job.
11 You should find out about special customs / if you need a visa / changing currency.
12 You shouldn't get back in touch / see what he or she is doing on Facebook / go out together again.
13 He or she has to correct homework / organize the classroom / prepare the class / have everything he or she needs.
14 You should consider what to cook / what food you need to buy / what drinks you need to buy.
15 You shouldn't exercise / go swimming / get cold.
16 A good student has to participate in class / do homework / go to class / pass exams.
17 You must reply to the invitation / buy a present / make sure you have some nice clothes to wear / plan how to get to the wedding.
18 You should take an aspirin / lie down / close your eyes / have a cup of coffee.
19 You must fill the gas tank / check the tires / plan your route. You must not smoke / forget your map / drive without taking breaks.
20 You should be punctual / have information about the job / look professional. You shouldn't get there late / talk too much / wear casual clothes.

5A What a cheat!
A pairwork activity

Sts complete different texts about cheating in sports with verbs in the correct tense (simple past, past perfect, or past continuous) and then memorize and tell each other their story. Copy one sheet per pair and cut into a and b.

> **Language**
> past tenses
> *Jane had already eaten when I got home.*

- Put Sts in pairs and get them to sit face to face if possible. Give out the sheets. Explain that they each have a different true story about cheating in sports.
- Focus on **a**. Give Sts a few minutes to read their story and then complete the numbered spaces with the correct form of the verbs in parentheses.
- Check answers by copying the key onto the board.

Did he cheat?
2 formed 3 included 4 was preparing 5 had sat down
6 showed 7 had chosen 8 was driving 9 crashed
10 gave 11 passed 12 went 13 had left
14 had crashed 15 accused 16 admitted

The Long Road to Ruin
2 banned 3 was competing 4 had won 5 had faced
6 was recovering 7 decided 8 returned 9 amazed
10 came 11 offered 12 confessed 13 had taken
14 announced 15 had cut

Extra support
- You could get two **A**s and two **B**s to work together to complete their stories.

- Focus on **b**. Explain that Sts are now going to tell each other their stories, and ask their partner a final question about the story.
- Give Sts time to re-read and memorize the story.
- Now get **A** to tell **B** from memory about Nelson Piquet, Jr., and then ask **B** the final question (instruction **c**). They should try to tell the story from memory but can use their texts as prompts where necessary.
- **B** then does the same for Lance Armstrong and asks the final question **c**.
- Get feedback by asking Sts whether they think Nelson Piquet, Jr. or Lance Armstrong was the worse cheat and why.

5B How did they change our world?
A pairwork activity

Sts talk about some inventions and what life used to be like before they existed. Copy one sheet per pair.

> **Language**
> used to / didn't use to
> *People used to use candles for light.*
> *They didn't use to stay up late at night.*

- Put Sts in pairs and give out one sheet per pair.
- Focus on the first invention (the electric light) and ask Sts *What did people use to do before it was invented?* Try to elicit at least one (+) and one (-) answer with *used to*, e.g., *They used to go to bed when it was dark. They didn't use to stay up late at night.*
- Sts continue in pairs with the other inventions. Get them to write the sentences if you think they need more written practice with *used to*. Stress that they should try to make at least three sentences per invention.
- Get feedback, asking pairs to tell you their different sentences.

- Now tell Sts that they have five minutes to choose three inventions that they couldn't live without, and three that they could happily live without. Then they compare choices and explain why.
- Get feedback to see which were the most / least popular inventions.

Extra idea
- You could cut the cards up and give each pair or group of three or four Sts a set, placed face down. Sts pick up the top card and continue as above.

Example answers
the refrigerator They used to go shopping every day. They didn't use to buy ice cream.
Google They used to use encyclopedias. They didn't use to look for information online.
GPS They used to use maps. They didn't use to be able to avoid traffic jams.
TV They used to play games or other activities. They didn't use to sit inside for a long time.
email They used to write lots of letters. They didn't use to communicate quickly.
MP3 players They used to listen to the radio. They didn't use to listen to music wherever they were.
the car They used to use horses for transportation. They didn't use to travel so fast on land.
cell phones They used to use phone booths. They didn't use to contact people at any time.
digital cameras They used to be careful of how many photographs they took. They didn't use to put photos onto a computer.
low-cost flights They used to pay a lot of money to travel by plane. They didn't use to travel so far.
ATMs They used to get money from a person inside the bank. They didn't use to be able to get money anywhere in the world.

6A Give me an answer
A group activity

Sts ask questions using the passive to other Sts in the group. Copy and cut up one set of cards per three or four Sts.

Language
question forms in the passive
Is the movie subtitled?

- Put Sts in groups of three or four and give each group a set of cards face down.
- Sts take turns picking up the top card and asking the question to the other people in the group. Remind them to use *What about you?* when they repeat the question to the second or third student.
- Demonstrate by picking up a card yourself and asking one group. Ask extra questions for more information to encourage the Sts to do the same.
- Sts then continue. Monitor and correct any mistakes with passive forms.
- Stop the activity when one group has asked all the questions, or when you think it has gone on long enough.

Non-cut alternative
- Copy one sheet per pair of Sts, and cut in half vertically. Put Sts in pairs (preferably sitting face to face) and give them one half each. **A** asks **B** his / her first question, **B** answers, and then returns the question by saying *What about you?* Then **B** asks **A** his / her first question.

6B Who do you think they are?
A pairwork activity

Sts have to match some people to their professions. Copy one sheet per pair.

Language
modals of deduction
He/she can't be… He/she might be… He/she must be…
She might be a hairstylist because she has beautiful hair.

- Put Sts in pairs and give out the sheets.
- Go through the list of jobs and make sure that Sts remember the meaning of all of them.
- Tell Sts to speculate about each person in turn, going through all the jobs. Tell Sts that they are all real people who do one of these jobs.
- Focus on photo 1 (Vince Cable) and **b**. Get Sts to give you a sentence with another reason why he can't be a boxer e.g., *He can't be a boxer because he looks very stylish.* Repeat with **c** and **d**. Remind Sts that they have to say why.
- Monitor while they discuss and encourage them to use *He | She can't be | might be | must be*, etc.
- When you think that Sts have had enough time, check that they have made a final decision for each person.
- Check answers, eliciting from different pairs sentences with *He | She must be a…* and their reasons, and see if any of the pairs guessed the correct answers.

Extra support
- You could write *We think he | she must be…* on the board.

1 Vince Cable is a politician.
2 Richard Ward is a hairstylist.
3 Mary Beard is a university professor.
4 Adam Phillips is a psychoanalyst.
5 Nicola Benedetti is a violinist.
6 Nicola Adams is a boxer.

7A Finish the sentences
A group activity

Sts race to complete sentences. Copy and cut up one sheet per four or five Sts.

Language
first conditional and future time clauses + *when, until*, etc.
I'll move to a new house when I get a promotion.
I'll do my homework as soon as I get home this afternoon.

- Put Sts in small groups (four or five) and number the groups. Give each group a set of 20 strips in an envelope.

- Each group picks a strip and tries to complete the sentence in a logical and correct way. They should then write their sentence. As soon as they've written it, one student comes to you with their sentence. If it's correct, the group gets a point. Keep the score for each group on the board. If the sentence is not correct, the group rewrites it.
- Set a time limit, e.g., eight minutes. When the time is up, the group with the most correct sentences wins.

Non-cut alternative

- Put Sts into pairs and give out one sheet per pair. Sts work in pairs to complete the sentences. Set a time limit. When the time is up, get the pair who has completed the most to read their sentences aloud. The pair with the most correct sentences wins.

7B If you had to choose...

A pairwork or group activity

Sts ask questions about preferences, either to a partner or small group. Sts have to say which alternative they would prefer and why. Copy one sheet per pair or small group. You can personalize this activity if you want by inventing more questions, giving alternatives yourself.

Language
second conditional
I'd prefer to have a vacation house on the coast, because if I had a house in the mountains, I'd miss the ocean.

- Put Sts in pairs or small groups and give out the sheets.
- Demonstrate the activity by getting a student to ask you one of the questions. Answer in as much detail as possible. Sts then continue either asking their partner the question or asking all the people in the group. Tell the other student(s) to return the questions using *What about you?*
- While Sts are talking, go around and monitor, correcting any mistakes with conditionals.
- When the activity finishes, get feedback from a few pairs or groups.

8A Ask and tell

A pairwork activity

Sts interview each other and then report questions and answers to a new partner. Copy one sheet per pair and cut into **A** and **B**.

Language
reported speech
I asked Pablo how many times he'd been abroad.
He said (that) he'd been abroad about five times.

- Put Sts in pairs **A** and **B** and give out the sheets. Focus on **a**.
- Stress that Sts just need to ask the questions on their sheet and write notes (not whole sentences).
- Sts ask and answer the questions alternately. Monitor to make sure that Sts aren't writing down everything their partner says or asking for more information.

- After Sts have finished asking all their questions, put Sts in new pairs so that all the **A**s are now working with a different **B**. Focus on **b**.
- **A** tells **B** what he / she asked his / her original partner and what he / she said (using reported speech). Sts do this alternately.
- Monitor and correct any misuse of reported speech.

Extra idea

- Fast finishers could write down the ten questions they asked their partner using reported speech.

8B Predict the story

A reading and predicting activity. Copy one sheet per student (or pair).

Sts read and predict the next paragraph of a short story.

Language
work

- Give each student a sheet. Make sure they have a piece of paper to cover the text before they start reading.
- Sts cover all the text except the first paragraph and question 1. Sts read up to the first question *What do you think the meeting was about?*
- Give Sts a minute to discuss question 1 with a partner, or elicit ideas from the whole class (someone will almost certainly guess right, but don't tell them).
- Sts then uncover and read the next part of the story and question 2, and find out if their predictions were correct.
- Repeat the same process with the remaining parts of the story and questions.
- When you come to the last two questions, elicit all possible suggestions from the class. Accept all ideas, but tell Sts that Keeler will probably be fired.

Tip

- Explain to the Sts that *The Firing Line* is a play on words: it refers to someone who is in line to be fired, and it also refers to the position from which someone with a gun shoots at a target.

9A Third conditional game

A group board game

Sts review third conditionals by moving around a board and completing sentences. Copy one sheet per group of three or four Sts.

Language
third conditional
If we had known it was your birthday, we would have bought you a present.

- Put Sts in groups of three or four and give each group a copy of the board game. They will also need counters (or pieces of paper) and a coin.

- Explain the rules of the game. Sts throw the coin and move one square for heads and two for tails. When they land on a square, they must finish the sentence so that it is grammatically correct and makes sense. Encourage them to use contracted forms. The rest of the group are "judges." Be the final judge in case of dispute. If the sentence is correct, they can stay on the square they have landed on. If not, they have to go back to where they came from.

- The youngest student in each group starts. If Sts land on a square where another student has been before, they must complete the sentence in a different way.

- The first student to reach the "Finish" wins.

Possible answers
1 would have won the game
2 you'd decided to come
3 wouldn't have had a table
4 you hadn't had that last cup of coffee
5 wouldn't have cooked lamb
6 I'd known who was calling
7 wouldn't have gotten lost
8 wouldn't have missed your call
9 I'd studied more
10 would have bought you a present
11 you'd told us you were coming
12 he'd been more careful
13 would have bought it
14 he'd arrived at work on time more often
15 it had snowed more
16 would have caught the train
17 I'd played the lottery last week
18 we would have won the game

9B Lifestyle survey
A pairwork activity

Sts compare information about their lifestyle and practice using quantifiers. Copy one sheet per pair and cut into a and b.

> **Language**
> quantifiers
> *How much time do you spend with your family every day?*
> *Not enough.*

- Put Sts in pairs and give out the sheets. Focus on **a** and give Sts a few minutes to read all their question prompts. Then focus on **b** and on the expressions Sts should use in their answers.

Extra support
- Drill all the questions with the whole class.

- Demonstrate the activity by getting an **A** and a **B** to ask you their first question. Answer each question with an expression from the list, and then explain it. Elicit follow-up questions.

- Sts ask and answer the questions in pairs. Get them to ask alternate questions, and, if there's time, to return the question with *What about you?*

- Get some feedback from the class.

10A Relative clauses quiz
A pairwork quiz

Sts complete questions using relative pronouns and then ask a partner the questions. Copy one sheet per pair and cut into **A** and **B**.

> **Language**
> relative pronouns
> *Can you tell me the sport that is played at Wimbledon?*

- Give out a copy of the questions (**A** or **B**) to each student.

- Sts complete the questions individually with a relative pronoun.

- When all Sts have completed their questions, check answers either orally or by writing the pronouns on the board.

> **A Sports** 1 that / which, 2 that / which; **Art and literature** 1 who, 2 whose; **Movies and TV** 1 who, 2 who; **Geography** 1 that / which, 2 where; **Technology** 1 whose, 2 where
> **B Sports** 1 where, 2 whose; **Art and literature** 1 whose, 2 who; **Movies and TV** 1 where, 2 who; **Geography** 1 where, 2 that / which; **Technology** 1 where, 2 that / which

- Put Sts in pairs **A** and **B**. Sts sit facing each other.

- Focus on **b**. Explain that first they must ask their partner the question without giving the three alternative answers. If their partner gets it right, he / she gets three points. If he / she gets it wrong, then they should give the three alternatives. If their partner chooses the correct option, he / she gets one point.

- When Sts finish, ask each pair who got the most points.

Extra challenge
- Get Sts to write some more quiz questions of their own.

10B Memory game: tag questions
A pairwork activity

Sts ask each other questions, remember the answers, and then check that they've remembered the answers correctly using tag questions. Copy one sheet per pair and cut into **A** and **B.**

> **Language**
> tag questions
> *Your favorite color is blue, isn't it?*

- In pairs, Sts sit facing each other. Give out the sheets and give Sts a minute to read their questions and instructions.

- **A** and **B** ask and answer each other's questions alternately (or **A** asks all his / her questions first, and then **B**). Stress that they must not write down their partner's answers, but must try to remember them. Encourage them to have a conversation rather than just asking / answering. This will help them to remember the answers.

- When **A** and **B** have asked all their questions, stop and get the class's attention. Ask one **A** if he or she remembers how **B** answered the first question (*When's your birthday?*) and explain that to check this he or she should say *Your birthday's on (May 18th), isn't it?* Get **B** to answer (*Yes, it is* or *No, it isn't. It's on…*).
- In pairs, Sts check their memory of their partner's answers. Monitor to make sure they're forming and pronouncing the tag questions correctly.
- Get feedback to see which student in each pair had the better memory.

Review

A pairwork speaking activity

- Sts ask each other questions about key vocabulary areas using a range of tenses and verb forms from the book. This could either be used as a final "pre-test" review or as an oral exam. Copy and cut up one set of cards per pair.

> **Language**
> grammar and vocabulary of the book
> *What does your brother look like?*

- Sts work in pairs. Give each pair a set of cards face down. Set a time limit, e.g., ten minutes. Sts take turns picking up the top card and talking to their partner about the topic on the card, using the prompts.
- Tell Sts to keep their cards and then if there is time, to exchange cards with their partner.
- Encourage Sts to ask follow-up questions.
- Monitor, help, and correct.

Non-cut alternative

- Make one copy per pair. Give Sts a few moments to read through the cards. **A** chooses a number for **B**. **B** then talks about what's on the card for that number. Sts continue taking turns choosing a topic for their partner to talk about.

COMMUNICATIVE Getting to know you

Student A instructions

a Read your instructions and write your answers in the correct place in the chart.

In the star, write your first and last name.

In square 1, write the year you started learning English.

In circle 2, write two things you really like doing when you have some free time.

In square 3, write the number of the month when you were born (e.g., October = 10)

In circle 4, write the name of a famous person you admire.

In square 5, write the name of the last movie you saw at home or at the movie theater.

In circle 6, write the name of the most beautiful place you've ever been to.

In square 7, write the names of two sports you think are really boring or interesting to watch.

In circle 8, write the name of the person you get along with best in your family.

In square 9, write the name of a famous group or singer you really like or don't like.

In circle 10, write the name of a TV show you often watch.

b Exchange charts with **B**. Ask **B** to explain the information in his / her chart. Ask for more information.

Why did you write "3"?

Because it's how many brothers and sisters I have.

What are their names?

c Explain your answers to **B**.

- -

Student A chart

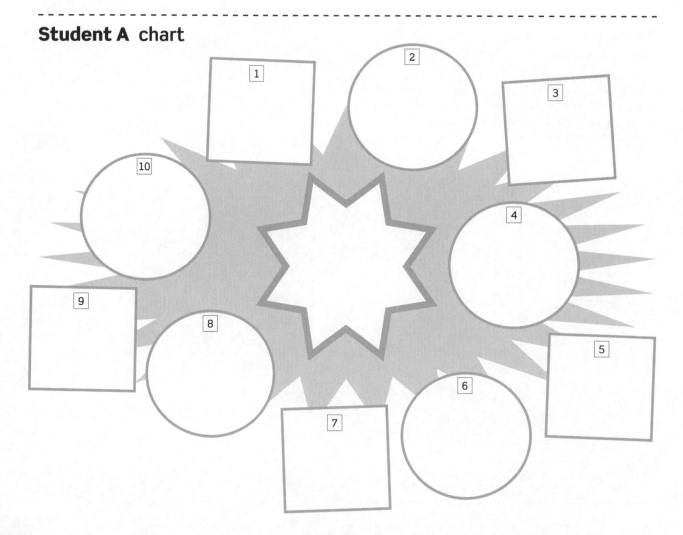

American English File 2nd edition Teacher's Book 3 Photocopiable © Oxford University Press 2014

COMMUNICATIVE Getting to know you

Student B instructions

a Read your instructions and write your answers in the correct place in the chart.

In the star, write your first and last name.

In square, 1, write the number of brothers and sisters you have.

In circle 2, write the two things you don't like doing on the weekends.

In square 3, write the number of the house or apartment where you live.

In circle 4, write the name of a really good friend.

In square 5, write the name of the place where you spent your last vacation.

In circle 6, write the name of a website you often visit.

In square 7, write the name of a subject you really love or loved in school.

In circle 8, write the name of two kinds of music you really like.

In square 9, write an animal you have or would like to have as a pet.

In circle 10, write the name of a TV personality you really like or don't like.

b Exchange charts with **A**. Ask **A** to explain the information in his / her chart. Ask for more information.

Why did you write "Sebastian"?

Who exactly is Sebastian?

Because it's the name of the person I get along with best in my family.

c Explain your answers to **A**.

- -

Student B chart

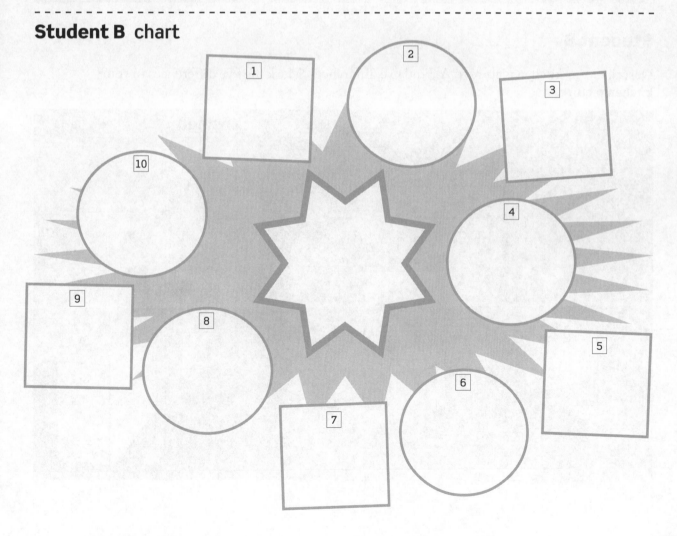

Student A

Describe your restaurant picture to **B**. Find five differences. Mark the five differences in your restaurant picture.

Student B

Describe your kitchen picture to **A**. Find five differences. Mark the five differences in your kitchen picture.

1B COMMUNICATIVE Who is it?

a parent **your best friend**
your boyfriend / girlfriend
a stepmother / stepfather **a brother / sister**
a nephew / niece
a co-worker **your husband / wife**
a grandparent

Person's first name _____

❶ Family

Where / born?
_____

Where / live?
_____

Who / live with?
_____

❷ Occupation / School

What / do?
_____

Where / work or go to school?
_____

/ like / job or school? Why (not)?
_____

/ going / change / job or school in the future?
_____

❸ Appearance and personality

What / look like?
_____

What kind / clothes / wear?
_____

What / like?
_____

What / best and worst quality?
_____

❹ Interests

What / like doing in / free time?
_____

/ play any sports or exercise? Which?
_____

What kind / music / like?
_____

/ speak foreign languages? Which?
_____

❺ Your relationship with this person in the present

How often / see each other?
_____

/ get along well?
_____

What / have in common?
_____

What / do together?
_____

❻ Your relationship with this person in the future

When / you / see this person next?
_____

What / do together?
_____

/ go on vacation together this year?
_____

Do you think / know this person / ten years from now?
_____

---

a You're going to tell your partner about someone in your family, or someone you know very well. Look at the question prompts in the table and think of your answers to the questions.

b **Student A:** Ask **B** about his or her person. Use the questions in the table but ask for more information, too. Try to guess who the person is.
Student B: Answer **A**'s questions. Give as much information as possible about him or her, but don't tell **A** who he or she is. **A** has to guess if the person is a parent, your boyfriend or girlfriend, your best friend, a coworker, etc.

c Change roles.

2A COMMUNICATIVE Money, money, money...

Student A

Ask your partner the questions. Remember to ask for more information.

Do you like finding bargains?

Why?

No, I hate going to sales.

1 Do you like finding bargains?

2 When do you prefer to pay by cash, and when do you prefer to pay by credit card?

3 Have you ever bought something you couldn't really afford?

4 Has an ATM ever "eaten" your bank card? If so, how did you get it back?

5 Have you, or anyone you know, ever won a lot of money?

6 Does anybody owe you money? Do you owe anybody money?

7 How much do you spend on food and drink every week?

8 Have you ever given money to a charity, like Save the Children or Goodwill?

9 Is your country expensive to live in right now? What kinds of things are expensive?

10 Who usually pays the check when you go to a restaurant?

- -

Student B

Ask your partner the questions. Remember to ask for more information.

Have you ever bought something and then regretted it?

Why didn't you like it?

Yes, I once bought a picture, but when I brought it home I decided that I didn't like it.

1 Have you ever bought something and then regretted it?

2 How much money have you spent so far today? What did you spend it on?

3 What kind of things do you normally buy online? Why don't you buy them in a store?

4 Have you ever taken out a loan from the bank? Why?

5 Is there anything you'd love to buy but can't afford right now?

6 Have you bought anything nice this week?

7 Have you ever inherited money or property, or something more unusual?

8 What's the most expensive thing you've ever bought?

9 What do you spend your money on aside from food, rent, etc.?

10 Have you, or anyone you know, ever had money stolen? If so, what happened?

American English File 2nd edition Teacher's Book 3 Photocopiable © Oxford University Press 2014

OCCUPATION

Where do you work or go to school?

How long / work or study there?

HOUSE

Do you live in a house or in an apartment?

How long / live there?

INTERESTS

Do you have a special hobby?

How long / do it?

GADGETS

What gadgets (e.g., e-reader, smartphone, etc.) do you have?

How long / have them?

SPORTS

Do you play any sports or exercise?

How long / do it?

VACATIONS

Is there a place you often go to for vacation?

How long / go there?

SOCIAL NETWORKS

Are you on Facebook or another social network?

How long / have an account?

GIVING

Do you give money to, or do you work for, a charity, e.g., the World Wildlife Fund?

How long / help them?

TV

Is there a TV show or series you regularly watch?

How long / watch it?

FRIENDS

Who's your oldest friend?

How long / know him or her?

LEARNING

Are you learning anything new at the moment (not English!)?

How long / learn it?

GYM

Do you go to a gym?

How long / be a member?

3A COMMUNICATIVE Questionnaire

Student A

a Complete the questions with a comparative or superlative.

What does "get stuck" mean?	**English**
	1 Which do you think is _____ to learn, your own language or English? (hard)
	2 What's _____ thing about studying English? (difficult)
	Traveling
	1 What's _____ vacation you've ever had? (bad)
	2 Which do you use _____, public transportation or a car? (often)
	Your life
	1 During a typical day, are you _____ in the morning or in the afternoon? (active)
	2 What's your _____ habit? (unhealthy)
	Friends and family
	1 Who's _____ person in your family? (good-looking)
	2 Who in your family are you _____ to? (close)
	Technology
	1 If you have a technical problem who's _____ person you know to help you? (good)
	2 Which do you think is _____, a laptop or a tablet? (practical)

b Ask **B** your questions. Ask for more information.

- -

Student B

a Complete the questions with a comparative or superlative.

LEARN Chinese in 5 DAYS	**English**
	1 Aside from English, what do you think is _____ foreign language to learn? (useful)
	2 Do you find listening is _____ than speaking? (easy)
	Traveling
	1 What's _____ trip you've ever been on? (long)
	2 Do you think traveling alone is _____ than traveling with friends or family? (enjoyable)
	Your life
	1 Which part of the day is _____ for you? (relaxing)
	2 Do you eat _____ than in the past? (healthily)
	Friends and family
	1 What's your _____ friend like? (good)
	2 Who's _____ English speaker in your family? (fluent)
	Technology
	1 Is it _____ to buy things online or in a store? (cheap)
	2 What's _____ gadget you've ever bought? (expensive)

b Ask **A** your questions. Ask for more information.

American English File 2nd edition Teacher's Book 3 Photocopiable © Oxford University Press 2014

Women have a better sense of style than men.

People who spend a lot of time on computers have no social skills.

Cyclists should pass a test before riding a bike.

Vegetarians are healthier than people who eat meat.

Young people today have easier lives than their parents.

Exercise is only good for you if it hurts.

School friends are for life.

Brothers and sisters don't usually get along well.

Designer clothes are a waste of money.

People who have a sports car are usually fast, aggressive drivers.

Food that tastes good is usually bad for you.

Cats make the best pets.

4A COMMUNICATIVE Language learning

a Look at the statements and check (✓) if you agree or put an ✗ if you disagree in the column next to it.

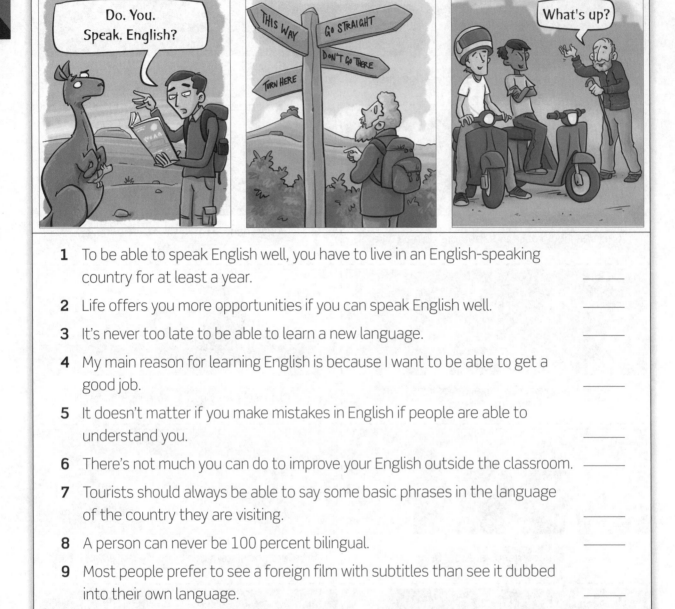

1   To be able to speak English well, you have to live in an English-speaking country for at least a year. _____

2   Life offers you more opportunities if you can speak English well. _____

3   It's never too late to be able to learn a new language. _____

4   My main reason for learning English is because I want to be able to get a good job. _____

5   It doesn't matter if you make mistakes in English if people are able to understand you. _____

6   There's not much you can do to improve your English outside the classroom. _____

7   Tourists should always be able to say some basic phrases in the language of the country they are visiting. _____

8   A person can never be 100 percent bilingual. _____

9   Most people prefer to see a foreign film with subtitles than see it dubbed into their own language. _____

10 The Internet can help you when you're learning a language. _____

11 Listening to other people speaking English is the only way I can improve my pronunciation. _____

12 Most young people in my country can communicate well in English. _____

13 A child can learn English just by watching TV in English. _____

14 A good teacher can influence how much you enjoy a language. _____

15 To be able to communicate well in a foreign language, pronunciation, and vocabulary are more important than grammar. _____

b Compare your answers with your partner and explain why you agree or disagree.

Take another turn!

START

1 Three things you **shouldn't** do before you go to bed.

2 Two things you **have to** do after class today.

3 Two things you **must** do before you catch a plane.

4 Three things you **don't have to** do when you're on vacation.

5 Two things you **shouldn't** do the night before an exam.

FINISH

Take another turn!

START

6 Two things you **don't have to** do if you shop online.

7 Two things you **must** do and two things you **must not** do when you're driving.

8 Two things you **should** think about before you buy a new phone.

9 One thing you **had to** do in your English class last year that you found very difficult.

10 Two things you **have to** do if you want to live and work in an English-speaking country.

FINISH

Take another turn!

START

11 Two things you **should** find out about a country before you visit it.

12 Two things you **shouldn't** do when you break up with your partner.

13 Two things a teacher **has to** do before a class.

14 Two things you **should** consider if you've invited friends to have dinner.

15 Two things you **shouldn't** do if you have the flu.

FINISH

Take another turn!

START

16 Three things a good student **has to** do to improve their English.

17 Two things you **must** do if you've been invited to a wedding.

18 One thing you **should** do if you have a headache.

19 Two things you **must** do and one thing you **must not** do when you are going on a long car trip.

FINISH

20 Two things you **should** do and two things you **shouldn't** do when you have a job interview.

Tell us about ...

5A COMMUNICATIVE What a cheat!

Student A

a Put the verbs in parentheses in the simple past, past perfect, or past continuous.

Did he cheat?

In the autumn of 2008, Nelson Piquet, Jr. ¹___*found*___ (find) himself in the middle of one of sport's greatest controversies – had he or hadn't he deliberately crashed his car during the Singapore Grand Prix?

Piquet Jr. ²_____ (form) part of the Renault Formula 1 team which also ³_____ (include) the Spanish driver Fernando Alonso. According to Piquet, the day before the race, while he ⁴_____ (prepare) to drive, two senior Renault F1 directors asked to speak to Piquet, Jr. He went to see them in their offices, and as soon as he ⁵_____ (sit down), the two directors took out a map of the Singapore circuit. They then ⁶_____ (show) him the exact corner on the map where they wanted him to crash his car, and the exact moment when they wanted it to happen. The directors ⁷_____ (choose) this corner because they knew rescue teams couldn't get to this part of the track quickly, so all the drivers would have to slow down. Piquet agreed to "sacrifice" his race so that his teammate, Alonso, could win. While Piquet ⁸_____ (drive) around the circuit for the 14th time, he ⁹_____ (crash) his car. This allowed Alonso to make an early pit stop and ¹⁰_____ (give) him an advantage. After Piquet crashed, Alonso ¹¹_____ (pass) the other drivers and ¹²_____ (go) on to win the race.

In 2009, after Piquet ¹³_____ (leave) Renault, there was an investigation. Piquet admitted that he ¹⁴_____ (crash) his car on purpose under instruction from Renault. At first, Renault ¹⁵_____ (accuse) Piquet of lying, but finally they ¹⁶_____ (admit) their guilt.

b Read the story again and remember it.
In your own words, tell **B** about Nelson Piquet, Jr.

> This happened to Nelson Piquet, Jr. in 2008. He was part of...

c Ask **B** *Who do you think is telling the truth, Nelson Piquet, Jr. or Renault Formula 1?*

- -

Student B

a Put the verbs in parentheses in the simple past, past perfect, or past continuous.

The Long Road to Ruin

One of the greatest sporting scandals ¹___*made*___ (make) the news headlines all over the world in August, 2012 when United States Anti-Doping Agency (USADA) ²_____ (ban) Lance Armstrong from cycling for life for taking performance-enhancing drugs while he ³_____ (compete) as a professional cyclist. Before the ban, Armstrong ⁴_____ (win) seven Tour de France races, but he ⁵_____ (face) numerous accusations of drug use during his career.

Many years earlier in 1996, at the age of 25, Armstrong was diagnosed with life-threatening cancer. Fortunately he responded well to the treatment, and while he ⁶_____ (recover) from the illness he ⁷_____ (decide) to set up the Livestrong Foundation to raise money for cancer research. Armstrong ⁸_____ (return) to cycling in 1998 and he ⁹_____ (amaze) his fans by winning the Tour de France again and again. But in 2011, witnesses and former teammates ¹⁰_____ (come) forward and ¹¹_____ (offer) unquestionable proof of Armstrong's guilt. In January, 2013, in an emotional interview, Armstrong publicly ¹²_____ (confess) that he ¹³_____ (take) performance enhancing drugs and he also ¹⁴_____ (announce) that he ¹⁵_____ (cut) all ties to the Livestrong Foundation. Armstrong's seven Tour de France wins were removed from the history books.

b Read the story again and remember it.
In your own words, tell **A** about Lance Armstrong.

> This happened in 2013.
> Lance Armstrong finally admitted...

c Ask **A** *Do you think the punishment given to Lance Armstrong was fair?*

the electric light

the refrigerator

Google

GPS

TV

email

MP3 players

the car

cell phones

digital cameras

low-cost flights

ATMs

6A COMMUNICATIVE Give me an answer

1 Has your car or bike ever been stolen?

2 What's the best present you've ever gotten?

3 Would you like to be painted by a famous artist?

4 How much are you influenced by advertisements on TV and online?

5 When you were a child, did you use to be punished a lot for doing something wrong?

6 At what age do you think people should be allowed to vote?

7 At what age do you think people should be allowed to drive?

8 Do you like being photographed?

9 Have you ever been caught a) cheating on an exam, or b) speeding?

10 Do you prefer driving or being driven?

11 Name the best thing that was invented or discovered by someone from your country.

12 When was the last time you were invited to a wedding?

13 Which jobs in your country do you think are a) not paid enough, or b) paid too much?

14 Have you ever been photographed by a professional photographer?

15 Are you often asked to show your ID? When was the last time?

16 How do you feel about being corrected when you are speaking English?

17 Do you think life skills, like cooking, should be taught in school?

18 Have you ever been attacked by an animal?

19 Has one of your vacations or flights ever been canceled?

20 How soon do you think e-books will be used in all schools instead of paper books?

a Look at the people in the pictures and the list of jobs below. Each person does one of the jobs from the list.

| boxer | hairstylist | politician | psychoanalyst | university professor | violinist |

b Discuss each person with your partner. Eliminate the jobs you think are impossible for that person. Use *He | She can't be a…* and say why.

*The man in picture 1 **can't be** a boxer, because he looks too old.*

c Now say which jobs you think are possible. Use *He | She might be …*

*He **might be** a college professor…*
but he doesn't look intelligent enough.

d Now make a final choice for each person. Use *He | She must be…* and say why. Your teacher will tell you if you're right.

*He **must be** a… because…*

7A COMMUNICATIVE Finish the sentences

I'll move to a new house **when**...

I'll do my homework **as soon as**...

Unless they pay me more money...

Laura won't buy a new phone **until**...

You'll soon feel better **if**...

When I'm 75, I...

Send me a message **as soon as**...

Don't do anything **until**...

You'll find the love of your life **if**...

As soon as I get home...

We'll miss the train **unless**...

When we get to the hotel...

The children won't go to sleep **until**...

We'll tell him the news **as soon as**...

I won't know which computer to buy **unless**...

If I can get tickets for the concert...

My parents won't let me go to the party **unless**...

I won't be able to pay you back **until**...

When I have enough money...

If you press this red button...

Talk to a partner.
Say why.

> I'd prefer to live in a new house because if I lived in an old house, I'd have to do so much work on it!

If you had to choose...

 Would you prefer to live in a new house or in an old house that you could renovate yourself?

 Would you prefer to have a vacation house on the coast or in the mountains?

 Would you prefer to have a house with solar energy or a house with traditional electricity?

 If you had space in your house, would you prefer to have a gym or a game room?

 Would you prefer to live in a four-bedroom house in the country or a one-bedroom apartment downtown?

 Would you prefer to live in a house next to an airport or a house next to a school?

 Would you prefer to live in a modern, spacious apartment or in an old, cozy house?

 Would you prefer to live in a fourth-floor apartment without an elevator or on the first-floor apartment with a dance club next door?

8A COMMUNICATIVE Ask and tell

Student A

a Ask your partner the questions and write down his / her answers in note form.

		notes
1	Can you play a musical instrument?	_____
2	How many times have you been abroad?	_____
3	Did you go to bed early last night?	_____
4	What do you usually have for breakfast?	_____
5	Are you going to go out on Saturday night?	_____
6	Have you ever won a prize or trophy?	_____
7	What are you going to do after class?	_____
8	What's your favorite time of year?	_____
9	When did you last get a letter written by hand?	_____
10	What do you do on Sunday mornings?	_____

b Change partners. Tell your new partner about what your first partner told you.

I asked Anna if she could play a musical instrument and she said she could play the piano.

- -

Student B

a Ask your partner the questions and write down his / her answers in note form.

		notes
1	Could you swim when you were five?	_____
2	Are you afraid of any animals or insects?	_____
3	Have you ever visited an English-speaking country?	_____
4	Do you have a favorite sports team?	_____
5	Where did you go to on vacation last year?	_____
6	What websites do you like looking at?	_____
7	Where are you going for your next vacation?	_____
8	Where will you be at four o'clock tomorrow afternoon?	_____
9	Have you played any sports or exercised today?	_____
10	Can you count to one hundred in three languages?	_____

b Change partners. Tell your new partner about what your first partner told you.

I asked Paul if he could swim when he was five, and he said he could swim when he was four.

 THE FIRING LINE *by* Henry Slesar

Part 1

Sheldon Keeler, marketing manager of Walford International, knew from experience that company meetings could be called at any time and in any place, even in the elevators. As he was going up to his office on Wednesday morning, Cliff Bowles, the head of personnel, got into the elevator with him. "We had a meeting last night, Sheldon… ," he said.

> 1 What do you think the meeting was about?

"One of your guys is out."
"Oh?" Keeler said. "Who?"
"Macauley. He's not the right man for the job. Tell him as soon as you can."
"Of course," Keeler said, desperately trying to remember who Macauley was of the 67 people in his department. "I'll tell him right now."
"No," said Bowles. "It will be better if you wait until Friday."

> 2 Why does Bowles want to wait until Friday to fire Macauley?

And do it late in the afternoon, when most people have gone home. It's not good for the company to have employees who've been fired complaining to everyone. They might even go on strike."

> 3 How do you think Keeler feels about having to fire a member of his department?

Keeler wasn't pleased. It wasn't the first time he'd had to tell someone to go, but he didn't enjoy it. And sometimes there were unpleasant scenes. Even the carefully-written company document. (*How to Fire a Walford Employee*) wasn't much help when the victim became emotional. The elevator stopped and Keeler got out. "Right," he said. "I'll tell him as soon as I get back from lunch on Friday."

Part 2

Thursday was a busy day for Keeler, and he completely forgot that he had to fire one of his men. But on Friday, he returned from lunch feeling tense. He knew the moment had come, and couldn't wait any longer. He called Eve, his secretary, and told her to tell Bob Macnally to come to his office. Macnally arrived promptly, a slim young man with a sensitive face.

> 4 What do you think might be the first question Keeler asks Macnally?

"Sit down," Keeler said with a friendly smile. "How long have you been working here, Macnally?" This was the standard first question, recommended by the company document.
"Almost two years," the young man said. "Let's see, it'll be exactly two years this November."
Keeler smiled. "And how do you feel about these two years?"
"Fine," the young man said, "Just fine, Mr. Keeler."
The manager sighed deeply. "Well, I suppose it must be our fault then," he said sadly.
"Your fault? What do you mean?"
"Look, Bob," Keeler said confidentially. "You're a good man and you've got great potential. When you leave here, your experience with Walford will be a really good recommendation. We'll give you a good reference. You can be sure of that."

> 5 Do you think Macnally knows now that he's going to lose his job?

"But I wasn't thinking of leaving, Mr. Keeler."

"Bob," Keeler said sadly, "Sometimes a man has to think about leaving."

Macnally suddenly realized the truth. "You mean I'm fired?" he said incredulously.

"Look Bob…"

"Don't call me Bob. You've never called me Bob in your life, Keeler. I bet you never even knew my first name until now."

"I'm only trying to make this easy for you…"

"I'm the best marketing man you've ever had, you told me that yourself."

"Did I?"

"You certainly did. Last year. You sent me an email, remember? Or didn't you know who you were sending it to? I've got the best record in the department, and now you're firing me! I don't believe it!"

"There are a few factors," Keeler said seriously. "The personnel department…"

"To hell with them!" the young man said furiously, standing up. "And to hell with you!" he shouted. "You're just a puppet!" He turned and walked towards the door.

6   Who do you think he's going to speak to and why?

"I'm going to see the CEO. I'm going to get some answers. I won't accept it unless he gives me a really good reason."

"Wait a minute!" Keeler shouted. "You'll only make things worse if you go and see Mr. Walford…"

But he couldn't stop him. Keeler sighed deeply and went back to the letter he was writing. At 5:10 he filled his briefcase with unread documents and went home.

Part 3

On Monday morning, Evelyn arrived at the office before him. She looked up as he entered. "Oh, Mr. Keeler, Mr. Walford called at nine and asked you to go and see him as soon as you got here."

7   Why do you think Mr. Walford wants to see Keeler?

Keeler got the elevator to the executive floor and went to Mr. Walford's office at the end of the corridor.

"Sit down, Keeler," said Mr. Walford. "This man of yours, Macnally…"

"Sorry about that, Mr. Walford. So he came to see you…"

"Yes, he did," said Mr. Walford. "A very emotional young man. A good man, too. I asked Mr. Bowles in the personnel department about him. He said he was the best young man in your department. I didn't want to lose him. But after the things he said to me, I couldn't let him stay. He called me an old… What a pity."

"Yes," said Keeler, "It is a pity, I didn't want to fire him, Mr. Walford. But the personnel department knows best… "

"Did you get the order from Mr. Bowles?"

"Yes, sir."

"When?"

"On Wednesday. It was in the elevator actually. He told me that Macauley wasn't the right man for the job…" He stopped.

"Macauley," he whispered.

"Yes," Walford said quietly. "Macauley. Tell me something, Keeler… How long have you been working here?"

8   Why does Mr. Walford ask Keeler the last question? What do you think is going to happen to Keeler?

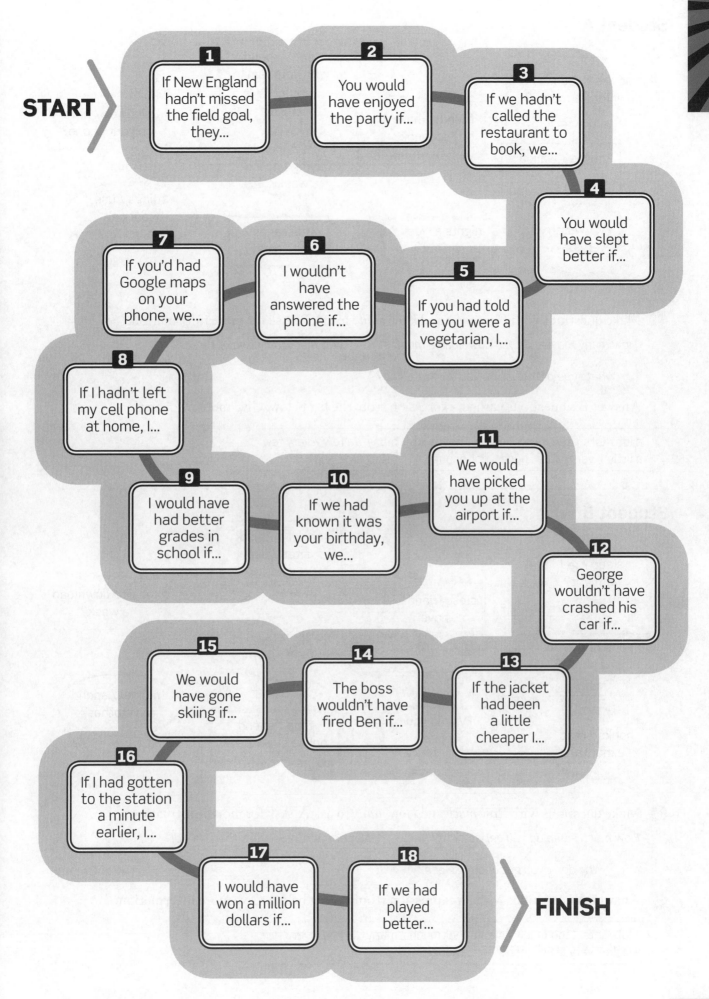

START

1 If New England hadn't missed the field goal, they…

2 You would have enjoyed the party if…

3 If we hadn't called the restaurant to book, we…

4 You would have slept better if…

5 If you had told me you were a vegetarian, I…

6 I wouldn't have answered the phone if…

7 If you'd had Google maps on your phone, we…

8 If I hadn't left my cell phone at home, I…

9 I would have had better grades in school if…

10 If we had known it was your birthday, we…

11 We would have picked you up at the airport if…

12 George wouldn't have crashed his car if…

13 If the jacket had been a little cheaper I…

14 The boss wouldn't have fired Ben if…

15 We would have gone skiing if…

16 If I had gotten to the station a minute earlier, I…

17 I would have won a million dollars if…

18 If we had played better…

FINISH

9B COMMUNICATIVE Lifestyle survey

Student A

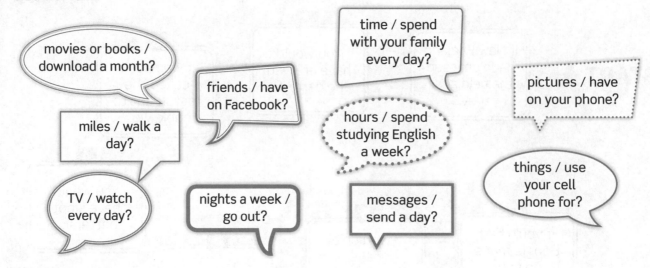

a Make questions with *How much* and *How many* to ask **B**. Ask for more information.

How many movies do you download a month?   *Not many, only two or three.*

What type of movies do you like watching?

b Answer **B**'s questions with an expression from the list below. Give more information.

a lot / lots   too much / many   not much / many   a few / very few
a little / very little   none   not enough

- -

Student B

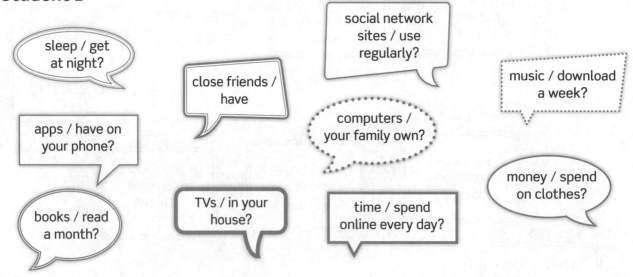

a Make questions with *How much* and *How many* to ask **A**. Ask for more information.

How much sleep do you get at night?   *Not enough, much less than I need!*

Why don't you get enough sleep?

b Answer **A**'s questions with an expression from the list below. Give more information.

a lot / lots   too much / many   not much / many   a few / very few
a little / very little   none   not enough

10A COMMUNICATIVE Relative clauses quiz

Student A	Student B

Student A

Can you tell me...

Sports

1 the sport _____ is played at Wimbledon?
   a cricket b polo **c tennis**
2 the year _____ the US last held the Olympic Games?
   a 1908 **b 2002** c 2012

Art and literature

1 the name of the person _____ wrote the Twilight series?
   a Stieg Larsson b Stephen King **c Stephenie Meyer**
2 the name of the famous artist _____ most famous work was the *Mona Lisa*?
   a Caravaggio **b Leonardo da Vinci**
   c Michelangelo

Movie and TV

1 the names of two actors _____ have played Batman?
   a Christian Bale and George Clooney
   b Christian Bale and Johnny Depp
   c Christian Bale and Daniel Day-Lewis
2 the name of the actress _____ played Margaret Thatcher in the 2012 film *The Iron Lady*?
   a Glenn Close b Judi Dench **c Meryl Streep**

Geography

1 the continent _____ has the largest population?
   a Africa **b Asia** c South America
2 the city _____ you can find the Spanish Steps?
   a Buenos Aires b Moscow **c Rome**

Technology

1 the name of the company _____ logo is a piece of fruit?
   a Apple b Cherry c Raspberry
2 the university _____ Facebook was invented?
   a Harvard b Stanford c Yale

(a) Complete the questions with *who, that, which, where,* or *whose.*

(b) Ask **B** the questions. (Begin with *Can you tell me…?*)
If **B** knows the answers, he / she gets three points.
If **B** doesn't know the answer, give him / her the three options.
If **B** gets it right, he / she gets one point.

Student B

Can you tell me...

Sports

1 the name of the stadium _____ the Chicago Cubs play?
   a Yankee Stadium b Fenway Park **c Wrigley Field**
2 the sports company _____ slogan is "Just do it"?
   a Adidas **b Nike** c Reebok

Art and literature

1 the name of the painter _____ works of art included a can of soup?
   a David Hockney b Damien Hirst **c Andy Warhol**
2 the name of the writer _____ wrote the James Bond books?
   a Albert "Cubby" Broccoli **b Ian Fleming**
   c John Le Carré

Movie and TV

1 the planet _____ Superman comes from?
   a Arrakis b Galileo **c Krypton**
2 the name of the actress _____ is married to Javier Bardem?
   a Penélope Cruz b Cameron Diaz c Salma Hayek

Geography

1 the U.S. state _____ Apple has its headquarters?
   a California b New York c Washington
2 two U.S. cities _____ have a Disney theme park?
   a Denver and Dallas b Dallas and Anaheim
   c Anaheim and Orlando

Technology

1 the place in California _____ they make electronic gadgets?
   a Fresno Valley **b Silicon Valley** c Simi Valley
2 the name of one of the two companies _____ helped develop "smart" cars?
   a Fila b Oakley **c Swatch**

(a) Complete the questions with *who, that, which, where,* or *whose.*

(b) Ask **A** the questions. (Begin with *Can you tell me…?*)
If **A** knows the answers, he / she gets three points.
If **A** doesn't know the answer, give him / her the three options.
If **A** gets it right, he / she gets one point.

10B COMMUNICATIVE Memory game: tag questions

Student A

a Ask **B** the questions below and remember his / her answers. Don't write anything down.

* When's your birthday?
* Do you like using Facebook?
* How long have you been studying English here?
* Have you been to an English-speaking country?
* Did you go out last night?
* Where were you born?
* Can you speak five languages?
* Where are you going after this class?
* What did you have for dinner last night?
* Are you talkative?

b Answer **B**'s questions.

c Now check if you remember **B**'s answers to the questions in **a**. Use a tag question.

Your birthday's October 25th, isn't it?　　　*Yes, it is.*

- -

Student B

a Ask **A** the questions below and remember his / her answers. Don't write anything down.

* Do you take sugar in coffee?
* Are you going anywhere next weekend?
* What's your favorite color?
* Can you play a musical instrument?
* Did you have breakfast this morning?
* How long have you been living in your house / apartment?
* Were you at home last night?
* Where would you like to go on vacation this year?
* Have you been to an opera?
* Are you stubborn?

b Answer **A**'s questions.

c Now check if you remember **A**'s answers to the questions in **a**. Use a tag question.

You don't take sugar in your coffee, do you?　　　*No, I don't.*

COMMUNICATIVE Review

1 Food and cooking

Talk for a minute about what and where you eat.

* Do you think you have a healthy diet? Why (not)?
* Do you eat or drink too much or not enough of anything?
* Are you trying to cut down on anything right now?
* Do you prefer eating out or eating at home?
* What's your favorite dish when you eat out?
* How do you usually like these kinds of food to be cooked? Fish   Potatoes   Rice

2 Family and friends

Describe a friend or a member of your family.

* What does he / she look like?
* What is he / she like? (Give two positive and two negative characteristics.)
* In what ways are you similar?
* In what ways are you different?
* Do you get along with this person? Why (not)?

3 Money

Tell your partner about your attitude to money.

* Are you good at saving money?
* Are you careful with money? How?
* Do you usually leave tips in hotels, taxis, or restaurants? Why (not)?
* Is there anything you don't like spending money on? Why (not?)
* Do you think credit cards are a good thing? Why (not?)

4 Transportation

Talk to your partner about transportation in your town.

* What's your favorite form of transportation? Why?
* What's the best way to get around your town / city?
* What's the worst way to get around your town / city?
* How do you get to the place where you work / study?
* If you could change one thing about transportation in your town, what would it be?

5 Sports

Tell your partner about...

* A sport you really like watching or playing.
* A sport you hate watching or playing.
* A sport you used to do and why you stopped.
* A favorite team. How long have you been a fan? Do you go and see them play?
* The sporting event you most remember.

6 Relationships

Tell your partner about a good friend of yours.

* How long have you known each other?
* Where did you meet?
* Why do you get along well together?
* Have you ever had a serious argument?
* How often do you see each other?

7 The movies

Think of a movie (but don't say the name). Describe it for your partner to guess.

* Where's it set?
* Is it based on a book?
* Who was it directed by?
* Who's in it?
* What's it about?

8 Your education

Tell your partner about your high school (or elementary school if you are still in high school).

* Did you use to wear a uniform?
* What subjects were you good at?
* What subjects didn't you like?
* Did you use to have a favorite teacher?
* Were there any teachers you didn't like? Why (not)?

9 Your home

Talk about your home.

* Where do you live?
* How long have you lived there?
* What kind of house or apartment is it? Can you describe it?
* What do you like about it? What don't you like?
* What do you like about the area where you live? What don't you like?

10 Work

Think of a friend or family member who has a job. Tell your partner about the good and bad side of his / her job. Talk about:

* The salary
* The hours
* The vacations
* The best thing about the job
* The worst thing about the job

Vocabulary activity instructions

Classroom language

- Give each student a sheet. Focus on each section and elicit / drill the meaning and pronunciation of each phrase.
- If Sts wish, they can write a translation of each phrase alongside it. You could get Sts to test themselves or each other by covering the phrase and looking at the translation.
- Tell Sts that these are phrases that you expect Sts to always use in English, and be strict about not letting them say them in their L1.

Extra idea
- You could copy and enlarge this sheet and put it up in the classroom to remind Sts to use the phrases.

1A Food and cooking
A card game

Sts define words / phrases for other Sts to guess. Copy and cut up one set of cards per pair or small group.

Language
food and cooking

- Put Sts in pairs or small groups. Give each pair or group a set of cards face down or in an envelope.
- Demonstrate the activity. Choose another word (not one of the ones on the cards) from the Vocabulary Bank *Food and cooking*. Describe it to the class, e.g., *It's the type of meat which comes from a cow*, until a student guesses the word (*beef*). Highlight that Sts are not allowed to use the word on the card in their definition.
- Sts put the cards face down. They play the game, taking turns picking up a card and describing the word / phrase. Sts describing the word / phrase shouldn't let their partners see what's on the card. Tell Sts to wait until their partner has finished his / her description before trying to guess the word.

Extra idea
- You could get Sts to play this in groups as a competitive game. Sts who correctly guess the word first keep the card. The student with the most cards at the end of the game wins.

Non-cut alternative
- Put Sts in pairs. Copy one sheet per pair and cut it down the middle. Sts take turns describing the words / phrases to their partners until they guess the correct answer.

1B Personality
An information gap activity

Sts define words to help their partner complete a crossword. Copy one sheet per pair and cut into **A** and **B**.

Language
personality adjectives

- Put Sts in pairs, ideally face-to-face, and give out the crosswords. Make sure that Sts can't see each other's sheets. Explain that **A** and **B** have the same crossword but with different words missing. They have to define words to each other to complete their crosswords.
- Give Sts a minute to read their instructions. If Sts don't know what a word means, they can look it up in Vocabulary Bank *Personality*. Make sure Sts understand the difference between *across* and *down*. Remind them that they can't use any part of the word in their definition.
- Sts take turns to ask each other for their missing words (e.g., *What's 1 down? What's 3 across?*). Their partner must define / describe the word until the other student is able to write it in his / her crossword. Sts should help each other with clues if necessary.
- When Sts have finished, they should compare their crosswords to make sure they have the same words and have spelled them correctly.

2A Money
A fill-in-the-blank activity race

Sts complete sentences. Copy one sheet per pair.

Language
money

- Put Sts in pairs and give out the sheets. Focus on the instructions. Set a time limit, e.g., three minutes. Tell the Sts that they have to fill in as many blanks as they can within the time limit. The first pair to complete all the phrases correctly wins.

Extra idea
- You could get Sts to do the exercise individually and compare their answers with a partner. Then check answers.

Extra support
- Give Sts a few minutes to review the money vocabulary in Vocabulary Bank *Money* before they start.

2 worth	3 live off	4 pay (very much) for		5 earn
6 pay back	7 bill	8 from	9 waste	10 save	11 pay by
12 lend	13 debt	14 bill	15 inherited	16 charge
17 ATM	18 mortgage	19 tax	20 account	

3A Transportation
A pairwork information gap activity

Sts describe their pictures to each other and find the ten differences between them. Copy one sheet per pair and cut into **A** and **B**.

> **Language**
> transportation

- Put Sts in pairs, ideally face-to-face and give out the pictures. Make sure Sts can't see each other's pictures.
- Explain that they both have the same pictures, but they have been changed so that there are ten differences.
- Tell **A** to start describing their picture starting on the left side, while **B** listens for differences. When **A** has reached the center of the picture (the middle of the road, where the policeman / woman is) they change roles.
- Continue until one pair has found the ten differences. Then let Sts compare their pictures.
- Elicit the ten differences from the class.

Extra idea
- Fast finishers can compare their pictures and write down some of the differences.

> 1 A The door of the taxi is open and the driver is reading a paper.
> B The door of the taxi is closed and the driver is drinking from a can.
> 2 A A policeman is directing the traffic.
> B A policewoman is directing the traffic.
> 3 A The double-decker bus is in front of the truck transporting sheep.
> B The truck transporting sheep is in front of the double-decker bus.
> 4 A There is one person on the motorcycle.
> B There are two people on the motorcycle.
> 5 A The car in the intersection in the background has a sofa on its roof.
> B The car in the intersection in the background doesn't have anything on its roof.
> 6 A There are three white taxis parked on the left-hand side of the road.
> B There are two white taxis and a black van parked on the left-hand side of the road.
> 7 A There's a bike lane on the right-hand side of the road.
> B There are parking spaces on the right-hand side of the road.
> 8 A A woman with a baby is crossing the street.
> B A woman and a dog are crossing the street.
> 9 A There's a 25 mph speed limit sign.
> B There's a 20 mph speed limit sign.
> 10 A There's an entrance to a subway station.
> B There's a parking sign.

3B Dependent prepositions
Fill-in-the-blank

Sts complete sentences with dependent prepositions. Copy one sheet per student.

> **Language**
> dependent prepositions

- Give out the sheets. Set a time limit, e.g., three minutes. Tell Sts that they have to write as many prepositions in the missing preposition column as they can within the time limit. Check answers.

> 2 about   3 to   4 with   5 to   6 in   7 about   8 of   9 for
> 10 on   11 for   12 between   13 about   14 to / for   15 in
> 16 to   17 with / about   18 to   19 for   20 of

- Focus on **b**. Give Sts time to review and then test themselves.

5A Sports
A pairwork vocabulary race

Sts read a series of clues and write the words. Copy one sheet per pair.

> **Language**
> sports

- Put Sts in pairs and give out the sheets. Set a time limit. Tell Sts that they have to write as many words as they can within the time limit. The first pair to write all the words correctly wins.

> 2 track   3 court   4 spectators   5 hockey   6 warm up
> 7 get injured   8 stadium   9 tie   10 referee   11 diving
> 12 golf   13 work out   14 train   15 win   16 players
> 17 kick   18 coach   19 fan   20 sports arena

5B Relationships
A vocabulary fill-in-the-blank activity

Sts complete different texts about relationships in the simple past tense. Copy one sheet per pair. Cut each sheet into three stories.

> **Language**
> relationships, simple past

- Put the Sts into pairs and give them a few minutes to read the first story, My best friend at school, and then complete the numbered spaces with the correct verbs in the list.
- Check answers and write them on the board.
- Now give each pair an **A** and **B** story.
- Give Sts a time limit to read their story and complete it with the simple past of the verbs in the list.
- Go around to check that they are completing their stories correctly.
- Ask the students to read the story they have just completed to their partner.
- Get whole class feedback and write the answers on the board.

> **My best friend at school**
> 2 felt   3 became   4 got along   5 were   6 lost touch
> 7 left   8 got in touch
> **A My parents**
> 2 fell in love with   3 gotten to know   4 went out together
> 5 proposed   6 got married   7 celebrated
> **B My disastrous date**
> 2 liked   3 asked   4 gave   5 asked (me) out
> 6 didn't get along   7 had

6A Movies
An information gap activity

Sts define words / phrases to help their partner complete a crossword. Copy one sheet per pair and cut into **A** and **B**.

> **Language**
> words associated with the movies

- Put Sts in pairs, ideally face-to-face, and give out the crosswords. Make sure that Sts can't see each other's crosswords. Explain that **A** and **B** have the same crossword but with different words missing. They have to define words to each other to complete their crosswords.
- Give students a minute to read their instructions. If Sts don't know what a word means, they can look it up in Vocabulary Bank *Movies*. Make sure Sts understand the difference between *across* and *down*.
- Sts take turns asking each other for their missing words (e.g., *What's 1 down? What's 1 across?*). Their partner must define the word until the other student is able to write it in his / her crossword. Sts should help each other with clues if necessary.
- When Sts have finished, they should compare their crosswords to make sure they have the same words and have spelled them correctly.

6B The body
A pairwork vocabulary race

Sts read a series of clues and write the words. Copy one sheet per pair.

> **Language**
> words associated with the body

- Put Sts in pairs and give out the sheets. Set a time limit. Tell Sts that they have to write as many words as they can within the time limit. The first pair to write all the words correctly wins.

> 2 stomach   3 eyes   4 mouth   5 hair   6 knees   7 nose
> 8 tongue   9 toes   10 clap   11 smile   12 nod   13 smell
> 14 touch   15 whistle   16 throw   17 tastes   18 ears
> 19 back   20 stare

7A Education
A team game

Sts have to explain the difference between two words / phrases. Copy and cut up one set of cards.

> **Language**
> words associated with education

- Divide the class into two teams (or more if you have a lot of students).
- Give a card to each team. Give Sts a minute to decide what the difference is between the two words or phrases.
- Write the two words / phrases on each team's card on the board.

- A spokesperson from each team takes turns trying to explain the difference to the rest of the class. If the explanation is correct, the team gets a point. If it isn't correct, the other team can try to win an extra point by explaining the difference correctly before taking their own turn.
- Then give each team another card.
- Keep a record of each team's points on the board. The team with the most points wins.

> **Bring somebody up** is to take care of a child and teach him/her how to behave. It's usually done by parents / family member.
> **Educate** is to teach somebody at a school / university.
> **A public school** is run by the government and is usually free. You have to pay to go to **a private school**.
> **Pupils** study in an elementary / middle / high school (especially in the UK).
> **Students** study at any age (US).
> A **teacher** teaches in any school aside from a college or university.
> A **professor** teaches at a college or university.
> **Terms** are one of the three periods of the year during which classes are held in schools, universities.
> **Semesters** are the two periods that the school / college year is divided into, especially in the US.
> **A high school** is for students between 14-18 years old.
> **An elementary school** is for students between 5-10 years old.
> **Pass an exam** is to achieve the required standard in an exam or test.
> **Fail an exam** is the opposite.
> **Learn** is to get knowledge or a skill.
> **Study** is to spend time learning about something.
> **Be punished** is to make someone suffer because they've done something bad or wrong.
> **Be suspended** is to officially make somebody leave school because they have done something wrong.
> **A boarding school** is a school where students eat, sleep, live, and study.
> **A school** is a place where students go to be educated.
> **Take an exam** is the same as take a test.
> **Retake an exam** is to take an exam again because you've previously failed it.
> Do **homework** is to do the work given by teachers at home.
> Do **housework** is to do the work involved in taking care of a home, e.g., cleaning, cooking, etc.
> **A single-sex school** is a school for either boys or girls, but not both.
> **A mixed school** is a school for both boys and girls.
> **A graduate** is a person who has a college or university degree.
> **A student** is a person who studies at any age.
> **A required subject** is one you have to study.
> **An optional subject** is one that you can choose to study or not.
> **History** is a subject that is the study of past events.
> **A story** is a description of events and people that a writer has invented in order to entertain.
> **IT** stands for information technology, which is a subject in a school or university.
> **PE** stands for physical education, which is a subject in a school or university.
> **A principal** is a person who is in charge of a school.
> **A teacher** is a person who teaches in any school aside from a university.
> **A university** is a place where you can study for a degree or do research.
> **A graduate** is someone who has completed all their classes at a university and graduated.
> **A score** is the result of a test or exam, given as a number.
> **A grade** is the result of a test or exam, given as a letter.

Non-cut alternative

- Put Sts in pairs. Copy one sheet per pair and cut it down the middle. Set a time limit, e.g., ten minutes, and Sts take turns to ask each other, *What's the difference between…?*, choosing words at random. Sts decide if the explanation is correct. Finally check answers with the whole class.

7B Houses

A crossword

A crossword to review vocabulary associated with houses. Copy one sheet per student.

Language
words associated with houses

- Give out the sheets. Give Sts five minutes to fill in their words. Tell them that if they can't remember a word, they can look it up in Vocabulary Bank *Houses*.
- When they've finished, they can compare their answers with a partner.
- Check answers with the whole class.

Across
2 balcony 4 ceiling 7 cottage 8 steps 9 cozy
10 fireplace 11 basement
Down
1 spacious 3 old-fashioned 4 chimney 5 gate
6 outskirts

8B Work

A pairwork vocabulary race

Sts read a series of clues and write the words. Copy one sheet per pair.

Language
words associated with work

- Put Sts in pairs and give out the sheets. Set a time limit. Tell Sts that they have to write as many words as they can within the time limit. Each word begins with (or in the case of **X** includes) a different letter of the alphabet. The first pair to complete all the words correctly wins.

apply boss charge do employees for gardener
hairstylist interview job kitchen look for musician
night overtime part-time quit retire self-employed
temporary up vet work extra year

9A Word building

A fill-in-the-blank word building activity

Sts complete the sentences with the correct noun, adjective, or adverb from the given words. Copy one sheet per student.

Language
making verbs, nouns, adjectives, adverbs

- Give out the sheets. Set a time limit, e.g., three minutes. Tell Sts that they have to complete the sentences with the correct form of the words in bold. They write as many words as they can in the column on the right within the time limit. The first student to write all the words correctly wins.

Tip
- The missing words in sentences 1–13 are nouns, and can be reviewed in the first part of Vocabulary Bank *Word building*. The missing words in sentences 14–20 are positive or negative adjectives and adverbs, which can be reviewed in the second part of the same Vocabulary Bank.

2 compensation 3 argument 4 delivery 5 success
6 achievement 7 explanation 8 attachment
9 agreement 10 demonstration 11 payment 12 loss
13 sale 14 uncomfortable 15 comfortable
16 impatient 17 unlucky 18 careful 19 carelessly
20 unfortunately

- Focus on **b**. Give Sts time to review and then test themselves.

Phrasal verbs

A fill-in-the-blank activity race

Sts read the sentences and write the phrasal verbs. Copy one sheet per student.

Language
phrasal verbs

- Give out the sheets. Set a time limit, e.g., three minutes. Tell Sts that they have to read the sentences and write as many of the phrasal verbs as they can in the column on the right within the time limit. The first student to write all the phrasal verbs correctly wins.

2 set up 3 plug in 4 cut down on 5 eat out
6 cut out 7 pay back 8 pick up 9 applied for
10 split up 11 turn off 12 bring up 13 work out
14 take out 15 look forward to 16 argue with
17 look for 18 run out of 19 watch out 20 turn up

- Focus on **b**. Give Sts time to review and then test themselves.

VOCABULARY Classroom language

Asking for help

Excuse me.
Can (Could) you say that again, please?
Can you help me, please?
Could I have a copy, please?
Could you explain something, please?
Is this right (wrong)?
What does _____ mean?
How do you say _____ in English?
How do you spell it?
How do you pronounce it?
Where's the stress?
What's the opposite of *fast*?
What's the past tense of *eat*?
What's the difference between *meet* and *know*?

Apologizing / Making excuses

Sorry I'm late.
I couldn't come to class on *Thursday*. I was sick.
I couldn't do the homework because...
I won't be able to come next week because...
I have to leave early today because...

Working in pairs / groups

What do we have to do?
What did he / she say?
We haven't finished (yet).
Whose turn is it?
It's my (your) turn.
What do you think?
Do you agree?
I agree (don't agree) (with you).

Leaving

A See you on (*Wednesday*)!   B Yes, see you!
A Have a good weekend!   B The same to you. / You too.

pear	grapes	grilled (salmon)	seafood
shrimp	mussels	peppers	takeout (pizza)
a cucumber	roast (lamb)	steamed (rice)	raw (meat)
boiled eggs	squid	(to) eat out	a peach
canned (fruit)	frozen (food)	(to) cut down on	fried (fish)
fresh (vegetables)	raspberries	(to) cut out	cherries

1B VOCABULARY Personality

Student A

a Look at your crossword and make sure you know the meaning of all the words you have.

b Now ask **B** to define a word for you. Ask for example, *What's 1 down? What's 4 across?* Write the word in.

c Now **B** will ask you to define a word.

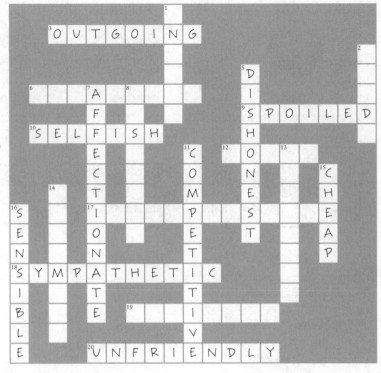

Student B

a Look at your crossword and make sure you know the meaning of all the words you have.

b Now **A** will ask you to define a word.

c Now ask **A** to define a word for you. Ask for example, *What's 3 across? What's 5 down?* Write the word in.

American English File 2nd edition Teacher's Book 3 Photocopiable © Oxford University Press 2014

2A VOCABULARY Money

What's the word?

Work with a partner. You have three minutes to complete the sentences.

1 We can't _a f f o r d_ to go on vacation this year, so we're staying at home.

2 That ring can't be _ _ _ _ _ _ $20,000. It looks like plastic!

3 Pete doesn't have any money, and basically he has to _ _ _ _ _ _ _ his parents. They pay for absolutely everything.

4 My brother didn't _ _ _ very much _ _ _ his car. It was secondhand.

5 How much do you think you'll _ _ _ _ every month in your new job?

6 Sorry, but I can't _ _ _ _ _ _ _ the money I owe you until the end of the month.

7 Do you have any change for the parking meter? I only have a $10 _ _ _ _.

8 Some people think it's a really bad idea to borrow money _ _ _ _ a close friend.

9 I get really angry with myself when I _ _ _ _ _ _ my money on things I don't really need.

10 I used to have a piggy bank when I was young. That's how I learned to _ _ _ _ money.

11 Is it OK to _ _ _ _ _ credit card?

12 Did the bank _ _ _ _ you the money to buy a new car?

13 Diana started spending a lot more money than she had in the bank. She got into _ _ _ _ after six months.

14 Our gas _ _ _ _ was really high this month because we had the central heating on all the time.

15 Our neighbor _ _ _ _ _ _ _ _ _ a beautiful house in the country when her aunt Jane died.

16 How can the lawyer _ _ _ _ _ _ _ you $200 for ten minutes' work?

17 My grandmother's afraid of using an _ _ _ on the street. She prefers to go into the bank to get money.

18 I've asked my bank for a _ _ _ _ _ _ _ _ because I want to buy a house.

19 The government is going to put a _ _ _ on gasoline and oil.

20 If you open an _ _ _ _ _ _ _ with this bank, you get an interest-free credit card for a year.

3A VOCABULARY Transportation

Student A

- -

Student B

3B VOCABULARY Dependent prepositions

a Complete each sentence with a preposition. Write your answers in the missing preposition column on the right. You have three minutes.

		missing preposition
1	I'm really tired ▓▓ listening to my sister. She complains about her boyfriend all the time.	*of*
2	Katy's worried ▓▓ her final exams. She thinks she's going to fail.	_____
3	The waiter was so rude ▓▓ us that we didn't leave a tip.	_____
4	They're not very pleased ▓▓ their new car. It's broken down three times in one month!	_____
5	My mother's been married ▓▓ my stepfather for 20 years.	_____
6	Tom's interested ▓▓ joining the army because he wants to see the world.	_____
7	Are you excited ▓▓ moving to your new house next month?	_____
8	That man over there reminds me ▓▓ my first boyfriend.	_____
9	How much did you pay ▓▓ your smartphone?	_____
10	What we decide to do tomorrow will depend ▓▓ the weather.	_____
11	Recent research shows that drinking mango juice is good ▓▓ your immune system.	_____
12	You'll have to choose ▓▓ this one and that one. You can't have both.	_____
13	My sister and I get along really well and hardly ever argue ▓▓ anything.	_____
14	I apologized ▓▓ the teacher ▓▓ being late.	_____ / _____
15	What time does your plane arrive ▓▓ Dallas?	_____
16	Who does this book belong ▓▓? Is it yours, Sarah?	_____
17	Is Carl still angry ▓▓ Monica ▓▓ what happened at the party?	_____ / _____
18	You should be kinder ▓▓ your brother. After all, you are the oldest!	_____
19	I never have to ask anybody ▓▓ directions anymore now that I have a GPS.	_____
20	He's the first person in his family to go to college so his parents are really proud ▓▓ him.	_____

activation

b Cover the missing preposition column on the right. Read the sentences aloud with the correct prepositions.

5A VOCABULARY Sports

Vocabulary race

1 In soccer or basketball, it's the most responsible player on the team.

`C A P T A I N`

2 It's a course used for running or horse racing.

3 You can play tennis and basketball on this.

4 The people who go and watch a sports event.

5 It's a sport you can play on ice or grass.

6 Before you do any kind of exercise, it's very important to do this.

7 When this happens to you, you may have to go to the hospital.

8 Fenway Park and Wrigley Field are both famous examples of this.

9 It's a verb that describes when two teams have the same score at the end of a game.

10 It's the person who calls a penalty in a football game.

11 It's a sport where you jump head first into a pool.

12 In this sport you go around a course of 9 or 18 holes.

13 It's a phrasal verb that means "go to a gym and exercise."

14 It's what professional athletes do every day.

15 It's the opposite of "lose."

16 There are 11 on a team in a soccer game, but only 9 in a baseball game.

17 It means to hit e.g., a ball with your foot.

18 It's the name of the person who gives instructions to the members of a team, but who doesn't play.

19 It's a person who cheers for a team.

20 It's where you play indoor sports.

5B VOCABULARY Relationships

My best friend at school

Read the story and complete it with the correct form of the verbs from the list. Remember to use the simple past.

---

be   become   get in touch   get along   feel   leave   lose touch   ~~meet~~

I first [1]___*met*___ Emily on my first day in elementary school. We both [2]_____ very lost and afraid, but we soon [3]_____ best friends. We [4]_____ very well from the beginning because we liked playing the same games together. We [5]_____ best friends for over 15 years, all the way through high school, but unfortunately we [6]_____ when we [7]_____ school to go to college. Recently I found her on Facebook, and I sent her a message. She [8]_____, and we're going to meet up again after all these years!

Student A My parents

ⓐ Read the story and complete it with the correct form of the verbs from the list. Remember to use the simple past.

---

celebrate   fall in love with   get married
get to know   go out together   propose   ~~see~~

My dad says that as soon as he [1]___*saw*___ my mom he [2]_____ her. My mom says that after a couple of months, when she'd [3]_____ my dad, she felt the same. I don't know if that's true or not, but what I do know is that they [4]_____ for seven months before he [5]_____ to her in 1961 at Carnegie Hall while they were listening to a concert! My mom said "yes," and they [6]_____ in 1963 in New York City. They [7]_____ their 50th wedding anniversary last year and are still incredibly happy together.

ⓑ Now read the story to your partner.

Student B My disastrous date

ⓐ Read the story and complete it with the correct verb from the list. Remember to use the past tense.

---

ask   ask out   like   not get along   give
have   ~~introduce~~

I'd just broken up with my boyfriend and a coworker [1]___*introduced*___ me to Paul, his roommate, at a restaurant in the summer of 2008. He was very good-looking and I really [2]_____ him. At the end of the evening, he [3]_____ me for my phone number so I [4]_____ it to him. I was really happy when he called me the next day and [5]_____ me _____ for dinner. Unfortunately, the date was sort of a disaster because although he was attractive, we really [6]_____. During the meal, I found out that we [7]_____ absolutely nothing in common! Of course, we never had a second date.

ⓑ Now read the story to your partner.

6A VOCABULARY Movies

Student A

a. Look at your crossword and make sure you know the meaning of all the words you have.

b. Now ask **B** to define a word for you. Ask for example, *What's 3 down? What's 5 across?* Write the word in.

c. Now **B** will ask you to define a word.

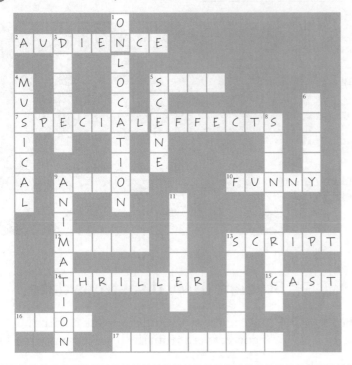

Student B

a. Look at your crossword and make sure you know the meaning of all the words you have.

b. Now **A** will ask you to define a word.

c. Now ask **A** to define a word for you. Ask for example, *What's 2 across? What's 3 down?* Write the word in.

American English File 2nd edition Teacher's Book 3 Photocopiable © Oxford University Press 2014

6B VOCABULARY The body

1 Most people have 32 of them and use them to eat.   `T E E T H`

2 The part of your body where food is digested after you've eaten it.

3 When you cry or peel onions, they turn red.

4 When you sit down in the dentist's chair, the dentist asks you to open this.

5 It can be straight, wavy, or curly.

6 They're half way down your legs.

7 When you have a cold, it's sometimes difficult to breathe through it and you can't smell anything.

8 A cat uses it to drink milk.

9 There are five of these on each of your feet.

10 At the end of a concert, the audience does this to show they like what they've heard.

11 When you want to show you're happy, you do this.

12 In most countries you do this if you want to agree with something someone says without speaking.

13 We usually do this to flowers when we are given them.

14 In art galleries you must not do this to the paintings or sculptures.

15 You make this sound with your lips to attract someone's attention in the street.

16 Basketball players move the ball to each other by doing this.

17 Food that has too much salt in it _____ horrible!

18 We have two of these to hear.

19 You should swim a lot if you have problems with this part of your body.

20 It's a verb and it means to look at somebody or something for a long time.

bring somebody up **AND** educate somebody	a public school **AND** a private school
pupils **AND** students	a teacher **AND** a professor
terms **AND** semesters	a high school **AND** an elementary school
pass an exam **AND** fail an exam	learn **AND** study
be punished **AND** be suspended	a boarding school **AND** a school
take an exam **AND** retake an exam	do homework **AND** do housework
a single-sex school **AND** a mixed school	a graduate **AND** a student
a required subject **AND** an optional subject	history **AND** a story
IT **AND** PE	a principal **AND** a teacher
a graduate **AND** a college	a score **AND** a grade

7B VOCABULARY Houses

Crossword
Look at the clues and fill in the crossword.

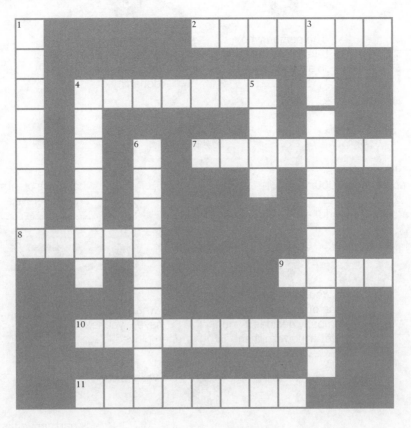

Across

2

4

7 A small and usually old house, especially in the country.

8 They're like stairs, but you can only find them outside.

9 This adjective describes a room or house that is warm and comfortable.

10 The open place in a room where you light a fire.

11 It's the lowest room or rooms of a building that are completely below ground level.

Down

1 This adjective describes a room or building which is large and has plenty of room for people.

3 It's the opposite of "modern."

4

5 It's similar to a door, but it's in the yard. You can also find them at an airport.

6 The part of the town or city that is farthest from the center.

8B VOCABULARY Work

A I'm going to _____ for that job I saw in the paper.

B The person who tells you what to do at work is your _____.

C I'm in _____ of the sales department.

D We ___ training courses twice a year.

E Microsoft has more than 90,000 _____ around the world.

F My friend Jack works ___ Apple.

G A person who grows plants and flowers is a _____.

H A _____ cuts your hair.

I You usually have one of these before a company decides if you get a job with them. _____

J It's what you don't have if you're unemployed. _____

K Chefs work in here. _____

L A phrasal verb that means the same as "search for." _____

M Someone who plays the violin is a _____.

N My partner works shifts: he works at _____ one week, then works during the day the next.

O If you work more than your usual hours, you get _____.

P It's an alternative to working full-time, but you work fewer hours. _____-_____

Q Another way of saying "resign." _____

R A verb that means when people stop working after the ages of 65 or 70. _____

S A person who works for him/herself is _____-_____.

T It's the opposite of a permanent job. _____

U He decided to set ___ his own business last year.

V She is an animal doctor. ___

W I _____ in an international company in downtown Chicago.

X A small, non–speaking job in a movie has this letter in it! _____

Y My brother is in his second _____ of college, and he loves it.

9A VOCABULARY Word building

Change the word!

a Complete the sentences with the correct form of the words in **bold**. You can make nouns, or positive or negative adjectives, and adverbs. Write your answers in the column on the right.

1 I wrote a letter of ▮▮ to the hotel manager because I wasn't happy with the service. **COMPLAIN** _complaint_

2 The airline didn't offer us any ▮▮ for the ten-hour delay. **COMPENSATE** _____

3 Listen! The neighbors next door are having another ▮▮. **ARGUE** _____

4 If you buy the washing machine today, we can guarantee next-day ▮▮. **DELIVER** _____

5 The dinner party wasn't a ▮▮ because Paul was rude to Richard. **SUCCEED** _____

6 My mother learned to swim when she was 67. I think that's a real ▮▮. **ACHIEVE** _____

7 What ▮▮ did Anna give you for not finishing her report? **EXPLAIN** _____

8 I got Jason's email, but he forgot to send the ▮▮. **ATTACH** _____

9 We have an ▮▮ at home that if my husband cooks, I do the dishes. **AGREE** _____

10 The salesperson gave me a very good ▮▮ of how the gadget worked. **DEMONSTRATE** _____

11 PayPal is a safe way of making a ▮▮ online. **PAY** _____

12 The company showed a ▮▮ for five years and eventually it had to close down. **LOSE** _____

13 The house next door is for ▮▮. I'd love to buy it! **SELL** _____

14 The bed was so ▮▮ that I wasn't able to sleep. **COMFORT** _____

15 These sandals are so ▮▮. It feels as if I'm not wearing anything on my feet. **COMFORT** _____

16 Having to wait for people makes me really ▮▮. **PATIENT** _____

17 Nick's ▮▮ in love. His partners always leave him! **LUCK** _____

18 Be ▮▮ not to break your leg on the first day of your skiing vacation! **CARE** _____

19 Paolo won't pass the written part of the TOEFL exam. He writes very ▮▮ and doesn't check for mistakes. **CARE** _____

20 ▮▮, it rained on our wedding day, but we had a great day anyway. **FORTUNE** _____

activation

b Cover the column on the right. Read the sentences aloud with the correct form of the words in **bold**.

VOCABULARY REVIEW Phrasal verbs

a How many of these phrasal verbs can you remember?

		phrasal verb
1	It's what you should do before you do any kind of exercise.	w a r m u p
2	It's another way of saying "start (a business)."	___ __
3	To charge your phone, attach it to the charger, ▓▓ it ▓▓ to the outlet, and wait until it is completely charged.	____ __
4	I think I need to ▓▓▓▓ ▓▓▓ ▓▓▓ Diet Coke – I drink too much.	___ ____ __
5	We often ▓▓▓▓ ▓▓ because neither of us likes cooking.	___ ___
6	My doctor told me I had to ▓▓▓▓ ▓▓ dairy products because I have an allergy.	___ ___
7	I need to ▓▓▓▓ ▓▓ the money my father lent me.	___ ____
8	I'll come and ▓▓▓▓ you ▓▓ in the car at six o'clock. We can go to the party together.	____ __
9	After she graduated, Ellen ▓▓▓▓ ▓▓ at least one job every day.	_____ ___
10	It's another way of saying "break up with somebody."	_____ __
11	When you get on a plane you have to ▓▓▓▓ ▓▓ your cell phone.	____ ___
12	Although his parents ▓▓▓▓ him ▓▓ quite strictly, Josh is a happy child.	_____ __
13	It's another way of saying "exercise at the gym."	____ ___
14	I need to go to the ATM and ▓▓▓▓ ▓▓ some money before we get the train.	____ ___
15	I really ▓▓▓ ▓▓▓ ▓▓ my weekly dance class. It's fun!	____ _____ __
16	My brother and sister often ▓▓▓▓ ▓▓ each other. Sometimes they don't speak to each other for days!	_____ ____
17	If you want to find a job, you could ▓▓▓▓ ▓▓ one on the Internet or in the newspapers.	____ ___
18	If you ▓▓▓ ▓▓ ▓▓ gas, your car will stop.	___ ___ __
19	You say ▓▓▓ ▓▓! to someone if you see that they might be going to have an accident.	_____ ___
20	Can you ▓▓▓ ▓▓ the music. I can't hear it.	____ __

activation

b Cover the phrasal verb column on the right. Read the sentences aloud with the correct phrasal verbs.

Song activity instructions

1B Our House
Listening for specific words (1)22))

- Copy one sheet per student.
- Give each student a sheet and focus on **a**. Highlight that the clues in parentheses will help Sts to decide what the missing words are when they listen.
- Give Sts a minute or so to read through the lyrics once before they listen. Tell them not to worry about the meaning of the song at this stage.
- Play the song once for Sts to try and write the missing words. Get Sts to compare their answers with a partner and then play the song again for Sts to fill in all the blanks. Play specific lines again as necessary. Then check answers.

> 2 tired 3 downstairs 4 Brother 5 always
> 6 mom 7 late 8 shirt 9 school 10 happy

- Now get Sts, in pairs, to read the lyrics with the glossary and to do task **b**. Check answers. Help with any other vocabulary problems that arise.

> 1 His memory of his home seems to be very positive. He talks about *such a happy time* and he describes his family and home life with affection. However, one line of the song says *Something tells you that you've got to move away from it*. Perhaps this is how he felt when he was a teenager and wanted to become independent of his family.
> 2 busy ✓ clean ✓ crowded ✓ traditional ✓

- Ask Sts to read the **Song facts**.
- Finally, if you think your Sts would like to hear the song again, play it one more time. If your class likes singing, they can sing along.

  For copyright reasons, this song is a cover version.

3A 500 Miles
Listening for extra words and sentence rhythm (2)16))

- Copy one sheet per student.
- Give each student a sheet and focus on **a**. Give Sts a few minutes to read through the lyrics. Then play the song once or twice as necessary. Check answers.

> 3 tonight 4 always 5 'll 6 ✓ 7 ✓ 8 ✓ 9 ✓ 10 and
> 11 ✓ 12 front 13 hard 14 ✓ 15 all 16 ✓ 17 ✓
> 18 ✓ 19 see 20 that 21 ✓ 22 ✓ 23 and 24 ✓
> 25 front 26 feeling 27 ✓ 28 ✓ 29 fun 30 just
> 31 ✓ 32 ✓ 33 always 34 ✓

- Now focus on **b**, and get Sts to do it in pairs. Check answers.

> **Example answers**
> 1 He's singing to someone that he's in love with and will do anything to be with.
> 2 He declares his love by saying that he would walk 1,000 miles (500 miles and 500 more) to be in the same place as her. He states his intention (using *going to*) to always be there for her.
> 3 Yes. In lines 20 and 21 he says *if I grow old well I know I'm gonna be the man who's growing old with you*.
> 4 To give almost all the money he earns to her, be faithful to her, dream about her, etc.

- Ask Sts to read the **Song facts**.
- Finally, if you think your Sts would like to hear the song again, play it one more time. If your class likes singing, they can sing along.

  For copyright reasons, this song is a cover version.

4B You Can't Hurry Love
Listening for specific verbs (2)49))

- Copy one sheet per student.
- Give each student a sheet. Focus on **a** and give Sts a few minutes in pairs to guess the missing verbs. Don't check answers at this point.
- Now play the song once for Sts to fill in the blanks. Get Sts to compare with a partner, and then play the song again for them to check. Check answers.

> 2 can't 3 have to 4 can't 5 have to 6 Must 7 must
> 8 can 9 can't 10 can't

- Now focus on **b**. Play the song again in the background while Sts read the lyrics with the glossary. Then give them a few minutes to answer the questions in pairs. Check answers.

> 1 f 2 a 3 d 4 b 5 c 6 e

- Ask Sts to read the **Song facts**.
- Finally, if you think your Sts would like to hear the song again, play it one more time. If your class likes singing, they can sing along.

  For copyright reasons, this song is a cover version.

5A We Are the Champions
Correcting words (3)14))

- Copy one sheet per student.
- Give each student a sheet and focus on **a**. Go through the phrases in **bold** and explain that Sts have to listen and decide if these phrases are right (what the singer sings) or wrong (different). The first time they listen, Sts just have to put a check (✓) or an ✗ next to each line. They shouldn't try to correct the phrases at this stage.

- Check answers (i.e., if the phrases are right or wrong), but don't tell Sts what the right phrases are.
- Now focus on **b**. Play the song again and this time Sts have to try and correct the wrong phrases.
- Let Sts compare with a partner and then check answers, going through the song line by line.

> 4 ✓　5 bad mistakes　6 ✓　7 kicked in my face　8 ✓
> 9 ✓ 10 we'll keep on　13 time for losers　15 ✓　16 ✓
> 17 you brought me　18 ✓　19 But it's been　20 ✓
> 21 the whole human race　22 ✓

- Focus on **c** and give Sts, in pairs, time to match the phrases 1–8 with their meanings a–h.
- Check answers, clarifying meaning where necessary.

> 1 f　2 d　3 a　4 b　5 c　6 g　7 h　8 e

- Ask Sts to read the **Song facts**.
- Finally, if you think your Sts would like to hear the song again, play it one more time. If your class likes singing, they can sing along.

  For copyright reasons, this song is a cover version.

6B I Got Life

Listening for specific words ③ 43))

- Copy one sheet per student.
- Give each student a sheet. Focus on **a** and give Sts, in pairs, a couple of minutes to say what they can see in the small pictures. Explain that these are the words which are missing from the song. The first group of pictures are for blanks 1–7, and the second group (the parts of the body) for 8–16. Reiterate that they shouldn't write anything down. Don't check answers at this stage.
- Play the song once and ask Sts to write the words in the blanks (**b**). Repeat if necessary and get Sts to compare answers with a partner before checking answers.

> 2 money　3 sweater　4 perfume　5 mother　6 name
> 7 ticket　8 head　9 ears　10 nose　11 mouth
> 12 tongue　13 neck　14 arms　15 fingers　16 toes

- Now focus on **c** and give Sts in pairs a few minutes to find the words. Check answers.

> 1 culture　2 alive　3 brains　4 soul　5 blood　6 freedom

- Focus on **d** and ask Sts if songs in their own language also use slang or incorrect grammar. Elicit that *I ain't = I'm not*. Then give Sts in pairs a few minutes to match the rest of the expressions. Check answers.

> 1 e　2 a　3 f　4 b　5 g　6 d　7 c

- Now get Sts to read the lyrics with the glossary and ask them if they think it's an optimistic or a pessimistic song (it's optimistic).
- Ask Sts to read the **Song facts**.
- Finally, if you think your Sts would like to hear the song again, play it one more time. If your class likes singing, they can sing along.

  For copyright reasons, this song is a cover version.

7B If I Could Build My Whole World Around You

Listening for the correct verbs ④ 25))

- Copy one sheet per student.
- Give each student a sheet. Focus on **a**, and on the example, and give Sts time to read the lyrics using the glossary to help them, and think about what the missing verbs might be.
- Play the song once for Sts to fill in the missing verbs. Get them to compare with a partner and then play again. Check answers.

> 2 grow　3 be　4 take　5 wash　6 make　7 put　8 give
> 9 keep　10 be　11 give　12 step　13 give　14 be　15 make

- Now focus on **c**. Get Sts to do this individually and then compare with a partner. Check answers.

> 1 c　2 d　3 b　4 e　5 a

- Ask Sts to read the **Song facts**.
- Finally, if you think your Sts would like to hear the song again, play it one more time. If your class likes singing, they can sing along.

  For copyright reasons, this song is a cover version.

Extra support

If you want to give your Sts more listening comprehension practice, play the song for the Sts to listen to without previously trying to fill in the blanks first.

8B Piano Man

Listening for rhyming words ④ 51))

- Copy one sheet per student.
- Give each student a sheet. Focus on **a**, and on the example, and give Sts time to read the lyrics using the glossary to help them, and think what the missing words might be.
- Play the song once for Sts to complete the missing words. Get them to compare with a partner and then play again. Check answers

> 2 clothes　3 alright (all right)　4 be　5 place　6 life
> 7 alone　8 while　9 here

- Now focus on **c**. Get Sts to do this individually and then compare with a partner. Check answers.

> 2　He said that it (the song) was sad and it was sweet.
> 3　He told Bill that he believed it (the bar) was killing him.
> 4　John said that he could be a movie star if he could get out of this place.
> 5　They asked the piano man what he was doing here.

- Ask Sts to read the **Song facts**.
- Finally, if you think your Sts would like to hear the song again, play it one more time. If your class likes singing, they can sing along.

  For copyright reasons, this song is a cover version.

9A Karma

Listening to choose the correct words (5 9))

- Copy one sheet per student.
- Give each student a sheet. Give them a couple of minutes to read the lyrics and familiarize themselves with the song.
- Focus on **a**. Sts listen and choose the word they hear. Play the song once all the way through and tell Sts to try to circle the correct words as they listen for the first time. Tell them you will replay the song if necessary.
- Replay any lines as necessary. Check answers.

> 2 space 3 give 4 stay 5 gone 6 leave 7 family
> 8 dream 9 say to 10 when 11 three 12 always
> 13 kind 14 when 15 knowing 16 before 17 thought

- Focus on **b**. Give Sts time to read the song with the glossary and help with any other vocabulary problems. Check answers.

> 1 And never knew what you supposed to do
> 2 Saying I'm your everything
> 3 I'm over you
> 4 You never come through
> 5 What goes around comes around

- Ask Sts to read the **Song facts**.
- Finally, if you think your Sts would like to hear the song again, play it one more time. If your class likes singing, they can sing along.

  For copyright reasons, this song is a cover version.

10A Greatest Love of All

Listening for missing verbs (5 33))

- Copy one sheet per student.
- Give each student a sheet. Focus on **a**, and on the example, and give Sts time to read the lyrics using the glossary to help them, and think what the missing verbs might be. They should write the verbs in the column on the right.
- Play the song once for Sts to listen and check. Get them to compare with a partner and then play again for Sts to correct any wrong answers, and write the correct verbs in the blanks in the lyrics. Check answers.

> 2 teach 3 possess 4 make 5 searching 6 need
> 7 depend 8 fail 9 believe 10 happening 11 learning
> 12 dreaming

- Now focus on **c**. Get Sts to do this individually and then compare with a partner. Check answers.

> fail (verb, line 14)
> succeed (verb, line 14)
> laughter (noun, line 5)
> beauty (noun, line 3)
> pride (noun, line 4)

- Now focus on **d** and get Sts to complete the text with the words from **c**. Check answers.

> 2 success 3 failed 4 proud 5 beautiful 6 laugh

- Ask Sts to read the **Song facts**.
- Finally, if you think your Sts would like to hear the song again, play it one more time. If your class likes singing, they can sing along.

  For copyright reasons, this song is a cover version.

Our House

Father wears his [1]_____Sunday_____ best *(a day of the week)*
Mother's [2]_____ she needs a rest *(adjective)*
The kids are playing up [3]_____ *(part of the house)*
Sister's sighing in her sleep
[4]_____'s got a date to keep *(member of the family)*
He can't hang around

> CHORUS
> Our house, in the middle of our street
> Our house, in the middle of our...

Our house it has a crowd
There's [5]_____ something happening *(adverb of frequency)*
And it's usually quite loud
Our [6]_____ she's so house-proud *(member of the family, colloquial)*
Nothing ever slows her down and a mess is not allowed

> CHORUS

Our house, in the middle of our street
(Something tells you that you've got to move away from it)

Father gets up [7]_____ for work *(adverb of time)*
Mother has to iron his [8]_____ *(something you wear)*
Then she sends the kids to [9]_____ *(a place)*
Sees them off with a small kiss
She's the one they're going to miss in lots of ways

> CHORUS

I remember way back then when everything was true and when
We would have such a very good time
Such a fine time
Such a [10]_____ time *(adjective)*
And I remember how we'd play, simply waste the day away
Then we'd say nothing would come between us two dreamers

> REPEAT FIRST VERSE
> CHORUS

Our house, was our castle and our keep
Our house, in the middle of our street
Our house, that was where we used to sleep
Our house, in the middle of our street *(to fade)*

a Listen to the song and write the missing words 1–10. Use the clues in parentheses to help you.

b Read the lyrics with the glossary and answer the questions.

1 Do you think the singer's memory of his home is positive or negative?

2 Which of these adjectives would you use to describe his house? Check (✓) the boxes.

busy ☐
quiet ☐
clean ☐
messy ☐
crowded ☐
traditional ☐

GLOSSARY

Sunday best = best clothes
playing up = behaving badly
sighing = making a sad sound
has got a date = has a meeting (with a girl)
hang around = stay somewhere for a long time
house-proud = spending a lot of time keeping a house clean and neat
you've got to = you have to

SONG FACTS

Our House was British group Madness's biggest international hit. In the summer of 2012, 20 years after they first recorded it, the song became popular with a new generation of music fans: Madness sang the song to an international audience at the closing ceremony of the London 2012 Olympics.

3A SONG 500 Miles

a Listen to each line of the song carefully. If you hear an extra word, cross (✗) it out. If the line is correct, check (✓) it.

500 Miles

1 When I wake up, ~~early~~ well I know I'm gonna be,
2 I'm gonna be the man who wakes up next to you. ✓
3 When I go out tonight, yeah I know I'm gonna be,
4 I'm gonna be the man who always goes along with you.

5 If I get drunk, well I'll know I'm gonna be,
6 I'm gonna be the man who gets drunk next to you.
7 And if I haver, yeah I know I'm gonna be,
8 I'm gonna be the man who's havering to you.

    CHORUS
9 But I would walk five hundred miles
10 And I would walk five hundred and more
11 Just to be the man who walked a thousand miles
12 To fall down at your front door.

13 When I'm working hard, yes I know I'm gonna be,
14 I'm gonna be the man who's working hard for you.
15 And when all the money comes in for the work I do,
16 I'll pass almost every penny on to you.

17 When I come home (when I come home),
18 Oh I know I'm gonna be,
19 I'm gonna be the man who comes back home to see you.
20 And if I grow old, well I know that I'm gonna be,
21 I'm gonna be the man who's growing old with you.

    CHORUS
22 But I would walk five hundred miles
23 And I would walk five hundred and more
24 Just to be the man who walked a thousand miles
25 To fall down at your front door.
    Da da da da, etc.

26 When I'm feeling lonely, well I know I'm gonna be,
27 I'm gonna be the man who's lonely without you.
28 And when I'm dreaming, well I know I'm gonna dream,
29 I'm gonna dream about the fun time when I'm with you.

30 When I go out (when I go out), well I just know I'm gonna be,
31 I'm gonna be the man who goes along with you
32 And when I come home (when I come home),
33 Yes, I know I'm gonna be I'm gonna be the man who always comes back home with you.
34 I'm gonna be the man who's coming home with you.

    CHORUS
    Da da da da, *etc.*
    REPEAT CHORUS

b Read the lyrics with the glossary and answer the questions.

1 Who is the singer singing to?
2 How do we know how the singer feels about this person?
3 Does he think their relationship will last for a long time? If so / not, where does it say this in the song?
4 What kind of things does he promise his partner?

GLOSSARY

gonna = going to
haver = (an old Scottish word) to say silly things
when the money comes in = when I start earning money
pass every penny on = give all my money
go along with = colloquial way of saying "travels beside"

SONG FACTS

I'm Gonna Be (500 Miles) was originally written and sung by the Scottish group The Proclaimers in 1988. It was the favorite song of Ling Hsueh, who lives in southeast China. When her boyfriend, Liu Peiwen, asked her to marry him in 2011, she accepted. However, she joked that it was on condition that he walked to her door from his home in Henan Province – 1,000 miles away. To her surprise, he did exactly that.

4B SONG You Can't Hurry Love

a Complete the song with *have to, need to, must, can,* or *can't.*

You Can't Hurry Love

I need love, love to ease my mind
I [1] ___*need to*___ find, find someone to call mine
But mama said,

    CHORUS
    "You [2] _____ hurry love
    No, you just [3] _____ wait"
    She said, "Love don't come easy
    It's a game of give and take."

You [4] _____ hurry love,
No, you just [5] _____ wait
You've got to trust, give it time
No matter how long it takes

But how many heartaches
[6] _____ I stand
Before I find a love
To let me live again?
Right now the only thing
That keeps me hanging on
When I feel my strength, yeah
Is almost gone

I remember mama said,

    CHORUS

How long [7] _____ I wait
How much more [8] _____ I take
Before loneliness will cause my heart
Heart to break?

No, I [9] _____ bear to live my life alone
I grow impatient for a love to call my own
But when I feel that I, I [10] _____ go on
These precious words keep me hanging on
I remember mama said,

    CHORUS

"You can't hurry love
No, you just have to wait"
She said, "Trust, give it time
No matter how long it takes"

No, love, love don't come easy
But I keep on waiting
Anticipating for that soft voice
To talk to me at night
For some tender arms
To hold me tight
I keep waiting
I keep on waiting
But it ain't easy
It ain't easy
But mama said,

You can't hurry love
No, you just have to wait
She said, "Trust, give it time
No matter how long it takes"

    CHORUS

b Match the phrases from the song (1–6) with their meanings (a–f).

1	ease my mind	a	it's hard to find love
2	love don't come easy	b	stops me giving up and want to continue
3	a game of give and take	c	I can't stand
4	keeps me hanging on	d	a matter of accepting things that the other person wants, and not doing some of the things that you want
5	I can't bear	e	give me a warm hug
6	hold me tight	f	make things less painful

GLOSSARY

don't come easy = doesn't come easy
heartaches = strong feelings of sadness
stand = endure or tolerate
strength = noun from the adjective "strong"
ain't = isn't

SONG FACTS

This song was originally recorded by The Supremes in 1966 and reached the top five in the UK that same year. The Supremes' version is included in the Rock and Roll Hall of Fame's list of "500 songs that shaped rock and roll". The song was used in the 1995 film *Runaway Bride*, with Julia Roberts and Richard Gere.

5A SONG We Are the Champions

a Listen to the song. Some of the phrases in **bold** are right, and some are wrong. Check (✓) the right phrases, and put an ✗ next to the wrong ones.

We Are the Champions

1	**I've paid** my dues	✓
2	Time after time	
3	I've ~~completed~~ *done* my sentence	✗
4	**Committed no crime**	___
5	And **terrible mistakes**	___
6	I've made **a few**	___
7	I've had my share of sand **thrown in my face**	___
8	**But I've come** through	___
	(And we can go on and on and on and on)	
	CHORUS	
9	We are the champions, **my friend**	___
10	And **we'll carry on** fighting till the end	___
11	We are the champions	
12	We are the champions	
13	No **time for winners**	___
14	'Cause we are the champions of the world	
15	**I've taken my bows**	___
16	**And my curtain calls**	___
17	**You showed me** fame and fortune and everything that goes with it	___
18	**I thank** you all	___
19	**And it's been** no bed of roses	___
20	No pleasure cruise	
21	I consider it a challenge before **the entire human race**	___
22	That I'd never lose	
	(And we can go on and on and on and on)	
	CHORUS	
	REPEAT CHORUS	

b Listen again and correct the wrong phrases.

c Match the phrases from the song (1–8) with their meanings (a–h).

1	paid my dues	a	the time when actors come out at the end of the show in a theater to receive the applause of the audience
2	come through	b	being well known and having money
3	curtain calls	c	not an easy or pleasant situation
4	fame and fortune	d	survive
5	no bed of roses	e	the people in the world
6	pleasure cruise	f	worked hard and paid what I owed
7	challenge	g	(literally) a trip in a boat, (in this context) something easy and fun
8	human race	h	something new and difficult that you want to try to do

GLOSSARY
'cause = because
I ain't gonna = I'm not going to

SONG FACTS
We Are the Champions was first recorded by Queen in 1977 and was written by their lead singer, Freddie Mercury. The song is about how the group made their way to the top of their profession and achieved great success. Freddie Mercury himself said that it could be interpreted as his version of Sinatra's *My Way* but that he also had the idea of a soccer anthem in mind. In fact, it's become the anthem of successful sport teams around the world.

6B SONG I Got Life

a Look at the pictures and identify them. Don't write anything yet.

1–7 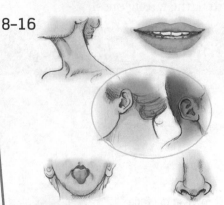 | 8–16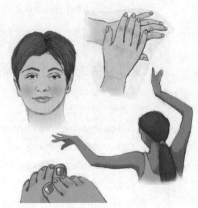

I Got Life

I ain't got no home, ain't got no ¹_____*shoes*_____

I ain't got no ²_____, ain't got no class

Ain't got no skirts, ain't got no ³_____

Ain't got no ⁴_____, ain't got no beer

Ain't got no man

Ain't got no ⁵_____, ain't got no culture

Ain't got no friends, ain't got no schooling

Ain't got no love, ain't got no ⁶_____

Ain't got no ⁷_____, ain't got no token

Ain't got no god

What have I got?

Why am I alive anyway?

Yeah, what have I got

Nobody can take away?

I've got my hair, got my ⁸_____

I've got my brains, got my ⁹_____

I've got my eyes, got my ¹⁰_____

I've got my ¹¹_____, I got my smile

I've got my ¹²_____, got my chin

I've got my ¹³_____, got my lips

I've got my heart, got my soul

I've got my back, I got myself

I've got my ¹⁴_____, got my hands

I've got my ¹⁵_____, got my legs

I've got my feet, got my ¹⁶_____

I've got my liver, got my blood

I've got life, I've got my freedom

I've got life

I've got life

And I'm gonna keep it

I've got life

And nobody's gonna take it away

I've got life

b Listen and complete the song with the words from **a**.

c Find words in the song which mean…

1 art, literature, music, etc. _____

2 the opposite of *dead* _____

3 the part of your body inside your head that controls your thoughts, feelings, and movements _____

4 the spiritual part of a person _____

5 the red liquid that flows through your body _____

6 the noun from *free* _____

d Match the colloquial expressions from songs (1–7) with the grammatically correct expressions (a–g).

Expressions in songs	Grammatically correct expressions
1 I ain't (rich)	a I don't have
2 I aint got no (money)	b I'm going to …
3 I wanna (be free)	c I've got
4 I'm gonna (leave you)	d because
5 Yeah	e I'm not …
6 'cos / 'cause	f I want to …
7 I got	g Yes

GLOSSARY

class = (in this context) style

schooling = education

token = a piece of paper or plastic that you can use to buy things

liver = the part of your body that cleans your blood

SONG FACTS

I Got Life was originally recorded by Nina Simone in 1968. She was a talented pianist, but she was rejected by music schools because she was black. She turned to pop music and used classical influences to give her songs a more complex sound.

7B SONG If I Could Build My Whole World Around You

a Read the song lyrics and think about what the missing verbs could be.

If I Could Build My Whole World Around You

---
be grow ~~put~~ take wash

Oh, if I could build my whole world around you, darling
First I'd 1 _put_ heaven by your side
Pretty flowers would 2_____ wherever you walked, honey
And over your head would 3_____ the bluest sky
And I'd 4_____ every drop of rain
And 5_____ all your troubles away
I'd have the whole world wrapped up in you, darling
And that would be all right, oh yes it would

---
be give keep make put

If I could build my whole world around you
I'd 6_____ your eyes the morning sun
I'd 7_____ so much love where there is sorrow
I'd put joy where there's never been love
And I'd 8_____ my love to you
For you to 9_____ for the rest of your life
Oh, and happiness would surely 10_____ ours
And that would be all right, oh yes it would

Doo doo doo doo doo, doo doo doo doo
Doo doo doo doo doo, doo doo doo doo

---
be give (x2) make step

Oh, if I could build my whole world around you
I'd 11_____ you the greatest gift any woman could
    possess
And I'd 12_____ into this world you've created
And 13_____ you true love and tenderness
And there'd 14_____ something new with every
    tomorrow
To 15_____ this world better as days go by

If I could build my whole world around you
If I could build my whole world around you
Then that would be all right, oh yeah
(repeat to fade)

b Listen to the song and fill in blanks 2–15 with a verb from the list.

c Read the lyrics and match the words and phrases.

1 build my whole world around you
2 be all right
3 put joy where there's never been love
4 happiness would surely be ours
5 there'd be something new with
   every tomorrow

a every day would bring something different
b make you happy when you've only ever been sad
c make you the center of my existence
d be OK
e there's no doubt we'd be happy

GLOSSARY

honey = a way of addressing
    someone that you like or love
wrapped up = enclosed
sorrow = a feeling of great sadness
joy = a feeling of great happiness
tenderness = gentleness, love

SONG FACTS

If I Could Build My Whole World Around You was released in 1967. It was the third single for the singing duo of Marvin Gaye and Tammi Terrell. Together they had a total of seven hit singles in the late 1960s. When Terrell died aged only 24 from a brain tumor, Marvin Gaye was devastated at the loss of the singing partner he regarded as a sister.

8B SONG Piano Man

a With a partner, read the lyrics and think what the missing words 1–9 could be. Each missing word rhymes with the word in **bold** with the same number.

b Listen and write the words in the gaps.

c Report the highlighted phrases in the song.

1 He told the piano man that he *wasn't really sure how it (the song) went*. *(line 6)*

2 He said that _____. *(line 7)*

3 He told Bill that _____. *(line 17)*

4 John said that he _____. *(lines 19–20)*

5 They asked the piano man _____. *(line 36)*

GLOSSARY

shuffles = walks without lifting their feet off the ground

we're all in the mood for = we all feel like

out-of-town folk = visitors who don't live in the town

real estate = property, such as land or buildings

bread = slang for *money*, in this context in the form of a tip

SONG FACTS

Piano Man was released as a single in 1973, and was the first big hit song for American singer-songwriter Billy Joel. Before Joel became a successful recording artist, he used to be a piano player and singer at the Executive Room bar in Los Angeles. *Piano Man* describes his experiences of working there, and tells of the failed dreams of the customers, the bartender, and the piano player himself.

Piano Man

1 It's nine o'clock on a Saturday
2 The regular crowd shuffles ¹ **in**
3 There's an old man sitting next to me
4 Making love to his tonic and ¹ _____*gin*_____

5 He says, "Son, can you play me a memory?
6 I'm not really sure how it ² **goes**
7 But it's sad and it's sweet and I knew it complete
8 When I wore a younger man's ² _____."

La la la di di da, la la di di da dum

CHORUS
9 Sing us a song, you're the piano man
10 Sing us a song ³ **tonight**
11 Well, we're all in the mood for a melody
12 And you've got us feeling ³ _____

13 Now John at the bar is a friend of mine
14 He gets me my drinks for ⁴ **free**
15 And he's quick with a joke for the out-of-town folk
16 But there's someplace that he'd rather ⁴ _____
17 He says "Bill, I believe this is killing me"
18 As the smile ran away from his ⁵ **face**
19 "Well, I'm sure that I could be a movie star
20 If I could get out of this ⁵ _____."

Oh, la la la di di da, la la di di da dum

21 Now Paul is a real estate novelist
22 Who never had time for a ⁶ **wife**
23 And he's talking with Davy, who's still in the Navy
24 And probably will be for ⁶ _____

25 And the waitress is practicing politics
26 As the businessmen talk to their ⁷ **phones**
27 Yes, they're sharing a drink they call loneliness
28 But it's better than drinking ⁷ _____

CHORUS

29 It's a pretty good crowd for a Saturday
30 And the manager gives me a ⁸ **smile**
31 'Cause he knows that it's me they've been coming to see
32 To forget about life for a ⁸ _____

33 And the piano, it sounds like a carnival
34 And the microphone smells like a ⁹ **beer**
35 And they sit at the bar and put bread in my jar
36 And say, "Man, what are you doing ⁹ _____?"

Oh, la la la da di da, la la da di da dum

CHORUS

9A SONG Karma

a Listen to the song and (circle) the correct word.

Karma

Come on
Come on
Come on

Weren't you [1]**the man** / **the one** who said
That you don't want me anymore
And how you need your [2]**space** / **place**
And [3]**give** / **send** the keys back to your door
And how I cried and tried
And tried to make you [4]**stay** / **be** with me
But still you said your love was [5]**gone** / **over**
And that I had to [6]**go** / **leave**

CHORUS
(Now you) Talking 'bout a [7]**baby** / **family**
(Now you) Saying I complete your [8]**dream** / **life**
(Now you) Saying I'm your everything
You're confusing me, what you [9]**tell** / **say to** me
Don't play with me, don't play with me, 'cause
What goes around, comes around
What goes up, must come down
Now who's crying, desiring to come back to me?
What goes around, comes around
What goes up, must come down
Now who's crying, desiring to come back?
I remember [10]**when** / **while** I was sitting home alone
Waiting for you 'til [11]**four** / **three** o'clock in the morn

And when you came home
You'd [12]**never** / **always** have some sorry excuse
Half explaining to me
Like I'm just some [13]**type** / **kind** of a fool

I sacrificed the things I want
Just to do things for you
But [14]**when** / **if** it's time to do for me
You never come through

CHORUS

Night after night, [15]**thinking** / **knowing** something
    going on
Wasn't long [16]**before** / **until** I be g-g-g-gone
Lord knows it wasn't easy, believe me
Never [17]**thought** / **knew** you'd be the one that would
    deceive me
And never knew what you supposed to do
No need to approach me fool, 'cause I'm over you

What goes around comes around
What goes up, must come down
Now who's crying, desiring to come back to me?
What goes around, comes around
What goes up, must come down
It's called karma baby, and it goes around

(repeat to fade)

b Read the lyrics with the glossary. Match the definitions (1–5) with the highlighted phrases in the text.

1 And always confused about what you
   should do
   _____

2 Telling me that you love me
   _____

3 I don't love you anymore
   _____

4 You never keep your promises
   _____

5 The way you behave towards other people
   will later come back to you
   _____

GLOSSARY

morn = morning
sacrificed = gave up something that is important to you
deceive = lie to

SONG FACTS

This song was a hit in 2004 for singer/ songwriter and actress Alicia Keys. Her real name is Alicia Augello Cook, but her stage name is "Keys" after the keys on a piano. She loves playing this instrument and often uses it in her songs.

10A SONG Greatest Love of All

a With a partner, read the lyrics and think what the missing verbs could be. Write your suggestions in the column on the right. The first letter has been given for you, but pay attention to the form of each missing verb.

Greatest Love of All

1

	Verbs
I ¹_____ the children are our future	b *elieve*
²_____ them well and let them lead the way	t_____
Show them all the beauty they ³_____ inside	p_____
Give them a sense of pride to ⁴_____ it easier	m_____
Let the children's laughter remind us how we used to be	

2

Everybody's ⁵_____ for a hero	s_____
People ⁶_____ someone to look up to	n_____
I never found anyone who fulfilled my needs	
A lonely place to be	
And so I learned to ⁷_____ on me	d_____

> CHORUS
> I decided long ago, never to walk in
>   anyone's shadows
> If I ⁸_____, if I succeed   f_____
> At least I'll live as I ⁹_____   b_____
> No matter what they take from me
> They can't take away my dignity
> Because the greatest love of all
> Is ¹⁰_____ to me   h_____
> I found the greatest love of all
> Inside of me
> The greatest love of all
> Is easy to achieve
> ¹¹_____ to love yourself   l_____
> It is the greatest love of all
>
> *Repeat verse 1*
> CHORUS

3

And if, by chance, that special place	
That you've been ¹²_____ of	d_____
Leads you to a lonely place	
Find your strength in love	

b Listen and check.

c Look at the words (1–6). Find the correct form of the words in the song and complete the column on the right.

1 belief (*noun*) ____*believe*____ (*verb*)
2 failure (*noun*) _____ (*verb*)
3 success (*noun*) _____ (*verb*)
4 beautiful (*adj*) _____ (*noun*)
5 proud (*adj*) _____ (*noun*)
6 laugh (*verb*) _____ (*noun*)

d Use the correct form of some of the words from the list in **c** to complete the summary of the song below.

We all need someone to respect and admire, but when you're alone in life you have to find the strength to ¹____*believe*____ in yourself. It doesn't matter if you've been lucky and you're a ²_____, or even if you've ³_____ in life, because you've learned to be ⁴_____ of yourself and what you can do. That's why we should teach children that they are all ⁵_____ inside: when children ⁶_____, they show us what we used to be like when we were younger.

GLOSSARY

pride = the feeling of pleasure that you have when you do something good

fulfilled my needs = made me feel happy and satisfied

never to walk in anyone's shadows = never feel inferior to anybody else

no matter = it doesn't matter

SONG FACTS

Greatest Love of All is a song about how to be strong when you are faced with life's challenges. It was originally recorded by George Benson for a 1977 film about the great sporting icon, Muhammad Ali. Whitney Houston released her version in 1986. It was a worldwide hit and became one of her most popular songs. Whitney Houston is a pop and soul icon whose sad death in 2012 gives this song extra poignancy.

Workbook answer key

1A

1 VOCABULARY

a 2 salmon   <u>meat</u>
   3 pear   <u>vegetables</u>
   4 eggplant   <u>fruit</u>
   5 beef   <u>seafood</u>
   6 cherry   <u>vegetables</u>

b Down: 2 baked   4 roasted
   Across: 2 boiled   3 fried   5 steamed

c 2 take-out
   3 frozen
   4 raw
   5 low-fat
   6 spicy
   7 fresh

2 PRONUNCIATION

a 1 chicken, squid
   2 beef, peach
   3 crab, mango
   4 carton, jar
   5 chocolate, sausage
   6 raw, salt
   7 cook, sugar
   8 soup, tuna

c 2 cabbage
   3 spicy
   4 roasted
   5 grapes
   6 fruit
   7 baked
   8 melon
   9 zucchini

3 GRAMMAR

a 3 Do you eat out
   4 ✓
   5 Do you think
   6 We have
   7 ✓
   8 I don't want
   9 ✓
   10 He's ordering

b 2 doesn't, cook
   3 are ('re) having
   4 aren't going out
   5 Do, spend
   6 serves
   7 do, eat out
   8 am ('m) not having
   9 don't, buy
   10 is ('s) cutting down

4 READING

a 2 D
   3 A
   4 B

b 2 F
   3 F
   4 T
   5 F
   6 F
   7 T
   8 F

5 LISTENING

a C

b 1 D
   2 B
   3 A
   4 C

1B

1 GRAMMAR

a 2 I'll pay
   3 I'll make
   4 you'll get married / you're going to get married
   5 We aren't going
   6 I'll have
   7 I'll be
   8 We'll pay
   9 I won't be
   10 We're having / We're going to have

b 1 are ('re) staying / are ('re) going to stay, are ('re) having / are ('re) going to have
   2 'll order, 'll call, 'll have
   3 are … leaving / are … going to leave, 'm taking / 'm going to take, 'll give
   4 are … doing / are … going to do, am ('m) seeing / am ('m) going to see, 'll love it
   5 'll help, 'll wash, won't break

2 each other

   2 don't know each other
   3 aren't speaking to each other
   4 don't understand each other
   5 respect each other

3 PRONUNCIATION

a 2 not, book, flight
   3 look, online
   4 Who, meeting, tonight
   5 meeting, friends
   6 not, meeting, girlfriend
   7 When, get, scores
   8 won't, this, week
   9 get, Monday

4 VOCABULARY

a 2 great-grandfather
   3 only child
   4 niece
   5 aunt
   6 immediate family
   7 stepmother
   8 father-in-law
   9 extended family
   10 nephew

b 2 jealous
   3 reliable
   4 selfish
   5 sensible
   6 aggressive
   7 self-confident
   8 ambitious
   9 stubborn
   10 independent

c 2 unkind
   3 hardworking
   4 immature
   5 disorganized
   6 insensitive
   7 quiet
   8 messy

5 READING

a They can help each other when they have a problem.

b 2 a
   3 b
   4 c
   5 a

6 LISTENING

a They decide not to move in with Terry's parents.

b 2 F
   3 T
   4 T
   5 F
   6 T

1 REACTING TO WHAT PEOPLE SAY

2 believe
3 kidding
4 mind
5 Really
6 pity
7 How
8 news
9 What

2 SOCIAL ENGLISH

2 How do you see
3 Not really
4 That's because
5 How incredible
6 Go ahead
7 things like that
8 I mean

3 READING

a 2 55 Bar
3 Barbès
4 Smalls
5 Café Carlyle
6 Smalls

2A

1 VOCABULARY

a 2 afford
3 save
4 earns
5 is worth
6 raise
7 owe
8 inherited
9 charged
10 lend

b 2 for
3 into
4 from
5 in / with / by
6 to
7 on
8 by
9 in

c 2 ATM
3 coin
4 salary
5 bills
6 loan
7 mortgage
8 taxes

2 PRONUNCIATION

a 2 clothes
3 done
4 worse
5 short

3 GRAMMAR

a 2 charged
3 I've been
4 didn't inherit
5 You've lent
6 did your TV cost
7 have you wasted
8 didn't have
9 Have you ever invested
10 earned

b 1 passed
2 did … borrow, have / 've … spent
3 Have … found / Did … find, agreed
4 Have … lent, needed
5 Has … made / Did … make, called

4 READING

a 3

b 2 c
3 a
4 c
5 b

d 2 retirement plan
3 discarded
4 era
5 stock market
6 sell-by date

5 LISTENING

a 2 a
3 c
4 b

b 2 T
3 T
4 F
5 F
6 T
7 F
8 T

2B

1 GRAMMAR

a **for:** a long time, a week, six months, the last two days, years and years
since: March, I was little, Tuesday, you last called

b 2 has ('s) been, since
3 have ('ve) known, since
4 has ('s) worked, for
5 have ('ve) lived, since
6 have been, for
7 have ('ve) wanted, for
8 hasn't spoken, since

c 2 We've been traveling
3 has he been working
4 She's been looking for
5 He hasn't been doing
6 Have you been waiting
7 I've been taking care of

d 3 has had
4 has Mark been playing
5 ✓
6 I've known
7 We've been going
8 You've been wearing

2 PRONUNCIATION

a 2 long, out
3 feeling, yesterday
4 haven't, living
5 cleaning, morning
6 haven't, sleeping

3 READING

a 1 B
2 A
3 C

b 2 C
3 A
4 C
5 A
6 B
7 C
8 A

d 2 make a contribution
3 the wild
4 underprivileged
5 shelters
6 lend a hand

4 VOCABULARY

a 2 delicious
3 excited
4 hilarious
5 enormous
6 filthy

b 2 tiny
3 furious
4 terrified
5 amazed
6 starving

5 LISTENING

a 3, 5, 6, 9, 10, 11, 12

b 2 14 and nine.
3 $300,000.
4 Twelve in Twelve.
5 They took care of elephants.
6 They taught them English.
7 Children who have HIV.
8 Encourage other families to do the same.

1 VOCABULARY

a Down: 2 scooter 4 light rail 5 train
7 truck
Across: 1 bus 3 platform 6 freeway
8 van 9 subway

b 2 parking
3 traffic
4 road
5 bicycle / bike
6 gas
7 rush
8 taxi
9 speed
10 traffic

2 PRONUNCIATION

a 2 seat belt
3 check-in
4 chemistry

3 GRAMMAR

a 2 than
3 the
4 more
5 worst
6 less
7 better / quicker / faster
8 most
9 as
10 least

b 2 Beijing is the most crowded of the
three destinations.
3 Beijing is easier to get to than
Sydney.
4 Sydney is less exciting than Cancun.
5 Sydney is hotter than Beijing.
6 Sydney is the most relaxing of the
three destinations.

c 2 Beijing isn't as difficult to get to as
Sydney.
3 Sydney isn't as exciting as Cancun.
4 Sydney isn't as cold as Beijing.

4 PRONUNCIATION

a 2 least enjoyable
3 most interesting
4 more expensive
5 bigger
6 as expensive as

5 READING

a Totora reed boats.

b 2 T
3 T
4 F
5 F
6 T
7 T
8 F

6 LISTENING

a 2 B
3 D
4 A
5 C

b 2 20 miles
3 In the middle of a field.
4 A little boy.
5 Green.

1 GRAMMAR

a 1 languages, boys
2 the door, the house
3 a Japanese, an engineer
4 fish, the salmon
5 the movies, a week
6 the end, the world
7 women, men
8 a beautiful, lunch

b 2 next weekend
3 Money
4 ✓
5 twice a year
6 the DVD that I lent you
7 ✓
8 What a noisy child
9 a doctor
10 cats
11 ✓
12 gets to work

2 PRONUNCIATION

a 2 flowers, table
3 What, do
4 open, window
5 doctor, headaches
6 go, walk

3 READING

a 1 C
2 A
3 B

b 2 c
3 b
4 c
5 a
6 a

d 2 poisonous
3 responsible for
4 more likely
5 have a reputation
6 vital

4 VOCABULARY

a 2 to
3 for
4 on
5 at
6 for
7 about
8 of

b 2 on
3 about
4 in
5 from
6 at
7 with
8 for

5 WHEN ARE PREPOSITIONS STRESSED?

a 1 argued, dad
2 laughing, at; laughing, you
3 excited, about; excited, vacation
4 listening, to; listening, radio

6 LISTENING

a 3

b 2 F
3 F
4 T
5 F
6 F
7 F
8 T

1 GIVING OPINIONS

2 think
3 right
4 opinion
5 agree
6 ask
7 agree
8 honest

2 SOCIAL ENGLISH

2 Hang on a minute
3 kind of you
4 Did you mean
5 It's just that

3 READING

a 2 F
3 T
4 F
5 F
6 T
7 T

4A

1 GRAMMAR

a 3 ✓
4 ✓
5 haven't been able to
6 ✓
7 been able to
8 ✓
9 used to be able to
10 ✓
11 must be able to
12 not being able to

b 2 could / was able to
3 can't / isn't able to
4 has been able to
5 to be able to
6 couldn't / wasn't able to
7 will ('ll) be able to

3 READING

a 1 C
2 A
3 D
4 B

b 2 F
3 F
4 T
5 T
6 F
7 F
8 T

c 2 dropped out
3 eventually
4 was fired
5 brands
6 box office

4 VOCABULARY

a 2 tiring
3 ✓
4 ✓
5 surprised
6 ✓
7 ✓
8 frustrated

b 2 embarrassed
3 frustrated
4 exciting
5 worrying
6 interesting
7 depressing
8 disappointed

c frustrated, excited, interested, disappointed

d 2 themselves
3 herself
4 itself
5 myself
6 ourselves

5 LISTENING

a 1 pharmacy clerks
2 Turkish, a salesperson
3 Spanish, his host family
4 Portuguese, a street vendor
5 Korean, a salesperson

b 1 vacuum cleaner
2 fresh bread, fresh young man
3 banana, large plate
4 ice cream, tickle
5 he's not here, he's dead

4B

1 VOCABULARY

a 2 hang up
3 message, voicemail
4 silent, vibrate
5 call back
6 ringtone
7 instant messaging
8 dial
9 busy
10 screensaver

2 GRAMMAR

a 2 must not
3 don't have to
4 have to
5 ✓
6 should
7 should
8 must not
9 shouldn't
10 ✓

b 2 I had to
3 ✓
4 You must not play / You can't play
5 he has to work
6 ✓
7 everyone will have to speak
8 You should go home.

3 PRONUNCIATION

a 2 recei̶p̶t
3 h̶our
4 shou̶l̶dn't
5 ex̶h̶austed
6 wa̶l̶k
7 cou̶l̶d
8 de̶b̶t

4 READING

a 1

b 2 b
3 a
4 b
5 c

d 2 gesture
3 appreciate
4 concept
5 offend
6 looked down on

5 LISTENING

a 1, 2, 3, 5

b 2 c
3 b
4 c
5 c

5A

1 GRAMMAR

2 were driving, remembered, hadn't turned off
3 had already started, turned on, were losing, were playing
4 didn't recognize, had changed
5 was waiting, called, couldn't, had broken down
6 beat, was winning, scored
7 ran, had already left, were waiting
8 started, was walking, called, wasn't wearing, didn't have

2 PRONUNCIATION

a 2 sports
3 worst
4 court

3 READING

a 1 Scrabble
2 the blank tiles

b 2 T
3 F
4 F
5 F
6 F
7 T
8 T

d 2 admitted to
3 disqualified
4 replace
5 suspicious
6 accuse
7 opponent
8 resorted

4 VOCABULARY

a 2 referee
3 slope
4 kick
5 fan
6 course
7 get, shape
8 field
9 coach
10 stadium

b 2 trained
3 won
4 warmed up
5 tied
6 lost
7 threw
8 beat
9 scored
10 got injured

5 LISTENING

a China.

b 2 F
3 T
4 T
5 T
6 F
7 T
8 F

5B

1 GRAMMAR

a 3 ✓
4 doesn't usually wear
5 ✓
6 usually walk
7 didn't use to talk
8 Do you usually get up
9 Did you use to watch
10 ✓

b 2 didn't use to like
3 usually call
4 used to take
5 used to eat out
6 don't usually work
7 used to be
8 usually give

2 PRONUNCIATION

b 2 especially
3 please
4 music

3 VOCABULARY

a 2 roommate
3 colleague
4 classmates
5 fiancé
6 ex
7 close friend
8 couple

b 2 got to know
3 became friends
4 had, in common
5 went out together
6 were together
7 broke up
8 lost touch
9 got in touch
10 got along
11 proposed
12 got married

4 READING

a 2.03

b 2 c
3 a
4 b
5 b

d 2 trust
3 the average person
4 serious matters
5 contrast dramatically
6 getting more isolated

5 LISTENING

a a 2
b 3
d 4

b 2 T
3 T
4 F
5 F
6 T
7 F
8 T

1 PERMISSIONS AND REQUESTS

a 2 join
3 meeting
4 visit
5 pass
6 take

b 2 a
3 e
4 f
5 b
6 c

2 SOCIAL ENGLISH

2 come
3 way
4 mind
5 days
6 talk

3 READING

a 2 They all charge different prices.
3 It operates in the US and Canada.
4 You can buy your ticket seven days in advance.
5 Students get a 15% discount on the regular fare.
6 They should take their own food.

6A

1 VOCABULARY

a 2 comedy
3 historical
4 thriller
5 horror
6 western
7 drama
8 romantic
9 war movie
10 musical
11 science-fiction
   Hidden kind of movie: action movie

b 2 plot
3 script
4 audience
5 review
6 scene
7 subtitles
8 sequel
9 soundtrack
10 special effects
11 extras
12 cast

2 GRAMMAR

a 2 was played
3 was being shot
4 will be released
5 are going to be invited
6 is being shown
7 has been dubbed
8 was written

b 2 was shot
3 were filmed
4 tells
5 falls
6 plays
7 is played
8 starts
9 has been seen
10 is introduced
11 is based
12 was composed
13 wrote
14 were nominated

3 PRONUNCIATION

c 2 hi<u>sto</u>rical <u>mo</u>vie
3 <u>co</u>medy
4 di<u>rec</u>tor
5 <u>dra</u>ma
6 <u>hor</u>ror <u>mo</u>vie
7 re<u>view</u>
8 <u>se</u>quel
9 <u>sound</u>track
10 <u>sub</u>titles

4 READING

a 3

b 2 F
3 T
4 T
5 F
6 F
7 F
8 T

d 2 ballroom
3 stately homes
4 open-air
5 venue
6 speech impediment

5 LISTENING

a a 4
c 7
d 3
e 2
f 6
g 5

b 2 stone
3 ✓
4 There are two
5 57
6 largest
7 ✓
8 1934

6B

1 VOCABULARY

a 2 shoulder
3 back
4 knees
5 feet
6 lips
7 face
8 nose
9 neck
10 stomach

b 2 kick
3 touch
4 taste
5 smell
6 smile
7 nod
8 clap
9 bite
10 whistle
11 throw
12 point

2 PRONUNCIATION

a 2 eyes
3 tongue
4 shoulders
5 outgoing

3 GRAMMAR

a 2 must
3 can't
4 might not
5 can't
6 must

b 2 can't
3 might
4 must
5 can't
6 might not
7 can't
8 might

4 LISTENING

a 1, 2, 5

b 2 F
3 T
4 F
5 T
6 T
7 F

5 READING

a 2

b 2 c
3 b
4 a
5 b

d 2 banned
3 altering
4 figure out
5 wrinkles
6 rating

7A

1 VOCABULARY

a 2 elementary
3 middle
4 high
5 grade
6 semesters
7 college
8 nursery
9 primary
10 secondary
11 head
12 terms
13 boarding
14 university

b 2 behave
3 cheat
4 suspended
5 fail
6 pass
7 study
8 punished

2 PRONUNCIATION

a 2 pull
3 cut
4 subtitles

3 GRAMMAR

a 2 e
3 b
4 f
5 a
6 h
7 d
8 g

b 2 unless
3 if
4 after
5 until
6 before

c 2 will ('ll) be, hurry up
3 will ('ll) have, go
4 won't wait, aren't
5 doesn't come, won't take
6 won't leave, finds
7 won't be able to, lend
8 gets, will ('ll) call
9 won't start, is ('s)
10 will ('ll) play, practice

4 READING

a 3

b 2 T
3 F
4 T
5 F
6 F
7 F

d 2 pillows
3 competitive
4 reluctant
5 common sight
6 tutors

5 LISTENING

a 1

b 2 fourteen
3 building
4 rock musician
5 English
6 an insult
7 cows
8 field
9 all right
10 Wednesday

7B

1 GRAMMAR

a 2 g
3 c
4 a
5 h
6 b
7 e
8 f

b 2 would be, cleaned
3 wouldn't take, didn't have
4 Would ... keep, won
5 wouldn't call, had
6 wouldn't eat out, wasn't / weren't
7 had, wouldn't move
8 wasn't / weren't, could
9 Would ... wake up, didn't set
10 had, wouldn't be

2 PRONUNCIATION

a 2 grow, vegetables
3 buy, house
4 would make
5 wouldn't work

c 2 f
3 e
4 a
5 d
6 c

3 VOCABULARY

a 2 in the woods
3 on the fourth floor
4 on the West Coast
5 on the outskirts

b 2 top floor
3 spacious
4 wood floor
5 balcony
6 basement
7 cabin
8 cozy
9 ceilings
10 logs
11 fireplace
12 deck
13 steps
14 entrance

5 LISTENING

a a 4
b 7
c 6
e 5
f 3
g 2

b 2 20 years
3 in 1967
4 One
5 three
6 4 p.m.
7 play cards
8 the first floor

6 READING

a 2

b 1 D
2 F
3 A
4 C

d 2 research
3 go back
4 previous
5 hang
6 instructions

Practical English Boys' night out

1 MAKING SUGGESTIONS

2 Let's
3 going
4 could
5 feel
6 don't
7 about
8 great

2 SOCIAL ENGLISH

2 why
3 make
4 off
5 not
6 word
7 happen

3 READING

a 2 $30
3 8:30 a.m.
4 Two
5 9 a.m.
6 Fridays

1 VOCABULARY

a 2 mall
3 fits
4 outlet store
5 book store
6 try ... on
7 pharmacy
8 sale
9 suit
10 department store

b 2 payment
3 complaint
4 attachment
5 response
6 explanation
7 success
8 compensation

2 GRAMMAR

a 2 it was
3 told me
4 she bought
5 ✓
6 ✓
7 had to
8 whether
9 I wanted
10 had forgotten

b 2 (that) he hated buying clothes
3 how much I had paid for my jacket
4 you would check the price online
5 where the shoe department was
6 if / whether the shirt fit me

3 READING

a 2 D
3 A
4 C
5 F
6 B

c 2 hackers
3 padlock
4 turn up
5 log out
6 landline

4 PRONUNCIATION

a 2 certain
3 said
4 raise
5 captain
6 brain

5 LISTENING

a 1 New York
2 two

b 2 c
3 c
4 a
5 d

1 VOCABULARY

a 2 resign
3 applied
4 shifts
5 promoted
6 downsized
7 training
8 set
9 self-employed
10 retire

b 2 translator
3 employment
4 pharmacist
5 retirement
6 promotion
7 lawyer
8 scientist
9 resignation
10 application
11 farmer
12 qualifications

c 2 in, temporary
3 for, in, of
4 in, well qualified
5 full-time, permanent
6 unemployed, self-employed

2 PRONUNCIATION

a 2 downsize
3 employment
4 farmer
5 lawyer
6 musician
7 overtime
8 permanent
9 promotion
10 qualify
11 resign
12 retire
13 salary
14 temporary
15 unemployed

3 GRAMMAR

a 2 making
3 to pay
4 to fire
5 not going
6 having
7 working
8 to sign

b 2 ✓
3 to get
4 taking
5 ✓
6 playing
7 ✓
8 Filling out

c 2 to meet
3 Lifting
4 to find
5 getting
6 applying
7 helping
8 to accept

4 READING

a All three of them.

b 2 A
3 C
4 C
5 B
6 A

5 LISTENING

a Speaker 2 ✗
Speaker 3 ✓
Speaker 4 ✓
Speaker 5 ✗

b 2 T
3 F
4 T
5 T

9A

1 GRAMMAR

a 2 would have arrived
3 hadn't forgotten
4 had ('d) checked
5 would ('d) have missed
6 wouldn't have made
7 would ('d) have worn
8 wouldn't have invited

b 2 if they hadn't had a problem
3 she would / might / could have gotten the job
4 he wouldn't have broken them
5 if you had ('d) followed my directions
6 we would have played tennis.

2 PRONUNCIATION

a 2 told, meeting
3 hadn't, expensive
4 known, driving
5 hadn't played
6 booked, month

3 VOCABULARY

a 3 fortunate
4 unfortunate
5 careful
6 careless
7 patient
8 impatient
9 lucky
10 unlucky

b 2 uncomfortable
3 lucky
4 desperately
5 Unfortunately
6 Luckily
7 comfortably
8 carefully

4 LISTENING

a A 3
B 5
D 4
E 2

b 2 e
3 c
4 a
5 d

5 READING

a A 4
B 2
D 5
E 3

b 2 They saw a car and a couple on their lawn.
3 He wanted to stop people from stealing his potted plants.
4 The driver lost control of it.
5 He was thrown out of the sunroof and he landed on the lawn.
6 One of them was taken to the hospital.
7 She said that she had seen them arguing.
8 Drivers often go around the corner too fast.

d 2 emergency services
3 around the corner
4 minor injuries
5 lose control
6 Passersby

9B

1 GRAMMAR

a 2 any
3 too much
4 big enough
5 a little
6 too quickly
7 lots of
8 no
9 very few
10 enough hours

b 2 enough, too expensive / much
3 a little, much / enough
4 too many / lots of / a lot of, enough
5 no, any
6 few, many

2 PRONUNCIATION

a 2 cough
3 through
4 laughed

3 VOCABULARY

a 2 turned it down
3 plugged it in
4 turned it up
5 I switched it off

b Clues across: 4 plug   6 outlet   7 remote control   9 screen   11 headphones   12 switch

Clues down: 2 adaptor   3 keyboard   5 USB cable   8 speaker   10 mouse

4 READING

a 3

b 2 T
3 F
4 F
5 T
6 F
7 T
8 F

5 LISTENING

a How to use the Wi-Fi access.

b 2 302
3 $10
4 25 cents
5 $30
6 advanced
7 3:10 today
8 3:10 tomorrow

Practical English Unexpected events

1 INDIRECT QUESTIONS

2 how much a one-way ticket costs
3 if / whether you have a Student Advantage Card
4 ✓
5 what time it arrives

2 SOCIAL ENGLISH

2 I guess
3 Of course
4 It's obvious
5 What if
6 either

3 READING

a 2 F
3 T
4 F
5 F
6 T
7 T

10A

1 GRAMMAR

a 3 whose
4 that, which, (–)
5 who, that
6 where
7 who, that

b 2 he
3 they
4 it
5 her
6 there
7 it

c 2 where the Mona Lisa can be seen
3 which is in the Himalayas
4 whose voice will never be forgotten
5 which was opened in China in 2011
6 who is a human rights leader
7 whose wife is Beyoncé
8 where Native Americans protected themselves from hot temperatures

2 VOCABULARY

a 2 seat belt
3 headphones
4 profile picture
5 traffic jam
6 first floor
7 bookcase
8 subway map

b 2 top floor
3 soundtrack
4 training course
5 roommate
6 high school
7 bicycle lane
8 rush hour

3 PRONUNCIATION

a 2 crosswalk
3 flash drive
4 parking ticket
5 ringtone
6 speed camera
7 subway map
8 tennis court

4 READING

a 1 one brother and one sister
2 his brother (and his best friend)

b 2 He admires his father.
3 He enjoyed playing outside.
4 He doesn't like waking up early.
5 He can't cook.
6 He likes the fruit trees in his yard.
7 He's afraid of snakes and spiders.
8 He likes Bob Marley.
9 He cried.
10 He worries about getting old.

d 2 weird
3 get real
4 legend
5 honorary degrees

5 LISTENING

a 2 tea bag
5 tin can

b 2 T
3 F
4 F
5 T
6 T
7 F
8 F
9 T
10 T

10B

1 VOCABULARY

2 murder
3 victim
4 evidence
5 witnesses
6 murderer
7 suspects
8 solve
9 prove

2 GRAMMAR

a 2 were you
3 didn't you
4 haven't you
5 aren't you
6 doesn't he
7 haven't you
8 wouldn't you

b 2 do you
3 is it
4 doesn't he
5 didn't they
6 has she
7 aren't I
8 won't you

3 PRONUNCIATION

b 1 weren't, hurt
2 brutal, prove, truth
3 discover, suddenly, suspect

4 READING

a the US

b 2 b
3 a
4 b
5 c
6 a
7 b
8 c

5 LISTENING

a He is murdered.

b 2 T
3 F
4 T
5 T
6 F